Subaltern Studies XI
COMMUNITY, GENDER AND VIOLENCE

Subaltern Studies XI

Community, Gender and Violence

Edited by
PARTHA CHATTERJEE
AND
PRADEEP JEGANATHAN

COLUMBIA UNIVERSITY PRESS
NEW YORK

Columbia University Press
Publishers since 1893
New York

© 2000 by Permanent Black
All rights reserved.

ISBNs: 978-0-231-12314-3 (cloth); 978-0-231-12315-0 (pbk.)
LCC: 90641861

Contents

Preface	vii
Notes on Contributors	ix
1 AAMIR R. MUFTI A Greater Story-writer than God: Genre, Gender and Minority in Late Colonial India	1
2 PRADEEP JEGANATHAN A Space for Violence: Anthropology, Politics and the Location of a Sinhala Practice of Masculinity	37
3 NIVEDITA MENON Embodying the Self: Feminism, Sexual Violence and the Law	66
4 FLAVIA AGNES Women, Marriage, and the Subordination of Rights	106
5 TEJASWINI NIRANJANA Nationalism Refigured: Contemporary South Indian Cinema and the Subject of Feminism	138
6 SATISH DESHPANDE Hegemonic Spatial Strategies: The Nation-Space and Hindu Communalism in Twentieth-century India	167

7 QADRI ISMAIL 212
Constituting Nation, Contesting Nationalism:
The Southern Tamil (Woman) and Separatist
Tamil Nationalism in Sri Lanka

8 DAVID SCOTT 283
Toleration and Historical Traditions of Difference

9 GAYATRI CHAKRAVORTY SPIVAK 305
Discussion: An Afterword on the New Subaltern

Glossary 335

Index 339

Preface

THE ESSAYS COLLECTED in this volume were presented at the Fifth Subaltern Studies Conference held in Colombo in June 1995, under the auspices of the Social Scientists Association of Sri Lanka (SSA), the International Centre for Ethnic Studies, Colombo (ICES), and the Subaltern Studies Society.

The theme of the conference was 'Community, Gender and Violence': the present volume is held together by that theme. The essays have taken their present form after a fair amount of discussion and correspondence between the contributors. To that extent this volume is a result of collaborative effort.

We are grateful to Gayatri Chakravorty Spivak for giving us an expanded written version of the remarks she made at the conference; this has been included herein as a 'discussion' piece.

Readers of earlier volumes of *Subaltern Studies* will have noticed the entry of new subjects and themes into discussions of the subaltern condition. The Fourth and Fifth Subaltern Studies conferences held at Hyderabad (1993) and Colombo (1995) foregrounded the theme of gender. This volume continues that project. We thank the editorial collective of *Subaltern Studies* for entrusting us with the responsibility of editing this volume. We are especially grateful to Jennifer DeWan for her help in preparing the manuscript for press.

We are grateful to SSA and ICES for hosting the conference, and for their support in bringing out this volume. Additionally, Jayadeva Uyangoda, in his earlier capacity as Chairman, Sri Lanka Foundation Institute, was generous in his assistance in hosting the conference. Kumari Jayawardena's support has been constant and crucial through this entire process, and we are particularly indebted to her.

We note, finally, with a sense of profound loss and outrage, the assassination on 29 July 1999, in Colombo, of Neelakanthan Thiruchelvam, the founder-director of ICES, whose ability to catalyse and enable intellectual communities was boundless, and whose generous, gentle and astute scholarly presence was so central to our meetings in Colombo. In the difficult years ahead, we will miss him more acutely than words can tell.

Calcutta PARTHA CHATTERJEE
Minneapolis PRADEEP JEGANATHAN
26 December 1999

Notes on Contributors

FLAVIA AGNES is a lawyer-activist in Mumbai.

SATISH DESHPANDE is Fellow in Sociology at the Institute for Economic Growth, Delhi.

QADRI ISMAIL is Assistant Professor of English at the University of Minnesota at Minneapolis.

PRADEEP JEGANATHAN is Assistant Professor of Anthropology and Global Studies at the University of Minnesota at Minneapolis.

NIVEDITA MENON is Lecturer in Politics at Lady Shri Ram College, University of Delhi.

AAMIR R. MUFTI is Assistant Professor of Comparative Literature and English at the University of Michigan.

TEJASWINI NIRANJANA is a Fellow at the Center for the Study of Culture and Society at Bangalore.

DAVID SCOTT is Associate Professor of Anthropology at Columbia University.

GAYATRI CHAKRAVORTY SPIVAK is Avalon Foundation Professor of English and Comparative Literature at Columbia University.

A Greater Story-writer than God: Genre, Gender and Minority in Late Colonial India

AAMIR R. MUFTI

> The short story ... sees absurdity in all its undisguised and unadorned nakedness, and the exorcising power of this view, without fear or hope, gives it the consecration of form.
>
> Georg Lukács[1]

IT IS REPORTED that when he died in 1955 at the age of forty-three from liver ailments caused by excessive drinking, Saadat Hasan Manto left behind an epitaph he had written for himself: 'Here lies Saadat Hasan Manto. With him lie buried all the arts and mysteries of short-story writing. Under tons of earth he lies, wondering if he is a greater short-story writer than God.'[2] At the time, he was firmly established as one of the greatest practitioners of the Urdu *afsana* or short-story form, but was also considered an *enfant terrible*, with a reputation for zealous drinking and carousing in the urban demimonde. He was widely criticized within the literary world and beyond

---

[1] Georg Lukács, *The Theory of the Novel: A Historico-Philosophical Essay on the Forms of Great Epic Literature*, tr. Anna Bostock (Cambridge, MA: MIT Press, 1989), p. 51.

[2] Mahnaz Ispahani, 'Saadat Hasan Manto', *Grand Street*, 7(4) (Summer 1988), p. 193. For the reported Urdu original, see Sahba Lakhnavi, *Manto: Ek Kitab* (Lahore: Maktaba-e Afkar, 1994), p. 66.

for the explicitness of sex in his stories, and he had been tried several times, by colonial and postcolonial governments, for violating obscenity laws. He had been hounded out of the All-India Progressive Writers' Association (AIPWA), the umbrella organization of nationalist writers founded in 1936, which had initially welcomed him as a patriotic and committed writer. At the time of his death, his connections with the Association had long been severed, his erstwhile friends now accusing him of having abandoned realism, and of being obsessed with abnormal personality and the morbid.[3]

Manto had barely survived the Partition of India in 1947. Both physically and artistically, he had suffered a paralysing breakdown upon his arrival in the (now Pakistani) city of Lahore from Bombay—where he had spent much of his artistic life associated in one way or another with the Hindustani film industry. The Partition and its aftermath became an obsessive theme in his later writing, and his stories of this period are widely considered among the most forceful accounts of the trauma of India's national fragmentation. It is very often for these that he is most remembered.

Given this enormous historical density within Manto's life and career, how may we begin to unpack the semantic baggage of his self-chosen epitaph in a register other than the biographical? What are the arts and mysteries of short-story writing? What is the debris under which they lie buried? Who is Manto? Who or what is God? To mock God and his Creation is of course to invoke the powers of the demonic. Irony itself, as Lukács once noted, is inherently demonic. For the novel form, which Lukács considered 'the epic of a world that has been abandoned by God', irony consists in 'the freedom of the writer in his relationship to God, the transcendental condition of the objectivity of form-giving.' In turning to irony, modern subjectivity achieves, Lukács writes, the highest freedom that it is possible to achieve in a Godless world. To be possessed of a demon is to 'overreach [oneself]

---

[3] Manto's own remarks on this stormy relationship are to be found in 'Jaib-e Kafan', in *Mantonama* (Lahore: Sang-e-Meel Publications, 1990), pp. 221–9. Also see Leslie Fleming, *Another Lonely Voice: The Life and Works of Saadat Hassan Manto* (Lahore: Vanguard, 1985), pp. 27–30.

in ways that have no reason and cannot be explained by reason, challenging all the psychological or sociological foundations of [one's] existence.'[4]

Manto's ironic epitaph is first of all a commentary on the type of form-giving that is the Urdu afsana or short-story, this concrete modern bid to give subjective 'freedom' a form. It is an invitation to consider the nature of the 'transcendental condition of the objectivity of [this] form-giving' and of the specific freedom to which it gives form. But Manto's epitaph gives this modern bid at freedom a further twist. For it is directed not so much at the existence of God as at God's epic ambitions: the possibility that Manto's stories might well be 'greater' than God's also implies that the stories of which God is author are indeed 'short' ones. It is not a disavowal of the 'transcendental conditions' that 'God' represents, but rather their immanent interrogation.

I suggest that we read in the epitaph Manto's ironic relationship to the culture of Indian nationalism, in particular the bourgeois universalism of its 'moment of arrival', which Partha Chatterjee has associated with the figure and influence of Jawaharlal Nehru.[5] This essay is concerned in part with Manto's relationship to the 'Progressive' literary culture of that Nehruvian moment. I have argued elsewhere that the figure of the Muslim poses unique problems for the Nehruvian discourse concerning the emergence of a secular Indian consciousness.[6] That discourse seeks to contain the crisis of cultural difference, which lies at the heart of the national community, by translating the problem of 'Muslim' difference into the problematic of minority culture and history. It is my suggestion here that we read Manto's entire oeuvre as a series of literary attempts to dislodge, from within, the terms of the attempted nationalist resolution of the question of collective selfhood and belonging. Manto's ironic epitaph makes explicit what is already implicit in his practice of the short-story form: an immanent critique

---

[4] Lukács, 1989, pp. 88, 92–3.
[5] Chatterjee, *Nationalist Thought and the Colonial World: A Derivative Discourse?* (London: Zed Books, 1986), chapter 4.
[6] See Aamir R. Mufti, 'Secularism and Minority: Elements of a Critique', in *Social Text* 45 (1996), pp. 75–96.

of nationalism's divine ambitions, of its claim to a God-like perch above society. Manto turns the Urdu short-story—itself a 'minor' genre that is made to do the work in Urdu, as I shall shortly argue, of a 'major' one—into a means of dislodging the resolutions of that nationalism from within. He renders an account of national modernity that is inscribed not with affirmations of identity and subjectivity, but with displacement and difference.

It is as part of such a move, I shall argue later, that we should read the proliferation in Manto's fiction of a figure that has been at the centre of the controversies surrounding his work: the subaltern figure of the prostitute. I shall read this figure as Manto's reinscription of what, to borrow Sandhya Shetty's words, is a conventional and tenacious 'moment in the Indian nationalist discourse's production of woman: the allegorical figuration of the nation as mother.'[7] Manto's is a rewriting that turns to irony as a means of opening up the familial semiotic of nationalism to interrogation. At the same time, Manto's impoverished and exploited prostitutes displace the high cultural figure of the courtesan (*tavaif*), through which narratives of a distinct 'Muslim' cultural experience have so often been mediated in Indian modernity.

Since the publication and progressively pan-Indian reception and success of Mirza Muhammad Hadi Rusva's novel *Umrao Jan Ada* (1899), the courtesan has been a stock figure of the Indian national imaginary, a means of signifying the distinctness of a 'Muslim' presence within the space of national culture. If nationalism mobilizes motherhood as metaphor—from its early canonization in Bankimchandra Chatterjee's novel *Anandamath* (1882), through Gandhi's utilization of the mother as sign in cow-protection campaigns, to such moments of postcolonial nationalist culture as Mehboob's classic film *Mother India* (1955) and Congress politics under Indira Gandhi[8]— the relation of a Muslim minority to national culture is posed in terms

---

[7] Sandhya Shetty, '(Dis)figuring the Nation: Mother, Metaphor, Metonymy', in *Differences: A Journal of Feminist Cultural Criticism*, 7(3) (1995), p. 50.

[8] Recent studies of north Indian literatures that include analyses of this trope include Sudhir Chandra, *The Oppressive Present: Literature and Social Consciousnes in Colonial India* (Delhi: Oxford University Press, 1992), pp. 27–30; and Sudipta Kaviraj, *The Unhappy Consciousness: Bankimchandra Chattopadhyay and the Formation of*

of an organization of affect whose characteristic figure is the courtesan. (In postcolonial popular culture, the so-called 'Muslim social' genre of Bombay cinema is perhaps the most famous instance of this articulation.[9]) A number of important studies have in recent years examined critically the gendered semiotics and sociology of the formation of nationalist identity in colonial India, but these analyses have for the most part confined themselves to the utilization (and instability) of the 'mother' signifier. I shall attempt here to move this exploration in a somewhat different direction. I argue that locating the 'mother' within the larger field of contested and conflictual significations of nation-space must lead necessarily to that other projection which mediates between the economy of sex and gender identifications and the vicissitudes of collective selfhood: the courtesan or prostitute.[10] In order to understand the nature of the home that stands under the sign of the mother, we must examine closely the inhabitants of that other gendered space, the brothel. If the domesticated and desexualized figure of the mother becomes a critical moment in the interpellation of the (male) subject as *national* subject, then the trouble that 'Muslim' represents for nationalist discourse is enunciated through the excessive

---

Nationalist Discourse in India (Delhi: Oxford University Press, 1995), 137ff. The history of the figure in modern painting is briefly touched upon in Partha Mitter, *Art and Nationalism in Colonial India, 1850–1922: Occidental Orientations* (Cambridge: University of Cambridge Press, 1994), part three.

[9] See Fareed Kazmi, 'Muslim Socials and the Female Protagonist: Seeing a Dominant Discourse at Work', in Zoya Hasan (ed.), *Forging Identities: Gender, Communities and the State* (New Delhi: Kali for Women, 1994), pp. 226–43; and Mukul Kesavan, 'Urdu, Awadh and the Tawaif: The Islamicate Roots of Hindi Cinema', in Hasan, *Forging Identities*, pp. 244–57.

[10] The more important of these include Partha Chatterjee, 'The Nationalist Resolution of the Women's Question', in Kumkum Sangari and Sudesh Vaid (eds), *Recasting Women: Essays in Colonial History* (New Brunswick: Rutgers University Press, 1990), pp. 233–53; Gayatri Chakravorty Spivak, 'A Literary Representation of the Subaltern', in *In Other Worlds: Essays in Cultural Politics* (New York: Routledge, 1988), pp. 241–68 and 'Woman in Difference: Mahasweta Devi's "Douloti the Bountiful"', in Andrew Parker and Mary Russo (eds), *Nationalisms and Sexualities* (New York: Routledge, 1992), pp. 96–117; and Sandhya Shetty, '(Dis)figuring the Nation'.

and 'improperly' sexual figure of the prostitute. I shall argue here that in Manto's stories the brothel and its inhabitants come to acquire a critical energy that makes visible the representational work of the nation. His stories suggest possibilities of national belonging in terms of forms of 'love' not subsumable under the discourse of filial piety and devotion.

Urdu and the Writing of India

My larger and more speculative concern here is to suggest some ways of thinking about the relationship of Urdu literature in the two decades before Partition to the canonical forms of Indian nationalism. Any reading of Urdu literary production during the period in question must confront the paradox that the period of modern Indian history that saw the most decisive bifurcation of national politics along religio-communal lines is perhaps the most secularist period in the history of modern Urdu literature. Thus, none of the writers who came to prominence in this period—Manto, Ismat Chughtai, Miraji, Faiz Ahmed Faiz, to name only a few—could see themselves as addressing a primarily Muslim audience, as Iqbal, for instance, had sometimes been able to do a mere two generations earlier. This aggressively 'national' stance came to be marked in Urdu literary culture in a number of ways. Urdu writers took the lead in the formation of the AIPWA in 1935–6 and continued to have a disproportionate influence on its affairs at the national level up to and even beyond Partition. The organization was founded in London by a group of Indian students who followed the development of anti-fascist cultural fronts with great interest, with the Urdu writer Sajjad Zaheer playing the leading role.[11] Within a year it had held its first all-India meeting in Lucknow, gathering together an astonishing range of the country's most distinguished writers, with the doyen of Hindi-Urdu narrative, Munshi

[11] See Carlo Coppola, 'The All-India Progressive Writers' Association: The European Phase', in Carlo Coppola (ed.), *Marxist Influences and South Asian Literature*, vol. I, Occasional Papers no. 23, South Asia Series (Lansing, Michigan: Michigan State University), pp. 1–34.

Premchand, as its president.[12] Urdu writers also filled in disproportionate numbers the ranks of such newly-established and emergent sites of national cultural production as All India Radio and the Bombay film industry. Furthermore, as even a cursory perusal of literary journals from the period will reveal, the personnel of Urdu literary culture cut right across communal lines so far as origin is concerned. This is especially true of Punjab, but also of the heartland of the Hindi–Urdu conflict, Delhi and the United Provinces (UP).

But above all, this national, rather than separatist or communal, posture must be read in the literature itself—for instance, in the development of what was taken to be a 'realist' practice in fiction—by such writers as Manto, Rajinder Singh Bedi, Chughtai, Krishan Chander, Muhammad Hasan Askari, Ahmad Naseem Qasmi, Upendra Nath Ashk and Akhtar Hussain Raipuri, among numerous others[13]—with narrative becoming the staging ground for a vision of national life as secular social landscape: the life of India's 'eternal' villages under the onslaughts of modernity, the psycho-sexual tensions and crises of the middle-class home, the multi-layered energy and movement of modern cities, each with its range of social types and problematics. In poetry, these changes are signalled by the transformation of the protocols of the classical Urdu lyric, in particular the *ghazal* form, a genre and tradition that came to be increasingly criticized in modern times—in

---

[12] For a documentary history of the AIPWA, see Sudhi Pradhan (ed.), *Marxist Cultural Movement in India, Chronicles and Documents*, vol. I (Calcutta: Pustak Bipani, 1985). For a collection of documents and interpretive and historical essays pertaining to the influence of the Association in Urdu literature per se, see Qamar Raees and Syed Ashore Kazmi (eds), *Taraqqi pasand adab: pachas sala safar* (Delhi: Educational Publishing House, 1987). For Urdu, the standard historical study is still Khalilurrahman Azmi, *Urdu men taraqqi pasand adabi tehrik* (Aligarh: Anjuman-e Taraqqi-e Urdu, 1972). Zaheer's own authoritative insider's account is to be found in *Raushnai* (Lahore: Danyal, 1986).

[13] Askari and Raipuri each wrote only a small but influential body of short fiction. The former of course went on to become a leading literary critic in Pakistan after Partition and a major antagonist of Progressivist aesthetics from a perspective that he described as Islamic, and the latter largely withdrew from literary life for the next several decades.

the cultures of both Indian nationalism and Muslim separatism—for its inwardness and imperviousness to Indian nature and reality.[14] But it is my argument here that we read these developments against the grain, that despite this secularist and 'national' posture of Urdu literary culture, the relationship of Urdu to nationalism remains an ambivalent one. What characterizes the distinctness of Urdu literary production is precisely the uncanonizability of its forms within the discourse of national culture, as indexed, for instance, in Gandhi's controversial identification of Urdu in 1936–7 as an exclusively Muslim register and style.[15]

The paradoxical posture of Urdu during the period in question—the 1930s and 1940s—in which Urdu literary production seems to be

[14] The critique of classical Urdu poetry (of the period from the late seventeenth to the middle of the nineteenth century) associated with Aligarh Movement 'reformers' like Altaf Husain Hali and Muhammad Husain Azad has been discussed at length by Frances W. Pritchett, *Nets of Awareness: Urdu Poetry and its Critics* (Berkeley: University of California Press, 1994). For the (Indian) nationalist view of the Urdu poetic tradition, a reliable source is Suniti Kumar Chatterji, author of *Indo-Aryan and Hindi* (1942): 'A language and literature which came to base itself upon an ideology which denied on the soil of India the very existence of India and Indian Culture [*sic*], could not but be met with a challenge from the sons of India, adherents of their natural culture; and that challenge was in the form of highly Sanskritized Hindi.' Quoted in Aziz Ahmad, *Studies in Islamic Culture in the Indian Environment* (Oxford: Clarendon Press, 1969), p. 255. It is significant that Ahmad, whose position throughout this book may be described as Pakistani nationalist, is in perfect agreement with Chatterji and cites the latter only as a cap to his own argument about the inwardness and autonomy of the 'Muslim psyche' in India as revealed in classical Urdu poetry.

[15] As is well known, from the 1860s onwards the status of Urdu itself had come to be increasingly embroiled in the communal conflict as it developed in northern India. The polarizing effects of the controversies concerning the official language of the colonial courts in the North-Western provinces and Bihar, for instance, are well known. See Paul Brass, *Language, Religion and Politics in North India* (New York: Cambridge University Press, 1974), part III; Amrit Rai, *A House Divided: The Origin and Development of Hindi/Hindavi* (Delhi: Oxford University Press, 1984); Christopher King, *One Language, Two Scripts: The Hindi Movement in Nineteenth-century North India* (Bombay: Oxford University Press, 1994); and Vasudha Dalmia, *The Nationalization of Hindu Traditions: Bharatendu Harischandra and Nineteenth-century Banaras* (Delhi: Oxford University Press, 1997), especially chapters 2 and 4. It was famously such

staking national-secular claims despite its increasing public identification by nationalists as a 'minority' culture and problematic, is further complicated by the fact that this is also the period that sees the near disappearance of the national form (supposedly) par excellence, namely, the novel. This is the period that sees the appearance instead of a new and self-confident short-story in the work of a whole new generation of writers.[16] Urdu is in fact unique among the major literatures of South Asia in the emphasis it places on the short-story as the primary genre of narrative fiction, even over the decades after Partition. In Urdu, the more common hierarchical relationship of the novel to the short-story is reversed. This is particularly striking because some of the kinds of transition associated with the move from epic to novel and modern narrative—picaresque, didactic and historical fictions, for instance—began to take place in Urdu much earlier than in the other

---

conflicts that provided the impetus for separatist, 'Muslim' cultural projects like Syed Ahmed Khan's Aligarh movement. See Syed Ahmad's classic biography by his follower and publicist, Altaf Hussain Hali, *Hayat-e Javed* (New Delhi: Taraqqi-e Urdu Bureau, 1990), pp. 139–44; David Lelyveld, *Aligarh's First Generation: Muslim Solidarity in British India* (Princeton: Princeton University Press, 1978), pp. 97–101; and Francis Robinson, *Separatism Among Indian Muslims: The Politics of the United Provinces' Muslims, 1860–1923* (Delhi: Oxford University Press, 1994), pp. 96–8. And when the Hindi-Urdu question resurfaced again in the mid 1930s, this time with Gandhi at its centre, the result once again was political polarization, with erstwhile admirers of the Mahatma finding themselves in the opposite camp. This was perhaps most notably the case with Maulvi Abdulhaq, the most prominent publicist of Urdu in the first half of the twentieth century, who broke publicly with Gandhi at the 1936 convention of the Akhil Bharatiya Sahitya Parishad in Nagpur. Among the more interesting accounts of this episode in the history of the Hindi-Urdu conflict are Ram Babu Saksena, *Gandhiji's Solution of the Language Problem of India* (Bombay: Hindustani Prachar Sabha, 1972), pp. 9–11; and Dr Akhtar Hussain Raipuri, *Gard-e Rah* (Karachi: Maktaba-e Afkar, 1984),pp. 102–7. For a selection of Gandhi's interventions in the language debates during this period, see the collection, in Anand T. Hingorani (ed.), *Our Language Problem* (Karachi: Anand T. Hingorani, 1942).

[16] On the novel and the nation, see Benedict Anderson, *Imagined Communities: Reflections on the Origin and Spread of Nationalism* (London: Verso, 1983), pp. 30–5; and Timothy Brennan, *Salman Rushdie and the Third World: Myths of the Nation* (New York: St Martin's, 1989), chapter 1.

major north-Indian languages.[17] Commissioned narratives were produced at Fort William College for the linguistic training of colonial officials in the first decade of the nineteenth century. These included collections of original fairy-tales in the classical Persian style, such as Mirza Rajab Ali Beg's *Fasana-e ajaib* (probably written in 1824–5); the standardization and translation of medieval epic cycles like *Dastan-e Amir Hamza* (1860s onwards); the *islahi* ('reformist' or didactic) works of Nazir Ahmad (also 1860s onwards); the immensely popular picaresque narratives of Ratan Nath Sarshar written under the influence of Cervantes (*Fasana-e Azad* was first serialized in the *Avadh Akh-bar* beginning 1778); the historical romances of Abdulhaleem Sharar (1890s onwards)—all these milestones in the development of modern narrative forms in Urdu should have presaged a prominent place for the novel form in twentieth-century literary culture. It is a source of constant concern and speculation in Urdu criticism that this in fact has not turned out to be the case. Despite the appearance of some accomplished practitioners—in particular Rusva and Premchand in the early decades of this century and Qurratulain Haider in the decades after Partition—the novel has in fact remained a less developed form than the short-story, to say nothing of lyric poetry.

It is my argument here that the two processes I have outlined are not unrelated, that this particular distribution of genres—this foregrounding of the short-story at the cost of the novel—is to be understood in terms of the ambivalent relationship of Urdu to the discourse of Indian nationhood, in terms of the particular *location* of Urdu within the larger space of Indian literature(s). The privileging of the short-story in modern Urdu literature is a function of this problematic

---

[17] The standard histories in English include Shaista Akhtar Banu Suhrawardy, *A Critical Survey of the Development of the Urdu Novel and Short-story* (London: Longmans Green and Co., 1945); and Ram Babu Saksena, *A History of Urdu Literature* (Lahore: Sind Sagar Academy, 1975), chapters 15–17; Also see the following somewhat impressionistic works by Ralph Russell: 'The Development of the Modern Novel in Urdu', in T.W. Clark (ed.), *The Novel in India: Its Birth and Development* (Berkeley: University of California Press, 1970); and *The Pursuit of Urdu Literature: A Select History* (Delhi: Oxford University Press, 1992).

of minoritization. The absence of a canonical novel form in Urdu is a historico-philosophical fact of great significance and is an inscription, at the level of literary form and institution, of the dialectic of selfhood in Indian modernity. For an enunciation of the 'major' claims of nationhood and belonging, Urdu turns to a 'minor' epic form, thereby lending to those claims an air of contingency.

Lukács argued in *The Theory of the Novel* that what distinguishes the nineteenth-century novel as a genre, what makes it the epic of the modern world, is its capacity to narrate the socialization of the individual, its inscription at the level of form of the claim that life is ethically meaningful. For the nationalist narrative in late colonial India—and this applies as much to Nehru's *The Discovery of India* (1946) as it does to Mulk Raj Anand's *Untouchable* (1935) or Premchand's *Godan* (1936)—the representative self that is the object of the narrative has a secular nationalist consciousness as its defining characteristic. For the Nehruvian, 'progressive' aesthetics that emerged in the 1930s under the influence of Popular Front conceptions of the artwork and society, telling the truth of society in fiction—'realism'— amounted to narrating the emergence of this consciousness—the abstract and secular citizen subject—as the highest form of consciousness possible in a colonial society.[18] The protocols of social realism, first formulated as a programme at the Soviet Writers' Congress in 1934 and adopted as official Popular Front policy in 1935, undergo a transformation in being transplanted to a colonial setting. What the language of realist aesthetics now seeks to define is a specific relationship between writing and the nation, so that it is more accurate to speak of *national* realism in this context.

A revealing document in this connection is the speech that Anand, a founding member of the Association from its London phase, delivered at the convention of the AIPWA at Calcutta in 1938. Anand argued that the goal of 'social realism' is as much the 'portrayal . . . of

---

[18] My discussion here is indebted to the analysis of these issues in another colonial setting, namely, Ireland, by David Lloyd, 'Violence and the Constitution of the Novel', in *Anomalous States: Irish Writing and the Post-Colonial Moment* (Durham: Duke University Press, 1993), pp. 88–124.

all those tragedies in the obscure lanes and alleys of our towns and villages' as is the imperative to 'release the dormant potentialities of our people buried in an animal biology and make them the creative will which may take us from the infancy of our six thousand years to milleniums [sic] of a less elemental struggle for individual perfection.'[19] 'Realism' here is therefore only as much a matter of mimesis as it is of narrating the (national) passage from primitivism to modernity. The degraded life of India's peasant masses is barely above the level of 'animal biology'. It is the task of the committed writer to narrate the conditions of possibility of the passage from this limited state of existence to the universal consciousness of the citizen subject—'individual perfection'. In Anand's novel *Untouchable*, the totality that is the nation is concretized as the formal tension between the universalist and secular consciousness of the narrator and the subaltern protagonist Bakha, a consciousness whose limits are defined by, and in struggle with, the socio-religious institutions of caste society.

Lukács had argued of the modern short-story that it, along with other 'minor epic forms', focuses on a fragment of social life rather than its totality, letting the whole enter 'only as the thoughts and feelings of [the] hero', thereby presenting 'completeness' in entirely subjective terms. Lukács considered the short-story 'the narrative form which pin-points the strangeness and ambiguity of life': 'It sees absurdity in all its undisguised and unadorned nakedness, and the exorcising power of this view, without fear or hope, gives it the consecration of form.'[20]

The Urdu short-story takes such an exorcising stance with respect to the narrative of Indian selfhood. Its staging of that selfhood remains ambivalent. Moreover, the fragments it isolates from the stream of life and elevates into form do not merely point towards a totality, however subjective, of which they are part. It puts the terms of this totality in question and holds at bay the resolutions whose 'end' is the form of consciousness that is the abstract citizen subject. It is this ambivalent relationship of Urdu to the forms of national culture that Manto's

---

[19] See Pradhan, 1985, pp. 22–3.
[20] Lukács, 1989, pp. 50–1.

work exemplifies. More than any of his contemporaries, Manto explores the possibilities of writing itself as a national institution. His post-Partition writings, with which I am for the most part not concerned in this paper, represent a complex and multifaceted exploration of the cultural reinscriptions and rearrangements out of which the fiction of two autonomous nationalities was being produced. But his earlier writings are also obsessed with the representational structure of national belonging, with the meaning of national culture, and with the ethical and aesthetic dilemmas of a writer in a colonial society on the verge of gaining at least formal independence. Above all, Manto raises these questions as an *Urdu* writer, a writer of a language itself embroiled in the crisis of national culture, from within a literary culture imputed with a minority consciousness and posture in the discourse of the nation. That is the ambition and larger distinctness of his oeuvre and his place in the literary history of not only Urdu but also India.

(M)other India: Manto's Women and National Modernity

In a number of mostly early, pre-Partition stories, Manto develops a set of themes around the national-allegorical possibilities of 'woman' as signifier. He simultaneously explodes such possibilities by turning to sexually and morally displaced figures, figures that are at the heart of the controversies concerning obscenity that his stories created. (The meaning of 'obscenity' in this connection is itself of great interest, and I shall return to it later.) In such stories as 'Khushiya', 'Hatak', 'Sharda', 'Babu Gopinath', 'Mera nam Radha hai', 'Janaki', 'Mammi', and above all 'Kali Shalvar', to which I shall turn at length below, Manto pays almost obsessive attention to such figures—in both senses—and in particular to the figure of the prostitute, returning to it again and again. He examines in more and more detail and from different angles and perspectives the world of the brothel, the characters who inhabit it, and the light he insists the brothel throws on the world outside. The figure of the prostitute emerges in his stories not simply in binary opposition to the virtuous wife and mother of the nationalist imagination, but as a means of exploring the complexities of the latter itself as signifier.

The uncanny mirrorings of brothel and home are the subject of 'Hatak' (Insult), for instance. Here the prostitute Saugandhi maintains a curious fiction with her lover Madho, who visits her in Bombay from time to time and always manages to extract money from her despite the repeated cautionings of her pimp, Ram Lal. Madho always promises to return what she gives by money order as soon as he returns home to Poona, and even to send her more money for her upkeep. He keeps insisting volubly that she should give up her profession and let him support her—even as they both know it is she and her trade that support him. He exaggeratedly threatens to leave her if she does not clean out her room of the paraphernalia of her trade—bottles of cheap perfume and make-up, garish clothing, pornographic prints on the wall. This feigned interest of Madho in her life, Madho's formulaic insistence that she turn her brothel into a home, draws Saugandhi to him and strengthens her love. In fact, Manto tells us, she is a person with an almost infinite capacity for loving, quite capable of willing herself into believing that each encounter with a client is a falling in love. Often, we are told, she is overwhelmed by a desire to take the man's head in her lap and sing him to sleep. Both Madho and Saugandhi were liars, Manto tells us, living a counterfeit life, like cheap costume jewellery with shiny gold or silver plating. Saugandhi was happy because 'those who cannot afford to own real gold can satisfy themselves with such trinkets.'[21] It is this ability in Saugandhi to find the basis of love in an untruth which is of interest for us here. Her pretense with Madho, her lover—that he visits her not in a brothel but a home—and her ability to imagine her anonymous clients as lovers, suggest a form of love whose truth has its basis in an untruth.

The precarious stability of this world is brought abruptly crashing down by a brief encounter with a bourgeois client ('seth'), the event

---

[21] Saadat Hasan Manto, 'Hatak', in *Mantonama* (Lahore: Sang-e Meel Publications, 1990), p. 904. The corresponding passage in the Tahira Naqvi translation is to be found in Fleming, 1985, p. 248. All further references to this text will also include the corresponding page in the Naqvi translation.

hinted at in the title—'Hatak' (Insult). One night, Saugandhi finds herself standing on a dimly lit street corner, trying to peer into the rolled up window of a car. The window is rolled down, as someone inside the car shines a flashlight in her face for a brief blinding moment. The light is then shut off, Saugandhi hears a grunt of displeasure—'Unh!'—the window is rolled back up, and before she knows it the car has driven off into the night. Ram Lal matter-of-factly walks away—'Didn't like you, I suppose'—and Saugandhi is left standing all alone, a storm having been unleashed in her mind as a result of that 'Unh!' (907/251).

The passages that follow are superbly crafted. They are an early Manto exercise in modernist prose which was to be fully developed only later in such stories as 'Phundne' (Tassles). Onomatopoeia abounds, familiar words take on unfamiliar meanings, there is an almost mantric repetition of words and sounds, and narrative voice is overwhelmed by interior monologue. The language here mirrors the crisis of self precipitated as a result of Saugandhi's encounter. As her head reels from the rejection, the 'insult', Saugandhi begins to wonder why it had wounded her so:

> She wondered why she suddenly longed for someone to sing her praises. Never had she wanted it so much before. So why did she now look even at the inanimate things around her in a way that begged for approval? Why was every fragment of her being becoming 'mother'? Why was she ready to gather all the things of the earth [*dharti ki har shai*] into her lap like a mother? Why did she want to embrace the lamp-post in front of her, to place her warm cheek against the cold metal and absorb all of its chill? (911/254)

First of all, this passage begins to render indistinct the opposition of mother to prostitute. The signs of motherhood and domesticity appear, uncannily, within the world of the brothel. But furthermore, the fantasy of motherly love and nurture that is elaborated here renders the 'mother' allegory itself visible as a fantasy of encompassment and containment whose ultimate object is 'the earth' itself. Manto's use of 'dharti' here is significant, for it signifies not just the living earth, but rather a particular portion of it, a known and meaningful portion, the bit of the earth that is *ours*. In other words, 'dharti' points to the territorial body of the nation. Manto draws attention here to the national-allegorical possibilities of the body of the woman. In its juxtaposing of the sexualized and commodified body of the prostitute to the desexualized and idealized body of the mother-nation—which appears here, furthermore, as fantasy—the text produces a multiplicity of meanings: the desexualized mother is revealed to be the icon of a particular sexual—but also communal and national—politics. The exploitation of the prostitute is presented as the truth of the idealization of the mother, and the prostitute herself is held up as an ethical figure—a tenuous and temporary icon of an alternative conception of human community and attachments.

Lying and the possibilities of love are also the theme of 'Babu Gopi Nath', another Bombay story, written in the mid 1940s.[22] The story is about the narrator Manto's encounter with and moral education at the hands of Babu Gopi Nath, a middle-aged man who has come from Lahore, bringing with him a prostitute named Zeenat, a beautiful and hopelessly naïve young woman whose marriage he wishes to arrange with a suitably wealthy man before retiring himself to live a hermit's life. On the day of the wedding, when Manto sees Zeenat in the bridal chamber, looking for all intents and purposes like a demure bride, he cannot resist shattering the illusion. 'What is this farce?' he asks Zeenat, reducing her to tears. From the position of the middle-class intellectual—Manto the narrator is a writer and journalist—such a configuration of human relations appears farcical, a mixing of categories and crossing of boundaries. But in the end it is Manto who is reduced to regret and embarrassment—Babu Gopi Nath, now visible in his full complexity as father, mother, lover, pimp and saint, turns to him with tears in his eyes and reproaches him for having so thoughtlessly ridiculed Zeenat.

Both these stories therefore present the brothel as a tenuous world

---

[22] 'Babu Gopinath', in *Mantonama*, pp. 276–91. A translation may be found in Saadat Hasan Manto, *Kingdom's End and Other Stories*, tr. Khalid Hasan (New Delhi: Penguin Books, 1987), pp. 133–48.

constantly under threat from the outside. The delicate fiction that sustains this world is destroyed in each case by a representative of the outside world of bourgeois respectability—in Saugandhi's case by a wealthy client and in Zeenat's by a middle-class intellectual. It has sometimes been argued that, despite his oft-stated intent to write about women who are (sexually) transgressive and rebellious, Manto most often produces characters whose rebelliousness is at best an ambivalent or even superficial affair, and that this intention is inscribed at one level in the narrative and undermined or taken apart at others.[23] The desire for a normalization of her (sexual) self that we have seen in Saugandhi, for instance, or again Zeenat's touching attempt to become the demure bride, might lead us to agree with this characterization of Manto's women. While I do not take this reading to be incorrect as such, I feel it misses the more important point—i.e. that this 'make-believe' is itself a figure for the politics of (nationalist) representation.[24] It marks a refusal to romanticize as autonomous those

---

[23] See, for instance, Dr Wazir Agha, 'Manto ke afsanon men aurat', *Timsal* 1(1) (1992), pp. 35–50. Bhisham Sahni, writing from a Progressive position far removed from the deconstructionism of Agha's argument, has also argued that Manto's women seem ultimately incapable of rebellion against their state. See 'Saadat Hasan Manto: A Note', in Alok Bhalla (ed.), *Life and Works of Saadat Hasan Manto* (Shimla: Indian Institute for Advanced Study, 1997), pp. 172–4. (I am grateful to Zoya Khan for bringing this latter reference to my attention.) Manto's classic statement on the question of his female characters is the following passage from an essay written in response to some of the obscenity trials to which he was periodically submitted: 'If in my neighborhood a woman is daily abused by her husband and then polishes his shoes, I feel no sympathy for her whatsoever. But when a woman fights with her husband, threatens to kill herself, and then goes off to the movies, and I see the husband for two hours in a state of great worry and agitation, I develop a strange sympathy for them both . . . The hard working woman who grinds grain all day and sleeps peacefully at night cannot be the heroine of my stories. My heroine can only be the prostitute who stays up all night and sleeps all day but wakes up suddenly sometimes from a nightmare in which old age is knocking at her door . . . Her filth, her illnesses, her irritation, her bad language—these appeal to me. I write about these and completely ignore the pure locution, the good health and the finesse of respectable women' ('Lazzat-e sang', in *Mantonama*, pp. 619–20).

[24] Sahni, 'Saadat Hasan Manto', in Bhalla 1997, p. 172.

locations in society whose resources of culture and affect provide the means for an ethical critique of nationalism—and, more precisely, what I have called national realism. It points to the subordinate and dependent position of these locations. At the same time, they are held up as models of human relations and emerge from the narrative in their complexity as possible resources for the representation of collective cultural practices made unimaginable in the pious projection of the middle-class family as microcosm of the nation.

Manto's most ironic comment on the solemnities of motherhood as signifier come in 'Mammi' (Mummy). This recounts a series of encounters in Poona between Manto and an older English widow named Stella Jackson, whom everyone addresses as 'Mummy'. Manto meets her through some friends in the film industry who are part of her circle of devoted young men and women. The very idea of family is turned on its head by this loose and voluntary association of individuals brought together by their love of Mummy's company. Motherhood itself is ironized in the excess of this figure—foreign, garishly made-up, drunk and sexually permissive. The foreign word by which she is addressed, and which stands as the title of the story, itself marks a rejection of the purity of the (Indian) family as produced in the icon of the desexualized and virtuous mother. But at the climactic moment of the story, at a moment of crisis for this family, Stella is able, paradoxically, to act as the mother of her brood of young bohemians and misfits, her adopted children, and manages to prevent the seduction of a young girl of fifteen in her charge by one of Manto's raucous friends. This paradox is a characteristic Manto gesture, put here in the service of unsettling and rearranging the qualities collected under the sign of the mother in the representative practices of nationalism.

But Manto's most complex exploration of the brothel and its inhabitants comes in 'Kali Shalvar' (Black Trousers), written most likely in 1940, a story to which I shall now turn in some detail. The story begins with a description of the life of Sultana, who has recently moved to Delhi from the military cantonment town of Ambala in Punjab. In Ambala, we are told, most of her customers had been British soldiers, and from them she had learned a few sentences of English. Business there was good and Sultana considered these Englishmen to be better than Indian men. Although they spoke a language she did not understand, even this had proved an advantage of sorts, for she could curse them in her own language if they bothered her too much or got too rowdy, smiling all the time and suggesting by her tone that she was speaking lovingly to them. Since she had moved to Delhi, however, her business had collapsed. Where previously she could make up to twenty rupees a day after a few hours' work, in Delhi she had made barely that much in three months. It was next to having no income at all, and slowly her meagre jewellery had had to be pawned off piece by piece.

I suggest that we read Sultana's move from Ambala to Delhi, from the provinces to the colonial capital, and her aspirations for success there, as a reorientation of life-expectations along national lines. She moved there not out of a desire on her own part—such concerns seem beyond her horizon, and she is portrayed as someone with strictly local concerns. It is not she but her lover and pimp, Khuda Bakhsh, who, Manto writes, was taken by a sudden and inexplicable desire to move to Delhi. She willingly followed him because her business had picked up after she met him in Ambala. Being a superstitious person ('zaif-ul-i'tiqad'), she considered him a source of good luck. (Manto uses the forms 'mubarak' and 'bhagyavan', the first of clearly Arabic lineage, the second of a Sanskritic one. His very name, Khuda Bakhsh, meaning 'God-given' or 'gift of God', suggests this aspect of their relationship.[25]) He is a man of the world, an ex-truckdriver, now with a small business as a pavement photographer outside the train station. He has some education and, though he is constantly chasing after one holy man or another and is a devotee of Nizamuddin Auliya (the patron saint of Delhi), his relationship to technology is carefully contrasted to that of Sultana's—she screams in terror when she accidentally pulls on the flush chain in the bathroom and the water rushes out below. The chief technological reference point for her is the railways, and she wonders, when she first sees the flushing chain, why the bathroom should have a chain like a passenger compartment in a train.

---

[25] Saadat Hasan Manto, 'Kali Shalvar', in *Mantonama*, p. 660. All further references to this text will also include the corresponding page in the Naqvi translation. All translations from the Urdu, unless otherwise indicated, are my own.

It is also interesting that Khuda Bakhsh's profession entails taking photographs of English soldiers stationed in Ambala cantonment, i.e. creating images of the colonial rulers. There is a hint of the dilemma of the native artist in this character's predicament: he is busy domesticating a foreign technology and form and relies for personal success alternately on the (rational) ethic of 'hard work' and (irrational) hopes of saintly intervention. The photographic images he creates of English clients hint at a recurring artistic threat for the native artist, namely the endless reproduction of colonial culture. At the behest of this man, functioning partly within an indigenous idiom but literate also in the use of Western forms and technology, Sultana moves to Delhi and exchanges English clients for Indian ones.

In Delhi, Sultana is at first lost, literally so, unable to find her way back to her apartment. She is living in a quarter built by the city authorities specifically for prostitutes, and all the buildings appear to her to be 'of the same design' (661/209). She eventually learns to recognize her building by the laundry on the ground floor. Sultana's initial inability to find her home, her bearings, in this place called 'Delhi', would suggest the uniform space of nation and citizenship, seemingly without the landmarks of status, difference and belonging that allow her to navigate within the regime of colonial sovereignty that in this story is given the name 'Ambala'. In other words, if Ambala signifies the militarily enforced relationship of a tributary colonial state to its subaltern subjects, Delhi represents the modern regime of power that Foucault called governmentality. This proceeds through the ability 'to structure the possible field of action of others', and which relies not so much on external supervision or discipline as on suggesting the possibility of freedom of action for those who are to be governed.[26]

It is to this place, where colonial subjects are to become citizens, that Sultana is brought by her lover-pimp. That transformation, however,

---

[26] Michel Foucault, 'The Subject and Power', *Critical Inquiry* 8 (Summer 1992), p. 790. For two recent studies of the governmentalization of power in South Asian colonial society, see David Scott, 'Colonial Governmentality', in *Social Text* 43 (Fall 1995), pp. 191–220; and Milind Wakankar, 'Body, Crowd, Identity: Genealogy of a Hindu Nationalist Ascetics', in *Social Text* 45 (Winter 1995), pp. 45–73.

does not proceed in the manner promised. When Sultana does gain a foothold in this space, it is only a tentative one, and it is secured by external, artificial means, the laundry on the ground floor becoming a means of recognizing the apartment above. It is a containment of terror rather than its final disappearance, like her eventual understanding of the chain in the bathroom: by pulling it, she could make human refuse disappear into the ground.

The incident in the toilet hints at the nationalist cult of technology. Furthermore, it highlights those distances and discrepancies between the subaltern and élite domains of the colonial world whose political dimension Ranajit Guha has described as 'dominance without hegemony'. For Guha, the defining characteristic of the native bourgeoisie in a colonial setting is that it lacks the historical ambition and will to reshape society in its own image. Like the foreign élite at the helm of the colonial state, it is content to rule the subaltern masses by coercion rather than through their conversion to the universalism of its projects and values. In 'Naya Qanun' (The New Law), another Manto story from the early 1940s, the bourgeois project in question is not technological modernization but the politics of constitutionalism.[27] The story centres around a horse-cart driver in Lahore named Mangu, who is generally respected in the community of cart drivers as a man with a certain knowledge of the world. One day Mangu picks up two passengers at the High Court, native ('Marwari') businessmen, and comes to understand from their excited conversation that a 'naya qanun' (new law, or constitution) is about to be implemented which will make Indians free to be Indians in their own country and protect them from the arbitrary insults and oppressions of the English.[28] Thrilled by this prospect, Mangu announces the news to his audience at the horse-cart stand and anxiously begins to count the days till the auspicious occasion. The day finally comes, and Mangu learns a lesson in the discrepancy between subaltern struggles and bourgeois aspirations. As he is taking a break from his work and thinking about when and where he will see the new *qanun*, Mangu is hailed rudely by an Englishman,

---

[27] Manto, *Mantonama*, pp. 707–19; and Manto, *Kingdom's End*, pp. 83–92.
[28] The historical reference here is of course to the Government of India Act of 1935.

whom the former recognizes as a passenger who had abused him once on a certain day the year before. The man asks to be driven to Heera Mandi, the prostitution district of Lahore's walled city. Mangu asks for an arbitrarily high fare, they get into an argument, and when the Englishman raises his cane at him, Mangu gives him a memorable thrashing, enlightening him in the process that the English would have to change their old ways now that the 'new law' has come. The police then arrive, and Mangu is himself thrashed and dragged off to the police station, uncomprehending and shouting all the way, 'the new law, the new law'. In 'Naya Qanun' Manto highlights the differing relationships of the subaltern and the bourgeois nationalists to colonial political 'reform'. Half understanding the nationalist interpretation of the law, the subaltern is willing to act and claim the new dignity and status ('citizen') he thinks it is promising him, only to be roundly disabused of that illusion. In 'Kali Shalvar', Sultana is similarly baffled by the workings of modernity, in her case the mysteries of planned urbanization and the introduction of sewage technology.[29]

Manto tells us that in Delhi Sultana languishes. Clients do not come, not even for a fraction of what she charged English soldiers in Ambala. Khuda Bakhsh disappears, sometimes for days on end, chasing after holy men in the shadow of Purana Qila (the ruined Old Fort of Sultanate and Mughal Delhi)—holy men who, he hopes, will change his luck and make business boom. She repeatedly tells him that she hasn't taken to Delhi, but he always turns down her suggestions that they move back to Ambala, saying that they are in the capital to stay and that things are bound to improve any day. Alone all day, Sultana finds herself drifting to the balcony of her flat, increasingly engrossed in watching the comings and goings of engines and freight carriages in the railway yard across the street.

If the incident in the toilet already hints at the nationalist cult of technology, the railway yard dramatizes more explicitly the workings

---

[29] If at first it appears faintly ridiculous to speak of nationalist hopes for the flush toilet, we need think only of the conclusion to Anand's *Untouchable*, where it is suggested that the practice of untouchability, socially tied to the demeaning labour of removing human filth, will disappear upon introduction of that modern technology.

of national modernity, the modernization of the nation, watched this time by Sultana, as it were, from afar. This function of the railways as a pristine sign of colonial modernity is well established in modern Indian fiction. But the real interest of these passages lies not so much in that signification itself as in the attention the story repeatedly draws to the uncanny resemblance between the two spaces described: the goings-on of the railway yard on the one hand, and on the other the world of the brothel. The effect is not so much allegorical as meta-allegorical. For instance, observing the railway lines glinting in the twilight, Sultana finds her gaze turning to her own arms, where her veins seem to her to be marking her body as the lines mark the ground, the territorial body of the nation. The clouds of smoke rising from the engines appear to her to take on the shapes of heavy-set men. Sometimes it seems to her as if this world of criss-crossing tracks, of billowing clouds of smoke and steam, is itself a brothel: a crowd of numberless carriages being driven this way or that by a few bloated and self-important steam engines. Sometimes the engines appear like the prosperous merchants who visited her in Ambala and she herself seems a solitary carriage, pushed down a track by she knows not whom, heading she knows not for what destination, as others throw the switches that determine her direction.

There is much of contemporary critical interest in these passages. Manto himself cites them, in an essay responding to the charge of obscenity, only to argue that his prostitute stories are realistic and not obscene, a question to which I shall return.[30] What concerns me here in the railway-yard passages, however, is the manner in which they make visible the representational practices of the nation. For Sultana's perception that the worlds of national modernization and the brothel are reflections of each other, that moment of allegory and counter-allegory is made possible only in this place called 'Delhi'. Even in Ambala cantonment, Manto tells us, she had lived near the railway station, but such thoughts had never entered her mind there. It is only within a *national* orientation, in other words, that such allegorical

---

[30] Saadat Hasan Manto, 'Safed Jhut', in *Mantonama*, pp. 674–83.

connections between the body of the woman and the body politic become possible. Furthermore, Manto's text draws attention to and comments upon the national allegory itself. The effect of the passage as a whole, in other words, is meta-allegorical. Manto's text therefore reproduces the classic tropic structure of the nationalist text, namely, the figuring of nation as woman, but ironically displaces its locus from mother to prostitute, commenting in the process on the allegories inherent in the nation as a representational form.

As Sultana languishes in Delhi's G.B. Road (infamous for its brothels), the holy month of Muharram approaches, and she realizes that she does not have a full suit of traditional black clothes that she needs to mark this month of ritual mourning. She has a white *kurta* (tunic) and *dupatta* (scarf), which Khuda Bakhsh had given her for Diwali, which she can have dyed black. But she is missing a black *shalvar* (trousers). Her two friends in the neighbourhood, also prostitutes, have shiny new black clothes of satin and georgette. One of them, Mukhtar, has a new satin shalvar that Sultana eyes with particular envy. One day, standing in the balcony, looking across at the rail yard, she notices a young man in the street looking up at her, and seeing her signal he comes up to her apartment. But this man, named Shankar, quickly disabuses her of any hope that he will prove a client. Insisting that *she* had called him up, and so should pay for his company with sexual services, he leaves her stunned at the sudden reversal of the roles of professional and client. She is initially angered but they quickly become friends and he a frequent visitor to Sultana's home.

As Muharram draws near, Sultana's panic mounts. She begs Khuda Bakhsh to somehow raise the money for a shalvar, but he leaves her with no illusions. Finally one day she approaches Shankar. Anxiously stressing that she is not asking payment for her services, Sultana asks him to get her not the money for a pair of trousers but the trousers themselves—in other words, a gift. Shankar tells her he has no money but nevertheless promises to get her a black shalvar by the first of Muharram. Then he points to Sultana's cheap costume earrings and asks if he can have them. Wondering what he could possibly want with such worthless jewellery, she hands them over. Sultana is not at all certain that Shankar will keep his promise, but early on the morning of the first there is a knock on her door, and it is Shankar, looking dishevelled, as if he has just stumbled out of bed somewhere nearby. He hands over a bundle to Sultana and leaves: it is a new black shalvar, rather like the one she has seen with her friend Mukhtar. Thrilled by the prospect of a complete suit of clothes, but thrilled even more because Shankar has kept his promise, Sultana changes into her new things, and just then there is a knock on the door. It is Mukhtar. As they meet at the door, the two women are stopped in their tracks by something—as Mukhtar eyes Sultana's new trousers and the latter recognizes Mukhtar's new earrings. They lie to each other about their new acquisitions, and the story ends with the intimation that after that the two had to remain silent for a moment. In that silence of the two women, in that silent, mutual recognition of love and betrayal, we may read Manto's relationship to that orientation of the nationalist subject that comes to us coded as love for the Mother-nation. For Shankar's betrayal of Sultana (and of Mukhtar) does not imply an *absence* of 'love'. On the contrary, it is precisely the simultaneity of faithfulness and betrayal that constitutes for Manto the variety of love he places in the brothel.

Although he appears near the end of the story, Shankar is an instrumental figure in it. When, on first meeting Sultana, Shankar makes fun of Khuda Bakhsh for chasing after holy men, she responds that he is making fun of 'our holy men' because he is a Hindu. Shankar's responce to Sultana is a typical Manto exercise in inversion: 'In places such as these [i.e. brothels], Hindu-Muslim questions do not arise. Even great *pandits* and *maulvis*, were they to come here, would become *sharif*' (668/215). Thus the brothel renders ironic the concept of *sharafat*, one of the most overcoded words in the glossary of modern north Indian history. Sharafat is at once decency, nobility of character, social respectability, and the fact of belonging to the diffuse and overlapping set of élite Muslim (and, to some extent, Hindu) castes, sub-castes and other social groupings known as the *shurafa* or *ashraf*. As the meaning of sharafat is transformed in the nineteenth century to incorporate the emerging experience of bourgeois respectability, it is rendered ironic in the figure of the courtesan, who is now simultaneously fallen woman and guardian of at least some high cultural forms—as *salonière*, arbiter of literary and musical taste, and instructor in élite social manners.[31] The tavaif belonged in very concrete ways to the pre-colonial social élites of cities like Lahore and Lucknow.[32] If, by the end of the nineteenth century, the figure of courtesan becomes a compelling representation of the problematic of Muslimness in the emergence of the Indian modern—most famously, as I have noted, in Rusva's novel—this is at least in part due to its ability to metonymically stand in for the culture of the *pre-modern* élites of north India. The courtesan, in other words, embodies the ambivalent articulation of 'Muslim' and 'bourgeoisie' that characterizes the Indian modern, an ambivalence that is typically misrecognized in secular nationalist discourse as the sign simply of a *lag* in development.[33]

If we may read the figure of courtesan in *Umrao Jan Ada* as a supplement to the nation-Mother, at what Partha Chatterjee has called nationalism's moment of departure, in Manto's bedraggled prostitutes we encounter its ironic reinscription at nationalism's moment of arrival. Rusva's élite courtesan encodes the relationship of the north Indian Muslim élites to nationalism's attempted reorientation of the subject towards a veneration of the nation-Mother, a reorientation whose most influential literary representation is generally held to be Mahendra's conversion at the hands of the *sannyasis* in Bankim's *Anandamath*.[34] In the élite programme of religious reform envisioned by nationalism at its moment of departure, the figuring of nation as mother therefore performs a central function: it seeks to fix the (élite) subject's orientation towards the nation as the love of the (male) child for its mother. In the courtly gatherings in Umrao Jan's *kotha*— neither 'salon' nor 'brothel' can quite capture the complex cultural and

---

[31] For a brilliant 'thick description' of sharafat and its vicissitudes in the nineteenth century, see Lelyveld, 1978, pp. 35–101.

[32] See, for instance, Veena Talwar Oldenburg, 'Lifestyle as Resistance: The Case of the Courtesans of Lucknow, India', in *Feminist Studies* 16(2) (Summer 1990), pp. 259–87.

[33] For an examination of this trope in Nehru's *Discovery of India*, see my 'Secularism and Minority.'

[34] See Shetty, 1995, pp. 55–6; and Kaviraj, 1995, p. 139.

sociological significations of this word—we see another model of human relations. Here the extraction of tribute by a culturally accomplished courtesan from her patron(s), rather than filial piety, governs the possibility of 'love', that is, of human attachment. The nation is a distinctly modern form—a form of (*gessellschaft*-like) association, but one that turns to the metaphorical possibilities of the family in order to claim (*gemeinschaft*-like) primacy, spontaneity and naturalness. The stylized figure of the courtesan both points to a distinct cultural ethos and marks 'Muslim' belonging as ambivalently modern—a simultaneously tributary and 'voluntary' or non-organic form of coherence of the collective.[35] It marks the inability of nationalist discourse to deal with the figure of the Muslim in terms of the familial imagery that governs its imaginary, and at the same time produces 'the Muslim' as a distinct problematic history and community.[36]

In Manto's stories, the elevated figure of the courtesan is stripped of the appurtenances of style, a move sometimes figured, as it were 'literally', in the figure of a naked woman—as we have already seen in 'Kali Shalvar', but as also is the case in 'Khushiya'—and is reduced to an ordinary prostitute. Manto's prostitutes eke out a tawdry and miserable existence in the back lanes of Bombay, in small cantonment towns, in the planned prostitutes' quarters of colonial Delhi. Thus we may read them in a literary historical register as accounts of the transformation of the representational practices of nationalist culture, as a fragmentary history of the (gendered) sign in the life of Indian nationalism. For, the meaning of 'Mother India' for nationalism at its moment of arrival is significantly altered from its significance at the moment of departure. For the secular nationalist—and again the canonical elaboration is to be found in *Discovery of India*, in the famous

---

[35] In its post-Partition rearticulations, for instance in the 'Muslim social' genre, the courtesan encodes (marked) Muslim selfhood as style only, that is, as an excess beyond the (unmarked) self that is representative. In other words, it encodes 'the Muslim' as minority.

[36] On the conception of India at the turn of the century as 'a collection of communities' rather than of 'citizens', see Gyanendra Pandey, *The Construction of Communalism in Colonial North India* (Delhi: Oxford University Press, 1990), p. 210.

passage in Chapter Three titled 'Bharat Mata'—it is a symbol that emerges spontaneously in the realm of subaltern life. It is a means not to the interpellation of the élite male subject himself but of his interaction with the masses. The urban, 'sophisticated' consciousness that is the nationalist has transcended its reliance on the modes of thought implicit in that symbol, which comes to appear to him as a variety of superstition. His use of it now is entirely self-conscious and instrumental: it is an element of the language he must speak when he addresses the peasant masses, with their 'limited outlook', even as his goal is to shake its hold over their minds, to lead them to a secular and rational sense of themselves as the nation.[37] This frankly instrumental mobilization of (a desexualized) motherhood is translated in Manto's fiction into the sexual exploitation of the prostitute. Thus such figures as Ram Lal and Madho in 'Hatak' and Khuda Bakhsh in 'Kali Shalvar', who put female sexuality in circulation, occupy the position of the nationalist in Manto's meta-allegory.

This is the position that Shankar, in his first meeting with Sultana, refuses to occupy. His reply to Sultana, as I have already noted, hinges around an interrogation of the meaning of sharafat, and, in the first instance, uncouples the latter term's moral and sociological significations. But sharafat is here also given a specifically political meaning. Were they to be made subject to the rules of 'places such as these', even 'pandits' and 'maulvis'—Hindu and Muslim religious scholars or priests—would become 'sharif,' that is, 'decent' or 'respectable'. What is being elaborated here are the terms of (political and cultural) 'decency' with respect to the crisis of Muslim, and hence national, identity. As with Nehruvian secularism, 'decency' here means a rejection of communal separatism, but this rejection does not take the form of a mere disavowal of difference. To the realm of (national-) bourgeois respectability and its familial elaborations of national belonging, Manto counters the brothel with its own unique resources of affect and attachment.

The prostitute has long been a paradigmatic figure for the literature

[37] Jawaharlal Nehru, *The Discovery of India* (Delhi: Oxford University Press, 1989), pp. 59–60. See Chatterjee, 1986, p. 147.

of the modern West; around her circulate a number of anxieties about chaos and social disruption. In the Paris of the Second Empire, according to Susan Buck-Morss's reading of Benjamin's arcades project, she represents the feminization of flânerie; she is the female flâneur par excellence.[38] What makes the prostitute threatening for the regulation of space in the industrial metropolis is her ability to circulate within social space across the internal dividers of bourgeois society: from private to public domains, across class boundaries, in violation of the distinction between seller and commodity. In the colonial city, as Claire Wills has noted, she also traverses the boundaries of race and nation.[39] And we may read Sultana's exchanging, at the behest of her pimp, of British tommy clients for Indian ones as Manto's inscription of nationalism's anxieties about the treacherousness of undomesticated female sexuality. But in Manto's Delhi, unlike Joyce's Dublin, to which Wills alludes here, the threat that the prostitute poses is not one linked to her as a figure of flânerie. On the contrary, as we have seen, she is at first literally lost in this uniform modern space characterized by anonymity and the chance encounter—both conditions for the activity of the flâneur—and if finally she is able to manoeuvre through it with some success, this proficiency is of a tentative, external and artificial nature. What she highlights is the alterity of the subaltern, not its subsumability within a narrative of ethical development. Therefore, she exposes the ambivalent universalism of the projects of colonial and nationalist modernity.[40]

But the larger threat that the prostitute poses in Manto's story is to the domesticated female sexuality that provides the idiom of national

---

[38] Susan Buck-Morss, 'The Flâneur, the Sandwichman, and the Whore: The Politics of Loitering', in *New German Critique* 39 (1986), pp. 99–140.

[39] Claire Wills, 'Joyce, Prostitution, and the Colonial City', *South Atlantic Quarterly* 95(1) (Winter 1996), pp. 79–95.

[40] While I admire and applaud the wide-ranging contemporary critical efforts—in the work, among others, of Edward Said, David Lloyd, Seamus Deane, Luke Gibbons, Joe Cleary, and Wills herself—to rethink Irish cultural experience in modernity as that of a colonial and postcolonial society, I do think that this move requires extra caution that we not simply conflate an experience such as Ireland's with that of Third World societies like India or Egypt.

belonging. The prostitute, the characteristic figure of deceitfulness and duplicity, provides Manto with a way to reinscribe the workings of faithfulness and loyalty in the narrative of national modernity. She and her environment—the brothel—hint at the possibility of another form of 'love' for the nation. It is a form of love that we may speak of as improper, both in the sense of being transgressive and of not being true to its own name—one that is less singular and totalizing, outside the discourse of filial nature, more open to 'doubt' and 'betrayal'. In this sense we may read Shankar as a figure for the Urdu writer himself. The latter's ambivalent relationship to the cultural protocols of the nation as they are produced in the culture of nationalism, the 'betrayal' inherent in his demystification of those protocols, and the paradoxical act of cultural and political fidelity of which in the end he proves capable—these features of Urdu literary culture find an appropriate representation in the relationship of Shankar to Sultana and Mukhtar in Manto's story.

I wish to stress here that, in arguing that we read the sexual circulation of women in Manto's stories as a representation of bourgeois nationalism's instrumental relation to the gendered sign in the public domain, I am not suggesting that we view the prostitute as simply a figure for capitalist modernity in its colonial-nationalist version. In 'Hatak', for instance, it is the brothel that makes possible at least a semblance of 'love', of human attachment, as against the impersonal forces of the market, and the possibility of this semblance is destroyed by the relentless logic of the market, whose agent in the story is the bourgeois client—the client's 'Unh' is his judgement on the woman as commodity. It is interesting therefore that neither the bourgeois nor the prostitute can truly traverse the distance between these two worlds of home and brothel—for the latter this traversal can only be the object of an unfulfilled desire—and they must meet in the street, the site proper for the negotiating of an exchange. As in 'Kali Shalvar', the brothel here for Manto is not simply synonymous with the logic of commodity exchange that regulates urban public space. The brothel is that which makes unstable the opposition of public and private, highlighting the gendered metaphor of domesticity that governs the 'public' domain of national belonging. It is also highly significant in this regard that, in 'Kali Shalvar', Sultana's new trousers do not come as payment for sexual services—from within the regime of commodity exchange in which she is administered by Khuda Bakhsh—but rather as gift. It is a remarkable conclusion to the story, one that carries an implicit critique of bourgeois modernity, of the exchangeability of values, but which in no way relies upon a gesture of recuperation or return to some uncomplicated past of presence and propriety, a preference for use- over exchange-value. For Manto, the (bourgeois) home is itself contaminated by the logic of exchange as it is put in circulation as sign by an instrumental nationalist rationality. And the gift here is itself improper, an exchange between two women with their common lover as the mediating term. By thus opening up the opposing terms 'gift' and 'commodity' to a mutual influence, the text complicates the opposition of tradition to modernity, of past to present. If through Shankar, Manto is able to produce a critique of religio-communalist sentiment, this is achieved neither through a narrative of ethical development—whose end-point is the abstract and 'secular' citizen subject—nor by reference to an eternal and undifferentiated India, but rather in the 'brothel', in the contingent give-and-take of human interaction. Shankar is the figure for an indigenous and vernacular modernity whose rejection of communalism rests on the assumption that it is *possible* to live otherwise, rather than inevitable.

The inhabitants of Manto's brothels are therefore significant figures in the contested field of significations that is national belonging. They allow us to see more fully the workings of gender in the crisis of national identity. If it is the case that the language of motherhood and veneration is itself implicated in the history of the Hindu-Muslim conflict in colonial India, this is not because the figure of the venerated Mother is derived from religious practices that are exclusively of the 'Hindu' majority, as is sometimes argued even by critics of Muslim separatism, and even from 'nationalist Muslim' positions.[41] Such

---

[41] See for instance Imtiaz Ahmad, 'Secularism and Communalism', in *Economic and Political Weekly* (July 1996), pp. 1137–58.

arguments are metalepses, a confusing of cause and effect, for the figuring of nation as Mother is itself instrumental in the division of the field of national experience into 'major' and 'minor' realms marked by religious difference. The function of this figure is to insert the subject within an economy of filial 'love' toward the nation-object, to produce the subject precisely as national subject. The male subject marked by 'Muslim' difference, even when offered a place in this tableau of familial love, cannot be figured as the *son* of the nation-Mother. The singularity of affect or 'love' implied in the veneration of the nation-Mother would, in other words, place 'the Muslims' in the position of minority, distinct from the sons of the mother even if allied with them, and make them subject henceforth, within the realm of politics, to the numerical logic of 'minority rights' and state 'protection'. It is this solution of the crisis of identity in colonial India, its successful minoritization, which is always implicit in the categories of nationalist thought, whose critique Manto's stories make possible by suggesting the possibility of imagining social cohesion and cultural belonging in terms other than that of filial love. Manto's prostitutes shatter this familial tableau and hint at possibilities of love unimagined in the affective economy of nationalism.

Exploited, abused and exhausted, Manto's prostitutes nevertheless continue to manufacture within their lives the signs of ordinary existence—religious-ritual observances, the pangs of human attachment, even love and marriage. Confined by law and custom to the margins of society, defined by ascendant bourgeois morality as those who live by the sale of their 'virtue', they somehow manage, perversely, to lead virtuous lives. Manto himself speculates about this inversion in one of his essays on the prostitute:

> I find strange talk of the repeated sale of virtue . . . Virtue, to the extent that I understand it, is sold only once. And that only if we equate it with the purity of character of the woman of the purely domestic sort . . . Because it is quite possible that, among prostitutes, that woman is considered virtuous who is true to the principles of her trade, who doesn't hand over her body for free.[42]

---

[42] 'Gunah ki betiyan, gunah ke bap', in *Mantonama*, p. 332.

The point of the prostitute for Manto is that she unsettles and puts in motion the antinomies of bourgeois respectability. Her ambiguous status as seller and commodity makes visible the exploitation of domesticated female sexuality in the bourgeois home. But once inscribed in the gendered troping of nation and national belonging, she also highlights this exploitation of woman as metaphor and stands as a rebuke to the frank instrumentalism with which bourgeois nationalism mobilizes the image of Mother. I am not suggesting here that we read Manto's reinscription of this figure as a proto-feminist critique of nationalist neo-patriarchal modernity. As with the prostitute in Benjamin's arcades project, she does not represent an unambiguous affirmation of a free female sexuality.[43] But Manto's lack of sentimentalism in this regard is itself salutary, avoiding any easy, and ultimately masculinist, gestures of representability. What these stories do make possible is a denaturalization of the work of gender in the representative practices of the nation. Furthermore—and this has been the larger point of my readings in this essay—for Manto, the form of improper and non-totalizing love of which she is the figure makes available possibilities of selfhood and human attachment that are denied and suppressed by nationalism. She exposes the claim of purity of the 'national family', of the 'chaste maternity' of the nation, and for this reason can become a site for opening up the question of identity precisely where nationalism would close it up.[44]

Conclusion: Nation, Fragment, Totality

As I noted earlier, Manto was eventually condemned by 'progressive' critics for taking an unhealthy interest in the abnormal and the prurient. In 1944, Zaheer described his story 'Bu' (Odour) at the All-India Urdu Congress as escapist and even reactionary, marking the beginnings of the break between Manto and the Urdu section of the

---

[43] See Buck-Morss, 1986, pp. 119–20.

[44] Wills, 1996, p. 93. Wills is referring here to the function of the prostitute in Joyce's fictions as an unmasking of the claims of Irish nationalism, but not, so far as I can tell, with respect to the question of minority.

AIPWA.[45] The charge of obscenity to which his stories became subject from a wide range of literary quarters obviously refers at one level to content, to Manto's relatively explicit treatment of sexuality. But it also contains a larger resonance, pointing to the transgression in Manto's stories of the protocols of what I have called national realism. The insistent irony of Manto's stories, his characteristic irreverence for all cultural and political pieties and solemnities, and his elevation of doubt and 'betrayal' to something like the imperatives of an ethical life—taken together these indeed cannot but translate within a national realist aesthetics as 'obscenity'. Perhaps the most revealing condemnation of his work from the Left came a few years after Partition from the leading poet and critic Ali Sardar Jafri. Comparing Manto's stories unfavourably with those of Krishan Chander, who was by then producing boilerplate and utterly forgettable narratives of rural life and Partition violence, Jafri wrote: 'The difference between Krishan's and Manto's stories is this, that Manto's heroes are mutilated men; therefore they cannot be representative, because they cannot represent the evolution of life. Krishan's heroes are courageous and conscious builders of life. They express evolution; therefore they are representative.'[46] What is 'obscene' about Manto's stories is, therefore, that they undermine the narrative resolutions through which the 'representative'—that is, national—self is produced. The real point of the debate about Manto's work is the cavalier attitude of his stories not towards sex itself, but rather towards the nation, or, more precisely, towards the gendered narratives of national belonging.

Following Lukács, I argued earlier that what is distinct about the short-story as a 'minor epic form' is that it 'singles out a fragment from the immeasurable infinity of the events of life', thereby making possible a relation of subject to totality that is distinct from that of the realist novel.[47] Urdu's emphasis on the short-story, I suggested, should be read in terms of this formal possibility. Urdu literary culture in late

---

[45] See Azmi, 1972, p. 93.
[46] Quoted in Fleming, 1985, pp. 28–9.
[47] Lukács, 1989, p. 50.

colonial India is located ambivalently at the cusp of 'nation' and 'minority', resisting precisely the resolutions that Partition is an attempt to implement: minoritization in India, nationalization in Pakistan. I have argued elsewhere that these resolutions remain still incomplete, that at its best Urdu literature continues to be the site for recovering forms of selfhood, community and collective memory at odds with the categories of the nation-state system.[48] The situation of Urdu therefore allows us to comprehend the categories of minority experience in a more complex manner than has often been the case in recent discussions of 'minority literature', many of them indebted to Gilles Deleuze and Félix Guattari's influential essay on the place of the Jewish Kafka in the literary history of European modernism. Minority emerges from this exploration as an ongoing process and pressure, necessarily incomplete, rather than a thing, simply a *type* of writing distinguished by its demographic and sociological situation: 'A minor literature ... is ... that which a minority constructs within a major language.'[49] The standpoint of Urdu allows a multifaceted interrogation of the formation of national and 'communal' identity in modern South Asian history.

But what has concerned us here is Manto's relationship as a writer to this wider literary and cultural problematic. It is not my argument that Manto is *typical* in the 'obscene' nature of his short stories, in the over-coded sense I have outlined above, or that in the two decades leading up to Partition there are literally no longer narratives produced in Urdu—the work of Premchand and Krishan Chander, for instance, would provide counter-evidence on both these counts. What I am arguing is that Manto is not so much a representative as an *exemplary* Urdu writer in his relationship to the discourse of nationhood. His work exemplifies in a unique manner the tensions that constitute Urdu as a literary formation at this key moment in its modern history.

---

[48] Aamir R. Mufti, 'This Self Which is Not One: Lyric and Partition in Faiz Ahmed Faiz', unpublished MS.
[49] Gilles Deleuze and Félix Guattari, *Kafka: Toward a Minor Literature*, tr. Dana Polan (Minneapolis: University of Minnesota Press, 1986), p. 16.

In his practice of the short-story form, Manto inscribes this tension as the paradox of a 'minor' narrative form mobilized for 'major' literary and cultural aims. The (gendered) 'fragment of life' that is the brothel appears with great frequency in Manto's stories, in particular the stories of the first decade of his career, the decade before Partition. But this fragment does not simply affirm the totality of which it is part—the modern life of the nation. It disturbs the serenity of the manner in which that totality is produced, pointing always to the possibility of ways of life that are less singular and more hospitable to human freedom.

A Space for Violence: Anthropology, Politics and the Location of a Sinhala Practice of Masculinity

PRADEEP JEGANATHAN

IN LATE APRIL 1992 I sat on a little stage on a small hillock in southern Colombo. Malathi de Alwis, who sat beside me, and I were to judge several contests. About 300 people, nearly everyone who considered themselves to be from Patupara, our community, had gathered for the event, which we all eagerly awaited. It was now mid-afternoon, but the day's activities had started much earlier, with several different sporting events, including road races and cricket matches. All this was part of New Year celebrations which in the urban neighbourhood where we lived, as in many similar communities, comes in two parts.

The first half of the astrologically marked week, usually encompassing the 13th and 14th of April, was commonly a private affair: if you got on particularly well with your neighbours you would expect some home-cooked sweets by the end of the week. The second half is far more public, a community event. Here a group of young working-class men of the area form a committee, gather money from anyone and everyone (but especially middle- and upper-middle-class people if they can be approached) and put together an extraordinary show that could include contests of strength, skill and beauty.

Malathi and I had moved in to this community in March of that year, three weeks before New Year. A week after we moved in, a group of men came by with a list for donations. I decided to ante-up, as I wanted to make a good impression. After all, people barely knew me in the area, even though a powerful family, the Pereras, had introduced me to a few notables as a friend and researcher. Therefore not only did I put my name down for a hundred rupees—ten times as much as anyone else had done—but I also handed over the money up front. This was very rare and it had a consequence I hadn't quite anticipated: the committee asked Malathi and me to be 'judges' for the contests. So, having bought my way into this not-very consequential position, I sat on the makeshift stage, waiting for the contest to begin. We had just been introduced on the booming sound system; we were no longer strangers in the area. We were now known as outsiders looking in.

This, I thought to myself, not unhappily, was the very moment I had been awaiting three years. Those years, at the University of Chicago, were geared to this moment where I would enter that place which my supervisor Bernard Cohn had written about with such wit, and guided me towards with great seriousness: anthropologyland.[1] I had, of course, grown up in Colombo, a few miles from where I now was, and had returned frequently for protracted visits after I had gone off to college in the US after the 1983 riots. But those were visits home; this was very different. Anthropologyland was for me a place where anthropology was possible, and I, having learnt in Haskell Hall, its protocols and practices, arguments and archive, canon and method, was now ready to practice. I had already tried my hand at the craft and had had some success the week before: a puberty ritual that a neighbour had invited me to compared reasonably well with its canonical description in the literature.[2] Yes, there were deviations to be noticed,

---

[1] Bernard Cohn, 'History and Anthropology: The State of Play', in *An Anthropologist Among the Historians and Other Essays* (Delhi: Oxford University Press, 1987), pp. 18–49. I note here, all too inadequately, the profound influence this essay has had in my understanding of 'anthropology'.

[2] The work I consulted while in Patupara was Geraldine Gamburd's description 'Rites of Passage and Kingship Ties', in Tissa Fernando and Robert N. Kearney (eds),

and transformations to be theorized, but in the main, as a normative account of what might be, the account was valuable.

The contest, as it turned out, would interrupt the smooth flow of my anthropology. It was a 'fancy dress contest' for children—twelve children had entered, they all wore different costumes and were to parade in front of us. We judges had to pick winners and runners-up. There were, represented among the children, schoolteachers and palm-readers, a postman and a snake charmer. But the kid who stole the show, and won first prize by general acclamation as it turned out, was a *chandiya*.

Vikum, who was nine, was dressed in a sarong tucked up high. His chest was bare of clothing, a medallion hung from his neck. On his chest was written in black marker pen: 'I am not afraid' (*mama baya nahe*). In his hand was a bottle of frothy liquid that was clearly meant to be moonshine. Vikum lifted one end of his sarong as he walked swaying, taking imaginary swigs from his bottle. In between his belt and skin, its handle sticking out, was a knife. The performance was superb, the parody perfect. Vikum had us in fits of laughter because he both represented and ridiculed something extraordinarily serious. We knew what he was representing: the *chandiya*, which I will gloss here as 'thug'. Such men come in all shapes, sizes and varieties. But they can, upon occasion, beat, cut, chop, maim, kill, loot and burn, or throw acid on your face so that you are disfigured for life. I saw then, surrounding Vikum, a masculine zone or an area which I will record in this essay: a space for violence. There it was, in front of me, the making of that space through an identifiable set of practices of masculinity, a way of being a *chandiya*. Clearly it was a habitus that could be learnt and performed, parodically or seriously, so regular that it was recognizable to a whole community either with laughter or with terror.

Even as I saw Vikum win first prize, I began to wonder how I would configure the practices at stake here as an anthropological object, or

---

Modern Sri Lanka: A Society in Transition (Syracuse, NY: Maxwell School of Citizenship and Public Affairs, 1979). The literature on this matter is, of course, too rich to be addressed here.

how, in other words, I would make this phenomenon apprehensible to my anthropology. For me this was and continues to be a matter for serious thought. It is possible to suggest, of course, that this is a false problem. By this line of reasoning, an anthropologist just studies what is in front of him. I disagree, arguing that the world is not transparently available to me. On the contrary, I suggest that the world is always mediated and constructed by archives of knowledge and protocols of knowledge production. Take my previous example, of a puberty ritual. This is a canonical object of anthropology, and it was therefore epistemologically available to me through anthropology, before I even set eyes on the event in my neighbour's house. The existence of a canonical knowledge on ritual that I had access to through the literature allowed that object a particular kind of visibility to my anthropological eyes.[3]

Just as the event in my neighbour's house had been visible to me through the category of ritual, Vikum's performance was visible to me under the sign of violence. This was because I had made it my business to view things around me in relation to that category: I was trying to produce an anthropology of violence. Yet, unlike ritual, violence is not a well worn, firmly canonized category in anthropology. In fact, the concern with violence in Sri Lankan anthropology is extremely recent, arising only after the massive anti-Tamil violence of July 1983.[4] This

---

[3] I only rehearse here a set of arguments that have been made with considerable sophistication elsewhere. Apart from Cohn, 1997, I have found Arjun Appadurai's 'Theory in Anthropology: Center and Periphery', in *Comparative Studies in Society and History*, 28(2), 1986, pp. 356–61, Dipesh Chakrabarty's 'Realist Prose and the Problem of Difference: The Relational and the Magical in Subaltern History' (unpublished mss. copy), David Scott's 'conclusion' in *Formations of Ritual: Colonial and Anthropological Discourse on the Sinhala Yakovil* (Minneapolis: University of Minnesota Press, 1994), and Kamala Visveswaran's *Fictions of Feminist Ethnography* (Minneapolis: University of Minnesota Press, 1994), helpful in different ways.

[4] During this 'riot', urban and suburban working- and lower-middle-class Sinhala men attacked the bodies, spaces and commodities of Tamils of all classes. It resulted in deaths in the thousands and economic disruption in billions of rupees. The political economy of the event, it has been argued in the most complex work available, is to be seen in relation to the under-capitalization of a Sinhala entrepreneurial class, in

event produces a profound rupture in the narration of Sri Lanka's modernity. Even as it does that, it becomes the historical and conceptual condition of possibility of an anthropology of violence. In other words, 1983, taken as a totality, makes available the category 'violence' to the anthropology of Sri Lanka.[5] It is this availability of violence that informed my reading of Vikum's parody under the sign of violence. My question then is this: how, given that anthropologization of violence, are the practices parodied by Vikum's performance, and others like it, to be made anthropologically apprehensible? This essay attempts an answer to that question.

To do so, I will need to make a critical or oppositional space in a particular strand of the Sri Lankanist anthropology of violence that bears a certain relationship to Vikum's parody. That literature is concerned with both the everyday and extraordinary practice of violence in Sinhala society, and seeks to explain both these forms of violence as culturally constituted phenomena.[6] Which is to say that this anthropology builds a causal bridge between the practice of violence and a larger field of Sinhala cultural practices. My effort will be to move through

---

contrast to their counterparts, in the post-1977 monetarist regime. Such uneven capitalization, it is argued, provides the structural conditions of possibility for the event. While I find such accounts important and useful, I shall not evaluate them seriously in the course of my argument here. See Newton Gunesinhe, 'The Open Economy and Its Impact on Ethnic Relations in Sri Lanka', Committee for Rational Development, ed., in *Sri Lanka: The Ethnic Conflict—Myths, Realities and Perspectives* (Delhi: Navrang, 1985) and Sunil Bastian, 'Political Economy of Ethnic Violence in Sri Lanka: The July 1983 Riots', in Veena Das (ed.), *Mirrors of Violence: Communities, Riots and Survivors in South Asia* (Delhi, Oxford University Press, 1990).

[5] I summarize here a more detailed argument on the canonicity of 'violence' which I make in the paper 'Violence as a Problem: Sri Lankanist Anthropology in the Wake of a Riot', presented at the South-South Workshop on Re-Thinking the Third World: History/Development/Politics, University of the West Indies, Mona, Jamaica, Dec. 1996. A revised and longer version of this paper is available as a chapter of my University of Chicago doctoral thesis, 'After a Riot: Anthropological Locations of Violence in an Urban Sri Lankan Community'.

[6] See for a location of this strand in relation to other such strands, Jeganathan, 'Violence as a Problem'.

this anthropological knowledge, traversing it critically, attempting at every turn to produce an object that will allow the 'space for violence' that surrounds Vikum to be anthropologized.

I choose this trope of space here to aid my critical project—to contrast it with what is a thinness or a lack of such space in the literature I want to consider. That literature positions violence as a 'fury' or an 'eruption', always uncontrolled and unthought. These explosions are then juxtaposed to 'restraint' or 'peace': the supposed state of ordinary life in Sinhala society. Therein lies the difficulty, or the need for a critical, oppositional project. For if this is the received anthropologization of practices of violence in Sinhala society, then how would the practices Vikum was parodying be anthropologized? For surely, the practices parodied cannot, as a rule, be reduced to unthinking explosions?

There is not then, simply put, an anthropological space to locate the practices Vikum was parodying. Or, in other words, there is no adequate 'space' for violence in this anthropological literature. Why? Why is violence, both everyday and extraordinary, anthropologized as an irruption or explosion? I will take this question seriously as I attempt to construct a space for violence, both anthropological and ethnographic, analytic and descriptive. In other words, I shall take this absence or lack of a 'space for violence' in the previous literature as the productive origin of my own counter-effort. In so doing, I hope not only to produce new knowledge about violence, but also perhaps about the nature of anthropological objects.

Let me start, as I must, with that celebrated anthropologist of the Sinhalese, Bruce Kapferer. His argument in *Legends of People, Myths of State*[7] is that there is a relationship between the 'riots' of July 1983 and 'exorcism', a Sinhala ritual practice that he had studied earlier. Let me read his statements closely. For Kapferer, the collective violence that was experienced by Sri Lankans in the summer of 1983 was a 'fury', as in 'the fury of the riots was demonic'.[8] Or take this sentence:

---

[7] Bruce Kapferer, *Legends of People, Myths of State: Violence, Intolerance, and Political Culture in Sri Lanka and Australia* (Washington: Smithsonian Institution Press, 1988).

[8] Kapferer, 1988, p. 29.

'I consider that there is a relationship between the passion of sorcery and the furious passion of ethnic violence.'[9] Now, having read these large claims, David Scott asks of Kapferer with considerable analytic justification: 'So tell us what precisely constitutes such an authentically "demonic" fury', so that particular kinds of fury can be then analytically distinguished from 'other equally . . . authentic *kinds* of fury' that might be available in Sinhala society.[10] But my question, or what I want to remark on here, is another categorical slippage in Kapferer's text: that between 'violence' and 'fury'. That is to say, in Kapferer's text, at the beginning of the lines we are reading, when he writes—'the fury of the riots was demonic'—what is for him simultaneously both ethnographic and anthropological is the 'was demonic' part of the equation. But there is a prior question here that does not seem to enter Kapferer's analytical field. And that is the first part of the equation, or in other words, the phrase: 'the fury of the riots . . .' Why would violence have anything to do with 'fury', or 'furious passion'? Kapferer, one might conclude, has naturalized 'furious' as a description of Sinhala collective violence. That naturalization proceeds simultaneously with another naturalization that has to do with the supposed opposite of this furious violence. Take this key sentence: 'Here is a reason, extraordinary as it may seem, for the sudden, almost inexplicable, transformation of a normally peaceful people into violent and murderously rampaging mobs.'[11] What I want to emphasize here is the contrast drawn between the two adjectives 'peaceful' *vs.* 'murderously rampaging'. Just as violence has, in Kapferer's Lanka, something to do with 'fury' and 'rampages', those very tropes of violence are to be juxtaposed, in this very same Lanka, to what is ordinary: 'normally peaceful people'. Once these two ethnographic poles have been established, as naturalized self-evident 'facts', as it were, it is then and only then, mind you, that anthropological theory emerges, or in other words 'an explanation' is required. For Kapferer's sentence on what I have called

[9] Ibid., p. 32.
[10] David Scott, 'The Demonology of Nationalism: On the Anthropology of Ethnicity and Violence in Sri Lanka', in *Economy and Society* 19(4), 1990, p. 494.
[11] Kapferer, 1988, p. 101.

the two ethnographic poles begins with the phrase: 'Here is the reason . . .' The contrast between peacefulness and furious violence has emerged then as a problematique which, in Althusser's words, is the 'constitutive unity of the effective thoughts that make up the domain of the existing ideological field with which a particular author must settle accounts in his own thought.'[12] It is my contention that this problematique is central to this strand of the anthropology of violence in Sinhala society.

Take another example, that of Jonathan Spencer, who was 'in the field' when 'violence broke out' in July 1983.[13] I will confine myself to Spencer's most concentrated analysis of this subject, 'Collective Violence and Everyday Practice in Sri Lanka'.[14] First, Spencer considers 'violence and aggression in everyday practice', and, as it turns out, there is very little violent practice in Sinhala everyday life, or even for that matter, 'very little public dispute'.[15] And this, as Spencer would have it, is a product of the Sinhala notion of 'restraint'. He says: 'the relative invisibility of violence in day-to-day life can be linked to the strong emphasis on restraint in village social life . . .'[16] Spencer produces a Sinhala practice of 'restraint' to ground his analysis of the Sinhala 're-pression'[17] of everyday violence. He learnt, he tells us, in 'village discussions' that there was 'no space between complete non-violence and the sin of the violence; so the appearance of violence—an inevitability in some situations of conflict and tension—tends to be impulsive and uncontrolled.'[18] So violence, in Spencer's argument, is contained in

---

[12] Louis Althusser, *For Marx*, trans. Ben Brewster (New York: Vintage Books, 1969), p. 66.

[13] See Jonathan Spencer, 'Popular Perceptions of Violence', in James Manor (ed.), *Sri Lanka in Change and Crisis* (New York: St Martin's Press, 1984).

[14] Jonathan Spencer, 'Collective Violence and Everyday Practice in Sri Lanka', in *Modern Asian Studies*, 24 (3), 1990, pp. 603–23.

[15] Spencer 1990, p. 605.

[16] Ibid., p. 606.

[17] Ibid., p. 616.

[18] Ibid., p. 609. Spencer goes on to tell us that there is 'a lot of evidence to support the view that violence comes suddenly and wildly in everyday [Sinhala] life.' There is more 'evidence' to this effect in Spencer's monograph, *A Sinhala Village in a Time*

Sinhala notions of restraint—emerging suddenly, breaking through, erupting as it were, 'impulsive and uncontrolled'. Murder, Spencer goes on, like all violence, also involves 'a loss of self-control and constraint'; it too is 'impulsive', 'unpremeditated' in the main.[19] And collective violence, or at least the murderous part of collective violence of July 1983, can be understood in this vein. As Spencer would have it, 'like murder in everyday life, collective murder was a product of a loss of control, of a breakdown of everyday restraint . . . the patterns which lie behind everyday repression.'[20]

This notion of restraint, then, is the primary anthropological category through which the reading of violence as anything other than a fury, an eruption or an impulse, is foreclosed. If then an analytic space for violence is to be produced, it will have to be through a reformation of this category of restraint. In Kapferer's work, 'restraint'—as in a 'normally peaceful people'—is assumed. What is theorized is the

---

of Trouble (Delhi: Oxford University Press, 1990), p. 185. To wit: 'violence . . . is often terrifyingly *out of control* when it does occur. Murders are very frequently associated with drink and tend to be *sudden*, brutal affairs, *exploding* out of some minor disagreement in a *matter of seconds*' (my emphasis).

Spencer cites Eric Meyer's short essay on '1983', 'Seeking the Roots of the Tragedy' in Manor (ed.), *Sri Lanka in Change and Crisis*, in support of his claims, but misses Joke Schrijvers' important monograph which directly addresses questions of masculine violence, *Mother's for Life: Motherhood and Marginalization in the North Central Province of Sri Lanka* (Delft: Eburon, 1985). Schrijver's feminist intervention is an important counterpoint in the Sri Lankan anthropological canon, but she does not break new ground, unfortunately, on the question of masculine violence.

Consequential threats of murder and suicide are traditional phenomena in Sinhalese society, Schrijvers tells us, citing as her authority Robert Percivals's colonial text, 'An Account of the Island of Ceylon in 1803'. Such threats are actualized 'frequently in such cases', she reports, going on to note that the 'extreme' of 'violence' is 'perhaps . . . relatively easily reached in Sinhala culture'. To concretize this claim, Schrijvers offers an ethnographic example, which reads to me as one of near-mindless actions: 'One day he [the son of Kalubanda] demanded that his wife give him money but she refused and he stabbed her to death. When his father-in-law asked him why he had done it, he stabbed him as well.' Schrijvers 1985, pp. 209–10.

[19] Spencer 1990, p. 614.
[20] Ibid., p. 616.

'demonic fury' of violence.²¹ As such, it is not a suitable site for pursuing an unpacking of 'restraint'. Spencer's text, on the other hand, does the opposite analytical work. Here the 'eruptions' of violence are untheorized, but restraint is thought in more detail. The question that I must pursue then is this: what are the contours of the production of this category of 'restraint'?

Let me pursue this category further. Importantly, in this regard, it is to be noted that Spencer's notion of 'restraint' is produced through an argument with the work of Gananath Obeyesekere. 'Restraint' for Spencer is a different 'gloss' on the Sinhala practice of *lajja-baya* which Obeyesekere glossed as shame-fear. Spencer is not alone in thinking with Obeyesekere's categories here. R.L. Stirrat's comprehensive exposition of Obeyesekere's mature work is another such example.²² Agreeing with Obeyesekere that *lajja-baya* is a constant theme in Sinhala life but suggesting that his specific ethnographic

---

[21] As David Scott has pointed out in a set of sustained and compelling arguments with Kapferer's work—*Formations of Ritual* (1983)—'demonism' in that anthropology is a descendant of a colonial Christian idea. Such conceptions are succinctly captured in James Emerson Tennent's contrast of 'demon worship' and 'Buddhism' as in this passage: 'Yet strange to tell, under all the icy coldness of this barren system [Buddhism], there burn below the unextinguished fires of another and darker superstition . . . demon worship,' *Christianity in Ceylon* (London: John Murray, 1850), pp. 229–30.

[22] R.L. Stirrat, 'A View from Britain', in *Contributions to Indian Sociology*, (n.s.) 21(1) 1987. The texts that concern Stirrat are *Medusa's Hair* and *The Cult of the Goddess Pattini* (Chicago: The University Press, 1981 & 1984). The essay is part of a special issue of the journal that celebrates the work of Stanley Tambiah and Obeyesekere. I pick this canon-building essay to demonstrate the categorical centrality of 'shame-fear' in contemporary Sri Lankanist anthropology, where it has the status of what Arjun Appadurai, 1986, p. 357 has called a 'gatekeeping concept . . . in anthropological theory, concepts that . . . seem to limit anthropological theorizing about the place in question and that define the quintessential and dominant questions of interest in that region.'

An alternative genealogy of this 'gatekeeping concept' can be constructed through the work of Michael Roberts, who, in work published simultaneously with *Pattini*, focuses also on 'practices of shaming'. See Michael Roberts, 'I Shall Have You Slippered: The General and the Particular in an Historical Conjuncture', in *Social Analysis*, 17, 1985, pp. 17–48.

discussion is restricted to 'ritual' and 'shame-language', Stirrat proposes that 'perhaps the focus could be widened to take in other aspects of modern Sinhala society.'[23] One of the areas that 'Obeyesekere's discussion of shame . . . might be useful in understanding' is 'aspects of . . . communal clashes is Sri Lanka.'[24] Here, Stirrat has in mind the collective violence of July 1983. I am struck here by the emergence of the question of violence, given an analytical field that has privileged the construct of shame/fear. For this move is the opposite of Spencer's logic, where the question of violence led to a discussion of restraint. Yet, what is remarkable are certain similarities of logic; the two arguments are not of course the same, but nevertheless inhabit the same logical terrain. So Stirrat does not tell us about violence in everyday Sinhala social life but notes, quoting Obeyesekere, the 'vulnerability of self' in that social life. This 'vulnerability of self', then, is seen in reciprocal equilibrium with the 'loss of self esteem'. Violence, its motives and logic, is then to be understood as a response to a perceived crisis in this delicate state of equilibrium, a response that remakes that disturbed balance. 'The killing of the soldiers in Jaffna', Stirrat writes, referring of course to the militant land-mine that led to the death of 13 men in July 1983 —which remains the proximate, symbolic point of 'origin' of that event of violence in its dominant narration—'could well be seen as triggering a "loss of self esteem" which led to the burst of "rage and uncontrollable violence" in July 1983.'[25] We have returned, albeit with a slightly different logic, to violence as an eruption of equilibrium.[26]

---

[23] Stirrat, 1987, p. 72.
[24] Ibid., p. 73.
[25] Ibid.
[26] Michael Roberts' views are an interesting variation on this dominant strand. Building on his own construction of 'shaming practices', Roberts 1985, goes on, in a recent brief contribution, to anthropologize the events of violence that took place in July 1983. He notes that the 'actions of assailants during a pogrom . . . could be cool, calculated Machiavellian operations. Or they could be acts of rage . . . [or] frenzy.' So for Roberts, violence is not always an 'explosion'. Nevertheless, he goes on to argue, that these practices of violence are visible, 'on the bodies and faces of the

If this is indeed a pervasive view, how then is a critique of it, in aid of a space for violence, to proceed? Perhaps historicizing these categories may be fruitful. To do so, I turn to that comprehensive and painstaking historian of crime in colonial Ceylon, John Rogers,[27] who produces a historiographic narrative that is rather proximate in logic to the colonial archives that he reads. By doing so I will be able to demonstrate the close relationship between problematiques of colonial and anthropological discourses in this context.

Homicide emerges as a problem in colonial discourse in the 1860s, simultaneously with the reorganization of the colonial police force in the wake of the 'grain riots' of 1866. By the 1890s, even as policing becomes more efficient and a wealth of statistics are increasingly 'available' in the colonial office in London, administrators in Ceylon realize that the 'rate of homicide [in the colony] is several times greater than that of both Britain and India'.[28] The reduction of the rate of homicide then becomes a colonial project and an ordinance restricting the carrying of knives is passed in 1890. In 1896, an additional ordinance is established to introduce 'flogging' as the 'standard punishment for anyone convicted of using a knife with intent to cause hurt, even if the injury was minor'. These measures, however, fail to bring down the rate of homicide. What is interesting to me is the discursive logic that is produced in the reading of these failures. Governor Ridgeway, John

---

practitioners' after the event of violence, as 'glee . . . joy . . . fun . . . [and] . . . exhilaration'. Such moments, Roberts suggests, are akin . . . to Sinhala 'practices of ritualized humiliation' . . . that 'have been described by observers over the centuries as shameless, beastlike or vindictive, and marked by 'unbounded license' and 'filthy obscenity'.

In my view, all this does is postpone the move to 'irruption' by one step—from during to *after* the event of violence. See Michael Roberts, 'The Agony and the Ecstasy of a Pogrom: Southern Lanka, July 1983', in *Exploring Confrontation—Sri Lanka: Politics, Culture and History* (Reading: Harwood Academic Publishers, 1996), pp. 323–4.

[27] John D. Rogers, *Crime, Justice and Society in Colonial Sri Lanka* (London: Curzon Press, 1987).

[28] Ibid., p. 143.

Rogers tells us, 'became disillusioned with the policy of corporal punishment.' Flogging, in the view of the governor, 'did not have any deterrent effect because the offender normally struck when enraged, and had no time to consider the eventual consequences of his action.'[29] Switching to what seems to be his own voice, Rogers writes then that 'most homicides were random, unpremeditated events arising out of everyday social intercourse . . . there was little the government could do to stop them.' The historian then goes on to write in his conclusion to that chapter, echoing the colonial texts he has read, to maintain that 'aggression was normally suppressed, and that this suppression increased tension which was sometimes suddenly let loose in adversarial situations.' We are on the now familiar terrain of societal 'restraint' encountered earlier, but when we are also told that 'homicides were largely irrational actions, a product of insecurity over personal status', I note that the argument has now moved to the also familiar understanding of violence as an eruption, given a disturbed equilibrium.

Having suggested in some brief way, then, that there is a close relationship between the logic of contemporary anthropological scholarship and colonial discourse and practices, it would be possible—armed as I am with a necessary postcolonial suspicion of that which is colonial—to propose an abandonment of the range of categories that have appeared in my inquiry here: restraint and its traces—that is to say, the anthropological category of *lajja-baya*. But that has not been the intent of this gesture towards colonial history and historiography. Rather, my effort is to point to the location of knowledge about eruptive violence in a context of social restraint; a location within a colonial project which is fundamentally concerned with order and control, a project which produces its categories, strategies and tactics in an effort to rule the unruleable. I think this is suggestive, not because I want to argue that contemporary anthropologists have written in bad faith, mean-spiritedly reproducing colonial accounts or misunderstanding the basics of Sinhala cultural practice through ignorance, but because I want to argue that these very categories of violence and restraint—

[29] Ibid., p. 144.

that is, the impossibility of a space for violence—are not only implicated in colonial projects of rule, but also in micro-projects of order and authority in Sinhala society. What have become canonical anthropological categories, I want to suggest, are themselves signifying practices of order and authority in Sinhala society.

I shall begin to demonstrate this by arriving, finally, at that extraordinary and magisterial text of Obeyesekere's, *The Cult of the Goddess Pattini*. I will not do justice to that text here, nor will I even produce an exposition of its extensive ethnographic account of *lajja-baya* in Sinhala society. For my purposes it will be adequate to read a passage from that rich description, one that will show the *location* of the signifying practice of *lajja-baya* in Sinhala society. Obeyesekere writes that *lajja-baya* is 'instilled' in young children by injunctions such as: '*Lajja nadda, mokakda minissu kiyanne*', 'aren't you ashamed, what'll people say?' 'This mode of socialization', Obeyesekere goes on, 'is carried on in school also, where shaming through ridicule is the most common method of control employed by teachers, particularly for the control of "brashness", "forwardness" or "impudence".' This practice is 'reinforced by authority figures, who like to pull up subordinates in front of others.'[30]

While these statements themselves lie in a normative account of *lajja-baya*, within what is a larger normative account of Sinhala society, even in producing this normative account Obeyesekere is concerned to show the operation of that normalization in a field of power. This is to be contrasted with the use of a norm of *lajja-baya*—always already assumed to be in place, pervading, and standing in for the Sinhalaness of Sinhala society—as a 'gatekeeping concept', in other words.[31] That is to say, Obeyesekere's account of *lajja-baya* in Sinhala society is acutely conscious of its place in relation to authority or its location in the micro-politics of power in a way that it is not in the writings of other scholars I have read here. And this I suggest, is its

---

[30] Gananath Obeyesekere, *The Cult of the Goddess Pattini* (Chicago: The University of Chicago Press, 1984), p. 505.

[31] Appadurai, 1986.

value. My point is that, given this particular locative move in the description of the practice, so visible in even this brief text of Obeyesekere's, a reading of the practice against its authoritative operation can be embarked on with some profit.

Given my concern to produce a space for violence, I propose then to read these descriptions of *lajja-baya* from the opposite angle, to turn them on their head, as it were. I want to re-locate the practice of *lajja-baya* from the position of the self that resists the imperative of such social interpellation. I want to position my analysis not with the teacher, but with the students that she thought were 'brash', 'forward' or 'impudent'. I am aided in my endeavours here by a parallel series of interventions made recently by Malathi de Alwis.[32] She has suggested that the practices that Obeyesekere contains under the sign of *lajja-baya* be glossed as those of 'respectability'. This formation of practices, she is able to suggest—after a fascinating reading of educational practices in the missionary schools of colonial Ceylon—is located historically as the gendered norm of bourgeois social life in the colony.

The practices I am about to read must be positioned in relation to that location of 'respectability'. Those practices that have been glossed here in English as brashness, forwardness, etc., can be named in Sinhala as 'lajja-nethi' or 'baya-nethi', with 'nethi' connoting the negative, and can be glossed as 'anti-respectability'. But since I will be particularly concerned with only one half of the set, the negation of 'baya' or 'baya nethi (kama)',[33] I will gloss the practice at stake as fearlessness. This, I suggest, is an important practice of Sinhala masculinity; one that is associated most closely with violence.

Lajja-baya, I argue, does not stand alone in Sinhala society; it is

---

[32] Malathi de Alwis. 'The Production and Embodiment of Respectability: Gendered Demeanours in Colonial Ceylon', in Michael Roberts (ed.), *Collective Identities, Nationalisms and Protest in Modern Sri Lanka* (2nd edition), vol. 1 (Colombo: Marga Institute Press, 1997) and also 'Gender, Politics and the Respectable Lady', in Pradeep Jeganathan and Qadri Ismail (eds), *Unmaking the Nation: The Politics of Identity and History in Modern Sri Lanka* (Colombo: Social Scientists' Association, 1995).

[33] The addition of the ending 'kama' to 'nethi' turns into a quality; it is equivalent to the English ending 'ness'. I used it here in aid of my anthropology.

practised in opposition to 'baya-nathikama' or 'fearlessness'. This is a repertoire of practices that can be learnt, taught and experienced, for example by masculine specialists, such as *chandi* or thugs. The practice of fearlessness is often a critical practice, and is so seen by its practitioners. It can produce, in its operation, a critical space in relation to the practice of *lajja-baya*. The production of this space is a condition of the possibility of violence. The practice of fearlessness, I contend, is a practice of masculinity that produces a space for violence in Sinhala society.

We are now ready, having traversed through this central strand of Sri Lankan anthropology, to return, as it were, to Anthropologyland. And more concretely, Vikum's performance at the fancy-dress parade. Recall now the simulated tattoo on his chest: *mama baya nahe* (I am not afraid). Here then, literally inscribed on the body,[34] is a sign of that practice of masculinity:[35] fearlessness. It was this inscription that drew

---

[34] I must note that 'the body' itself, as an anthropological object, is not under investigation in this essay, even though following Jean Comaroff's work I use the category to apprehend the relationship between the 'self' and the 'world', and I use that insight to locate the body in relation to 'violence' in my ethnography. See Jean Comaroff, 'Bodily Reform as a Historical Practice: The Semantics of Resistance in Modern South Africa', in *The International Journal of Psychology* 20, 1985, pp. 541–67.

As an aside, I am in disagreement with David Scott's recent suggestion, 1994, pp. 51–8, that there is a Sinhala body that has a definitive set of qualities, that can be marked off, as in 'the Sinhala body is constituted of humors'. I believe his insights to hold only in relation to the practices of Yaktovil, and an associated field of practices. My suggestion, in the pages that follow, and in general, is that the Sinhala body is as it is practised and located.

[35] I note that this essay is not a study of masculinity as such, but rather an effort to locate particular practices of Sinhala masculinity in relation to 'violence'. As such, my effort here differs but resonates with interesting recent work that seeks to produce an anthropological object of masculinity as such, or re-think, in general, the configuration of the 'honour-shame' problematique. I have in mind, for example, the explicit efforts of Nancy Lindisfarne's 'Variant Masculinities, Variant Virginities: Rethinking Honour and Shame', in Andrea Cornwall and Nancy Lindisfarne (eds), *Dislocating Masculinities: Comparative Ethnographies* (London: Routledge, 1994) and Philippe Bourgeois, *In Search of Respect: Selling Crack in El Barrio* (Cambridge: Cambridge University Press, 1995).

my anthropological eye to Vikum, and it was that inscription that could not be read before into a space for violence. I will now describe in further ethnographic detail the practices of masculinity at stake in this space, or, in other words, attempt to enter into spaces of violence.

Ruwan, a fifteen-year-old boy who lives in Patupara, and I are at a crossing point on a four-lane highway. Traffic is always heavy on this road and vehicles rarely stop for pedestrians. When I was a child, my mother told me to wait for a break in the flow of traffic before I crossed. Following her advice, I waited. Ruwan, whose mother had probably cautioned him in the same way, was not, however, interested in waiting. He dashed across the road, weaving through the traffic. He waited for me on the opposite side of the road as I crossed a few minutes later.

'Elder brother', he said, 'you are afraid to cress the road.' Ruwan, had an insolent grin on his face, similar to the one that he had displayed when he had picked berries off a tree in our yard, without our permission.

He used the word *baya—Para paninna bayayi.*

'No', said I, 'what nonsense.'

I was angry. As Ruwan and I walked down to the little road—Patupara—that we both lived on, I tried to figure out why I was angry: Ruwan was saying I wasn't man enough to cross the road, to ride the line of danger between the on-rushing traffic and the running body. Holding myself in, I said nothing.

Later, I was typing at my computer at home when I saw Ruwan through my window in the field across the path at the edge of the house. This land, even though a wide expanse, was private property. Hence the owners had fenced its boundary with the road with barbed wire. This wire was thick, with inch-long spikes knotted in at six-inch intervals along its length. Each knot had four spikes pointing out haphazardly. Not only were those spikes strong, they were sharp; the edges glinted in the hot afternoon sun.

Ruwan was standing away from the fence, eating his berries. He could see me, and he could see that I could see him. The fence came halfway up to his chest. He seemed to measure it up and ran towards it from an angle, just as he might in his school's PT class. But it was too high to jump. Ruwan stopped himself in time, feet skidding, arms thrust out, eyes screwed shut. Yes, it had been a near thing. I thought he would stop now, since there was not, from where I was sitting, any point to this exercise. In fact there was quite a large gap, a few feet away. Ruwan went back and tried again; I watched, mesmerized by this performance. He made it the third time, then dusted his body off and grinned his grin.

If Ruwan had collided with the fence, his skin would have been torn to pieces. There is, I want to suggest, a space of danger produced by the practice of fearlessness, where danger is about the possibility of violence done to the body. In Sinhala, danger and fear, as glossed in English, have the same root.

In a few years, Ruwan will be a thug—a *chandiya*. A man who does not know fear. When I lived in Patupara, Gunadasa still aspired to be a *chandiya*. The first time I met Gunadasa, it was in the heat of the afternoon sun. He was drunk, staggering slightly. He knew I was a newcomer to the neighbourhood: he looked me up and down, and I him. He wasn't very tall, but his body looked strong. His muscles were well defined, and on his chest and arms were tattoos. Some of the tattoos were of fierce animals, others of weapons like knives and swords that moved with the muscles under his skin.

'There is no *chandiya* like me in this area,' he said. I nodded, impressed by the forthrightness of this introduction.

'Where do you work?' he asked me.

'In the University.'

'Where?'

I yelled my reply, 'UNIVERSITY'.

'Police beatings have split my ear drums', said Gunadasa in a matter-of-fact way. There was thick, yellow pus coming out of his ears.

Gunadasa's body is a surface so sharply inscribed by the impact of violence that it seems to seep out of its extremities. The man rarely wore a shirt; he walked with the back end of his sarong held in his hands, which were usually crossed behind his back. There was, it seemed to me, always a powerful space around his body as he moved, and no one else would walk with him or by him. Any companion would

A Space for Violence 55

keep his distance. Gunadasa made that space as he walked, by travelling slowly, nonchalantly, but not carelessly, moving as if every step was important. He would look around himself as he did so, glancing, probing and pricking as if to push any and every one out of his way by his mere presence. More often than not, he walked alone.

But having fallen in with Gunadasa, and having spent a lot of time together, I walked by his side. I was well aware that this habit had drawn both attention and comment in the neighbourhood. Once, Gunadasa and I were walking down Patupara to get cigarettes; he had come along to bum one and my packet was empty. When we got to the store, Anura, the grocer, cast a long, sour look at Gunadasa before turning to get my cigarettes.

'He is a bad fellow', said Anura to me in English. Now Anura and I usually spoke in Sinhala, but English was spoken, I assume, so that the uncouth thug Gunadasa wouldn't get the drift of Anura's critical insights. I was being warned, as I had been by other 'respectable' people, about Gunadasa. But this was hard to do, because the point had to be made without letting on to me, an outsider in a small, closely knit community, that Gunadasa had served time for attempted homicide.

'Look at him', Anura went on, taking on a sign that was both visible and apprehensible, 'walking on the road without a shirt on.' The comment was sharp, both seemingly low key, yet telling. I got the point, and as we walked back I told Gunadasa what had been said. Gunadasa got the point too, but he thrust back with finesse. 'He must have thought I would be *baya*, if he said that [*Mama bayavei kiyalla hithannathi, kiyawata*]' said Gunadasa, laughing as if it was the joke of the week.

There is clearly a point, a stake, in Gunadasa's bare torso. His body is produced to contest, to occupy a counterpoint to the authoritative practice of *lajja-baya*, namely, the practice of being clothed in public, of not walking the streets in one's 'home clothes.'[36] Most working-class men would at least wear a T-shirt over their upper bodies when

---

[36] See, for a historicization of these practices through the missionary school in colonial Ceylon, Malathi de Alwis, 1997. A rich reading of a South African case is in John Comaroff and Jean Comaroff, 'Fashioning the Colonial Subject: The Empire's Old

walking on the road. Those who wanted to occupy the place of respectability, such as a lawyer's aide who needed to be at the courts everyday, or a working-class man going into a government office, or visiting relatives outside the neighbourhood, would be fully covered in clean clothes, either long pants and shirt or white sarong and 'national' shirt. If a woman went to the store in her 'house coat', or in other words with only one layer of clothes over the clothes she had slept in, she would be open to censure by others, even other working-class women, who cared to comment privately. But Gunadasa rode through withering glances and snidely muttered asides. That was what he was about. And even though here the contestatory space around his body is a small eddy, wrapped in the exchanges of the everyday, it is that very space that Gunadasa produces even as he walks that can be enlarged to be a space for violence.

But before I move to enlarge that space and enter it in its fullness, I will make a detour in order to specify the particularities of the masculinity at stake in the practice of fearlessness. I shall do so by exemplifying an instance of the failure of an attempt to create a space for violence, a failure that I suggest must be tracked together with the failure of that particular masculinity that is necessarily at stake in the space.

Suda and friends, who were in their early twenties and much younger than Gunadasa, were lying back on the playing field after a game of cricket. They were, Gunadasa liked to say patronizingly, boys who were coming along nicely. More likely, they were men who were biding their time, a time after which Gunadasa would be no more.

Piyal, a little boy of eight, passed by and said something in their general direction. I didn't hear it, but Suda did. He turned towards Piyal and asked, 'What did you say?'

Piyal had apparently uttered an obscenity and had had the impertinence to repeat it. He was by Suda's measure, 'just too much [*Ganata Vadi*]'. Piyal was in big trouble. Soon he was on his knee with his hands tied behind his back, his face smeared with charcoal. Doing

---

Clothes', in 'Of Revelation and Revolution: Christianity, Colonialism and Consciousness in South Africa', vol. 2 (unpublished mss. copy, 1995).

this to Piyal had greatly amused this group of young men, and there was much sniggering all round. Piyal was crying, not howling, but there were tears on his cheeks. Suda then got a stick, and pushing down on the back of Piyal's head, so bending him in there, began to swat gently on the boy's buttocks.

'Will you say bad words again?' he asked.

'No,' whimpered Piyal, really crying now.

There was more trouble to come. The boys couldn't see what I could: coming along the street, into this slowly simmering moment of homo-erotic domination, as it were, was Violet, Piyal's mother. Violet was not quite like other women. That is to say, unlike other women, she did not practice *lajja*—modesty/shame—which is the companion term of *baya*, the negation of which can produce a space for sexuality, just as fearlessness produces a space for violence.

There are many ways to practice *lajja* normatively. A succinct example would be its performance at the very same New Year celebration with which I began. There, just after we had judged the fancy-dress contest, came another contest, that of 'Avurudu Kumari' or 'new year princess'. Half a dozen young women from the neighbourhood had entered, and we were to be the judges. Malathi looked appalled at what I had got us into; she, I think, was ready to leave Anthropologyland then and there. 'Look', I said to her, invoking the last refuge of the anthropologist, 'this might be interesting.' 'Hmm', she replied.

This event was significant anthropologically because it produced before us performatively, with extraordinary elegance, a particular kind of gendered 'Sinhalaness' which is at the heart of *lajja*. Take for example the way the women were dressed. The women were dressed unusually: it was not just that they were wearing nice things, as they might when going to the movies with their families. Rather, the clothes themselves were special. The frilly, tight blouses and chintz cloths were not worn for the movies, but just for occasions such as this contest, when a certain kind of young woman, both beautiful and modest, practising a certain kind of Sinhalaness, stands in for and constitutes that identity. The contest, as it turned out, was judged not on clothes that were similar, not on face and figure that might have entered into the calculations in comparable configurations. It was judged on the walk or gait of the winner. Our judging practice was governed by 'crowd response' and especially the muter comments of the male organizers who were hovering behind us. 'There is no grace in her movement [*Kisima lathavak nahe*],' one young man said early on in reference to one of the first contestants, and I knew externally what he meant. The women, in short, did not move as fluidly as she might have. She did not, as did the winner—Shamila—produce her sexuality in the movement of her body; not openly and blatantly, but shyly, as if embarrassed but also excited by its very production.

Violet did not produce herself through *lajja* in this way, but in turn, neither was she so immodest—*lajja nethi*—so that she could be always already marked as a slut/whore within masculinized sexuality. Rather, she inhabited and operated the cusp between *lajjanethi* and *bayanethi*, producing anxiety and concern through that practised movement. Violet wore her hair long, but it did not appear to be combed and oiled as the hair of other women. Her clothes were often torn, sometimes dirty and always dishevelled. It seemed her body was, by her own reckoning, too bony, too angular, for anything to sit well on her frame: her efforts at straightening her clothes lacked conviction. For a living, Violet gathered various salad leaves that grew wild in the marshes that surrounded Patupara, bundling them in little lots and selling them in the market near the highway. She was, in the crude language of the everyday, a *vatti amma*, a woman of the market.

'What are you doing to my child?', asked Violet loudly, hands on hips. She always spoke loudly in a half hoarse, deep voice, which had got that way, she said, from all the crying out she had to do in the market, but now she was shouting.

'He said bad words', said Manju, who had been pinching Piyal's buttocks.

'Stop this nonsense', yelled back Violet.

'Why are you loitering on the street, don't you have a man to cook for?' sniggered Suda

'I don't need to cook for any man', snapped back Violet.

And so it went on. With Suda taunting Violet with her lack of a resident male partner and Violet, her arms stabbing the air—as if the strength of her actions would amplify the growing hoarseness of her voice—retorting repeatedly that she had no use for men, that she could live her life without them.

But Suda's move had success. For even as Violet attempted to inhabit the practice of *bayanethikama*, Suda's repeated positioning of her *lajjanethi* needed to be refused. Hence the necessity of repeating, for Violet, the refusal of grooming, coyness, modesty and shyness; the necessity, in other words, of refusing herself as a woman in relation to men. And in this refusal, even as Violet teetered on that uncertain, unstable cusp of *lajjanethikama* and *bayanethikama*—even as she, to put it more concretely, broke a short stick of a tree, and advanced at the boys—she lost to them, for she could not stop their laughter.

She lost out in the sense that, even as Piyal was released from his bonds, and pushed towards his mother, there was not for Suda and friends a high and dangerous stake; there was not a space for violence in that moment, because Violet could not produce the necessary move out of *lajja*, given the construction of her sexed body that would have allowed a space for violence to be made.

Gunadasa, on the contrary, had practised the art, with some aplomb, for years. But he was getting old. We all knew that his authority was on the wane. But one absentee landlord, who wasn't in the know, had asked Gunadasa to guard his coconut trees which stood on a quarter acre of land on the opposite side of our house, across the road. So when the coconuts ripened Gunadasa was supposed to count them and see that no one plucked them. Now this land wasn't even fenced, so the point wasn't that Gunadasa was to watch over the coconuts all day and night. Rather the logic of the operation was this: Gunadasa was a *chandiya*, it was known that the trees were on his turf, and no one would dare cross him.

And so it happened. Kulkul Sira, who liked the soft white meat inside the young coconut as much as the next fellow, decided to take his pick. Gunadasa, of course, wasn't around at the time; in fact, Sira was way up the tree, dropping the nuts down, when Gunadasa arrived.

'Get down, you devil', Gunadasa yelled.

Sira, who was probably thinking through Plan B at this point, said nothing. Another coconut came shooting down; Gunadasa had to jump back to avoid it. It was obviously impossible for Gunadasa to climb the tree after Sira, since there were still many nuts left at the top. Gunadasa retreated about ten feet, crossed his arms authoritatively and waited; Sira, after all would have to climb down. Sira took his time, but climb down he did.

'Come here', ordered Gunadasa, standing tall and still.

Now Sira could have made a run for it, but then the coconuts would have been lost. So he picked them up, and carrying all five of them by their stalks, made his way to Gunadasa. In his right hand was the large curved knife he had used to cut the nuts off the tree.

'Who asked you to pick nuts?' asked Gunadasa.

Now Sira could have invoked his aged mother, his pregnant wife or his sick children. That is, he could have positioned himself as a family man, trying against the odds to make ends meet. Sira would have tried that line with me, or with the landlord if he was around.

But this was Gunadasa and the stakes were different.

Sira looked Gunadasa in the eye, instead of shuffling and looking down.

'I haven't eaten Kurumba in a long time', he said, dropping the nuts down at the same time.

Gunadasa picked up a nut. Tucked in to the waist of his sarong was his short sharp knife.

'These trees are in my charge', he said, waving the large orange nut in his hand.

Fast, faster than my eye could see, Sira grabbed the nut out of Gunadasa's hand, his knife flew through the still air, slicing through the soft husk at the top of the fruit. The stalk of the nut and a silver of husk fell down gently to the ground.

Then, keeping Gunadasa in his sights, Sira took a long swig of the clear cool liquid. Gunadasa, whose hand had gone to his knife even as Sira had struck, said nothing. He had lost out.

'So what's the big deal if I cut a few', said Sira.

'I will skin you alive if I catch you again', said Gunadasa, who then

A Space for Violence   61

picked up two of the nuts and walked home. He left three nuts on the ground for Sira. After that the coconuts were fair game.

I have in these descriptions held back from a representation of violence itself, to draw attention not to violence but its space. I have been trying to produce a space, both ethnographic and anthropological, within which violence may be located. Ethnographically, I have done so by pointing to an oppositional Sinhala practice of masculinity (*baya nethikama*). It is this practice, then, that on the ethnographic level does the work of making a space for violence. This move then enables a critical space in the anthropological literature that de-centres the pervasive problematique of 'eruption' *vs.* 'restraint' in that literature.

But what then of 'violence?' I have not, I maintain, produced as yet in this essay an analytic of violence as such, an analytic that is capable of grappling with the signifying practices that make up that anthropological category. Rather, I have only delineated, through an engagement with anthropological knowledge, using well-known protocols of anthropological practice, the conditions of possibility of violence. This is what I have called a 'space for violence'. These conditions of possibility do not necessarily lead to violence: we have seen in my ethnographic text so far, examples not of the development of violence, but its foreclosure, not its production but its abatement.

But my argument so far can be read to imply that fearlessness and respectability make up an opposition, perhaps even, if we take just the practices of *baya* and *baya nethi* (fear/danger and fearlessness), a binary opposition. Is such an opposition stable? Is there, in other words, a normative core of respectability/restraint/fear in Sinhala society that is always in opposition to anti-respectability/anti-restraint/ fearlessness? If this were the case, we would be able to return, albeit more complexly, to the original problem of 'lajja-baya' positioned as the normative practice of 'Sinhalaness'. This would allow fearlessness and the 'spaces for violence' it produces to be the anti-normative moments of Sinhala social life. A straightforward anthropology of fearlessness as the anti-normative might then be possible.

The work of such an anthropology, I wish to suggest, may not be straightforward. For the opposition I have constructed here is not, in fact, stable. It cannot be, since the central argument of its construction was that fearlessness has a certain micro-political location in the ethnographic field of Lanka. That that location can be an anti-normative one, that it is indeed an oppositional counterpoint in numerous social interactions, does not necessarily imply that it must always be so. The point, rather, is that these practices have micro-political locations, and these locations may indeed shift contextually. Or, in other words, it is not possible to know, *a priori,* the location of fearlessness in relation to social norms, because these norms themselves are made and re-made in fields of power. This is what I seek to demonstrate, forewarned and forearmed with these arguments, by making and then entering into, finally, a space for violence.

Kukul Sira strutted around a little cockily after he had bested Gunadasa over the coconuts. In fact, I think he got a little careless when he hawked his packets of Kudu (powder)[37] at the lonely, dark end of Patupara. Now Sira had done this for some years, by all accounts. His clients were usually upper-middle-class teenagers who would come by on motorbikes for a quick transaction. But he did also trade locally, and this caused much dissension among the men. Some, like Gunadasa, who never strayed very far from his alcoholic high, would hurl a string of abuse at Sira's practices. But others who had tried the stuff wanted in on the action to keep costs down. In any event, Sira kept at it in his own way, not stopping his trade or cutting anyone in.

Now selling drugs was a difficult business in another way. The police had to be factored in. It wasn't a simple matter of the illegality of Sira's work. The police after all knew about Sira and what he was up to; they didn't take him in because be was protected, as is usually the case, by an arrangement worked out by his suppliers high above his head. As long as Sira didn't cross the police, he was safe.

The police were a visible sign in Patupara; two men walked a beat through Patupara every night. Straight and tall like broomsticks, rifles hanging from their shoulders, batons under their arms, they would

---

[37] Akin to 'brown sugar', a rather impure form of heroin that can be smoked or ingested.

march crisply through the neighbourhood at about ten o'clock each day. They spoke to no one, never stopped or looked back. The men, who hung out on the street, knew enough to give these two a wide berth, for they, like Gunadasa, made a space as they moved.

But Sira, as I said, grew careless. So sometimes, even when the policemen were in sight, Sira would be still hanging around at the corner of the road, seemingly chatting with a boy on a bike. It didn't seem to matter, for the policemen said nothing and did nothing. But Sira didn't really watch his back. At that intersection, literally behind where he stood, a new upper-middle-class house was being built. Sira, in fact, always shuffled around between the mounds of rubble that the construction workers had piled up on the edge of the narrow road. The shingles and crushed bricks there were so sharp that the soft, pink bottoms of my feet were cut open when I once tried to walk over to the building barefoot. Even Sira would sometimes feel a prick break through his hardened soles as he hung around the corner.

They got him from behind, but it did not matter, for it would have been impossible to run away even if Sira had seen them coming. They were bigger and stronger than he was by far and there were six of them, plain-clothes policemen who had been waiting in the half-built structure by the road, biding their time. They seemed to pounce at once, getting their man by the scruff of his neck and throwing him on to the shingles so that his body bounced once from the impact, and then again and again from the pain of the cuts. They set upon him then, with the yard-long rubber hose pipes they had brought, laying into him, hitting him as he lay there prone, both in unison and sequentially, repeatedly, taunting Sira as he rolled there on the shingles, writhing, begging and screaming for mercy. Even as they did so, the two policemen walked by on their beat, for it was that time of night. They only glanced at the direction of the violence, not stopping, not joining in or even exchanging words with their colleagues, but only confirming, for their own satisfaction, who was who, what was what, before they moved on into the night. But the beating went on for a few more minutes yet, until Sira whose back and chest were cut and swollen so badly that the colour of his skin could not be told, was given a respite and told finally to keep clear of the filth he was selling. Then the six men left, walking slowly up the road, to where their van was parked.

But later, even though the story was told again and again in the neighbourhood, there was not an ounce of condemnation to be heard. Sira, everyone agreed, had got his just deserts: 'I will not say it is a sin' (*Mama pavu kiyanneha*), said one woman echoing the sentiments of many. To call something a 'sin' in this context is not an act of deep faith; it means, rather, that the event was not 'wrong' in the straightforward terms of 'right' and 'wrong', or in other words that it was legitimate.

This event for me was the profoundest moment of violence I had seen in Patupara up to that time. But it was not produced locally, as a *sanduwa* (fight), a *valiya* or *goriya* (brawl), that can well be taken as categorical names for social spaces within which 'violence' can and is produced. What happened to Sira was thought to be a *guti-kama* (a beating, literally 'eating blows'), an entirely legitimate activity, so moral, so normative that it did not even occupy that space of anti-respectability, of a *valiya*, that the exchange between Gunadasa and Sira under the coconut trees had occupied. A beating, in this sense, is what policemen do to a drug dealer, what Suda and his friends did to Piyal, and also, to return to Obeyesekere's text, it is what teachers do to 'brash', 'forward' and 'impudent' students. It lies, in other words, at the very heart of respectability.

I have tried, in this essay, to construct an anthropological object: a space for violence. The analytical construct of a 'space' has allowed me to wrap 'violence' in its conditions of possibility, whether those conditions be those of the anthropological literature or the ethnographic field. That allowed me to approach 'violence' through the archive and method of anthropology to arrive at places where it might in fact be visible in an ethnographic field. Sira's beating is such a site. But it is not possible to know, in turn, if violence will appear in the centre of its space, for what counts as violence, and what does not, cannot be known *a priori*, before one enters its space. It cannot be, for what is violence and what is not, is always constituted by a politics. It is under the sign of that politics, finally, that violence, in all its power, is made visible to anthropology.

This, it seems to me, marks a limit of anthropology, a limit that marks the end of anthropology and the beginning of the political. I read this essay in fact, as a collection of such anthropological limits which I have reached and then interrogated, time and again, through an examination of the constitution and location of the discipline's objects. In so doing, I have traversed the basic problem of anthropology, which is to make the particular available through the categories of the universal.[38] Or in this particular instance, I have tried to make 'violence' available to my anthropology. But even as I have done so, proposing universalizable categories that might be available to an anthropological canon of violence, I have found my work interrupted by the politics of those very categories. In the face of these limits, however, I do not advocate an abandonment of anthropology, or a move to 'ethnosociology'. Rather, I suggest an exploration of those limits of anthropology, repeatedly and meticulously, leaving these limits always open to the possibility of political interruption.

---

[38] See, on this point, Partha Chatterjee, *Nationalist Thought and the Colonial World—A Derivative Discourse?* (London: Zed Books, 1986), p. 17.

Embodying the Self: Feminism, Sexual Violence and the Law

NIVEDITA MENON

THE UNIVERSALITY OF women's experience of sexual violence has always provided an immediate entry point for feminist intervention. Whatever the analysis of patriarchy and its relationship to class, caste, community or race, feminist politics of all hues is able to relate directly to sexual violation—experienced in different ways and to differing degrees—but an intrinsic part of women's lives. What are the codes which enable such immediate recognition of 'sexuality' and 'sexual' violence? Are they indeed so universally recognized by all cultures, by all women? And is this recognition something that *enables* feminist politics, or does it paradoxically *limit* the possibilities of feminist transformation? These questions become even more critical when sexual violence is sought to be made meaningful in legal terms, as the logical culmination of feminist intervention in this area.

In the last decade, in particular, the women's movement in India has reacted to every instance of violence against women by demanding legislative action. These efforts have been successful in that every campaign from 1980 to 1989 has resulted in legislative changes. However, as feminist activists have pointed out, not only has the implementation of laws remained partial and conservative, but since these changes have mainly involved the incorporation of more stringent punishments, there have been, in rape cases, fewer convictions than before. At the same time, each new law vests more power with the state enforcement machinery.[1] This situation has led to some rethinking on the efficacy of the law and a growing awareness in the women's movement not only that laws should be framed more carefully, but that legal changes cannot transform patriarchal power structures in society.

However, the issue that arises is more fundamental than the simple fact that the law is not enough. Focusing on the discourse of rape as it is produced by feminist and legal practices, we come up against two assumptions:

(a) The belief that it is possible for the law to establish, where it is the case, the culpability of the accused and the violation of the victim. If this happens very rarely, it is because (from the feminist perspective) the law needs to more clearly reflect the reality of women's experience. Once this is achieved, a demonstration of the guilt of the accused and his punishment will deliver justice to the woman and strike at the dominant misogynist values of our culture.

(b) The understanding that 'the body' is a natural and physical object and that 'sex' is a phenomenon which exists prior to all discourse, simply distinguishable from other kinds of human interaction.

This essay questions both assumptions, arguing not only that

(a) The binary logic of the law cannot comprehend the complexity of the way sexual experience is constituted. Even when justice appears to be done, the very demonstration through legal discourse of the violation of the woman re-enacts and resediments dominant patriarchal and misogynist values.
(b) More fundamentally, 'the body' and 'sex' are not 'natural' but produced by discourses. This is not to deny their 'reality' but

[1] Flavia Agnes, 'Protecting Women Against Violence? Review of a Decade of Legislation', in *Economic and Political Weekly*, 25 April 1992.

to question the assumption that this reality can be accessible outside particular contexts. It would then become necessary to rethink the attempt to universalise one particular 'reality' through law.

Is there a strength we can lay claim to precisely in accepting 'sex' as constituted by different discourses rather than as a natural, prediscursive reality? Legal discourse functions by fixing meaning, by creating uniform categories out of a multiplicity of possibilities, by suturing open-endedness. The experience validated by feminism as 'real', on the other hand, acquires meaning precisely through an interplay of contexts, and may be rendered sterile within the rigid codification required by legal discourse.

The first section of this essay looks at legal and feminist definitions of what constitutes rape. It argues that the feminist position simultaneously (a) sets up sexual violence as having an existence and reality prior to the law; and (b) looks to the law to recognize this reality and grant it legitimacy. The second section examines the implications of this, that is, of reinforcing the status of law as the primary legitimating discourse. In the section following, it is established that the binary logic of the law cannot comprehend the complexity of sexual violence. A pivotal instance is the notion of 'consent', which is unravelled next, laying out the manner in which consent gets rigidly defined in terms of biological age. The discussion on consent flows into the notion of 'honour'. In Indian legal discourse, 'honour' is the value which informs judgements which take a progressive position, from the feminist point of view, on lack of consent and the need for corroborative evidence. Consequently, the section that follows next examines the reinstatement of such dominant norms as honour and chastity through the rape trial, even when the verdict is favourable, that is, when conviction has been secured. The two concluding sections attempt to deconstruct the assumptions underlying the feminist understanding of 'rights over our bodies' and of 'sexuality', so that we can extricate ourselves from what has come to be an increasingly frustrating and counter-productive engagement with the law.

Defining Rape: The Legal Discourse

Section 375 of the Indian Penal Code explains rape in the following way: 'Penetration is sufficient to constitute the sexual intercourse necessary to the offence of rape.' A man is said to have committed rape, according to this section, if he has sexual intercourse with a woman in circumstances falling under any of the six following descriptions:

— against her will
— without her consent
— with her consent when the consent has been obtained by putting her or any person in whom she is interested, in fear of death or hurt
— with her consent if her consent is given because she believes the man to be her lawfully married husband, when the man knows he is not
— with her consent if she is unable to recognize 'the nature and consequences' of that to which she gives consent because of intoxication or unsoundness of mind
— with or without her consent if she is under sixteen years of age

The exception to these circumstances is that sexual intercourse by a man with his wife, the wife not being below fifteen, is not rape.

Apart from Sections 375 and 376 (which deals with punishment for rape), other related sections of the IPC are 354 (assault or use of criminal force with an intent to outrage a woman's modesty), 377 (sexual intercourse 'against the order of nature', which is understood to refer to sodomy), 509 (violating a woman's modesty with word or gesture), 511 (attempt to commit rape), 109 (aiding and abetting rape), and 34 (common intention or gang rape).

In India the issue of rape was placed on the public agenda in the late 1970s, when women's groups mobilized around a Supreme Court judgement acquitting police rapists of a young tribal girl, Mathura. Since then, rape and sexual violence against women have been among the most visible and strongly articulated issues in the women's movement. Sections 375 and 376 of the IPC were unchanged in the statute books since 1860. A sustained campaign was mounted against these antiquated laws after the Mathura case. Redefining 'consent' was one of the major thrusts of the campaign, since the case had shown that it is extremely difficult for a woman to prove that she did not consent 'beyond all reasonable doubt', as was required under criminal law. In response to the campaign, the government set up a Law Commission whose recommendations included the main demand of the campaign, that in rape cases the onus of proving consent should shift to the accused. That is, once sexual intercourse was proved, if the woman states that it was without her consent, the court should presume she did not consent. However the Criminal Law Amendment Act which was passed in 1983 accepted this demand only partially—in the case of custodial rape alone—that is, rape by police, public servants, managers of public hospitals and remand homes, and wardens of jails. Also, the mandatory minimum punishment was made more rigorous.[2]

One of the leading activists in the campaign against rape, Flavia Agnes, who has been writing extensively about her misgivings on the use of the law by feminists, urges the necessity to evolve a new definition of rape. She regrets that the campaign did not succeed in this:

> In fact the same old notions of chastity, virginity, premium on marriage and fear of female sexuality are reflected in the judgements of the post-amendment period. Penis penetration continues to be the governing ingredient in the offence of rape. The concept of 'penis penetration' is based on the control men exercise over 'their' women. Rape violates these property rights and may lead to pregnancies by other men and threaten the patriarchal power structure. We have not gone beyond this definition.

It is in keeping with this understanding of rape, she points out, that while in all other criminal offences injury and hurt caused by weapons is considered more grievous and deserving of greater punishment than that caused by limbs alone, in the case of sexual assault injury caused by iron rods, bottles or sticks does not even amount to rape. She urges therefore the use of the term 'sexual assault' to replace the categories

[2] Agnes, 1992.

of rape, attempt to rape and violation of a woman's modesty. The latter two categories at present entail lighter punishment, regardless of the harm done to the woman. As some countries have already done, the use of 'sexual assault' to cover all such attacks would ensure that the punishment would be determined by the injury caused to the woman.[3]

Defining Rape: Feminist Discourse

If we look at how feminist definitions constitute rape in an attempt to contest legal definitions, we can discern broadly three positions:

(a) Rape is violence, not sex.
(b) Rape is violence, but a unique form of violence because of its sexual character.
(c) Rape is violence and violence precisely *is* sex.

(a) The first position is exemplified by two pieces of legislation which have served as models for feminists around the world—Michigan State's Criminal Sexual Conduct Act of 1974 and the Canadian legislation on rape, 1982. These had considerable input from feminist lawyers, academics and women's groups both at the level of research as well as public awareness-raising.

The Michigan Act created 'a ladder of offences', each of which is described as criminal sexual conduct. Each degree covers a range of sexual assaults, differentiated according to the amount of coercion used, whether or not penetration has taken place, the extent of physical injury inflicted, and the age and incapacitation of the victim. In this way it was hoped that defendants who are guilty will plead guilty. Under the present system, in other parts of the world, the penalty is so high and the prospects of conviction so low that most defendants feel it wiser to plead not guilty. Also, the word 'rape' has connotations and conjures up images which very often do not match actual incidents of sexual assault. It was hoped that juries might be more willing to convict a crime called 'criminal sexual conduct in the third degree' than to convict for 'rape'. The law has had no appreciable effect on cases of

[3] Ibid., p. WS-21.

rape reported but there has been a clear increase in the number of arrests and convictions for conduct of this kind.[4] In the Canadian legislation the central proposition is that rape is a form of assault. As the Working Paper on which the legislation is based put it, 'the concept of sexual assault more appropriately characterizes the actual nature of the offence of rape because the primary focus is on the assault or the violation of the integrity of the person rather than sexual intercourse.'[5] By this legislation, the crime of rape no longer exists in Canada. Instead there is a gradation scheme which creates three offences of sexual assault, distinguished in terms of the violence used, with no distinction made between penetration and other sexual acts.

(b) The second position can be illustrated by a document suggesting amendments to the rape law in India. This was prepared in 1993 on behalf of the National Commission for Women by a group of lawyers and feminist activists in Delhi and was widely circulated for debate among women's groups all over the country. This draft bill recognizes 'the unique character of the nature of sexual assault' and aims to 'provide a comprehensive definition of sexual assault to cover the full range of such crimes against women and children.'[6] It points out that the legal definition of rape at present, recognizing as it does only vaginal penetration by the penis as rape, does not take into account a wide range of assaults which are sexual in nature. Particularly in the case of very young children, especially those below twelve, 'rape' can be committed without penetration and a number of serious injuries caused. The definition of rape has therefore to be expanded to 'take in a wide range of violations in addition to actual penetration.'[7] The expanded definition suggested by the draft bill would be covered by Sections 375(1) and (2), while the existing Sections 375, 376, 377, 354 and 509 will be deleted. (The offences covered by these have been outlined already.)

[4] Jennifer Temkin, 'Women, Rape and Law Reform', in Sylvana Tomaselli and Roy Porter (eds), *Rape* (Oxford: Basil Blackwell, 1986).
[5] Ibid., p. 31.
[6] 'Draft Amendments to Rape Law 1993', Committee for Redrafting Sexual Assault Law (unpublished), p. 11.
[7] Ibid., p. 1.

The amended Sections 375 (1) and (2) set out the content of sexual assault, which includes the penetration of any orifice by a penis or any other object, as well as, 'for a sexual purpose', touching, gesturing or exhibiting any part of the body, if any of these activities are carried out against the will or without the consent of the other person. If the other person is a minor then the question of consent is irrelevant. A further explanation clarifies: 'Any consensual sexual activity between two adults does not fall within the purview of this section.'[8]

A category of aggravated sexual assault has been introduced in Section 375A, the offences under this section being considered to be 'grievous' and deserving of more severe punishment. These are—sexual assault on a minor, a mentally or physically handicapped person, or a pregnant woman; on a woman or minor by a person abusing a position of power or authority; sexual assault which results in grievous bodily harm, is protracted over a period of time, or is by more than one person. The family is recognized as the 'greatest threat' where sexual assault is concerned, specially for minors.

The two radical points of departure that this draft bill makes from common conceptions of rape as well as from prevalent legal wisdom in India are that:

(i) it reformulates entirely the harm perceived to be caused by rape. The harm of sexual assault, it is argued, lies not in the causing of physical damage but in the 'violation of a person's bodily integrity';[9] and—

(ii) it introduces the possibility of recognizing rape within marriage by dropping the exception to the present Section 375, which reads, 'sexual intercourse by a man with his own wife, the wife not being under 15 years of age, is not rape.' The draft document explicitly states, 'the continuous rape of adult females within marriage or by other adult members of the family has also been covered.'[10]

We might formulate the main principle animating each of these

[8] Ibid., p. 12.
[9] Ibid.
[10] Ibid., p. 4.

two positions in the following way. The Michigan and Canadian legislations try to establish rape as a crime of violence, not sex. Such an understanding had been theorised most notably by Susan Brownmiller,[11] who holds that the human anatomy is such that men can rape women while women cannot rape men. This, according to her, is the root of women's subordination. Rape then is not an act of sex at all but one of power and domination. By taking the 'sex' out of rape, as it were, feminist strategies tried to combat the sexism of the legal system. It was seen as a way of improving the treatment of raped women by the criminal justice system so that they could be seen as the victims of violent assault rather than accomplices in a consensual act.[12]

Indian feminists on the other hand, seem to stress the 'unique character of *sexual* attack'.[13] Although the position taken in the Indian draft legislation that rape is a violation of bodily integrity seems to parallel the notion of 'violation of the person' in the Canadian legislation, there is nevertheless an emphasis on the 'sexual purpose' of touch, gestures or sounds/words which would make these actionable under the law.[14] The understanding here is that rape is a form of violence, but a unique form of violence because of its sexual character.

(c) A third position on this continuum is one which collapses the distinction between sex and violence in the opposite direction to that taken by the Canadian and Michigan legislations. That is, *not* 'rape is a crime of violence, not sex,' *but* 'rape is a crime of violence and violence *is* sex.' This position is exemplified by Catharine MacKinnon, whose work has arguably been one of the most influential analyses of rape in the last ten years. She sees the social relation between the sexes as organized so that 'men may dominate and women must submit and this relation is sexual—in fact, is sex.'[15]

---

[11] Susan Brownmiller, *Against Our Will: Men, Women and Rape* (New York: Bantam, 1976).

[12] Carol Smart, *Feminism and the Power of Law* (New York and London: Routledge, 1989), p. 44.

[13] 'Draft Amendments to Rape Law', p. 10 (emphasis added).

[14] Ibid., p. 12.

[15] Catharine MacKinnon, *Feminism Unmodified* (Cambridge and London: Harvard University Press, 1987), p. 3.

Embodying the Self 75

Gender in MacKinnon's understanding, then, is not a difference which suggests equality, but a hierarchy. To construe gender as a difference is to obscure the power relations which impose it by force. Violence against women has been eroticised, and 'men violating women' therefore has a sexual content. What this critique does that is different from the 'violence, not sex' critique is to 'ask a series of questions about normal heterosexual intercourse and attempt to move the line between heterosexuality on the one hand—intercourse—and rape on the other, rather than allow it to stay where it is.'[16] MacKinnon is arguing that the sharp distinction that men make between 'normal' sex and rape does not exist for women—'What we are saying is that sexuality in these normal forms often *does* violate us.'[17]

For MacKinnon, then, rape is inextricably bound up with heterosexuality. In other words, 'instead of asking, what is the violation of rape, what if we ask, what is the non-violation of intercourse?'[18] The difficulty that courts have in distinguishing between rape and seduction is precisely because there is not much difference between the two—all heterosexual sex is coercive. And exactly what 'heterosexuality as a social institution is fixated around' is what legally defines rape—that is, penetration.[19] This is a very male point of view, says MacKinnon, on what it means to be violated, for penetration is not all there is in rape which is 'intrusive or expropriative of a woman's sexual wholeness.'[20]

What is the understanding of 'sex' that emerges from the three positions discussed above? The first two—the Canadian and Michigan legislations and the Indian draft bill—assume a universal understanding of what 'sex' is. Neither statement, 'rape is violence, not sex', nor 'rape is a unique form of violence because of its sexual character' undertakes an explanation of what makes an act sexual.

The third position, that of MacKinnon, does clearly define what it understands to be 'sex'—the hierarchical and violent relationship be-

---

[16] Ibid., p. 89.
[17] Ibid., p. 86 (emphasis in original).
[18] Catharine MacKinnon, 'Feminism, Marxism, Method and the State: Towards Feminist Jurisprudence', in *Signs*, vol. 8, no. 4, 1983, p. 647.
[19] MacKinnon, 1987, p. 87.
[20] Ibid.

tween men and women is sex. However, such an understanding, that all (hetero)sex is violence, reduces one to paralysis. It denies one the possibility that women can redefine and affirm themselves outside the rigid codes of a male-defined sexuality. If violence is sexuality and sexuality is male, there is a daunting seamlessness to male dominance—where does MacKinnon see the space for feminists to refigure received notions of pleasure, pain or fulfilment?[21]

Even from a merely legal point of view, if rape cannot be distinguished from intercourse, then it would seem to be impossible to prosecute for rape at all. And yet MacKinnon does see the law as a crucial weapon to fight sexual violence against women. The ordinance on pornography that she drafted with Andrea Dworkin is a landmark in feminist politics in the USA.[22] The focus of her legal campaign is the recasting of all forms of sexual assault as civil, not criminal offences, which she believes is a more effective way of ensuring convictions. Civil wrongs are wrongs against individuals, criminal wrongs are offences against the state. MacKinnon argues that civil suits would leave the legal procedure in the control of the victims, rather than handing over control to the state. However, there remains the inconsistency involved in characterizing all (hetero)sex as rape on the one hand, and, on the other, seeking recognition for and punishment of sexual assault as a crime.

Finally, feminist critics also have a problem with MacKinnon's essentialising of 'women' into a natural category whose relations with men are fixed into static patterns of domination and power. Although she accepts that gender is socially constructed, the reduction of women to their sex becomes inevitable given that the only perspective available

[21] For a critique along these lines, see Drucilla Cornell, *Beyond Accommodation. Ethical Feminism, Deconstruction and the Law* (New York and London: Routledge, 1991), pp. 124–5, and Carol S. Vance, 'Pleasure and Danger: Towards a Politics of Sexuality', in Carol S. Vance (ed.), *Pleasure and Danger* (Boston: Routledge and Kegan Paul, 1984), pp. 1–28.

[22] This legislation has come under attack from the Feminist Anti-Censorship Taskforce which warns that it would be used by the right wing and by conservative governments to stifle a wide range of sexual expression.

Embodying the Self 77

to us is the male gaze. As Drucilla Cornell points out, with such a rigid understanding of the way gender is constructed, the 'social' category of gender becomes as irrevocable as if it were biological.[23]

An exercise that is central to each of the three positions discussed above is the attempt to enable women to recognize that they have a right to feel violated even if what they have experienced is not 'rape' as it is generally understood. In other words, the explicit purpose is to criminalize a whole range of behaviour which women accept as 'normal', but by which they feel humiliated and oppressed, or at the very least uncomfortable. As a survey in the USA revealed, many women did not know the legal definition of rape, but felt victimized even if they believed that the legal standards for 'rape' had not been met.[24]

Thus, a handbook issued by two Indian activists working in the area of sexual violence spells out:

> You have been sexually assaulted if . . . Against your will you have been:
> 1. Kissed
> 2. Fondled
> 3. Handled
> 4. Forced to have sexual intercourse
> 5. Sexually violated through oral or anal intercourse
> 6. Penetrated with a foreign object.
>
> The law recognizes only no. 4 as the very serious crime of rape and all others as lesser crimes. But for women, all six constitute equally serious violations of their freedom and their being.[25]

Further, the booklet notes, these sexual violations 'constitute a crime. The state defines them as crimes and they are not simply social misdemeanours even if men and society would like us to believe so.'[26]

There are, then, two simultaneous impulses at work in feminist analyses of rape. The one revealing the limitations of the law and its

---

[23] Cornell 1991, p. 120.
[24] Sharon Johnson, 'Rape: The Conservative Backlash', in *Ms*, March/April 1992.
[25] Jasjit Purewal and Naina Kapur, *Have You Been Sexually Assaulted?* (New Delhi, n.d.), p. 3.
[26] Purewal and Kapur, n.d., p. 5.

inability to encompass the lived experience of women; the other seeking to legitimate this experience precisely through having it recognized by the law as authentic, 'to write the experiences of women and minor children into the law.'[27] In other words: (a) certain experiences assumed to be clearly recognizable as 'sexual' are posited as having a reality and an existence prior to legal discourse, and the latter is seen as limited and incomplete to the extent it is incapable of recognizing these experiences, but at the same time: (b) these experiences need to be authenticated by law to have social value and be recognized as 'real'. To this extent then, they are to be constituted as real and legitimated by legal discourse.

Law as the Primary Legitimating Discourse

Recourse to the law is seen as necessary and inevitable because it is believed that designing a law around an experience proves 'it matters'; law is 'the concrete delivery of rights through the legal system.'[28] For example, activists in Britain fighting to get male rape classified as 'rape' and not merely 'sexual assault' argue that recognizing male rape as a crime 'would give men a signal that this is ... very serious ...'[29] Or, as another writer puts it, publicizing private injuries, that is, making them legally cognizable, politicizes them. 'The specific legal strategy advocated here is that we publicize and thus politicize those injuries—those intimate intrusions into our lives—which we want to make legally cognizable.'[30] Law is seen as the primary legitimating discourse and it is believed therefore, that legal criminalization would socially delegitimise a practice.

However, dominant modes of constituting the self—as woman, as

[27] 'Draft Amendments to Rape Law', p. 1.

[28] MacKinnon, 1987, p. 103.

[29] Mick Brown, 'Male Rape is not even Recognized as Crime' in *The Pioneer*, 16 December 1992.

[30] Adrian Howe, 'The Problem of Privatized Injuries: Feminist Strategies for Litigation' in Martha Albertson Fineman and Nancy Sweet Thomadsen (eds), *At the Boundaries of Law* (New York and London: Routledge, 1991), pp. 148–9.

criminal, as victim—are maintained and reinforced through the conventions of legal language. The rejection of these categories can come about, in fact, only through resistance to legal discourse.[31] As Foucault points out, judgement is passed not only on the 'crimes' defined by the code, but on 'the shadows lurking behind the case'—'on passions, instincts, anomalies...' In short, on the deviations from dominant norms.[32] Thus, what the law legitimates ultimately is precisely what feminist practice contests.

Moreover, in post-colonial societies, the establishing of law as the only legitimating discourse has meant marginalising and 'devalidating' other legitimating discourses. As a substantial body of historical scholarship shows for India, the colonial intervention decisively transformed indigenous notions of justice, honour and property and brought them in line with the requirements of modern legal discourse. This process was not necessarily unambiguously emancipatory. In fact, it had devastating consequences for many subaltern sections who were drastically marginalised and disciplined by the operation of modern codes of identity and governance—for example, tribes which were categorized as criminal, such as the *sansiah*, Nayar women in matrilineal arrangements who lost their rights to property, and female mill-workers in Bombay whose customary and traditional freedoms were curtailed by colonial law.[33]

In this context, let us examine a judgement which awarded a conviction in a rape case on the grounds that the Hindu Marriage Act supersedes all other forms of custom.[34] Three men had forcibly abducted a girl, said to be fourteen or fifteen years of age, and one of them had raped her. Though medical examination had shown her to be above the age of consent, the district court accepted her word that she

---

[31] Kristin Bumiller, 'Fallen Angels: The Representation of Violence Against Women in Legal Culture', in Fineman and Thomadsen, 1991, p. 94.

[32] Michel Foucault, *Discipline and Punish: The Birth of the Prison* (New York: Vantage Books, 1977), p. 17.

[33] See the essays by Sandria Freitag, G. Arunima and Radha Kumar in Michael Anderson and Sumit Guha (eds), *Changing Concepts of Rights and Justice in South Asia* (Delhi: OUP, 1998).

[34] *Nattu* vs. *State of Madhya Pradesh, Criminal Law Journal, 1990,* p. 1567.

had submitted passively on fear of death, and the men were sent to two years in prison. Considering the circumstances, this was a very short term in prison. On appeal, the accused men deposed that, being Bhils of Jhabua District, they had only been following the tribal custom of Bhagoriya marriage by which the woman is abducted, the couple have sexual intercourse, and then the boy pays an agreed amount to the father of the girl. They alleged that the girl's father lodged a complaint with the police because the bargaining was unsatisfactory and a quarrel took place. In the meanwhile, pending the appeal, the prosecutrix and her father entered into an agreement with the appellants and wished to discontinue prosecution. However, the judgement held that:

(a) Offences under Sections 366 and 376 (abduction and rape) are non-compoundable, i.e. cannot be settled out of court, and;
(b) '. . . it is difficult to take legal notice of custom opposed to law be it in the tribals or non-tribals' (at Para 16).

Nevertheless, the sentence was reduced from two years to six months in view of the appeal for compounding. In other words, the crime was treated as a light one even before the plea for compounding was made, when it had been clearly established that the woman had been forcibly abducted and raped. On appeal the already light sentence was further reduced. At the same time, the principle that has been embodied by the law as precedent is that 'law' supersedes 'tribal custom'. Serious negative implications may arise from the judgement for tribal communities and particularly women. Since many tribes have customs which give women more autonomy in marriage than the Hindu Marriage Act does, it can be detrimental to the interests of women in some tribes to have the law supersede tribal custom.[35]

[35] Hindu laws as codified through acts passed between 1955 and 1956 were based on inegalitarian Victorian English patterns of marriage and inheritance and on the customary practices of some of the dominant communities in North-West India, among whom women's rights have been seriously eroded. The practices of the Nairs in Kerala, Meitei in Manipur, Meenas in Rajasthan, and Jains, which provided better rights to women in many respects, were presumed to be nonexistent or non-Indian. Thus the Hindu codified law is in many ways a step backward for some communities. See Bina Agarwal, 'Rural Women, Poverty and Natural Resources', in *Economic and*

This argument is not intended to valorize pre-colonial communitarian values as egalitarian and just. On the contrary, 'the community' is marked by exclusion along the axes of caste, gender, class and so on; inegalitarian power relations are the fulcrum on which 'the community' turns. At the same time, it would be simplistic to assume the neutrality of the modern legal system. Social movements tend to work on the belief that even if the law is as enmeshed in the power structures of society as 'the community', it can be forced into the service of progress and change by the pressure of democratic movements. However, as Upendra Baxi points out, underlying the concept of 'Rule of Law' (the due observance of procedures prescribed for making a valid decision) is the idea that power should become impersonal and be constrained through rules applied by an independent judiciary and autonomous legal profession. But this formal legal rationality does not always constrain the arbitrary exercise of power; Baxi argues that, on the contrary, it often helps to camouflage the latter.[36]

What does it mean for feminists to insist that this 'formal legal rationality' should delimit the contours of a particular experience, and that it should legitimate this experience? Do we not, by implication, accept that without such validation the experience itself has no reality? We need to recognize that legal rationality cannot comprehend the complex ways in which sexual violence is constituted.

Sexual Violence and the Binary Logic of Law

It is a well documented fact that, all over the world, only a fraction of instances of rape/sexual violence are reported, and only in a fraction of these are there convictions. In Bombay in the period 1985–9 for

---

Political Weekly, 28 October 1989; Madhu Kishwar, 'Codified Hindu Law: Myth and Reality', in *Economic and Political Weekly*, 13 August 1994. See also G. Arunima, 'Colonialism and the Transformation of Matriliny in Malabar 1850–1940' (Ph.D. dissertation, Department of History, Cambridge University, 1992).

[36] Upendra Baxi, *The Crisis of the Indian Legal System* (Delhi: Vikas Publishing House, 1982), pp. 36–7.

example, of 504 cases registered, only 469 were chargesheeted, of which there were 13 convictions and 10 acquittals, and 441 were pending trial in 1990. Also, a large number of convictions in the sessions courts are overturned on appeal, or the sentences reduced.[37]

This is partly because, as Flavia Agnes points out, the criminal justice system envisages an all-powerful state prosecuting the vulnerable accused, and so the maxim on which it functions is that the benefit of doubt should go to the accused. In cases of rape however, she holds, the woman 'stands outside the power equations between the State and the accused.'[38] In crimes against women, 'which are private and personal in nature', it is virtually impossible to prove the case beyond reasonable doubt, as required by the criminal justice system. She urges the evolution of 'totally different criteria' for convicting the accused and a 'totally different concept of justice.'[39]

Another factor that hampers the conduct of rape cases, according to Agnes, is that rape is a criminal offence. Since under the Criminal Code all offences are crimes against the state, only the state can prosecute in a rape case. The woman raped is represented not by her own lawyer, but by the public prosecutor. The positive aspect of this is that it is the responsibility of the state to make preliminary investigations and collect evidence. On the other hand this also means that apathy on the part of the police and the public prosecutor can seriously hamper the progress of a case. Defence lawyers engaged by the accused are paid high fees and are in general more motivated.[40] Thus, treating rape as a criminal offence, which is meant to establish the greater magnitude of the crime, in effect seems to hamper prosecution.

Nevertheless, in the case of custodial rape by police or rapes by army personnel there is agreement among feminists that the state should accept responsibility. A recent case which focused on the responsibility of the state in a different context was the rape of a village-level worker (*sathin*) of the government's Women's Development Programme in Bhateri village, Rajasthan. In 1992, the sathin was punitively raped by

---

[37] Flavia Agnes, *Journey to Justice* (Bombay: Majlis, 1990), p. 48.
[38] Agnes 1990, p. 7.
[39] Ibid., pp. 10–11.
[40] Ibid., pp. 35–6.

two men of a family which had been prevented from conducting a child-marriage by the district authorities on the basis of her reports. The authorities colluded with the family, which belongs to the dominant caste in the village, to hamper registration and investigation of the case, and women's groups in the country rallied around. The case was transferred to the Criminal Bureau of Investigation (CBI), and later the district court acquitted the rapists on the grounds that upper-caste men would not even touch, let alone rape, a lower-caste woman. The appeal is pending in the High Court.

The point that women's groups have been stressing is that the sathin is a government employee carrying out responsibilities given to her by the government. The state, therefore, is responsible for what amounts to injury in the course of work. Nevertheless, the fact that this particular injury is sexual situates it firmly in the law's binary logic, and the CBI inquiry too has followed predictable paths, casting doubts on the victim's testimony, humiliating her, and so on.

No wonder then that exhausted feminists have come to feel that 'even though the law exists to protect your rights . . . It is often put into effect by men who have no understanding of what a sexual assault means to a woman.'[41] Or even more strongly, that 'liberal legalism' is itself misogynist.[42] At the very least there is the recognition of 'the limited ability of the law to provide a complete remedy to the problem of rape.'[43] However, this is usually understood to be a result of the sexist interpretation of the law by insensitive judges and lawyers. In other words, the limitation is seen to lie in the interpretability of the law, not its rigidity. It should follow that if a foolproof law were to be enacted according to feminist norms and administered strictly, 'the problem of rape' can be solved more satisfactorily. It is the contention of this study that the more foolproof the law in feminist terms, the more it refracts the ethical and emancipatory impulse of feminism itself.

Let us begin by examining whether the 1983 Amendment to the Criminal Law was necessary, from a feminist perspective. Flavia Agnes

---

[41] Purewal and Kapur, n.d., p. 11.
[42] MacKinnon 1987, p. 5.
[43] 'Draft Amendments to Rape Law', p. 1.

points out that the legal position regarding consent before the Mathura trial was not as adverse as might be assumed. In fact, the judgement in the Mathura case was contradictory to the generally accepted legal position set by the Rao Harnarain Singh case of 1958 in which the court had held that there is a distinction between submission and consent and that submission under terror is not consent.[44] An even earlier case than the one Agnes mentions is *Rameshwar* vs. *State of Rajasthan, 1952*, in which the Supreme Court had taken the view that in the case of rape the necessity of corroboration was to be treated only as 'a rule of prudence'. 'There is no rule of practice that there must be in every case, corroboration before a case can be allowed to stand.'[45]

Later judgements which Agnes lists include *Rafiq* vs. *State of UP, 1980*, in which the Supreme Court held that the testimony of the rape victim should not be rejected 'unless there are very strong circumstances mitigating its veracity. . . .' In 1981 in *Harpal Singh and Another* vs. *State of Himachal Pradesh*, the opinion of the court was that 'the fact that . . . the girl is used to sexual intercourse is immaterial in a rape trial.' In 1983, in *Bharwada Bhogibhai Hirjibhai* vs. *State of Gujarat*, the court held that corroborative evidence of the woman's testimony is not necessary. This last judgement came in the course of the public campaign to amend the rape laws and was probably influenced by feminist propaganda.[46]

While there have been progressive judgements on the issue of corroborative evidence even before the amendment, equally there have been retrogressive judgements after the amendment. These have stressed the necessity of injury both to the accused as well as to the victim, or the imputed promiscuity of the raped woman.[47] In the USA too, a survey of rape law in six states showed that pre-reform rulings had accomplished much of what reform laws were designed to do.[48]

---

[44] Agnes 1992, p. WS-20.
[45] *Rameshwar* vs. *State of Rajasthan*, AIR 1952, SC 54, Paras 46–7.
[46] Agnes 1992, p. WS-21.
[47] Ibid.
[48] Carole Goldberg Ambrose, 'Unfinished Business in Rape Law Reform', in *Journal of Social Issues*, vol. 48, no.1, 1992, p. 175.

From her analyses of judgements in rape cases, Agnes' conclusion is that the law can be interpreted progressively if the judiciary wishes. The 1983 amendment was supposed to close off the possibility of retrogressive interpretations by providing certain guidelines, but, as she establishes, in the post-amendment period provision for more stringent punishment has in fact resulted in fewer convictions.[49] The new law, it would seem, has served no purpose, and, if anything, has reduced the prospect of securing convictions. Could better-framed guidelines have made the law tighter, less prone to interpretation, more able to secure convictions? Or is sexual violence incapable of being comprehended by law?

Carol Smart outlines the contours of this complexity in the following way. Law's claim to truth is based on a binary logic which sets up oppositions like truth/untruth, guilt/innocence, consent/non-consent. This binary logic, she argues, is completely inappropriate to what she calls 'the "ambiguity" of rape.'[50] In criminal law, the object is to establish guilt or innocence, and in rape cases the establishing of either turns on another pair of opposites—that of consent/non-consent. The dualism of consent/non-consent is

> completely irrelevant to women's experience of sex. Neither begins to approach the complexity of a woman's position when she is being sexually propositioned or abused . . . [T]he 'telling' of a story of rape or abuse inevitably reveals ambiguities. Hence a woman may agree to a certain amount of intimacy but not to sexual intercourse. In the legal model, however, consent to the former is consent to full intercourse . . . [I]n legal terms submission fits on the consent side of the dichotomy. The only alternative when non-consent is not established is to presume consent.[51]

Smart's argument can be worked out through the consideration of a judgement by the Calcutta High Court in a case of a woman seduced with the promise of marriage and abandoned when she became

---

[49] Agnes 1992, p. WS-24.
[50] Carol Smart, *Feminism and the Power of Law* (New York and London: Routledge, 1989), p. 33.
[51] Smart 1989, pp. 33–4.

pregnant. She sued the man for rape, contending that her consent to sexual intercourse was given on the basis of a false promise and hence was not valid consent. The court rejected her plea, holding that 'Failure to keep the promise at a future uncertain date does not amount to misconception of fact. If a fully grown girl consents to sexual intercourse on the promise of marriage and continues to indulge in such activity until she becomes pregnant, it is an act of promiscuity.'[52]

Flavia Agnes cites this judgement as displaying 'an extremely negative view of women's sexuality.'[53] Her criticism arises from the notion of 'promiscuity' underlying the judgement, which immediately contextualises it in terms of the moral norms sanctioning only marriage as a legitimate forum for sex. At the same time, as feminists, we are sharply critical of these moral norms; Agnes would not use 'promiscuity', with all its derogatory connotations, to refer to sex outside marriage. If then an adult woman consents to sex outside marriage, and we object to this being termed 'promiscuity', rightly holding that this is a sexist term redolent of sexual double standards—if in other words we see such a description of the case as a 'negative view of women's sexuality'—then we cannot also support the woman's claim that her consent was not valid since she had given it on the promise of marriage. Her contention is valid only within a discourse which constitutes 'non-promiscuous' women as those who would not agree to sex outside marriage.

This case is clearly illustrative of what Smart calls 'the "ambiguity" of women's experience of sex.' For it is not my contention that the girl was not cheated and exploited. Rather, I would point to the law's inability to respond to complexity and ambiguity. Seen purely in the context of consent/non-consent, there is no doubt that the woman did consent, and not out of fear. Unless we accept MacKinnon's position that all heterosex is violent and male-directed (and we have discussed earlier how taking this position would make it impossible to engage with the law at all, as well as entail the rejection of the possibility of

---

[52] *Jayanti Rani Parda* vs. *State of West Bengal*, Cr. L.J. 1984, p. 535.
[53] Agnes 1992, p. WS-21.

female subjectivity altogether), we have to retain the space to comprehend 'women's experience of sex' as other than simply 'consenting' to male pressure. A judgement convicting the man of rape in this case could only have been on the basis of a reaffirmation of patriarchal norms of marriage and female sexuality. At the same time, the judgement as it stands has not given the woman 'justice' in any sense. Thus, while recognizing the relative powerlessness and lack of autonomy that characterize women's relations with men, the point here is to radically question the possibility of addressing this experience in the realm of legal discourse.

One way of inserting this particular case into the clear-cut dualism of the law might be to empty it of its 'sexual' content and see it as a case of cheating, for there is no disagreement on the fact that the man had promised marriage. Under Section 90 of the IPC, General Exceptions are listed and it lays down the conditions under which consent is not consent as intended by the code. One of these is: if the consent is given under misconception of the fact and the other person knows consent was given under these circumstances, would it have been possible to convict the man for cheating and fraud rather than rape? It seems unlikely that this would have worked, because the trial would have been inevitably 'sexualized', given the nature of the issues involved. This is what happened in a case in 1955.[54] Two constables lied to a woman that they had a warrant for her arrest and induced her to have sex with them in order to avoid being arrested. She did so, but later went to court claiming that her consent was vitiated by the fact that the policemen had lied to her. The court acquitted the accused since the woman had given her consent, even though under a misapprehension of fact. The precedent relied upon was an English judgement of 1888[55] in which it was held that consent obtained by fraud still must be considered consent—'If a man . . . gives [a woman] bad money in order to procure her consent to intercourse with him he obtains her consent by fraud, but it would be childish to say that she did not consent.' Would

---

[54] *Moti Ram* vs. *State of Maharashtra*, AIR 1955, p. 121.
[55] *Queen* vs. *Clarence*, 1888, 22 QBD, 23 at 2.

the judgement have been the same if a man had given bad money to buy property? Clearly the 'sexualisation' of consent transforms its meaning.

Consent and the Age Factor

The question of consent becomes crucial in the case of sexual assault in a way in which it does not in an act of nonsexual violence. The victim of a violent assault is never assumed to be an accomplice, but if such an assault can be described as sexual, the victim must establish her lack of consent, which is otherwise assumed. If consent is established, the act is considered legitimate. At the same time, sexual acts not sanctioned by prevailing codes of conduct are illegitimate, regardless of whether consent was given, as with people who do not have 'adult' status (in terms of age or mental capacity) or between parents and children, or, in India, sexual acts 'against the order of nature', which refers to sodomy, with men or women. Conversely, the consent of both parties is assumed in sexual acts sanctioned by the social order which are therefore perpetually legitimate, as for example sex within marriage. 'Marital rape' does not exist except within the feminist lexicon, unless it is sodomy, in which case both husband and wife are guilty of a criminal act if the wife consented, and the husband alone if she did not.

A crucial factor which decides the legitimacy of consent is age. In India, the legal age of majority, also the minimum age for marriage, is eighteen. Under Section 375 of the Indian Penal Code, however, the age of consent for marriage has been accepted as fifteen: 'Sexual intercourse by a man with his wife, the wife not being under 15 years of age, is not rape.' Feminists have pointed out often enough that the marriage of a woman below eighteen is not legal and to recognize such marriages as legal through Section 375 is a great anomaly.[56]

[56] This anomaly can also be interpreted in a startlingly different way. In his evidence to the Joint Committee of Parliament considering the Criminal Law Amendment Bill passed in 1983, a DIG of police argued that since the legal minimum age of marriage is 18 years, the law must assume a 'wife' to be 18. Once married, a woman must be

The proposed bill drafted by feminist lawyers and activists therefore seeks to correct this anomaly by fixing the age of majority at eighteen for the purposes of the bill. However, from the note accompanying the bill it is clear that this decision was arrived at after considerable debate: 'Some members were concerned that if the age was as high as 18 then even consensual sex between adolescents in the 16–18 age group would be an offence. This position could be constructed [*sic*] as highly puritanical and moralistic.'[57] The decision was finally taken on the consideration that the age of majority for voting is eighteen. At the same time, in order to deal with the sexual assault of minors while not unduly penalizing the possibility of consensual sex between adolescents, greater punishment has been laid down for the assault of children below twelve than in the age group twelve to eighteen. Thus the state of mind labelled 'consent', which is constituted in a complex way, as feminists would be the first to acknowledge, must be pegged rigidly to a linear notion of physical growth if it is to make sense within legal discourse.[58]

With the development of forensic medicine, it is possible to codify 'the body' more and more rigorously, and ossification tests to determine age are routinely ordered when there are no documents to attest to the age of the raped woman, which is very often the case. Courts tend to give credence to ossification tests even when documents are available. In one case for example, the judge held that the school-leaving certificate of the woman, which showed her to be a minor, appeared

---

considered to be 18, and therefore he held that the exception should read 'sexual intercourse by a man with his wife is not rape', J.P. Atray, *Crimes Against Women* (Delhi: Vikas Publishing House, 1988), p. 144.

[57] 'Draft Amendments to Rape Law', p. 4.

[58] See Tanika Sarkar on the Age of Consent debate in the nineteenth century. She demonstrates how all strands of opinion, whether colonial, revivalist-nationalist or medical-reformist, defined consent in terms of a purely biological category, that is, the stage when the female body was ready to accept sexual penetration without serious harm. They only differed, she points out, in assessing when this stage was reached: Tanika Sarkar, 'Rhetoric Against Age of Consent: Resisting Colonial Reason and Death of a Childwife', in *Economic and Political Weekly*, 4 September 1993, p. 1875.

to be suspect. The ossification test, which established her to be over the age of consent, was accepted, and since she had gone with the accused of her own will, the case was dismissed.[59] This judgement overruled an earlier one which had held that the best evidence of age is the date of birth according to the school register if available, since the ossification test is not infallible.[60] No permanent precedent has been set in this regard, and individual judges continue to decide whether they will give greater weight to medical evidence or to birth and school certificates.

Once again, it might seem that the law is infinitely interpretable but, far from demonstrating the elasticity of the law, this discussion on age points to precisely the opposite—the inevitable movement within legal discourse to codify, fix and regulate meaning. Different judgements may validate different kinds of evidence as more reliable, but 'more reliable' in the sense of 'better able to establish conclusively whether the woman was above or below the Age of Consent.' Below this age, a woman cannot be deemed to have acted on her own volition in matters of sex; that is, she can be understood only as Victim or Dupe. Above this age, even if it is by a few months, she is radically transformed from Victim to Accomplice.

The draft bill to amend the IPC is marked by a deep discomfort with the fixing of one specific physical landmark as the point at which 'consent' changes its meaning. As a result, much ambiguity remains. The definition of 'minor', for example, is given as 'a person who is 18 years of age or under.'[61] The age was arrived at on the consideration that the voting age is 18, but in this formulation a person who is 18 is a minor. Similarly, in the section explaining the conditions vitiating consent, one condition is, 'If the person is or *appears to be* a minor.'[62] The concern underlying this deliberate ambiguity is clear. The attempt to fix 'minority' at a higher level in terms of age and simultaneously to leave the boundaries of 'minor' status permeable results in opening up the possibility of more people being classified as minor,

---

[59] *Kanchan Das* vs. *the State*, 1991, Cri L.J. 2036, Delhi High Court.
[60] *Sachindranath Mozumdar* vs. *Bistupada Das*, 1978.
[61] 'Draft Amendments to Rape Law', p. 13.
[62] Ibid. (emphasis added).

so that more cases of rape can be classified as Aggravated Sexual Assault, deserving greater punishment. This must be seen in the context of the growing number of sexual attacks on children, and the growing awareness of sexual abuse of women and children within families. The committee makes it clear that it feels that the danger of sexual abuse of minors going unpunished is greater than the possibility of adolescents being punished for consensual sex.[63] However, the final form of the law cannot possibly retain the sort of ambiguity the draft embodies.

More importantly, we cannot be blind to the implications of constructing 'sexuality' for young women entirely in terms of victimhood. And yet, perhaps the very logic of legal discourse leaves us with little room to deal in complexity. We are forced into the language of patriarchy despite ourselves—for instance, the committee, while discussing the possibility that defining 'minority' so broadly could criminalize consensual sex between adolescents, came to the conclusion that there would be very few cases in which a family would make a false charge of sexual assault because such a charge would 'implicate their "family honour and dignity".'[64] The quotation marks around the phrase do indicate that it is self-consciously used. Also, this argument has been used in many judgements to dismiss the need for corroborative evidence in cases of rape. However, as the next section will demonstrate, accepting the notion of 'honour' as the basis for believing women's testimony in rape cases has serious consequences antithetical to the feminist project.

The Reinstatement of Dominant Norms through the Rape Trial

Feminists are increasingly becoming aware of the rape trial acting as pornographic spectacle. Even where convictions have been secured, the process of the trials as well as the judgements powerfully reinstate patriarchal and sexist norms of female sexuality and legitimate codes

[63] Ibid., p. 4.
[64] Ibid.

of female behaviour. Kristin Bumiller's analysis of the 1984 rape trial of six Portuguese immigrant men in New Bedford, Massachusetts, raises many of these issues.[65] The woman who had been raped received general public support and sympathetic media coverage, and four of the defendants were convicted, so it would seem to have been a 'successful' rape trial from the feminist point of view. And yet the law's demand to provide objective evidence to prove the abuse of the victim makes it necessary to establish the victim's 'innocence'—that is, her non-complicity and non-consent according to commonly held notions. The demand for 'objectivity' also makes it difficult to establish the woman's 'innocence' in more ambiguous situations where rape differs from the kind of act recognized as 'real' rape which involves strangers, the use of weapons and a public scene, or what Flavia Agnes calls an 'ideal' situation for the police, a gang rape of an infant girl resulting in multiple injuries and with eye-witnesses ready to give evidence.[66]

In the New Bedford case, the fact that the victim and the defendants were Portuguese was used to reinforce stereotypes of immigrant communities as violent and uncivilized. At the same time, the behaviour of the woman in going to a tavern at night, alone, came under scrutiny in terms of being compared to 'reasonable' standards of women's propriety. The trial in effect turned on the victim's freedom from guilt, reinforcing the presumption that punishing violent men is justified to the extent that women are worthy of trust and protection.

In India, particularly, judgements which have taken a progressive position on the issue of corroborative evidence in rape trials have been based on the most patriarchal notions of a woman's 'virtue' and 'chastity'. For example, in the 1983 judgement cited earlier,[67] the explanation for not needing corroborative evidence was that 'a girl or woman in the tradition-bound, non-permissive society of India would be extremely reluctant even to admit that any incident which is likely to reflect on her chastity had ever occurred.'

---

[65] Bumiller 1991, pp. 95–110.
[66] Agnes 1990, p. 8.
[67] *Bhogibhai Hirjibhai* vs. *State of Gujarat*, AIR, 1983, Sc. 753.

However, Justice Thakkar adds: 'Corroboration may be insisted upon when a woman having attained majority is found in a compromising position and there is a likelihood of her having levelled such an accusation on account of the instinct of self-preservation.' That is, the very values which Justice Thakkar cites as the reason why false accusations of rape would be unlikely in India—the values informing a woman's overwhelming desire to preserve public belief in her 'chastity' and 'virtue'—could equally motivate, in his understanding, a consenting woman found in a 'compromising situation' to preserve her reputation by denying that she had consented.

The implication is more serious, therefore, than feminist critiques recognize. It is not simply that in such decisions the court passively accepts rather than challenges the belief in the need to protect women's chastity, as one writer argues.[68] The seriousness lies in recognizing the assumption that if the 'tradition-bound society' of India would make 'innocent' women reluctant to level false accusations of rape, it would at the same time motivate 'promiscuous' women to hide their promiscuity precisely through such accusations. The rape trial thus turns once more on the 'guilt' or 'innocence' of the raped woman. Thus, the trend of decisions over the past decade to reduce the importance of corroborative evidence in rape cases is not really an indication that there is growing recognition of the fact that women rarely make baseless allegations of rape. On the contrary, it merely reinstates the duality of the innocent woman who should be protected from rape and the promiscuous woman who cannot be raped.

The *National Law School Journal* (*NLSJ*) points out that the problematic assumptions about women's sexuality are clearly seen when judgements make comparisons of the Indian context with 'the West'. Such comparisons suggest that 'more stringent rules of corroboration may be justified in 'the West' because Western women attribute no value to chastity and are thus more likely to make false allegations of rape. Implicit in these arguments is the assumption that the more aware women are of their sexuality, and the more obvious they are in

---

[68] Anonymous, 'Rape: Challenging the Pedestals of Patriarchy', *National Law School Journal*, vol. 1, 1993, p. 170.

the expression of their sexuality, the less they can be trusted to speak honestly and in turn the more likely they will become to lie about rape.'[69]

Another example of a problematic assumption that was validated by a judgement convicting a rapist is the belief that rape and sexual violence are impossible within marriage. Overturning the defence argument that the woman's injuries were caused by her husband and not by the defendant, the Supreme Court stated: '[It] is not possible to believe that when a married woman has sex with her husband in the privacy of their bedroom she would suffer abrasions.'[70] Thus the judgement reinforces 'traditional and sexist assumptions about women's sexuality and the nature of violence in their lives.'[71]

An analysis of the debate in the Lok Sabha on the Criminal Law Amendment Bill of 1983 (at which most of the benches were empty, as Geeta Mukherjee, the late Member of Parliament, pointed out) reveals that the discussion was far removed from the feminist concerns of dignity, selfhood and bodily integrity of women. The bill was passed, but it is significant that the instances of MPs' views given below were the rule rather than the exception.[72]

— Fears about the trapping of innocent men by women willing to claim falsely that they were raped: 'In such a situation the woman would not have been raped, but the poor man will certainly be raped in court.' (Moolchand Daga)[73]
— A statement approvingly quoted from the 8th Report of the National Police Commission: 'Women, largely because they have come out of their homes to study and to work, are now more exposed to dangers in society . . .' (Ram Singh Yadav)[74]
— The recommendation that any sexual relationship between a man and a woman who are not married should be treated as

---

[69] Ibid., pp. 170–1.
[70] Ibid., p. 167.
[71] Ibid.
[72] *Lok Sabha Debates*, 1983, vol. 42.
[73] Ibid., p. 431. Translated from Hindi.
[74] Ibid., p. 456.

rape. This would be more in keeping with 'our own sexual morality'. Conversely, the concept of rape by a husband should not be entertained. (A.T. Patil)[75]

— Opposition to the suggested amendment to debar publicity for rape cases. Apart from arguing that publicity ensures a fair trial, the MP held that social attitudes must change; merely protecting the identity of the woman could perpetrate 'the greater horror' of the girl later getting married without her husband or his family knowing about her rape. (N.J. Shejwalkar)[76]

— Objection to the clause vitiating consent if given when intoxicated. What if the woman intoxicates herself and then disclaims responsibility: 'after all, we're not dealing all the time with virtuous women. We may also deal with some women who unfortunately, do not conform to normal standards of womanhood.' (R. Jethmalani)[77]

These then are the values and assumptions that animate the 1983 amendment which was passed by parliament. The fear of the autonomous sexuality of women is the spectre that haunts the entire discussion. If rape is to be punished, it is because the enforced chastity of women is the cornerstone of patriarchal society. It is clear the law's comprehension of sexual violence can only be through misogynist and paternalist categories, even as it condemns and attempts to punish sexual violence.

Activists working in the area of sexual violence are increasingly coming to feel that there is a need to adopt strategies other than legal reform. Having conducted a workshop on sexual assault, a lawyer and feminist activist reports that the participants felt that they should shift focus from 'mainstream remedies to a sense of justice within'. This meant focusing on the victim's sense of self, denied to her by both the rapist and the enforcement agencies. More importantly, they felt they should work towards reinstating her within her community through

[75] Ibid., pp. 366–9.
[76] Ibid., pp. 375–6.
[77] Ibid., p. 413.

gender education and awareness.[78] This growing awareness that 'rape' needs to be reconstituted in ideological terms is also evident in the campaign on the rape of the sathin in Bhateri, discussed earlier. One of the central slogans was—'*Izzat gayi kiski? Bhateri ki, Bhateri ki*' (Whose honour has been lost? The village Bhateri's).

What are the implications of reconstituting 'a sense of self' after sexual assault? We are pushed inevitably into questioning 'sexuality' itself, a term assumed to be clearly comprehensible to everyone. And in one sense it is. We need to radically deconstruct this apparently universal, shared understanding of 'sexuality' to reveal the tenuousness of its foundations. The *NLSJ* concludes a feminist critique of judgements in rape cases with a statement which lays down the agenda for feminist practice:

> While we welcome the reduction of the corroboration requirements in rape cases, we must vigilantly reveal and challenge the problematic assumptions about women's sexuality that continue to inform these decisions. Feminist understandings of female sexuality and of women's rights to control our bodies, stand in stark opposition to the patriarchal pedestals of 'chastity and virginity'—pedestals that are securing the conviction of rapists at the cost of reinforcing the very assumptions that subordinate and oppress women.[79]

This statement fails to comes to terms with the fact that the reduction of corroboration requirements in rape cases is not just incidentally linked to problematic assumptions about female sexuality, as we have seen. More fundamentally, the statement fails to question the assumptions that underlie feminist understandings of—(a) 'women's rights to control our bodies'; and (b) 'female sexuality'.

The next two sections problematize these assumptions.

Rape and Rights-talk

Let us examine some of the implications of setting rape within the discourse of rights so that it can 'make sense' within law.

---

[78] Naina Kapur, 'CBI's Approach Discouraging for Rape Victims', in *The Pioneer*, 21 September 1993.

[79] Anonymous 1993, p. 171.

The draft bill to amend the rape law in India contains a note from one of the members of the committee, urging further debate on Section 375 (2)(a) as it has been drafted. This section classifies the sexual assault of pregnant women as aggravated sexual assault, for which harsher punishment is awarded. The implication is that non-consensual sexual activity causes greater harm to the pregnant woman than to a nonpregnant one. The note raises the question, 'We need to be aware of how this provision could be interpreted by a judge—would s/he understand that the harm is supposed to be to the woman herself and not to the foetus . . .? Would the latter position not conflict with pro-choice arguments?'[80] The 'broader ideological significance' of making sexual assault a more serious crime in the case of pregnant women, the note continues, is that it reinforces the 'value of women as wombs, rather than as individuals.'[81] Further, if it is assumed that pregnant women suffer a particular type of physical harm on being assaulted, then presumably the harm could change over the course of the pregnancy. How, asks the note, could this be worked into the legislation? 'Is it a more serious offence in the ninth month than in the first? How do we make these distinctions?'[82] The note also points out that if a miscarriage results from the assault, it is already punishable for life under Section 313 of the IPC. However, this section seeks to protect 'the rights of the unborn child', once again a problematic assertion for feminist pro-choice arguments.

The issues raised by this note unavoidably forefront the impossibility of simultaneously defining the 'harm of rape' so exactly that legal discourse can comprehend it and so retaining ambivalences that the ethical impulse of feminism is undamaged. Underlying the note is the whole history of feminist discussion on the ethics of abortion, on whether the foetus and the woman are to be seen as separate 'individuals' and on the unique nature of the 'pregnant body'.

Clearly, rights over our bodies are constituted in very complex ways. They come into being and are comprehensible only within

---

[80] 'Draft Amendments to Rape Law', p. 8.
[81] Ibid.
[82] Ibid., p. 9.

specific sets of agreements as to what constitutes one's 'own' body, the meaning of 'consent' and 'responsibility', the degree to which present social and economic arrangements are equitable, and the nature of the future desired society. Thus, rights come into being and have meaning only within particular discourses, and therefore alter significantly in meaning if they are displaced from one discourse into another. Thus, the 'right over one's body' is set within a particular matrix within feminist discourse but, once in the arena of law where diverse discourses of rights converge, its effects are not within the control of the originating discourse. To recognize the right to abortion, laws can permit the selective abortion of female foetuses, and laws to curb the latter can be used to restrict the right to abortion itself. Or, in the context of the present discussion, as the note appended to the draft bill points out, there are serious implications for women's access to abortion if sexual assault is seen as specially harmful to pregnant women.

The note attempts to resolve the dilemma by denying a unique status to pregnancy: 'Wouldn't it be more appropriate to draw a line between the severity and non-severity of the harm rather than pregnant and non-pregnant women?'[83] But this kind of 'sameness' approach towards pregnant and non-pregnant women is precisely that applied by courts between men and women, in order to strike down special provisions for women.[84] When the law treats pregnancy as a difference between persons and not between men and women, it becomes possible to argue that discrimination against pregnant women is not sex-discrimination because the distinction is being made between pregnant and non-pregnant people, and the latter category can include women as well.[85] Catharine MacKinnon has discussed how 'women's capacity to gestate children in utero' is sometimes used to

---

[83] Ibid., p. 8.

[84] The writer of the note has herself co-authored an incisive and comprehensive critique of this approach to equality as demonstrated by Indian courts: Ratna Kapur and Brenda Cossman, 'On Women, Equality and the Constitution: Through the Looking Glass of Feminism', *National Law School Journal*, vol. 1, 1993.

[85] Mary Joe Frug, *Postmodern Legal Feminism* (New York and London: Routledge, 1992), p. xii.

restrict employment for women and sometimes treated as so 'normal' a physical condition that special facilities are not required.[86]

A case in the USA involving sexual assault on a mentally retarded adult woman is illustrative of the double-edged nature of rights-talk when juxtaposed with the ambivalence of the notion of consent. The woman was sexually assaulted by a group of men known to her. She appears, from her testimony, to have 'consented' to these acts, but how capable can she be considered of 'informed' consent? Her attackers were convicted on the argument that she could not comprehend the nature of that to which she consented, but there has been considerable unease about the implications of such a judgement for the rights of the mentally handicapped. It is feared that there could be a setback in the struggle to win fair treatment for them in other areas like housing and voting rights.[87]

This discussion does not necessarily mean that feminists must reject altogether the possibility of using the language of rights. It does mean however, that we must be cautious about using this language to describe the nature of 'sexuality'.

Deconstructing 'Sexuality'

What is a 'sexual' act? The answer might appear to be self-evident. As an American judge said of pornography, 'I know it when I see it.'[88] So an act involving contact with the breasts or the genital region would appear to be a sexual act. In that case, what of the judgement in a case in Canada which concluded that an assault on a woman's breasts was not sexual because a person's 'secondary sexual characteristics' or 'erogenous zones' should not come under this category? The court gave as an example a man's beard, the touching of which it would be absurd to consider as a sexual assault.[89] On the other hand, what of harassment

---

[86] MacKinnon 1987, pp. 36–8.

[87] Catherine S. Manegold, 'A Rape Case Worries Advocates for the Retarded', in *The New York Times*, 14 March 1993.

[88] MacKinnon 1987, p. 163.

[89] Christine Boyle, 'Sexual Assault and the Feminist Judge', *Canadian Journal of Women and the Law*, 1985.

by strangers that may involve a 'nonsexual' part of the body such as arms or hands; which may not involve contact with the victim's body at all, as when men expose themselves; or which may be verbal or aural? Clearly, there are circumstances in which these kinds of performances could be identified as sexual attack too.

It would appear that sets of ideas, values and representations construct a mesh which trap some acts as 'sex'. Moreover this mesh is constantly shifting and sieves the material passing through it in different ways at different times. In other words, 'sex' is not a clear and specific physical phenomenon always recognizable as such under all circumstances.

Once identified as sexual, the significance of the event is radically transformed. One, the event, if it was physically violent, is no longer an act of violence alone, but of 'sexual' violence which radically alters qualitatively the terror and pain of the victim. Sexual assault has been so constructed that it is the most feared, most terrifying and humiliating form of attack. A booklet written by a feminist activist, outlining the procedures to be followed in a rape case, while discussing the tendency of courts to assume consent if the woman did not put up a struggle, points to 'the paralyzing effect on a young girl' that 'the sight of an erect penis can in itself have.'[90] This sense of paralysis and horror in the face of an attack recognized as sexual is not restricted to women. A counsellor in Britain heading Survivors, the principal counselling service for male rape victims, says that even 'big guys' 'freeze' when they are victims of a sexual attack. They talk of being literally unable to move, unable to offer any resistance.[91]

Even without physical violence or physical contact, 'sexual' performances in which people are involved against their will are traumatic in a way in which other encounters are not. Such encounters are also invariably faced more by women and children and more painful for them.

Can this explosive impact of sexual violence on its victims be explained entirely by the empirically verifiable physical acts that

[90] Agnes 1990, p. 10.
[91] Brown 1992.

constitute it? Or does the impact, and maybe even sexual violence itself, flow from the discourse which constructs 'sex', 'sexual violence' and 'sexuality' as aspects of the individual's 'real' and 'private' self, so that to violate the sense of wholeness in this area is to threaten one's belief in one's unique selfhood?

Feminist analyses share this in common with the misogynist and sexist assumptions they critique—both are squarely situated within the discourse which mystifies 'sexuality' as the truest, deepest expression of selfhood. Sexual violence, then, is seen as having 'a unique character',[92] as the 'violation of a woman's physical and mental being',[93] as 'a serious violation of (women's) freedom and their being'.[94] 'By sexual assault, men assume power over the most private part of a woman's life; her body.'[95] Thus, at the same time as 'sexuality' is constituted as the truest expression of selfhood, it is made clearly and easily identifiable with 'the body', itself unproblematically delineated as a material object with clearly definable boundaries—hence the redefinition of rape as 'violation of bodily integrity' in feminist legislative efforts. Simultaneously it is emphasized that the harm of sexual assault lies not so much in the physical assault, but in the transgression of the victim's conceptions of selfhood and sovereignty.

The repeated feminist emphasis on recognizing that rape is a crime points to the positioning of sexual violence in the realm of morality and ethics rather than in the category of definable physical acts. However, as I have argued, morality and ethics cannot be encapsulated within legality. Therefore, in order to be comprehensible within legal discourse, feminists must cast 'sexuality' and 'sexual violence' in physical terms, and catalogue as exhaustively as possible all the kinds of actions that can constitute sexual assault. Thus the proposed Section 375 (2) lists as sexual assault, gestures, sounds or words or the exhibiting of any part of the body 'for a sexual purpose'. This phrase is not explained. Similarly, Section 375 (3)(b) lists the conditions vitiating

---

[92] 'Draft Amendments to Rape Law', p. 10.
[93] Agnes 1990, p. 8.
[94] Purewal and Kapur, n.d., p. 3.
[95] Ibid.

consent, and (vi) reads: 'No consent is obtained for the purposes of Section 375 (1) when the woman is mistaken about the sexual nature of the act or mistakenly believes that the sexual activity is for medical, ritualistic, purificatory, therapeutic, psychological or spiritual purposes.'[96]

In both these instances, the physical act has been qualified in terms of the 'sexual' intention of the perpetrator as well as the intention as perceived by the victim. Under what circumstances can one establish the 'mistaken-ness' of the belief that a particular activity is for medical, ritualistic or spiritual purposes? What would be the implications of such a formulation for traditional practices not necessarily exploitative of women? Besides, the notions of 'intention' and 'perception of intention' will certainly lose their complexity within the binary logic of the law. My contention is not that this increases the possibility of 'innocent' men being prosecuted by women who misunderstood their intentions (although this possibility will certainly be one of the principal fears expressed in forums like the parliamentary committees). On the contrary, the ambiguity in phrases like 'for a sexual purpose' will be concretized in familiar misogynist and/or paternalist patterns in the process of the trial. One can see, then, the pressure from legal discourse to cast sexuality in terms of clearly recognizable physical boundaries. Simultaneously, the impossibility of doing so is also evident.

Feminists are increasingly becoming frustrated with the law in their struggle against sexual violence on women, but we continue to leave unquestioned the assumptions that are unravelling because they are being pushed by our own work. The argument so far suggests that the harm of rape cannot be comprehended in physical or material terms and so long as 'the body' is understood to be a physical object, prior to all discourse, the notion of 'violation of bodily integrity' would not appear to be very useful either. We have seen how 'consent' can figure and refigure 'bodily integrity' and how consent itself is refigured repeatedly in different contexts. For it is not a set of clearly discernible physical acts themselves which constitute rape but the discourse which

---

[96] 'Draft Amendments to Rape Law', p. 13.

constitutes these acts as 'sexual', and therefore as attacking the root of 'identity' itself. We have so far assumed as 'natural' the symbolic order which produces this identity, which inscribes the body as body, as separate from other bodies, as healthy/unhealthy and so on, and which constructs the gendered and heterosexual body as the norm. Can we begin to conceive of a feminist politics which radically contests the production of this identity?

It is useful to consider here Judith Butler's discussion of Freud's *The Ego and the Id* (1923) in which Freud argues that the body does not precede and give birth to the idea of the body but rather it is the idea that makes the body accessible as a body. Any description of the body, therefore, takes place through the circulation and validation of imaginary schema. There are two points that Butler is making here:

(a) That the boundaries of the body are defined by psychic projection. It is the psychic conception of the body which constitutes it as a unity—the very contours of the body are not merely implicated in the 'irreducible tension' between the psychic and the material but *are* that tension.

(b) At the same time, she is not positing the materiality of the body as an effect of the psyche. She affirms an array of materialities that pertain to the body, signified by the domains of biology, anatomy, illness, age and so on. Each such domain is constituted by what its boundaries exclude, and is marked by the history of its constitution. In other words, as Butler puts it, they are both 'persistent and contested regions.' We could claim, she argues, that what persists in these contested domains is the materiality of the body.[97]

If we work on the belief that it is the idea that makes the body phenomenologically accessible, feminist practice would be liberated from the stranglehold of the discourse that designates the body as the site of selfhood. The boundaries of the stable, gendered, heterosexual

---

[97] Judith Butler, 'The Lesbian Phallus and the Morphological Imaginary', in *Differences*, vol. 4, Spring, 1992, pp. 135–43.

self would be seen to be cultural and historical constructs, and not the natural immutable 'reality' that we are apparently irrevocably faced with.

What can this mean for us in our very real struggle against constant dehumanisation and humiliation through sexual assault? The discussion in this paper seems to point to the tentative recognition that the possibility of realizing the emancipatory impulse of feminism lies not in concretizing and more fully defining the boundaries of 'our bodies' through law, but in accepting 'the self' as something that is negotiable and contestable. The indeterminacy of identity need not lead to political paralysis—on the contrary, it could dislocate feminist practice productively, from sterile engagement with legal discourse and hegemonic cultural productions of selfhood to a realm of radical doubt and constant negotiation of what constitutes 'me' as a 'woman' in some contexts. Emancipation itself must be recognized as disaggregated, split along different axes, just as identity is not merely a positive conglomerate of different subject positions, but an ever-temporary construction, forming anew at the intersections of shifting subject positions.

It might be possible then, in the case of sexual violence, to see the feminist project not as one of 'justice' but of 'emancipation'. It is a characteristic of the discourse of justice that it leaves unproblematized the harm that is sought to be redressed—that the harm is a 'harm' does not have to be proved within its terms, only whether the harm actually was perpetrated. Thus, in the case of sexual violence, once 'rape' can be proved in legal terms, its harm is not in question. It is assumed by all the discourses that circulate around and produce 'sexual violence' as a category (including feminist discourses) that women can always be raped, and that rape is an attack on the very self-hood of woman. The issue then becomes one of 'proving' that rape did in fact take place, and ensuring justice through securing conviction by law. This leaves the ever-open possibility of other (all) women continuing to get raped.

What if our struggle were rather to emancipate ourselves from the very *meaning* of rape? Does the ever-present threat of sexual violence flow from the locating of the 'female' self inside the sexually defined body of woman? The attempt then should be to redraw the map of our body to make it accessible to new codes, to new senses of the self, so that at least some of these selves would be free of the limits set by the body.

Acknowledgements

I have learnt and rethought a great deal through the presentation of earlier versions of this paper at a workshop organized by Action India, Delhi, the conference out of which this volume has emerged, and the presentation at the Gender and Society workshop of the University of Chicago (made possible by Malathi de Alwis). I particularly want to thank Pradeep Jeganathan for his painstaking reading and Hannah Rosen for her insightful comments.

Women, Marriage, and the Subordination of Rights

FLAVIA AGNES

I. Introduction

THE DEMAND FOR a uniform civil code (UCC), with its contradictory origins and diverse implications, is one of the most controversial issues in contemporary Indian politics. The two most unlikely partners who consider it a priority are women's organizations and communal parties. This has not only placed the Indian women's movement in an awkward position but also compelled us to examine equations which have hitherto been overlooked while formulating strategies of gender justice.

It is true that the hardships and sufferings experienced by women of all communities—minorities as well as the majority—cannot be swept under the carpet nor glossed over with the rhetoric of 'freedom of religion'. However, placed in the unenviable position of juxtaposing women's rights and minority rights, the demand for legal equality can no longer be limited to a simple and straightforward task of preparing a *model draft* which ensures uniform rights to women of all communities.

The challenge today is to release matrimonial laws from their narrow and archaic confines of marriage defined as mere marital conjugality (explained in simple language, this means free access to sexual intercourse), and the consequential presumption of divorce as a termination of this conjugality (i.e. a release from sexual access and control of the spouse). We need to broaden its scope to encompass the economic rights of women and children who are trapped within a complex socio-economic system.

In India, the rights of women which flow from a marriage contract are defined within archaic laws formulated within the framework of a feudal society of agrarian landholdings. These will have to be redefined in the present context of urbanization, the capitalist mode of production, the evolution of the working class and its fragmentation into organized and unorganized sectors, and the current trend of liberalization and structural readjustment via new economic policies.

Historically, most religions viewed marriage as a sacrament, an indissoluble spiritual bond. Deemed as the basic unit of society, this sacramental aspect seemed to provide the basis for its indissolubility. The transition from feudalism to modernity necessitated a restructuring of the institution into a dissoluble contract, but the institution did not lose its trappings as a kind of spiritual bonding. Hence, even legal scholars and academics are sceptical about the introduction of the notion of women's right to property (which is deemed a *Western* concept), arguing that it may only reduce the institution of marriage to a financial transaction devoid of pious ideals, particularly in the Indian setting.

In response to such misgivings, this essay attempts to explore: (a) whether, historically, the concept of property and women's access to it was an integral part of the institution of marriage; and (b) the extent to which English notions of women's right to property influenced the Indian legal system.

II. Women's Right to Property Under Ancient Legal Systems—The Notion of Coverture

Contrary to popular myths regarding the sublime nature of marriage and its holiness, the concept of property and women's access to it governed all ancient systems of law.

Women's rights to property varied significantly, depending upon the three phases of their lives—maidenhood, coverture and widowhood. While at every stage of their life women were confined within an inferior status, the worst phase was coverture. Under the Roman (continental) and English (common law) legal systems, during coverture women were placed under the tutelage or guardianship of their husbands and deprived of all control over property. Since divorce was not recognized, only widowhood could end a period of coverture.

Three ancient legal systems—the Islamic, the Hindu and the Roman—are examined here from the perspective of married women's economic rights. Of these, the Islamic system appears the most progressive, followed by the Hindu system, with the Roman system exercising the most stringent control of all over women and their property.

I. ISLAMIC LAW

Islam was the first legal system to release women from the concept of coverture and recognized women's right to property during marriage. Right from its inception in the seventh century, Islam redeemed marriage of the trappings of sacramental indissolubility and elevated it to the level of consensual, contractual unions.[1] A thousand years later, this concept was adopted by the Continental legal system, from where it spread to England, and through this route was subsequently incorporated into Hindu law. *Offer* and *acceptance* formed the basis of the contract, with certain mandatory stipulations built in to provide women with additional safeguards. The custom of *bride price* in tribal Arabia—an amount paid to the father of the bride—was converted into *mehr*, which was meant to be a mark of respect to the woman, and this formed an essential ingredient of a marriage contract.[2]

---

[1] According to Paras Diwan, a leading authority on family law in India, the Hindus perfected the concept of gift (*dan*) and hence viewed marriage as dan (*kanyadan*: gift of a daughter), whereas Muslims perfected the concept of sale and found it convenient to express many transactions, including marriage, in the language of sale. P. Diwan, *Muslim Law in Modern India*, Sixth Edition (Allahabad: Allahabad Law Agency, 1993), p. 62.

[2] The following judgments in Indian courts, ranging over a period of a hundred years, have held that a Muslim marriage is a civil contract and that *mehr* is an integral

According to the *Hedaya*,[3] an accepted authority of Muslim law in India, a woman has the right to refuse cohabitation if the husband does not comply with prompt payment of the stipulated amount. According to accepted authorities, this is not a consideration proceeding from the husband to the wife out of the contract of marriage, but an obligation imposed by the law. Most Anglo-Islamic legal texts deal with this issue elaborately under a separate chapter titled Mehr or Dower.

Mehr could take the form of money, gold coins, or movable and immovable property. Once stipulated, the woman's power over it was absolute. This stipulation was meant to balance the husband's power of arbitrary oral divorce. The fact that mehr was not just a formality but a concrete right and women used this adequately can be gauged by various reported judgements.[4] In two states, Oudh (1876) and Jammu and Kashmir (1920), legislations were enacted to rescue husbands from paying exorbitant amounts by empowering courts to award reasonable amounts provided the amount stated in the contract of marriage was so high as to be deemed unreasonable. This was an indication of the wide use of this safeguard by Muslim women during the pre-independence period.

Since the Islamic system did not subscribe to the notion of coverture, the legal status of a married woman was not suspended during coverture. The position of a married woman in respect of her separate property was no different from that of a single woman. A woman had the right to own her separate property during the subsistence of the marriage and the husband could not access it without her consent.

The contractual aspect also helped women to stipulate conditions in the marriage contract (*nikahnama*) or enter into pre-marriage agreements (*kabin nama*) regarding their individual property; access to the husband's income and property; location of matrimonial home;

---

part of this contract: *Kamer-un-nissa* vs. *Husani*, ILR, 1880, 3 All 266; *Ameerunnissa* vs. *Muradunnisa*, 1985, 6 MIA 211; *Hamira Bibi* vs. *Zubaida Bibi*, ILR, 1919, 46 IA 294; *Kapoor Chand* vs. *Kedar Unnissa*, 1950, SCR 748.

[3] Charles Hamilton (trans.), *Hedaya* (London: S.G. Grady, 1870).

[4] F. Agnes, 'Economic Rights of Muslim Women', in *Economic and Political Weekly*, v.xxxi (41–2), 1996, p. 2832.

the right to exclusive use of a house or at least a room; housekeeping allowance; the right not to do housework or breast-feed the children (from this a further concept is developed within Muslim law, i.e. *fosterage*, which forbids marriage between the woman breast-feeding and the child who is breast-fed); the right of separate residence upon a husband's subsequent remarriage; etc. Courts in India held these contracts as binding and enforceable.[5] But this could be done only if judges relied upon Islamic precepts. When judges relied upon English notions of morality and public policy, such contracts were invalidated.[6]

The Anglo-Islamic law prevalent in India also entitled a woman to a personal allowance, termed as *kharch-i-pandan* or *mewa khori*. In fact a leading case which forms the basis of the law of contract with a minor is in respect of a contract between a minor Muslim girl and her father-in-law, namely *Khwaja Mohammed versus Hussaini Begum*.[7] In 1910 the Privy Council held that a contract between a father-in-law and a minor girl regarding a personal allowance to be paid to her was valid and binding, despite the commonly prevalent legal premise that a contract with a minor is not enforceable.

---

[5] The courts have held that the following pre-marriage agreements are valid and enforceable:
- Agreement providing for maintenance after divorce (*Mohd Muin-uddin* vs. *Jamal*, 1921, All 125)
- Agreement regarding the right of a second wife for separate residence and maintenance (*Mansur* vs. *Azizul*, AIR, 1928, Oudh 303)
- Agreement to live separately and claim maintenance (*Ali Akbar v Fatima*, ILR, 1929, Lah 85)

[6] The Bombay High Court, in *Mehrally* vs. *Sakerkhanoobhai*, 1905, 7 Bom, LR 602, relying upon the English doctrine of public morality, invalidated marriage agreements which stipulated the wife's right to separate residence, maintenance and return of ornaments in the event of the failure of an attempt at reconciliation. This was on the grounds that agreements which provide for a future separation are bad under English law. Subsequently, this principle was applied to an agreement to pay maintenance in the event of a future separation on the basis that such agreements encourage separation and hence are against public policy, in *Bai Fatima* vs. *Ali Mahomed Aiyab*, ILR, 1913, 37 Bom 280.

[7] *Khwaja Mohd* vs. *Husaini Begum*, ILR, 1910, 37IA 152.

If the husband died without paying his mehr dues the woman was deemed a creditor, and if she was in possession of her husband's property she could retain it till her mehr dues were paid. There is substantial case law which holds that the widow's right to retain her deceased husband's property is heritable and alienable.[8] Hence the widow could sell or gift the property or, after her, her heirs could retain it until the mehr was paid.

II. ANCIENT HINDU LAW

The superior position of Muslim women under their own personal law can be assessed only when we compare it with the position of women under other contemporary legal systems. For instance under both the Christian and the Hindu systems women lost their rights to acquire and control property upon marriage. Indissolubility of marriage under these systems and the notion of monogamy under Christian law proved further detriments to women's rights.

Property rights under the various schools of Hindu law, originating from the Mitakshara (Vijnaneshwar, eleventh century) were based on the notion of coparcenary or Joint Family Property, with ownership devolving jointly on four generations of male members. Collective ownership was more notional than actual, as the property was inalienable and was controlled by the head of the family, the *karta*, for the benefit of the entire household. Even the karta did not have the power to alienate the property, except at times of distress or for religious purposes (the technical terms used in legal texts were *legal necessity* and *pious obligation*). The men could demand partition of the property, but until it was partitioned their right was limited only to maintenance. Since women did not own the property even notionally, they did not have the right to demand partition. But a widow could claim a share equal to that of her sons upon partition.

However, all women had a right to be maintained from the property. Since most property was in the form of land, which was immovable and inalienable, male members of the family could not easily

---

[8] *Maina Bibi* vs. *Vakil Ahmed*, ILR, 1924, 52IA 145.

deprive women of their right to maintenance out of the income of the joint family property or the right of residence. Women's right to maintenance also included the right to demand marriage expenses out of the earnings of the joint family property and the right to be maintained for life if unmarried.

After marriage, within a patriarchal family structure, the bride was physically transferred from her natal family into her matrimonial family and she lost her right of residence and maintenance within her natal home. The husband and his family were entrusted with the legal obligation of maintaining the woman during coverture and widowhood.

But along with the concept of male coparcenary, the ancient law givers or Smritikars, from the time of Gautama Buddha and Manu (*circa* second century BC), recognized a concept of woman's property called *stridhan*. Manu laid down the following six categories as a woman's stridhan: gifts received from father, mother, brother, husband and in-laws, gifts at marriage, and a marriage fee on the occasion of the husband's subsequent marriage. Later Smritikars dealt with the subject elaborately and expanded its scope. Prominent among these were Vishnu, Yajnavalkya, Katayayana and, the last among them, Devala (seventh century AD).[9]

Stridhan could be both movable and immovable property. While Mitakshara specifically included inherited property as a woman's stridhan, the Dayabhaga of Jimutavahana (twelfth century), an authority of the Bengal School, specifically excluded inherited property from its scope.[10] Although several Smritis dealt with stridhan, none provided an exact definition. The texts were enumerative and descriptive and differed a great deal from each other, which resulted in wide regional variations within the same concept. But according to later commentators, who gave generous and dilatory interpretations to the six categories enumerated by Manu, the enumeration was to prevent a denial

---

[9] For a detailed discussion on stridhan, see S.T. Desai, *Mulla's Principles of Hindu Law* (Bombay: N.M. Tripathi, 1994), pp. 153–74.

[10] Desai 1994, p. 161.

Women, Marriage, and the Subordination of Rights 113

of the essential categories rather than a restriction against the inclusion of wider categories. Hence Vijnaneshwar in Mitakshara expanded the scope of the term *adhya* found in the Yajnavalkya Smriti to include a wide variety of property as a woman's stridhan.[11]

The woman had absolute power of ownership over stridhan and could alienate it by way of sale, gift or will. The Smritikars clearly laid down that a woman's husband, father, brother or son have no control over this property.[12] A Hindu woman was not bound by the husband's contracts in respect of her individual property. He had no power to part with her property without her consent or execute any document affecting her right to her property. The husband could use it with the woman's consent only in times of legal distress.

The line of succession of stridhan was also laid down by the Smritikars, the unmarried daughter being the first in succession, then the married daughter who has not been provided for, followed by the married daughter who has been provided for. In the absence of these, the daughter's daughter, and the daughter's son were the next heirs. The woman's own son was sixth in line.[13]

But the notion of stridhan underwent a change during coverture. While all gifts received by the woman during maidenhood and widowhood were termed as stridhan, gifts from strangers during coverture were excluded.[14] The woman's earnings from her own labour and skills during coverture were also excluded from the category of stridhan and deemed the property of her husband. This meant subscribing to the notion that a woman's person and labour power belonged to the husband. This concept, in fact, is similar to that of Roman law.

---

[11] Ibid., p. 159. Also see K. Gill, *Hindu Women's Right to Property in India* (Delhi: Deep & Deep, 1986), for an elaborate discussion on this issue.

[12] Manu's clear warning: 'Friends or relations of a woman, who out of folly or avarice live upon the property belonging to her, or the wicked ones who deprive her of the enjoyment of her own belongings, go to hell', and Katyayana's injunction: 'Neither the husband nor the son nor the father nor the brother has a power to use or alienate the legal property of a woman', are relevant in this respect.

[13] Desai 1994, p. 173.

[14] Ibid., pp. 170–1.

But scholars like Gooroodas Bannerjee have pointed out that Hindu law imposes fewer restrictions on married women than English law, which imposed far more stringent restrictions upon the woman's right over her property.[15]

While discussing the property rights of women under various schools of Hindu law, I have not talked about local customs which gave women better rights to property. The discussion here is limited to scriptural texts. The aim is only to examine how and to what extent it was possible to negotiate women's right to property within the strict orthodoxy of the upper castes, where women were hemmed in due to traditions based on anti-women biases.

Customs were an important source of Hindu law and there were wide regional variations of local customs as well as variations among different castes in the same region. In several regions there were local customs giving the daughter a plot of land, the earnings from which could be used by her for her own personal expenses. This was known as *manjal kani* in Tamilnadu,[16] *katnam* in Andhra Pradesh[17] and *haldi, kumkum* or *bangdi choli* in Maharashtra.[18]

Women of the lower castes were out of the varna system prescribed by Manu, and hence the Smriti code of sexual morality did not apply to them. Consequently they enjoyed greater freedom in matrimonial relationships. The custom of bride price prevailed in most communities and wives could obtain their freedom by returning the bride price.[19] Divorce by mutual consent was accepted and negotiated

---

[15] See the comments by Gooroodas Bannerjee, *Hindu Law of Marriage and Stridhana* (Calcutta: Tagore Law Lectures, 1878), p. 340.

[16] K. Mukund, 'Turmeric Land—Women's Property Rights in Tamil Society since Medieval Times', in *Economic and Political Weekly*, v.xxvii (17), April 1992, p. WS-2.

[17] C. Upadhya, 'Dowry and Women's Property in Coastal Andhra Pradesh', in *Contributions to Indian Sociology* (n.s.), 24(1), 1990, p.29.

[18] Reference was made to this in *Yadeorao Jogeshwar* vs. *Vithal Shamaji*, AIR, 1952, Nag. 55.

[19] M.N. Srinivas, *Caste in India and Other Essays* (Bombay: Modern Promoters and Publishers, 1986 [1962]).

through local caste panchayats. As wage earners these women contributed to the household. Since these were not landowning communities, the issue of maintenance from family property was not very crucial to these women. (The concept of maintenance envisages a non-working, dependent woman. The working class woman did not fit this description.)

There were also matrilineal societies where property was inherited through the female line. Such practices prevailed among the Nairs of Kerala, in Tulunad of coastal Karnataka and the various tribes of the North-east. These families were matrilocal and hence upon marriage women were not transferred to their husband's home. The concepts of natal home and matrimonial home did not apply to these women. In their own homes women had greater sexual freedom and economic security.[20] Among certain North-eastern tribes, property devolved upon the youngest daughter who was expected to live with and look after both her parents in their old age.

The customs of the Nair community as well as that of coastal Karnataka were transformed or abolished with land-reform legislations during the nineteenth and twentieth centuries and in the process the practice of inheritance through the female line was replaced by patrilineal inheritance patterns.[21]

III. CONTINENTAL AND COMMON LAW

The Roman law of marriage and property, which derived its roots from Judaic law, was based on the notion of a patriarchal family consisting of wives, sons and slaves. Hence, the suppression of women's rights after marriage was effected to a greater extent under Roman jurisprudence. Under the concepts of *patrias potestas* and *patrias*

---

[20] L. Dube, 'Kinship and Family in South and Southeast Asia: A Comparative View', paper prepared for 'Women's Work and Family Strategies Project' of the United Nations University, 1984.

[21] K. Saradamoni, 'Progressive Land Legislations and Subordination of Women', in L. Sarkar and B. Sivaramayya (eds), *Women and Law: Contemporary Problems* (Delhi: Vikas Publishing House, 1994), p. 155.

familias, the head of the family acquired total control over the person, property and labour of all members of his household. The wife was treated as the ward of the husband and she had no independent identity.

By the twelfth century, the power of the Roman church over marriages was well settled and marriage was granted recognition as a sacrament. By the early thirteenth century, a series of ecclesiastical courts were set up to enforce canon law throughout Europe. The influence of canon law spread to England after the Norman conquest in 1066 but England continued to recognize the prevailing system of common law marriages. During the reign of Henry VIII, the English Reformation transformed the Roman church into an English church. Later, the regulation of ecclesiastical courts in family law matters was transferred to the English courts.[22]

Divorce was not recognised in Europe (including England) until the advent of the industrial era. In pre-industrial Europe economic wealth and power were regulated through concepts of status. Marriage became a crucial link in determining the status of both spouses and their children. This system facilitated the accumulation of property and power within recognized groups and enabled the landed families of England, Europe and colonial America to retain and increase their possessions. The Christian concept of holy wedlock gave a sacramental character to these unions. Divorce would have disrupted production, undermined security of land tenure, brought families into conflict and created acute problems over the succession of land.[23]

The merging of husband and wife into a single legal personality was an appropriate legal form for a feudal society in which the home and the land around it formed the centre of production. This principle was first enunciated in the Dialogus de Scaccario in the twelfth century. In 1769 the English jurist William Blackstone explained the concept further:

---

[22] P.N. Swisher, H.A. Miller and W.J. Weston, *Family Law: Cases, Materials and Problems* (New York: Legal Education Analysis and Skills Series, 1990), pp. 5–6.

[23] A. Sachs and J.H. Wilson, *Sexism and the Law: A Study of Male Beliefs and Judicial Bias* (Oxford: Law in Society Series, 1978), p. 138.

By marriage, the husband and wife are one person in law, that is, the very being or legal existence of the woman is suspended during the marriage or at least is incorporated and consolidated into that of the husband under whose wing, protection and cover, she performs everything and is therefore called in our law, a *femme-covert*; she is said to be covert-baron or under the protection and influence of her husband, her baron or lord; and her condition during marriage is called coverture. Upon this principle of a union of person of husband and wife, depend almost all the legal rights, duties and disabilities, that either of them acquire by the marriage.[24]

Under the principle laid down by Blackstone, upon marriage the woman lost her legal existence. Marriage meant legal death. The woman could not contract, sue or be sued. All her individual property belonged to her husband and he could not only use it but even alienate it without her consent. While freehold and leasehold property reverted to her upon the husband's death, under common law property in terms of *pure personality* or *choses in action* devolved upon the husband's heirs and she lost all access to it. Only the woman's clothing (apparels) and jewellery reverted to her, but if the husband was insolvent his creditors could claim even these.[25]

The woman held no corresponding interest in her husband's freeholds, copyholds or leaseholds during coverture. But during widowhood, she had a right of *dower* (one-third of the interest of all his property even after it was alienated). This right was limited only to women who, during marriage, were capable of producing a male heir for the husband.

Women's rights in equity were similar to that of common law. However, if a husband approached a court of equity to reclaim the property of his wife, relying upon a legal concept, namely *the one who seeks equity must do equity*, the court could insist upon the husband settling a part of the property which was reclaimed, for the benefit of the wife.

The husband's right to his wife's property was held in such high

---

[24] P.M. Bromley, *Family Law*, 5th Edition (London: Butterworths, 1976), p. 107.
[25] For comments in this and the following paragraphs regarding the Married Women's Property Rights in England, I am relying upon Bromley 1976, pp. 425–35.

esteem that, even after betrothal, if the woman alienated her property without the consent of the groom, he could sue her for fraud of his marital rights.

From the seventeenth century onwards the demands of emerging capitalism rendered it necessary to redeem the land of its inalienable characteristics. So a gradual change in the nature of land tenures is discernible, culminating in the enactment of several legislations in the nineteenth century. The object of these legislations was to facilitate alienation of feudal manors and agricultural land tenures for the construction of factories, mines and townships. It is only during this period that women in England could stake their claim to hold and alienate their individual property.[26]

The Continental legal system changed its character after 1800 under the French *Code Civilii* (the code of Napoleon). Under this, marriage assumed the characteristics of a civil and dissoluble contract. Both spouses could make agreements in respect of their separate property at the time of marriage, and in default the concept of community of property prevailed. Under this concept, women acquired a right to the husband's property. Property which belonged to the spouses was deemed to be the joint matrimonial property of both spouses, and upon divorce or separation they could claim a division of this property.

In England the change was more gradual. In 1857 matrimonial jurisdiction in England shifted from the Ecclesiastical (Canon Law) courts to civil courts, and the Matrimonial Causes Act of 1857 secured Englishwomen the right to a judicial separation. Legally separated women could also hold separate property under a legal fiction, *femme sole*, and could apply to the court for a protective order against the husband and his creditors. In 1882 the Married Women's Property Act empowered married women the right to hold separate property acquired after 1883. From this period on, married women's right to hold property was consolidated gradually through a series of legislations enacted along with land-reform legislations. In 1935 the Married

[26] E.H. Burn, *Cheshire's Modern Law of Property*, 11th Edition (London: Butterworths, 1972), pp. 73–5, gives a detailed analysis of this phenomenon.

Women's Tortfeasors Act finally abolished the notion of *married women* and alleviated their status to that of single women.[27]

Despite the near-complete subordination of women, the position of the English woman was extolled throughout the commonwealth as being without compare. It was suggested that the honour and respect in which women were held was one of the glories of British civilization and among the blessed fruits of Christianity. These mystical sentiments served not only to obscure the true position of the great majority of women in Britain, but also to suggest a false status for Englishwomen when compared with that of women in the colonies.[28]

III. Colonial Influences in the Realm of Family Law in India

1. LEGISLATIONS STRENGTHENING THE RIGHTS OF INDIVIDUAL MEN AGAINST JOINT FAMILY PROPERTY

The notions of women's right to property and the changes that occurred in England are crucial milestones for the study of women's right to property in India because these notions governed judicial interpretations and statutory laws not only during the colonial period but do so even today. A judicial bias crept into the Indian legal system by the introduction of principles of Anglo-Saxon jurisprudence such as *justice, equity, good conscience* and *public morality*, and through the legal concept of *stare decisis*. Despite the stated policy of the British crown, namely non-interference in the personal laws of the natives, these concepts moulded personal laws in India.

Through these legal precepts, British jurists assumed the role of commentators and interpreted the ancient texts or Smritis according to what they believed were the new requirements of contemporary Hindu society. By overemphasizing the ancient scriptures, they undervalued the role of later commentaries as well as local custom. Since

[27] Bromley 1976, pp. 432–3.
[28] Sachs and Wilson 1978, p. 139.

they could not comprehend the plurality of the prevailing non-state legal systems, and locally-evolved practices, British jurists disturbed established customs of the community.

The harm caused became irrevocable as there was no scope for retracting under the notion of *stare decisis* or legal precedent. The decisions of the Law Lords of the Privy Council became the binding principles governing all subordinate courts in India. So at this stage the process of evolving laws at the local level through commentaries, which incorporated the local customs within them, was arrested. Gradually the non-state legal systems were transformed into state-controlled and state-regulated legal systems. British interpretations of ancient texts became binding on Indians and made the law certain, rigid and uniform. This could have been welcomed as a positive intervention if only these notions of modernity and uniformity had benefited women. But ironically the concepts provided a forum for the collusion of local patriarchal interests with the anti-women biases of British jurists and laid firm legal ground for the diminution of women's rights in India.

The first law reform of this period was the much-publicized Bengal Sati Regulation Act of 1829. This was followed by other legislations, such as the Age of Consent acts of 1860 and 1891, the Prohibition of Female Infanticide Act of 1872, and the Child Marriage Restraint Act of 1929. These highly acclaimed and widely publicized penal legislations were projected as the redeemers of Indian women from the barbarism of the indigenous system, as ushering them into an era of modernity. A popular notion prevails—that by incorporating these concepts of modernity into native jurisprudence, the status of women in India was improved. The overemphasis on the alleviating effect of these legislations served to justify colonial rule and its modernizing mission by projecting indigenous systems as pre-modern and barbaric.

British intervention did not stop at the level of penal legislation. It extended into two other spheres which have not received much attention. One set of legislations carved out a space for men's individual property rights into a system based on joint-family property and rigid caste affiliations of an agrarian feudal society, and laid the grounds for the introduction of the capitalist mode of production in an urban setting by making land alienable and transferable. The land-reform legislations of England which helped the process of changing the feudal land tenures to the capitalist mode of production were also gradually introduced in India, serving the interests of individual men. Unfortunately for Indian women, instead of an enhancement of their right to property, the scope of this was curtailed and became redundant within the changing character of property—which now became alienable and transient. The developments seem to have formed a pattern which is the reverse of that formed by women's rights in England during the same period.

The following legislations are an example of this tendency: the *Caste Disabilities Removal Act* of 1850 invalidated the provisions of Hindu law which penalized the renunciation of religion by denying the convert his right to a share in the joint family property. The *Hindu Inheritance (Removal of Disabilities) Act*, 1928 prohibited the exclusion from inheritance of certain disqualified heirs. This helped to loosen the rigid caste-based family structure. But the most significant among these was the *Hindu Gains of Learning Act* of 1930 which helped English-educated males to safeguard their individual earnings out of the realm of the joint-family pool. The act stipulated that all gains of learning (income earned through professional qualifications) would be the exclusive and separate property of a Hindu male even if he had been supported from the funds of the joint-family property. The other members of the joint family could have no access to these earnings.

So the benefits of maintenance from the earnings of joint-family property, upon which a woman could stake a claim by way of a charge on the property, became diminished in this process. Urban property was no longer valued for the land and income from it, but changed its character to facilitate factories and business establishments, small entrepreneurs, and salaries and wages from employment in such an urban setting. In this scheme the mode of production shifted from the domestic sphere, and women's access to resources became scarce.

Property was rendered alienable and transient and concentrated in the hands of individual men to the detriment of the rights of individual women—who had now no means of accessing it.

II. JUDICIAL DECISIONS THWARTING THE CONCEPT OF STRIDHAN

Along with the consolidation of individual male property rights, the Privy Council curtailed women's rights to hold and alienate property under the institution of stridhan and reduced it to a concept accepted in the English law: that of limited estate.

Through a series of decisions during the period 1850 to 1930, the courts held that whether the property was inherited through her male relatives (father, son, husband) or through her female relatives (mother, mother's mother, daughter) it was not her stridhan. Women lost the right to will or gift away their stridhan and it assumed the character of a limited estate. The British concept of 'revisioners' was introduced into the Indian legal system; through this all property dealings by Hindu widows could be challenged by the husband's relatives. Gradually, the Hindu widow lost her right to deal with her property and, on the least pretext, the property would revert to the husband's heirs.

For instance, in *Bhugwandeen Doobey* vs. *Myna Baee*, the Privy Council reversed the judgment of the lower court and proclaimed: 'Under the law of the Benares School, *notwithstanding the ambiguous passage in the Mitakshara,* no part of her husband's estate, whether movable or immovable to which a Hindu woman succeeds by inheritance forms part of her Stridhan.'[29]

The courts also ruled that property inherited by a daughter from her father is not stridhan. This principle was then extended to the property inherited by an unmarried daughter from her mother and later stretched to include the property inherited from all female relatives, thus sealing all avenues for the continuation of stridhan in the female line.

A case decided by the Privy Council in 1903, discussed in detail, illustrates this trend.[30] A woman had inherited property from her

---

[29] *Bhugwandeen Doobey* vs. *Myna Baee*, p. 1868, 9 WR (PC), p. 23.
[30] *Sheo Shankar* vs. *Debi Sahai*, 1903, 30 IA 202; ILR 25, All 468.

mother. After her death her sons claimed the property as heirs of the mother and grandmother, and deprived their sister. The subordinate judge of Gorakhpur, on 7 December 1897, held that property inherited through the female line was the woman's stridhan and hence her sons had no right over it. In appeal, the Allahabad High Court reversed the judgment. This resulted in an appeal to the Privy Council. In February 1903 the Privy Council upheld the decision of the High Court and laid down that property inherited by a woman from her mother is not her stridhan and hence will not devolve upon her daughter, who is her stridhan heir, but will devolve upon her son. Only the Bombay school, which relied upon the local authority Vyavahar Mayuka of Nilakanta Bhatt and the customary practices of the region, provided slightly better scope for women's rights.[31]

While the most negative interpretations of the Smritis were relied upon to deprive women of their well-established customary rights over property, in other instances custom was upheld against clear scriptural mandates granting women property rights. The Privy Council's decision of 1847 upholding the validity of custom among the Khojas and Memons of Gujarat is a classic example of this trend.

The Muslim trading communities of Gujarat—Khojas and Memons—followed the local custom of holding the family property jointly as coparcenars, thereby denying women their right to a stipulated share in the property. (Under the rules of Shariat coparcenary is not recognised and the daughter has a right to her father's property along with the son. The daughter is entitled to half the share to which a son is entitled.)

In a case adjudicated in 1847 a woman challenged this practice and claimed her share of the family property. On her behalf, it was argued that the Hindu custom of disinheriting daughters, which has been adopted by Mohammedans, is most unreasonable and that public policy would dictate the adoption of the wiser rule laid down by the Koran—by which daughters are allowed a defined share in the succession. A contrast was drawn between the relative position which

---

[31] See *Venayak Anandrav* vs. *Lakshmi Bai*, 1 BHCR 117 and *Pranjivandas Tulsidas* vs. *Devakuvarbai*, 1 BHCR 130.

women hold in the Hindu and Muslim systems. The woman's advocate pointed out that since the Muslim system was more beneficial to women, it was the duty of the court to give it effect when the two collide.

The comments of the judge, Lord Erskine Perry, while disallowing the woman's claim, make interesting reading:

> *A custom for females to take no share in the inheritance is not unreasonable in the eyes of the English law for it accords in great part with the universal custom as to real estates where there are any male issue and with some local customs mentioned by Blackstone by which in certain manors females are excluded in all cases.*[32]

Blackstonian views became the governing principle for deciding women's right to property, superseding both Manu and Mohammed with a claim of universality.

A clear convergence of the patriarchal interests of the Indian, Hindu and Muslim systems, aided by the biases of English jurists against women and their right to property, is reflected in the legal history of this period. The edifice of the present legal structure rests on this foundation.

IV. Reflections of British Notions in Indian Statutes

1. THE WIDOW REMARRIAGE ACT

Despite the moral view that marriage alliances are sacramental and economic transactions should not dominate this alliance, it is interesting to see the extent to which matters of property dominated matrimonial statutes. A classic example is provided by the Hindu Widow Remarriage Act of 1856, one of the earliest matrimonial legislations enacted during the British period.

This highly acclaimed act, which was meant to liberate Hindu widows, consists of seven sections. One section provides for the legalization of remarriage, another section deals with the ceremonies of remarriage, the third section deals with the consent of the parties, and

---

[32] Khojas & Memons' case decided in 1847, POC [1853], 110, emphasis added.

the remaining four sections deal with women's right to property or rather curtailment of their right to property upon remarriage.

The preamble of the act states: 'Hindu widows, with certain exceptions, are held to be incapable of contracting a second marriage and whereas it is just to relieve all such Hindu widows from the legal incapacity it is enacted as follows.' It is relevant that the preamble makes a reference to and acknowledges the fact that there are certain exceptions to this rule and that certain categories of Hindu widows do not suffer from a legal incapacity with regard to remarriage.

A woman marrying under this act lost her right to her husband's property and the right to be maintained from the joint-family property. Even if one concedes that it would be logical to apply these constraints to women who acquired the right of remarriage with this statute, it is difficult to accept the perverse logic through which even women who had a pre-existing right of remarriage under the custom of caste were deprived of their property. The statute needs to be contextualised within the legal status of women in England, who obtained the right to divorce, and subsequent remarriage, only in 1857; and legally separated women could own property only in 1882.

The rationale for denying Hindu women the right to retain their property was based on judicial interpretations of Hindu law. These interpretations said that the notion of holding her former husband's property was abhorrent to Hindu law. According to British jurists, a woman could hold property as part of her husband's body. When remarried she ceased to be a part of her former husband's body and so had no right to hold his property. The prohibition against remarriage has no scriptural foundation. In any case, women from the lower castes were out of the purview of such scriptural doctrines.

These interpretations of the principles of Hindu law continued to govern judicial notions from 1860 until 1956, the year in which the Hindu Succession Act granting women an absolute right in their husband's property was enacted. Regional and caste-based diversity in the property rights of women did not seem to have any influence upon these notions, and the courts continued to apply these principles even to women of lower castes who were not governed by such principles. For instance, in the Maraveer caste widows could remarry even prior to the 1856 enactment. But in 1877, while deciding the case of a woman from this community, the Madras High Court held:

> The principle upon which a widow inherits is that she is the surviving half of her husband. So it cannot apply where she remarries. The law cannot permit the widow who has remarried to retain the inheritance. As per the principles embodied in Steele's Hindu Law and Custom, the custom in the shudras is that a widow on remarriage gives up all properties of her former husband's relations except what has been given to her by her own parents.[33]

The court relied upon a quote which is attributed to Brhaspati: 'Of him whose wife is not dead half his body survives. How should any one else take the property while half his body lives?' This metaphor became a legal maxim in all subsequent judgements. The Madras High Court applied this rule in 1884 in the case of a woman from the Lingait Gounda community which followed the custom of remarriage prior to the act.[34]

In the Deccan region, widow remarriages in the name of *pat marriage* or *natra marriage* were performed among several castes. But following the trend set by the Madras High Court, in 1898 a judge of the Bombay High Court, Justice Ranade, held:

> So far as this Presidency is concerned, it is obvious from the information collected in Steele's Law and Custom of Indian Castes in Deccan among whom *pat* marriages were allowed or forbidden [*sic*]. But when a widow performed *pat*, her husband's relatives succeeded to her husband's estate. There is not a single caste mentioned in which any custom to the contrary prevails.[35]

The recording of customs within the Bombay Presidency, which was hastily and haphazardly done by Steele during the early phase of the Presidency and was published in 1827, seemed to have provided the basis for denying women from the lower castes their right to property in litigation several decades later.

[33] *Murugayi* vs. *Viramakali*, ILR, 1877, 1 Mad 226.
[34] *Kaduthi* vs. *Madhu*, ILR, 1884, 7 Mad 321.
[35] *Vithu* vs. *Govind*, ILR, 1989, 22 Bom 321 FB.

A dissenting and more rational view was expressed by the High Court of Allahabad in the year 1933. Since the act was a beneficial legislation, the court ruled that it could not be interpreted so as to impose further disabilities upon women who were not burdened with such disabilities before the enactment. The court held: 'A custom of remarriage does not necessarily carry with it a further custom of forfeiture upon marriage. Anybody who claims there has been forfeiture by reason of remarriage, must prove affirmatively that such forfeiture is an incident of the custom under which the remarriage took place.'[36]

Ironically this decision was not followed by the High Courts of Bombay, Madras, Calcutta or Andhra Pradesh even in the post-independence period. These courts continued to apply the principle of forfeiture to an increasing section of lower-caste women. Since the right was so well established despite a century of negative interpretations, the issue kept cropping up in several litigations right into the post-independence period.

In 1952 the Calcutta High Court applied the rule of forfeiture to a woman from the Bairagi community who remarried under the custom of the caste.[37] In 1954 the Bombay High Court reversed the decision of the subordinate courts and applied the rule to a woman from Kolhapur district, which was a Princely State till independence and hence the Widow Remarriage Act was not applicable and widows could retain the property of their former husbands. Ruling against the premise that as per the custom of the caste the rule of forfeiture upon remarriage did not apply, the court declared:

> The foundation that a widow is the surviving half of her husband does not disappear merely because certain communities recognise a custom of remarriage of widows. It would indeed be a startling proposition to say that even though she takes the property of her deceased husband by inheritance as his surviving half, she is entitled to take away that property with her to her new husband on remarriage when she can no more be regarded as the surviving half of her first husband.[38]

[36] *Bhola Umar* vs. *Kausilla*, ILR, 1933, 35 All 24.
[37] *Lalit Mohan* vs. *Shyamapada Das*, AIR, 1952, Cal 771.
[38] *Roma Appa* vs. *Sakhu Dattu*, AIR, 1954, Bom 315.

Hyderabad was another princely state which came under the new dominion. In 1952 a full bench of the Hyderabad High Court overruled, by a majority view, several of its decisions granting women the right to retention of property, despite a strong dissenting note from a section of the judiciary which vociferously argued that Manu did not lay down rules for shudras and was concerned only with the three higher castes: and hence his views could not govern shudra women.[39]

The significant factor here is that these decisions of the post-independence period with the constitutional mandate of equality were not even following the established rules of the community. They were setting new precedents for these communities through which women's right to property was being further curtailed, at a point in history when the debate about the reform in Hindu law and women's rights within it was raging in the country.

II. CHANGING NOTIONS OF PROPERTY IN ENGLAND AND ITS REFLECTION IN INDIAN STATUTES

Changing notions of property, along with Victorian concepts such as chastity and morality, influenced all statutes enacted during the last century. These trends are discernible in the Indian Divorce Act of 1869, the Parsi Marriage and Divorce Act of 1865 (re-enacted in 1936 and amended in 1988), and the Indian Succession Act of 1865 (re-enacted in 1925). This is the period when the concept of a right to hold property after judicial separation was gaining ground in England. Women got the right of judicial separation in 1857 and, in 1870, the first statute granting judicially-separated women the right to acquire and hold independent property was enacted by the British Parliament. A reflection of this development can be found in the Indian Divorce Act of 1869, which is applicable to Christian marriages in India.

Sections 24 and 25 of this act stipulate that, after separation, a woman would be deemed a spinster with respect to her property acquired after separation. Section 27 provides that a separated woman is

---

[39] *Basappa* vs. *Parvatamma*, AIR, 1952, Hyd FB.

entitled to apply to the court for an order protecting her property from her husband and his creditors. Such statutory protection was essential under the English system as, without such a protective order, the husband's creditors could attach a woman's property even if the property was acquired by her after a legal separation.

In India the established principles of both Hindu and Muslim law granted due recognition to a woman's right to hold property even during coverture. And the indigenous Christian community followed local customs based on these principles. Hence, these provisions were irrelevant and meaningless in the Indian context. They could only be beneficial for European Christians and British subjects residing in India. But even though they were not relevant, it is possible to overlook them as stipulating beneficial provisions.

But other provisions of the English system which crept into the Indian matrimonial statutes were (and remain) more detrimental to women's rights. Section 39 of the Indian Divorce Act and Section 50 of the Parsi Marriage and Divorce Act empower courts to settle the properties of an adulterous woman in favour of her husband and children. Section 35 of the Indian Divorce Act entitles the husband to claim damages from the adulterer. While the Indian Divorce Act of 1869 has remained unchanged in our statute books and governs all Christian marriages in India, the Parsi Marriage and Divorce Act went through major amendments in the year 1988, presumably to strengthen women's rights. Despite this, these derogatory provisions have been retained.

Section 20 of the Indian Succession Act of 1925 stipulates that the property of husband and wife will be deemed separate and the marriage will not entitle them to acquire any additional interest or powers in respect of their spouses' property. This notion had relevance to the progress being made in England in the nineteenth century where, upon marriage, a woman was granted the right to hold separate property. But it would be counter-productive in the twentieth century, where new concepts like a married woman's right to the husband's home and property were emerging under concepts like matrimonial home and property.

III. Monogamy, Maintenance, Morality and Conjugality

1. THE IMPLICATIONS OF HINDU MONOGAMY

Anglo-Saxon jurisprudence contributed two important concepts to Indian matrimonial law, i.e. monogamy and the restitution of conjugal rights. Both these essentially Christian concepts are aimed at regulating sexuality but have deeper implications for women's right to property.

Hindu marriages, which were often polygamous, were rendered monogamous by the codification in 1955. Through this process of codification during the years 1955–6 ancient Hindu law and the plurality of customs that had evolved under various schools and customary practices were transformed and modelled on English law. But they were devoid of all safety measures either under the traditional or customary system, or under more recent provisions of the English legal system.

Before this, under Hindu law, which recognised both polygamy as well as concubinage, women in polygamous relationships acquired a legal status and the right of maintenance from family property. As stated earlier, in the event of a subsequent marriage the first wife had a customary right to *sulka* or supersession which was her stridhan or exclusive property. In this context, Narada's dictate that the husband must give one-third of his property to the first wife at his second marriage is relevant.

But after the enactment of 1955, women in polygamous relationships lost their right to maintenance and legitimacy. So, while polygamy (or informal adulterous relationships) continued in practice, the marriages were deemed illegitimate under the law. This dealt a severe blow to women's right to maintenance, without in any way curbing polygamy. The fact that the diverse customary practices and rituals of a pluralistic Hindu society were brought under the banner of one codified law, without sufficient knowledge of cultural diversities, provided sufficient legal loopholes through which a Hindu man could escape the criminal consequences of bigamy as well as the financial responsibility of polygamous relationships.

The act provided for the solemnization of marriages either through Brahminical rituals of *homa* and *saptapadi* or the age-old and well-established customary practices. But as an unevenly developed pluralistic society in the process of transition, India adopted several new and informal rituals, including the exchange of garlands, applying *sindoor* to the bride's forehead, or couples declaring themselves married either before a deity, or through the celebration of a marriage feast, or by signing on stamped paper in a lawyer's chamber. The media, and more particularly popular films, contributed to the confusion by portraying these as valid forms of Hindu marriage.

This plurality of customs and rituals provided a Hindu male ample scope to contract bigamous marriages and, further, the right to validate any of his relationships and escape from financial responsibility towards the 'other' woman. (In contrast, while Islamic law permits polygamy, each wife is entitled to claim maintenance from the court and the privileged status of 'wife' is not reserved only to one woman.)

Later studies revealed that, in spite of the provision of monogamy under the reformed Hindu law, the percentage of polygamy among Hindus is greater than polygamy among Muslims.[40] So the progressive-sounding provision of monogamy not only turned out to be a mockery but in fact even more detrimental to women than the uncodified Hindu law which acknowledged the economic rights of wives in polygamous marriages.

When a woman approaches the court for maintenance, it is a routine ploy adopted by husbands to deny that the woman is the legally married wife. The husband pleads towards invalidating the marriage either on the grounds that essential ceremonies were not performed as per the codified Hindu law,[41] or that a prior valid marriage subsists.[42]

---

[40] Report on the Status of Women Committee, *Towards Equality*, p. 104.
[41] Sections (1) & (2) of Hindu Marriage Act, 1955
[42] Section (i) of Hindu Marriage Act, 1955.

The alarming number of husbands pleading invalidity of marriage is reflected in the following table:[43]

	Number	Percentage
Reported cases relating to maintenance	40	100
Cases where validity of marriage was an issue	9	36
Cases where the husband's plea was upheld	4	16
Admittedly polygamous marriages	6	24

In an interesting case, where the husband pleaded that since the woman was his second wife he was not entitled to pay her maintenance, the court took recourse to the uncodified Hindu law and held that since the marriage had taken place under the older Hindu law (which permitted bigamy) and not under the reformed code, the second wife was entitled to maintenance.[44]

In criminal prosecutions for bigamy, years of litigation failed to end in conviction for the errant male because the courts adopted a rigid view about certain shastric ceremonies. While the Hindu Marriage Act proclaimed that Hindu marriage has been transformed from the ancient concept of a *sacrament* to a modern notion of a *contract*, it continued to uphold ancient vedic and Brahmanical rituals like *saptapadi*, *vivahahoma* and *kanyadan* (which is in any case a custom derogatory to women), or ancient customs as the only means of formalizing this modern contract. If these ceremonies are not proved in prosecution for bigamy (by the first wife), the man can wriggle out of conviction for bigamy even though he has lived with the second woman openly as her husband, or has also fathered children from this contract.[45]

II. RESTORING CONJUGALITY

The remedy of a restitution of conjugal rights found in all current matrimonial statutes is yet another example of the incorporation of

---

[43] *Divorce and Matrimonial Cases*, vol. 1, 1994.

[44] *Anupama Pradhan vs. Sultan Pradhan*, 1991, Cri.LJ 3216 Ori.

[45] For a further discussion on the judicial attitude to Hindu bigamy, see Agnes 1996.

British (Christian) concepts into the Indian matrimonial legal system. This concept was not recognised in Islam as it provides for contractual marriages which can be dissolved. The woman has a right to stipulate conditions, and if these conditions are not met she has a right to divorce. Even under Hindu law, which prescribes a sacramental marriage, the remedy of restoring conjugality through legal injunctions did not prevail. At best, the king had the power to stipulate a fine for abandoning the wife.

The concept of restitution developed in medieval Europe, where marriages where deemed indissoluble unions and the husband had control over both the wife's person and property. If she escaped from his dominion, he could petition an ecclesiastical court to restore her to him. The control of ecclesiastical courts upon the laity was so overwhelming that they could physically force the woman back into her husband's custody. The remedy was retained when the jurisdiction over matrimonial matters was transferred from the ecclesiastical courts to the civil courts in England in 1857 and was incorporated into the Indian Divorce Act of 1869 (applicable to Christians), modelled on the Matrimonial Causes Act of 1869. Simultaneously, the remedy crept into the Indian legal system through the Civil Procedure Code.

While the remedy was used in England to restore adult wives who had left the company of their husbands, in India, where cultural conditions differed, it was applied to minor wives who had not instituted a conjugal relationship with their husbands—and hence the question of 'restoring' conjugality did not arise. In 1875, in an appeal filed by a husband against the order of a lower court which denied him remedy on the ground that his wife was a minor, the Calcutta High Court held: 'According to Hindu law, after marriage the husband is the legal guardian of his wife's person and property, irrespective of whether she is a major or minor.'[46]

In the controversial case *Dadaji Bhikaji* vs. *Rukhmabai*,[47] Justice Pinhey explained the history of this remedy as follows:

[46] *Kateeram Dokanee* vs. *Mst Gendhene*, 1875, 23 WR 178.
[47] *Dadaji Bhikaji* vs. *Rukmabai*, 1885, 9 ILR, Bom 529.

> the practice of allowing suits for the restitution of conjugal rights . . . originated in England under peculiar circumstances, and was transplanted from England into India. It has no foundation in Hindu law. . . . For many years after I came to India such suits were not allowed. It is only of late the practice of allowing such suits has been introduced into this country from England (I think only since the amalgamation of the old Supreme and Sadar Courts in the present High Courts has brought English lawyers more into contact with the mofussil). It is, in my opinion, a matter for regret, that it was ever introduced into this country.

And further: 'It is a misnomer to call this a suit for the "restitution" of conjugal rights. When a married couple, after cohabitation, separate and live apart, either of them can bring such a suit. Here, the husband has asked the court to compel the wife to go to his house, so that he may complete his contract with her by consummating the marriage.' The judge tried to differentiate between the 'restitution' and 'institution' of conjugal rights. But on appeal the court rejected the argument that there is no authority for a decree of 'institution' of conjugal rights under Hindu law and said: 'The gist of the action for restitution of conjugal rights is that married persons are bound to live together. Whether the withdrawal is before or after consummation, there has been a violation of conjugal duty which entitles the injured party to the relief prayed.'[48]

The decree could be enforced either by delivering the wife physically to her husband or by imprisoning her and attaching her property. Since a civil court did not have the power (as had the ecclesiastical court) to hand over the wife's person, nor to imprison a woman for this purpose, it was not an easy proposition, and attaching her property was often seen as the best solution. It worked in the woman's favour that, in most cases, she did not own property which could be attached in execution of a decree of conjugal rights. Since none of the three propositions was feasible, eventually the decree became only of a declaratory nature and could not be enforced. But ironically, although the remedy has been abolished in England, it subsists under all

---

[48] *Dadaji Bhikaji* vs. *Rukmabai*, 1886, 10 ILR, Bom 301.

matrimonial statutes in India. The Andhra Pradesh High Court, in T. Sareetha's case,[49] struck down the provision as unconstitutional. But subsequent decisions of the Delhi High Court and Supreme Court restored the section on the grounds that it provides for reconciliation measures.[50]

Conclusions

Since property, and not just regulation of sexuality, is an integral part of the marriage contract under all systems of law, it is surprising that the codified Hindu Marriage Act has not paid attention to this aspect of a marriage relationship. Women's rights are relegated to maintenance, which again is contingent upon their sexual purity and dependent status. The provision of maintenance under the Hindu law applies equally to both spouses, with a duty cast upon the wife to maintain her husband under an absurd notion of legal equality between the spouses. The seemingly liberating aspect of divorce can only release the sexual bond but not protect her economic rights.

To elaborate this point further, a Hindu woman under the customary law had a right of residence and maintenance which could be a charge on the husband's property. Since divorce was not recognised, this meant life-long economic security. The right was granted statutory recognition under the *Hindu Woman's Separate Residence and Maintenance Act* of 1946. But the Hindu Marriage Act, which provided for the divorce of the Hindu wife, did not protect her right to shelter or separate residence if the husband was cruel. Under the new act her only relief was a petition for divorce. The husband could also file a similar petition against her to terminate the matrimonial bond and deprive the woman of her right to residence. Hence, it appears that the Hindu woman has bartered away her right of economic security to her right of divorce—and consequent destitution.

It is very surprising that after incorporating within itself the severest

---

[49] *T. Sareetha* vs. *Venkatasubbiah*, AIR 1983, A.P. 356.
[50] *Harvindar Kaur* vs. *Harmender Singh*, AIR, 1984, Del 66 and *Saroj Rani* vs. *Sudarshan Kumar Chandra*, AIR, 1984, SC 1562.

subversions of women's rights under English law, attempts to restore the Hindu woman's economic rights—which had been protected under both customary law and scriptural doctrines—by the method of adopting more recent developments in English law are deemed 'Western' and therefore bad. The concept of a sacramental marriage and its supposedly sublime nature is invoked only when women attempt to seek economic protection and not while denying women these provisions.

In this context, any formulation of laws and rights needs to contextualise the economic rights of women as central within the marriage contract. Only then can the trend of destitution as a consequence of divorce be arrested. Unfortunately, the recent demand for a uniform civil code by progressive and pro-women lobbies has not taken into account the plurality of customs, nor has it made property the central theme of reforms. The primary focus continues to be the regulation of sexuality, and that is only bound to constrain women's economic rights further.

Unless property is situated at the centre of the discourse on women and legal reform, and unless the changing economic structure and uneven developments within a pluralistic society are kept in mind, any attempt at reform will be ineffective in protecting the economic rights of women and preventing their destitution.

List of Abbreviations

ACJ	— Appellate Case Journal
AIR	— All India Reporter
AP	— Andhra Pradesh
BLR	— Bengal Law Reporter
Bom.LR	— Bombay Law Reporter
BHCR	— Bombay High Court Reports
Bom	— Bombay
Cal	— Calcutta
Cri.LJ	— Criminal Law Journal
Del	— Delhi
FB	— Full Bench

HC	— High Court
ILR	— Indian Law Reports
IA	— Indian Appeals
MIA	— Moore's Indian Appeals
SC	— Supreme Court
SCC	— Supreme Court Cases
SCR	— Supreme Court Reporter
SCW	— Supreme Court Weekly
TLLS	— Tagore Law Lecture Series
WR	— Weekly Reporter

Nationalism Refigured: Contemporary South Indian Cinema and the Subject of Feminism*

TEJASWINI NIRANJANA

Gender and the Indian Modern

A NEW NATIONALISM IS in the air today, a nationalism suffused with romantic love, with the most intimate and 'private' of emotions. Popular cinema in India draws our attention to this phenomenon: *Roja* (1992), for example, is advertised as 'a patriotic love story', and one of the more successful films of 1994 was called *1942: A Love Story*. This nationalism appears to be premised on a detaching of the new middle class from the Nehruvian state of the post-Independence years, a process that has led to changes in the meaning of some of the key terms in our political life, such as 'secularism', for example. It is almost as if the hitherto hidden logic of the national-modern is now acquiring visibility owing to a new configuration of forces which include the rise of the Sangh Parivar[1] and the liberalization of the Indian economy.

---

*Versions of this paper have been presented to audiences in Calcutta, New Delhi, Colombo, Madras, Hyderabad and Chicago. My thanks to all of those who have taken issue with me both orally and in print.

[1] The term Sangh Parivar literally means the Sangh family. The reference is to the loose group of Hindu right-wing political and cultural organisations headed by the Rashtriya Swayamsevak Sangh, and including the Vishwa Hindu Parishad, the Bharatiya Janata Party and the Bajrang Dal.

The portrayal of 'mainstream' characters—unexceptional, not particularly 'heroic'—in commercial cinema provides one point of access to this complex configuration. Central to the shift in the national imaginary, as I shall show, is the figure of *woman*. In this negotiation of the new modernity, the woman is not presented as just a passive counter; rather, her agency is shown as crucial for the shifts that are taking place.

The Indian 'woman' is produced at a particular conjuncture between Nation (imaged as an autonomous, sovereign, nation-state) and Modernity (including both processes such as democratization or the spread of mass communication, and discourses such as those which produce the very distinctions between 'tradition' and 'modern'). Unlike gender, however, *caste* and *community* (or religious identity) are not privileged sites for the representation or staging of modernity and nationhood. (I refer here to lower caste-class and Muslim.) Quite the contrary. The pre-modern or non-modern, as well as the anti-national, is often staged *as* caste and community. To put it differently, invoking identities based on community and caste would be unacceptable to the secularist, the 'modern citizen', who has laid hegemonic claim to the nation in the post-Independence period. The leaving behind of caste/community by the national-modern, curiously enough, is facilitated by the claim of 'woman' to modernity and the nation.[2] The claim, however, is incomplete, and an analysis of it might well point to multiple fault lines and incoherences in the formation of the national imaginary.

This claim of women to entitlement is supported by the new identities fashioned by/for them in the post-Independence period on a host of different sites, a fashioning that seems to have taken new directions in the 1990s. My interest in popular cinema as a major site for such identity formation derives from the fact that it is perhaps the single most powerful medium, until the fairly recent coming of television, in which identities have been publicly displayed, negotiated and

---

[2] See Susie Tharu and Tejaswini Niranjana, 'Problems for a Contemporary Theory of Gender', in Shahid Amin and Dipesh Chakrabarty (eds), *Subaltern Studies IX* (Delhi: Oxford University Press, 1989).

narrativized. The three films discussed here at some length, *Geetanjali* (1989), *Roja* (1992) and *Bombay* (1995), all directed by Maniratnam, were produced in Tamil and Telugu, the second and third having been successfully dubbed into Hindi as well.[3] What I intend to investigate in these films is: (a) how they feed into, and endorse, even as they produce in the cinematic medium, the new Indian nationalism; and (b) how the post-Independence feminist subject is imbricated in the fashioning of this new nationalism. Perhaps I should clarify here that I do not necessarily think of my analysis as a contribution to film criticism. Instead, I see it as an attempt to understand how a historical-political conjuncture is structured by focusing on one kind of cultural artefact produced in it. My aim, therefore, is not to present a complete account of the films in terms of their formal devices, but to suggest how we might be able to account for the films' appeal in the present conjuncture.

Although chronologically speaking *Geetanjali* is a pre-Mandal film and *Roja* a pre-Babri Masjid one (they are, however, uncannily close to the two events—September–October 1990 and December 1992—named here), I would like to suggest that their representations of feminine identities are emblematic, in the first case, of the anti-Mandal woman, and in the second of the (Hindu) woman who stands for the nation (but is not necessarily the openly communal woman).[4] Primarily because she is Muslim, the central woman character in *Bombay* is portrayed somewhat differently from the heroines of *Geetanjali* and *Roja*, as I shall demonstrate later. I use the term 'anti-Mandal woman' to designate the self-identity of those who, by disavowing caste, are able to lay claim simultaneously to both the modern and the secular. This is not to suggest that 'modern and secular' is *the same as* 'anti-Mandal'; it is merely one way of indicating the convergences that occurred, or became evident, in the 1990s. The agitations in 1990

---

[3] Maniratnam sometimes re-shoots parts of his films to incorporate regional or linguistic differences. It becomes a little difficult therefore to say where the reshooting stops and the dubbing begins.

[4] One could also add that the structuring of these two feminine figures is similar, in terms of how they make a claim on the modern, the secular and the national.

against the recommendations of the Mandal Commission for reservation of government jobs and educational opportunities for the Other Backward Castes had framed the modern *as* the secular, and the secular as that which transcended caste differences.[5]

One of the major conceptual difficulties in talking of the new nationalism is that its vocabulary does not seem so very different from that of the older nationalism. National interest, national security, national integration and modernization are terms familiar to us since the 1950s. So is the term secularism, which has been central to liberal and left politics in India. My contention is that the continuity of terms obscures the real shifts that are taking place. In some ways, the process is one in which the contours of the national-modern are made evident, its exclusions of caste (the lower castes) and community (the non-Hindu) legitimized. Using a rather awkward term, we should perhaps speak of the 'post-national-modern' (not the postmodern, not the postnational) to describe this situation in which old terms are acquiring new significations.[6] I focus here on the mobilization of these terms in contemporary popular cinema and the new subject-positions which are being produced in the films.

Today, while the composition of the national-modern is being centrally challenged by the assertion of political identities based on caste and community, the question of gender occupies a very different position.[7] In spite of the considerable gains made by the women's movement over the last twenty years, the idiom in which feminist questions were raised is being mobilized today in very different kinds of initiatives, including the consolidation of the national-modern that feminists set out to criticize. The woman who chooses, the woman

---

[5] Note that the anti-Mandalites talked of 'differences', not 'inequalities'.

[6] The modes of access to, the negotiation of and with, and the deployments of this post-national-modern would have to be understood as necessarily different for different kinds of groups, depending on their caste/community/gender configuration and the position of relative advantage or disadvantage from which they access it.

[7] See Susie Tharu and Tejaswini Niranjana, 'Problems for a Contemporary Theory of Gender', and Vivek Dhareshwar, 'Caste and the Secular Self', *Journal of Arts and Ideas*, nos 25–6 (1993), pp. 115–26.

who acts independently, who takes the initiative, are today admired figures in popular cinema. If we examine closely the structuring of the agency of these female (or should we say feminist) subjects, like for example Maniratnam's protagonists Geeta, Roja and Shaila Banu, we might begin to perceive the modes of their implication in the refiguring of the national-modern.

The Anti-Mandal Woman

In this section I attempt an analysis of female subjectivity in *Geetanjali* in the light of the anti-Mandal agitation. The announcement in August 1990 of the implementation of the Mandal Commission recommendations by Prime Minister V.P. Singh, as we all remember, set off large-scale rioting by upper-caste youth who were, by and large, urban.[8] Many of these young people were women who took part enthusiastically in the activities of the Anti-Mandal Commission Forum (AMCF), which included organising batches of students to sweep the streets, polish shoes, carry luggage at railway stations, and orchestrate processions and rallies. The press represented such upper-caste youth as engaged in a heroic struggle to save the nation from impending chaos, supporting the idea that implementing reservations would lead to a derecognition of merit and a consequent destruction of the country. In the battle for 'merit', the truly patriotic and truly secular Indian was the one who rose above caste divisions; anyone who asked for reservations on the basis of caste was simply being casteist.

Prominently woven into the anti-Mandal discourse on merit was the figure of the Nation, and that of Modernity. Caste or the reservations policy (used interchangeably in this context) was described as that which had trapped India in a residual feudalism, preventing the country from achieving the progress and efficiency which would allow it to take its equal place in the world. By decrying caste, the modern middle-class subject also proclaimed its concern for the nation.

To take a slight detour into my own discipline, English, and see

---

[8] The Mandal Commission recommended additional reservations or quotas for Backward Castes in job and educational opportunities.

how it responded to the Mandal crisis, may not be inappropriate here. The study of English Literature, introduced in the nineteenth century by the British, had played a significant part in the formation of the liberal humanist subject who would be both modern and nationalist.[9] In India, the 'secularism' of the English-educated subject enabled a displacement of both caste and community from the middle-class sphere, so that these got marked as what lay *outside*, was *other* than, the middle class. During the anti-Mandal agitation, upper-caste English Department students in many universities boycotted classes *en masse* to demand the abolition of reservations altogether.[10]

There are connections, no doubt, between the fact that the (old) middle class which used to stand in for the nation is marked, above all, by its *Englished*-ness, and the phenomenon of middle-class/upper-caste female 'Englished' students emerging so decisively into the public realm to express the outrage of their class. Of all student agitations in post-Independence India, the anti-Mandal one was surely unique in its legitimization by the media and in the fond parental approval it generated. The acclamation, curiously enough, was related to the imaging of this student politicization as being 'above politics'.[11] Precisely because of what was seen by the media as the purity and distance from conventional politics of the anti-Mandalites, their protest became the rage of the righteous who had suffered far too long because of their innate courtesy and politeness, who were now forced to take action to prevent the nation from 'going to the dogs'.[12] The fact of women

---

[9] For a discussion of some of these issues, see Susie Tharu, 'Government, Binding and Unbinding', Introduction to the Special Issue of the *Journal of English and Foreign Languages* (June–December 1991); Gauri Viswanathan, *Masks of Conquest* (London: Faber, 1990); Tejaswini Niranjana, *Siting Translation: History, Post-structuralism and the Colonial Context* (Berkeley: University of California Press, 1992).

[10] However qualified the demand sometimes appeared, it was evident for instance from the proclamation of the national association of IAS officers that reservations in general (even for Scheduled Castes and Scheduled Tribes [SCs] and [STs] were being targeted, and not only the new Other Backward Castes (OBC) reservations.

[11] See Veena Das, 'A Crisis of Faith', in *Statesman* (3 September 1990).

[12] A phrase heard constantly during the anti-Mandal agitation. Another common remark of the time framed the upper-caste speaker in a discourse of Selflessness: 'I'm

appearing on the streets in public protest made the media recall the idealism of the freedom struggle. 'Women' were imaged as morally pure, and thereby entrusted with the task of saving the nation. The enthusiastic participation of 'women' in the anti-Mandal agitation along with their men, not as sexed beings but as free and equal citizens, suggests that these articulate and assertive subjects define themselves against 'caste' (read lower castes). As middle class, upper-caste 'women' thus claim a space in the post-national-modern, both men as well as women of the lower castes become invisible. A parallel process can be seen with regard to Muslim men and women.

It would be inaccurate, however, to think that the upper-caste anti-Mandal women were marked primarily by their Englished-ness. Interestingly, South Indian women of this class—positioned within the national -modern—would not, for example, have watched popular Telugu films, their first choices being English and Hindi movies. But today they are ardent admirers of films like *Geetanjali*, and 'vernacular' directors like Maniratnam. What makes Maniratnam's films unique in commercial cinema is their use of realistic modes of representation, their technical sophistication,[13] and the seeming naturalness and spontaneity of his actors, as well as the careful shaping of a seamless 'Indian modernity'. Importantly, Maniratnam's films mark the insertion of regional difference into the nation-space; witness the audacity with which the filmmaker puts a Tamil couple in Kashmir, or in Bombay, and claims for *them* the characteristics of the new national-modern. The films produce as well as take shape within a 'modern' space, having either discarded or de-emphasized the elements of farce and melodrama that are staple aspects of Indian-language commercial films. They make themselves available, therefore, to be celebrated without embarrassment, even with a certain pride, by the middle-class Indian. The growing popularity of Maniratnam's films across class

---

not concerned for myself. I can always get a job in spite of reservations. I'm only worried as to where this is taking us.'

[13] 'Rajiv Menon's cinematography [in *Bombay*] is of an international calibre', says well-known film critic Khalid Mohammed in his review in *The Times of India* (9 April 1995).

and region, in fact, indicate the near-hegemonic emergence of a 'cosmopolitan' taste, mediated by MTV and cable television programming.[14] In these films new subjectivities, and a new femininity, are being fashioned, this being perhaps a key element in their successful appeal to younger women. This new femininity holds out the promise of a modernity without the perils of feminism or feminist politics, which are frequently ridiculed in the media, and sometimes vilified, as imitative of Western aberrations.

The redefinitions of femininity produced and circulated today in films like Maniratnam's feed at many levels into, and reinflect, popular debates around questions of 'modernity' and 'tradition'. These debates, it seems to me, are helping to constitute an aggressive cultural nationalism which is beginning to articulate itself alongside and into the vocabulary of the multinational market economy. The re-figuring of femininity in popular cinema is linked to the emergence of a new consumer economy supported by the ongoing reconstitution of the national imaginary. It is premised on what I have been calling the idea of a post-national-modern, an idea that articulates at the level of everyday life—and in the life of commodities—the construction of an 'Indian' modernity which has resolved the older contradictions.

On the surface, some of Maniratnam's heroines don't match our conventional notions about good Indian women. The teenaged heroine of *Geetanjali*, for instance, is constantly saying, '*Lecchipoddaama*, shall we elope?', and not always to the same person. However, Geetanjali's daring and her sexual aggressiveness are presented in the narrative merely as a manifestation of her high spirits and sense of humour. Her 'abandon' in some sense comes from being abandoned, by an absent or dead mother, and by Life. The boldness of the heroine becomes literally possible only on the verge of death.

---

[14] Sunil Sethi writes of the 'lower middle-class ethnically mixed' Delhi audience he watched *Bombay* with: 'Film-goers seemed genuinely appreciative of the movie. I myself was greatly cheered to notice that not the subtlest nuance or bits of passing dialogue was lost on the audience, which laughed and clapped and gasped and cheered in all the right places...' ('Celluloid Metaphor of "Bombay",' *Newstime*, 16 April 1995).

What is the narrative trajectory that creates the space of feminine assertion in the film? *Geetanjali* is the story of two young lovers, both dying of incurable illnesses, the boy from leukaemia and the girl from heart disease. Set amidst the swirling mists of Kodaikanal, where the protagonists seem to have gone to die, the film unfolds into breathtaking landscapes whose lush greenness (and the yellows and reds of the heroine's 'ethnic' clothes) counterpoint the tale of imminent death. Interestingly, the only images of death foregrounded in the film are the tombs and ghosts of the graveyard where Geeta, as she is called, lures unsuspecting men in order to play an elaborate practical joke on them with the help of her young siblings. Death, as far as the female protagonist is concerned, is just a joke. The tombs are simultaneously 'real' as well as parodic images out of a horror film. The graveyard is therefore what awaits 'the inevitable end', as well as what sanctions a life lived in the present continuous tense. One of our first impressions of Geeta is of a prankster in ghost-like attire who has adopted the dress for fun and out of choice, for it is not until the intermission that the audience finds out about her incurable disease.

Throughout the narrative, however, love and death are closely intertwined, as for example in the lyrical Ilaiyaraja composition 'Om Namaha' with its background music dominated by a magnified heartbeat. Although the film was not well received in non-urban areas, middle- and lower-middle-class young people in large cities saw it again and again, shouting, chanting or whispering, according to context, every crucial piece of dialogue. What the film seems to reaffirm is that one should live as though one will die tomorrow. In living for today, the new consumers who form the bulk of the audience confirm their intuition that what is important is to look wonderful now, to buy their fashionable clothes (Nagarjuna's jeans and sweatshirts, Girija's neo-ethnic *salwar-kameez* and *ghagra-choli*) now, for tomorrow they will be as good as dead.[15] In fact, impending death is the only context in which 'love' begins to make sense, for it is a love that is reinforced

---

[15] The *Geetanjali* version of *ghagra-choli* did indeed create a new line of clothing for teenagers as well as little girls.

by the pretty clothes, a love that never disturbs the assumptions of the audience because not only does it have no future, it rests on the almost complete erasure of differences.

The protagonists are obviously metropolitan, but they are totally distant from, and uninvolved with, their normal context. The hero seems to be Hindu and the heroine Christian, but this is a trivial detail, used mostly for comic effect, as in the church scene where the boy calls out to God during Mass to complain about his lover. (Contrast this with *Roja*, in which another minority identity—Muslim—imaged effortlessly as both pre-modern and anti-national, is counterpointed to that which is invisibly Hindu and part of the national-modern.) Nowhere in the narrative is religious difference a point of contention, for everything is permitted to those who are about to die. The new consumer economy in which films like *Geetanjali* occupy a nodal position constitutes a new ethical self, a self premised on the need for 'authenticity'. Only the inauthentic, those who experience death-in-life, are afraid of death. Not the ones who truly experience life-in-death, whose moments, lived solely in the present, are authenticated by the imminence of their end.[16]

The centrality to *Geetanjali* of the new consumer ensures that *work* is never really represented in the film, except for the fruit-sellers who function as local colour, and the doctor and nurse who in any case are working *for* the lovers. The hero, although recently graduated from college, is exempt from work partly because of his parents' affluence and partly because of his impending death. Class differences, therefore, are not represented here, except for the lecherous caretaker and his weepy wife in the parodic sub-plot, and they too are subsumed in the general movement of the narrative. The heroine and her sisters again don't work, except to clean the house now and then or prepare elaborately for oil baths. Geeta is not even shown studying, for she lives in a kind of 'slack' time where all she has to do is entertain herself, and others. This film, unlike the later *Roja* and *Bombay*, erases regional

---

[16] I owe this point to Susie Tharu, who also drew my attention to the counterpointed images of 'modernity' in the film.

differences, except only in as much as the language spoken by the characters is Telugu; there is no other marker to *place* the film in any specific region. The look of the protagonists is not unlike those of college students from Delhi or Bombay or Bangalore. Obviously, the hero is dressed in Western clothes like other fashionable urban, middle-class youth; but the urban heroine in many South Indian films is increasingly dressed in North Indian 'ethnic' clothes. Instead of being through her clothes (*langa-daavni* or sari) the bearer of regional specificity, the film-heroine is now marked as 'Indian', like present-day urban young women themselves, through her Rajasthani-Gujarati apparel. In other films by Maniratnam (for example, the award-winning *Mouna Raagam*), we find obligatory fantasy sequences with a love song set in the desert, replete with camels, turbans, mirrorwork, and chunky jewellery. The visual imagery provided by mass media for our 'private' fantasies thus includes pictures of the new Indian.[17]

Geeta, then, is the 'new woman', the strong heroine, both modern as well as feminine. While her casual clothes and 'spontaneous' gestures represent her as 'liberated', she simultaneously carries a double burden—the burden of woman as saviour and teacher. Geeta helps the hero understand his mortality and reconciles him to the fate she also shares. The heroine is not thereby exempt from sustaining the image of the truly feminine. She is allowed to take the initiative in the relationship because, in spite of her shoulder-length hair, she is 'Indian', and a signifier of the *good* modernity. The film deploys a series of images which suggests a contemporary reappropriation of that which had, for the urban middle class, been relegated in the post-Independence period to the realm of tradition (shots of herbal

---

[17] In a perceptive essay, 'Beaming Messages to the Nation", *Journal of Arts and Ideas*, no. 19 (1990), pp. 33–52, Ashish Rajadhyaksha discusses the impulses behind what he calls the new definitions of indigenism. Rajadhyaksha suggests that since 'geographically defined regionalist identities are closely linked to geographically defined markets', the internationalization of markets obviously demands the formation of new identities. Mass media, especially TV and popular cinema, have contributed in important ways to the imaging of the new indigenism, an indigenism that takes up elements from diverse and anthropologized folk traditions and combines them into the authentically and timelessly 'Indian'.

preparations, Geeta with oil in her hair, the large courtyard where the women sit). This reappropriation, it must be obvious, is once again centred around the woman. The *bad* kind of modernity is signified by the army major's lusty wife, played by Disco Shanti, dressed in tight jeans or miniskirts or sometimes only a bath-towel. This bad modernity is inevitably associated with an insatiable sexual appetite, portrayed in the 'comic' scenes of Disco Shanti's seduction of the caretaker. Both women are sexually aggressive, but whereas Geeta's actions are sanctioned by death and the audience only laughs *with* her, the other woman's actions are ultimately presented as reprehensible, or as something to be laughed *at.*

Geeta has no mother in the film, only a grandmother, who passes on to her 'traditional' knowledge, imaged for the new consumer through herbal cosmetics. This 'grandmother's knowledge', mobilized by multinational capital, is authenticated and refashioned in the chemical laboratory in order to create new markets in 'traditional' societies. And why doesn't Geeta have a mother? If she had been part of this narrativization of contemporary female subjectivity, Geeta would have had to be schooled by her into the older femininity, to claim a place in the national-modern; she would have to be groomed for a future continuous, for the kind of austerity enjoined on us by the years just after Independence. Geeta, however, can challenge conventional models of femininity precisely because she is presented as having no future. Her father tolerates all her transgressions in the light of her imminent death. Her daring, her abandon, are permissible because they will not last, since they find full expression only on the verge of dying.

To come back to the anti-Mandal agitation with which I began this section of my essay: the anti-Mandal woman is prefigured in *Geetanjali* with regard to her occupation of an equal space with middle-class men, a space where differences of caste or community do not matter because they have been left behind by the secular subject. In its transition to the post-national-modern, this subject is articulated into the consumer economy, an economy naturalized by the film in its valorization of the present moment. And it is the consumer economy that legitimizes the demand for efficiency at all costs that a welfarist, pro-reservation state cannot provide.[18] This inefficient state is centrally thematized in *Roja*, which is set in present-day Kashmir.

The Romance of Nationalism

Whereas *Geetanjali* narrativizes the fantasies of the new middle class in a setting seemingly distant from the everyday world, *Roja*, which incidentally won the National Integration Award for 1993, dramatizes—as does the controversial *Bombay* (1995)—the politics of this assertive and self-confident class.[19] Although Maniratnam's representative technique has as its immediate ancestor the Hindi middle-brow film of the 1970s (either in its wistful Hrishikesh Mukherjee mode or the social-critique mode of Saeed Mirza), there is no *angst* apparent in his characters. Unapologetic about their protagonists in every way, Maniratnam's films celebrate rather than critique their aspirations and lifestyles.

The opening sequence of *Roja* shows a Kashmiri militant leader being captured by soldiers of the Indian army. This is followed by another beginning, which depicts the splendid waterfalls and coves and shining green fields of the village of Sunder Bhanpur (somewhere in India), with the heroine Roja singing and romping through the landscape.[20] In this rapidly-presented sequence—its slickness that of

---

[18] During the anti-Mandal agitation of 1990, the commonly held middle-class perception was that India's public sector had become corrupt and inefficient because of the reservations policy followed by the government.

[19] *Roja* was publicly endorsed on hoardings by Chief Election Commissioner T.N. Seshan as a film every patriotic Indian must see. The BJP's L.K. Advani confessed to having been moved by the scene of the hero saving the burning Indian flag. In an interview, the Shiv Sena's Bal Thackeray, who asked for and got certain cuts in the film, acclaims *Bombay* as 'a damn good film'.

[20] I have chosen to focus on the Hindi version of *Roja*, although I am familiar with the Telugu version as well. The Hindi version was a national success, and marked a confident occupation of a 'national' rather than just a 'regional' space (in terms of political agendas as well as markets) by the new South Indian cinema. Unlike the Tamil version, which might have interpellated its audience along very different axes, the

Nationalism Refigured 151

a TV commercial—we see Roja, sometimes accompanied by her youngest sister, driving a tractor (for fun, since they don't 'work'), playing pranks on the older villagers, dressing up in men's clothes, wearing a graduate's convocation robes, and dancing through a field where women are transplanting seedlings. As in other Maniratnam films, actual labour serves as a backdrop that enhances the light-heartedness of the heroine. Then we see her and the other girl driving a flock of goats down a hill and across the road (not work but play again) to block the hero's car so that he can be scrutinized before he enters the village. Roja is a good deal like Geeta, in spite of the 'rural' origins of the one and the 'urban' background of the other. Both are portrayed as uninhibited, high-spirited, self-assertive, never at a loss for words. These are women whose articulateness has been made possible by the women's movement, which has created certain kinds of spaces for women and helped bring them a new visibility, although they are recuperated into the very spectacularization that some feminists might challenge. Interestingly, Roja's high spirits, like Geetanjali's, seem to be made possible by the exemption of the heroines from 'real work',[21] so their assertiveness is not part of their interaction in a workplace situation.[22]

Rishi Kumar, the urbane hero, has come to 'see' Roja's sister, since he wants to marry 'a girl from a village'. Not only that, he would like

---

Telugu and Hindi versions were quite similar in their structures of address. However, the Hindi version of the film does flatten out and clarify some of the ambiguity of the Tamil and Telugu versions, especially around the question of language. Also, the question of 'patriotism' would be attached to very different debates in the context of Tamilnadu politics. When the film was released in 1992 in Tamilnadu, many people are supposed to have seen it as an exorcism of the collective guilt felt by Tamilians over Rajiv Gandhi's assassination in Sriperumbudur the previous year.

[21] Earlier commercial cinema also portrayed frolicking heroines exempt from the compulsions of the everyday world. What I'm trying to mark here is the difference in Maniratnam's young women, given the *realism* of the film's narrative style which distances it from dominant Indian commercial cinema, and which makes the women both 'real' and 'natural'.

[22] This exemption from 'work' helps contain the heroines' assertiveness, making it cute and attractive rather than threatening.

his bride to be from the beautiful village with which he has fallen in love ('I love the very soil of this place', as he says later). But clearly he will not marry just anyone—when the match with Roja's sister falls through because she wants to marry someone else, he turns immediately to Roja, whom he has glimpsed exactly twice until then.

Roja, who is fair, sharp-featured, obviously upper-caste, is quite different from the village women of the neo-realist 'art' films of Shyam Benegal, Adoor Gopalkrishna and others. She addresses her father as Daddy, has a television set at home, is accustomed to talking on the telephone; and, except that she does not know English, she is quite at ease in urban surroundings, adapting without difficulty to Rishi's upper-middle-class home and milieu. Roja does not therefore belong even to the genre of the 'village belle' of older commercial Hindi and regional-language cinema. Her old world and her new one are not represented as opposed to each other; rather, they exist in an almost seamless continuum. Given the rapid urbanization of the rural upper class/castes, English is no longer a sufficient marker of cultural difference or even a marker of non-Indianness. Instead, 'English' can be acquired through training in consumerism; what is more curious, English is closely associated not with the non-Indian but with that which is not only assertively Indian but clearly nationalist: as indicated by the words which signify Rishi's profession and his daily activity, a point to which I will return.

What the village stands for in Rishi's eyes is a newly formulated traditionalism: the 'ethnic' wedding, so much unlike the hotel or function-hall reception now seen as so tasteless by the upper-middle-class, the colourful saris of the old women who dance for the couple, or the sexual frankness of the 'rustic' wedding song, which is sung in playback partly by the rap musician Baba Sehgal. All this displayed ethnicity is not at variance with Rishi's cosmopolitan modernness; on the contrary, it helps strengthen its self-confidence. Except for the *dhoti-kurta* of his wedding day, Rishi usually appears only in jeans and shirt or sweater. On the other hand, the Kashmiri militants always appear in clothes which mark them as ethnically Muslim; it is an ethnicity which reveals them as anti-modern (therefore anti-national or anti-Indian), intolerant and fundamentalist, while Hindu ethnicity as displayed by Roja or Rishi is merely part of the complexity of being Indian. The Hindu wedding rites are so normalized that we do not pay them any special attention, or even mark them as 'religious', just as we do not really see Roja's frequent attempts to pray to her idols as significant to the story. The militants, however, especially Rishi's main captor Liaqat, are always shown praying—an action shored up by intercutting and by the soundtrack in such a way as to make it seem not only an assertion of religious difference but a menacing or sinister portent. Whereas their religiosity is always portrayed as grim and humourless, Roja's prayers are funny and endearing, inviting the spectator to share her hopes and anxieties.

Rishi's occupation is 'cryptologist', a word uttered in English and left unexplained, until he tells Roja in passing that she should get 'security clearance' since he deals with 'confidential matters' involving 'coding and decoding' (all these phrases uttered in English). Rishi is shown a few times in front of a computer monitor and keyboard, working on decoding a message. His work, directly related to the security interests of the country, is presented to us as truly nationalist; and, interestingly, his nationalism, I would argue, is not anti-Western, but although never stated as such, anti-Muslim. It has been asserted by some writers that since Nehruvian nationalism was pro-Western but not anti-Muslim, the argument about contemporary nationalism being pro-Western and *therefore* inclined to be anti-Muslim cannot be sustained.[23] There is, it seems to me, a major difference between 1950s Nehruvianism and 1990s middle-class neo-nationalism.[24] The conjuncture of nationhood and modernity in which the new citizen emerges

---

[23] See Arun Kumar Patnaik, 'Idealist Equations', *Economic and Political Weekly*, vol. XXIX: 32 (6 August 1994), p. 2108.

[24] To elaborate this, we would have to look into the composition of the citizen-subject in India. As Susie Tharu and I have argued in 'Problems for a Contemporary Theory of Gender', in *Subaltern Studies IX*, the 'Indian' in the nineteenth century emerges marked, or *coded* (since the marks are not visible) as upper-caste/middle-class, Hindu and male. The Indian comes into being, as several scholars have demonstrated, simultaneously unequal to the colonizer and claiming superiority to him in certain realms. The post-Independence Indian, therefore, professes to be more egalitarian and

also produces a secularism that proclaims its transcendence of caste and religion. The point to be made about Nehruvian nationalism is not simply that it was not anti-Muslim. (It was not simply pro-Western either, but that needs to be debated elsewhere and at length.) The formation of the 'Indian' in the 1950s was not explicitly dependent on an anti-Muslim discourse, because the citizen-subject was *coded*, among other things, *as Hindu*. Today, in the context of globalization, the hidden markings of the Indian citizen-subject are being revealed, and claimed *without embarrassment* by the upper-caste Hindu middle-class. This lack of embarrassment can go unremarked in a post-Cold War 'new world order' in which Islam is being relentlessly demonized. One kind of display of the markers of 'difference'—here, difference as privilege and not inferiority—emerges as part of the positive agenda of liberalization and globalization. Difference as mark of privilege is linked, I would like to suggest, to the comprehensive claiming of the space of the nation by the new middle class. This kind of claim is clearly manifested in the middle-class representation of the Kashmir 'problem'.

When Rishi's boss, who is supposed to go to Kashmir to help the army, falls seriously ill, he asks Rishi to take his place. His 'You don't mind going, do you?' is answered by Rishi's 'Of course not. I'll go anywhere in India. Isn't Kashmir in India?' (loud audience applause.) Roja insists on accompanying her new husband, although she has initially rejected all his advances due to a misunderstanding. So, like many earlier Hindi-film honeymooners, they arrive in 'Kashmir'. But to an official welcome, to be put up in a five-star hotel where there are obviously no other guests. As they are driven through deserted streets, Roja asks why the town looks so empty and Rishi merely answers 'curfew'. When asked why there should be curfew, he uses a favourite word: 'security'. No other explanation is seen as necessary for the spectator-position the film creates. Hardly any ordinary Kashmiris are

---

more welfarist than the liberal citizens at the heart of empire, and claims to strive for the eradication of all forms of 'backwardness'. The secular Indian citizen, then, presents 'him'self as transcending caste and community identities, the assertion of which work against the dominant narrative of emancipation.

shown in the film, except for a newspaper boy and some people selling souvenirs. In two fantasy/song sequences, we do see Kashmiris—either women, or children dressed in elaborate costumes. All the other Kashmiris (with one exception) are militants, and male. This depiction helps mark off Roja as the bearer of both femininity and Indianness, both implicitly marked as Hindu.[25]

Coming in search of Roja, who has gone to the temple to pray, the hero is kidnapped by the militants who have been following him, and who demand in exchange for his release their captured leader Wasim Khan. Roja goes to the police, to report that *'raakshas jaise aadmi'* ('men like demons') took away her husband, who is a *deshpremi* (patriot, lover of the nation). The aid of the state is invoked for the 'good citizen' against the militant 'demons'. Roja, although all she demands is her husband's return ('I don't care about the country'), is patriotic by implication, through her representation of both Rishi and the militants, as a patriot and as monsters respectively.

Rishi's love for the nation is driven home through two dramatic acts performed by him in captivity. First, when his captors want him to speak into a tape recorder and ask for the release of Wasim Khan, all he says into the machine is a firm 'Jai Hind'. Even after repeated blows which leave his face bleeding, he continues to say the phrase over and over again, making the audience cheer aloud. When the news arrives that the government has refused to release their leader, one of the militants picks up an Indian flag and rushes outside holding a flaming torch with which he sets fire to the flag. Rishi leaps through a window, shattering a glass pane, knocks over the militant, and throws his body on to the burning flag, driving the audience delirious. Having put out the fire, Rishi rises to his feet, partially aflame. In his jeans and sweater,

---

[25] Ravi Vasudevan's assertion, that 'regional identity in the figure of the woman ultimately seems to elude its translation into the rationality of the nationalist self' (Vasudevan, 'Other Voices: Reading "Roja" Against the Grain', *Seminar* 423, November 1994), pp. 43–4 is an interesting one that could be explored further. However, it seems to miss the crucial fact that Maniratnam's films increasingly construct an 'ethnic' identity rather than a specifically 'regional' one. This might account for the phenomenal success of his films in 'South Indian' languages as well as Hindi.

with the flames licking his clothes, he looks uncannily like the full-colour pictures with which the media glorified upper-caste anti-Mandal agitators in 1990, agitators who claimed that they were truly secular because they did not believe in caste but only in merit. Whereas in the anti-Mandal agitation, caste difference was coded as lack of merit, in *Roja* religious or ethnic difference (specifically Islamic) is portrayed not only as anti-national but as signifying lack of humanity. In this encrypted image, as Rishi 'burns', the soundtrack rises to a crescendo, the words of a nationalist poem blending into a triumphant chant. Throughout this sequence, intercut shots show the militant leader Liaqat deep in prayer inside the building, unconcerned about the struggle over the burning flag outside.

At the end, however, Rishi does escape, with the help of Liaqat's sister, who is mute throughout the film, though always depicted as shocked/weeping/distressed at the militants' rough treatment of their captive, and at the death of her youngest brother. The girl's femininity and her humanness ultimately oblige her to help the patriot, make her overcome her loyalty to her community, thus attaining the secular and, presumably, becoming *Indian*. In spite of Roja's determined appeals to the army and to the minister who arranges to have Wasim Khan released, the exchange of prisoners does not take place, and Rishi, although he is an employee of the state, does not depend on the state to regain his liberty. Roja pleads with the minister who is inspecting the army in Kashmir: my husband is not a big man, but '*Bharat ki praja to hai*' ('he is after all a citizen of India'), and we need security. The new middle class, in claiming its complete identification with the nation, has to demonstrate that demands made on the state are not met. The new class has to show its self-reliance instead, for the state apparatus is outworn, out of date, however large and impressive it may seem.[26] This middle-class imperative to detach itself from the state to

---

[26] While acknowledging the point made by S.V. Srinivas ('*Roja* in Law and Order State', *EPW*, vol. XXIX: 20 (14 May 1994), pp. 1225–6 and Arun Patnaik, 'Idealist Equations' about the increasing coercive activity of the state in the time of liberalization, I would argue that this is one of the signs of the *changing* state which indicates reallocation of functions, that is, different things are now being demanded of the state as it evacuates its older functions.

mark its coming to maturity can be seen, as I have suggested earlier, as a rejection of the Nehruvian state which had been compelled to write into its policies a vision of democracy and egalitarian socialism. (I see the absence of the mother in *Geetanjali* as another symptom of this rejection.) Among the consequences of these failed policies, the middle class would argue, is the situation in Kashmir, which can no longer be dealt with by the state but only by individuals like Rishi, who has shaken Liaqat to such an extent that the militant lets him go even when he has a rifle trained on him. Liaqat is shown to have been made *human*, through suffering and through Rishi's goodness (i.e. patriotism). Go, he says, '*ugravaadi aansu pochega*' ('the militant will wipe his tears'). Rishi's patriotism or nationalism, I would contend, is not centred around the nation-state; in fact, the state in this film is one that has failed in all respects—it cannot defeat the militants, cannot rescue its employee, cannot help Roja; its failure, then, can be made to justify a middle-class rejection of it in favour of a new economic order which in endorsing privatization will ensure greater efficiency.[27]

If Rishi is in many ways the central character of the film, Roja is integral to his vision of love for the nation. What makes this film's portrayal of the heroine different from older representations of woman-as-nation (such as *Mother India*) is that the woman is no longer mother but lover. In the song '*Roja jaaneman*', for instance, in Rishi's reverie the rose (red/green) he sees outside his cell merges into the figure of his bride (who is especially towards the end of the film dressed in green sari/red or saffron blouse or red sari/green blouse). In turn, the beauty of the Kashmiri landscape blends into the physical beauty of the heroine, who appears in this particular song-sequence dressed in Kashmiri clothes and jewellery, followed by little children also wearing Kashmiri dress. The early autonomy and assertiveness shown by Roja before marriage all but disappears in the sober woman who attempts to win back her husband's life, and whose agency actually comes to naught. In the concluding sequence, Rishi sprints to safety across a bridge

---

[27] This is where I disagree with Venkatesh Chakravarthy and M.S.S. Pandian who have argued that 'the apparent inability of the state in the film actually masks its silent and powerful ability'. See their 'More on *Roja*', *EPW*, vol. XXIX: 11 (12 March 1994), pp. 642–4.

while Roja runs towards him and falls at his feet, woman-as-nation grateful for his return, before he lifts her up for his embrace.

It is evident from *Roja* that the conjuncture between romantic love and nationalism does not provide the same kind of space for the woman as it does for the man. For Roja, the conjugal space is configured very differently from the national space, and her love for her husband finds utterance in statements such as 'I don't care about the country, all I want is my husband back'. For Rishi, on the other hand, love for wife and love for nation converge, as in the '*Roja jaaneman*' song sequence, so that romantic love comes to be figured *as* nationalism. The authentic subject of modernity in the post-national-modern, then, is the one who can be both lover and citizen, in fact is lover-as-citizen. The narrative logic does not permit Roja the heroine to be this desiring subject, for she has to be assigned the role of that which is desired. The representation of her agency in the film, therefore, relates to her function as the crucial mediator who enables the manifestation of love as nationalism.

The Secularism of Love

The good citizen accomplishing what an inefficient state machinery is incapable of is as central to the narrative of *Bombay* as it is to *Roja*. In *Bombay*, the capacity for romantic love is not only a significant marker of modernity, it is also seen as the highest form of secularism. The film was the focus of intense controversies in several parts of India. Let me take the example of one city, Hyderabad.

Bombayi (the Telugu version of *Bombay*) was released all over Andhra Pradesh on 10 March 1995, playing to full houses in every theatre. On 14 March, screening of the film was banned in the twin cities of Hyderabad and Secunderabad as well as the adjoining district of Rangareddy.[28] Newspaper reports indicated that stray incidents of audience violence and representations to the Home Minister from the Majlis-Ittehadul-Muslimeen and the Majlis Bachao Tehreek had resulted in the ban order. It was also reported that leftist organisations

[28] The film was re-released with three cuts a few weeks later.

such as the Students' Federation of India (SFI) and the Democratic Youth Federation of India (DYFI) as well as the right-wing Bharatiya Janata Yuva Morcha had opposed the ban. A statement by the SFI and DYFI declared that 'the film depicted nationalist feelings and had nothing communal about it'.[29]

The reaction to Maniratnam's films in Hyderabad may not be representative of a general South Indian response to them, nor of the response in Andhra Pradesh either. Due to its atypical demographic profile (a Muslim population that is over 50 per cent in the old city and over 20 per cent even in the new city), Hyderabad's political scenario and the space occupied in it by the agendas of specifically 'Hindu' and 'Muslim' parties may very well be unique in southern India. Maniratnam's earlier film *Roja*, first in its Telugu version and then in Hindi, had elicited considerable applause in new Hyderabad for its unabashed patriotism and its categorical denunciation of Kashmiri militancy. A national(ist) commonsense about what constitutes the truly secular was articulated here in its convergence with Hindutva; in fact, 'secularism' in *Roja* was indistinguishable, as it is in other contemporary cultural formations, from the attitudes produced by the making invisible of a 'Hindu' ethnicity. *Bombay* is in many ways not very different from *Roja* in its portrayal of the secular and the Indian. It is worth investigating, therefore, why the film seems to have evoked from the minority community, which made no public protest about *Roja*, a very different kind of response. In my view, the response allows us to reflect anew on major questions of cultural politics today, in particular the question of what constitutes the secular.

While the film follows *Roja* in the framing of its central problem—the question of the nation and the question of communalism (community identity in *Roja*)—it is, to my mind, marked by a certain stuttering, not so evident in *Roja*, when it comes to the issue of gender. This might partly account for the hostile reception in certain quarters of a film that, compared to a *Roja* which depicted the Muslim almost entirely as terrorist and anti-Indian, represents in its syrupy secularism

---

[29] Report in *Newstime* (15 March 1995).

'nothing ... that hurts Muslim sentiments',[30] and indeed is framed as an attempt to '[balance] the viewpoints of the opposing communities'.[31] 'How sad', exclaims a journalist writing in *The Hindu*, 'every time sincere efforts have been made towards national integration we end up in protests and riots'.[32] There appears to be a general consensus that Maniratnam is indeed a 'nationalist' filmmaker, as evidenced by *Roja* winning the 1993 award for national integration. It is perhaps then the very composition of the national-modern—a composition which legitimises some identities and marginalises others—that was being contested by those who were demanding a ban on *Bombay*. And it is precisely around the question of gender, I would suggest, that the fracturing of this composition became visible.

But first, an outline of the narrative. Shekhar, a young upper-caste Hindu from Bheemunipatnam, Visakha District, has just finished his studies in Bombay and started working as a proof-reader in a newspaper, with a view to becoming a journalist. On a visit to his village he sees Shaila Banu, the daughter of the Muslim brickmaker Basheer, and instantly falls in love with her. After a brief courtship, and after encountering the hostility of his family and Basheer's to the possibility of his marriage with Shaila Banu, Shekhar returns to Bombay, to be joined there by the girl. They commence wedded life as paying guests in a rickety old apartment building; Shekhar gets promoted to reporter, Shaila Banu gives birth to twins; Shekhar's father Narayanamurthy (who has tried to send bricks marked 'Sri Ram' to Ayodhya as penance for his son's act) comes to visit, fearing for the safety of Shekhar's family after the fall of the Babri Masjid, and is overwhelmed to learn that the twins are named Kabeer Narayan and Kamal Basheer. Shaila Banu's parents also come on a visit at the same time. The January 1993 Bombay riots take place; the parents of both hero and heroine die in a fire; the children are lost; amidst scenes of rioting the chief protagonists search

---

[30] Nasreen Sultana, 'Lift Ban on "Bombay"', Letter to the Editor, *Newstime* (20 March 1995).

[31] Interviewer (Lens Eye), in 'Truth or Dare', interview with Maniratnam, *Times of India* (2 April 1995).

[32] Bhawna Bomaya, 'The "Bombay" Problem', *The Hindu* (31 March 1995).

for the twins. In the concluding scenes, Shekhar makes impassioned speeches to the rioters to stop killing each other, and the children are found, even as Hindus and Muslims drop their weapons and hold hands. This bare narrative cannot possibly account for the many ingenious ways in which Maniratnam achieves his cinematic effects, some of which I shall refer to.

What I earlier called the 'stuttering' of *Bombay* has to do, it seems to me, with the portrayal of the Muslim woman. When the film was first shown, some of the audience kept asking why the protagonists could not have been a Muslim man and a Hindu woman. Given the logic of gender and nation in Maniratnam, this equation would have been clearly impossible. The (Hindu) female in *Roja*, for instance, is shown as imperfectly secular, imperfectly nationalist, because her concern is not for the security of the nation but for her husband. It is the Hindu male, therefore, who must take on the task of making the Muslim 'human', which implicitly means becoming secular and nationalist as well. Whereas in *Roja* it is the male militant Liaqat who is portrayed as being made human, his silent sister who helps the hero escape is shown as already human by virtue of her femininity. By aiding the hero, she transcends her community identity and in the process stands revealed as both human and 'Indian', rather than Kashmiri and militant-separatist.

Bombay is even more subtle: Shaila Banu marries the Brahmin Hindu hero (who is never shown as marked by caste or community) but does not give up her religion; neither does she dress like a South Indian Hindu woman, especially since she does not wear a bindi except in two song sequences. The secular hero is obviously tolerant about all this, is in a sense attracted by the very 'difference' of the heroine. While male Muslim ethnic markers in the film (prayer caps, or scenes of mass praying for example) are ominous portents of the rioting to follow, female Muslim markers of ethnicity—the burqa, primarily—are glamourised and eroticised.[33] Shekhar's first glimpse of Shaila Banu is

---

[33] I should point out that BJP/Shiv Sena men are also shown in the film as engaging in aggressive public worship of Hindu gods. I would see this, however, as part of the problematic equalizing of Muslim and Hindu 'fundamentalism' in *Bombay*.

when the wind accidentally lifts up her veil, and many of his subsequent encounters with her, including on the night when they consummate their marriage, thematise this visibility/invisibility as tantalising.

While in *Roja* the hero tries to *change* the militant Muslim's beliefs without necessarily comprehending why the latter might hold them, in *Bombay* the secular citizen attempts to *understand* the ethnic other, but it is an understanding that can only be accomplished through the erotic gaze. It is the feminine other who is the embodiment of the erotically mysterious and unapproachable, and who therefore compels an unveiling in the act of making intimate, while the relationship of the secular nationalist with the ethnicised male can only be contentious and combative. This ethnicised male in the logic of these films, and indeed in the dominant cultural logic of our times, cannot possibly be the hero of a narrative about the need for national integration. The only acceptable hero is the urbanised, westernised Shekhar who, like Rishi Kumar in *Roja*, does not need to draw attention to his caste or religion because in espousing nationalism he has transcended such identities.[34] If one examines the composition of the Indian citizen-subject of the 1990s, the Hindu female appears as the necessary bearer of ethnicity. Thus, the initiator of the integration process, or the initiator of the romantic relationship in the film, cannot but be a man from the majority community. *Bombay*, then, could not have had a Muslim hero and a Hindu heroine.

This inevitability is also related to the sharp demarcation of gendered 'secular' spaces in *Bombay*. While the hero's secularism (read tolerance) does have a domestic aspect to it, it is made manifest in this sphere only as playfulness, as in the scene where a relay of little children conveys to his bride his question—'Shall I change my religion?' or the song sequence ('Halla gulla') in which he briefly dons Muslim headgear. His publicly secular acts, on the other hand, are shown as acts of consequence, when during the riots he berates his two colleagues for claiming to be Hindu and Muslim instead of saying they are Indian, or in the climactic scenes when he splashes petrol on his body and urges the rioters to burn him in order to shame them into throwing down

---

[34] It is not entirely fortuitous that the actor Arvind Swamy plays both Rishi Kumar in *Roja* and Shekhar in *Bombayi*.

their arms. In contrast, when Shaila Banu makes a rare appearance outside the home, it is most visibly when she and Shekhar are looking for the children during the riots, and she is called upon only to show distress and horror. Early on in the film, the heroine expresses her secularism in a mode reminiscent of popular Western feminist analyses of Islamic women: running to meet Shekhar of her own volition, her burqa snags on a piece of rusting metal (actually an old anchor!); she tugs but cannot loosen it, and finally (in slow motion) leaves it behind and dashes towards the hero.

The domestic space is constantly defined in the film as a counterpoint to communalism; the increasing familial harmony (the birth of the twins, the reconciliation of the grandparents, Shekhar's desire for more children) is matched against increasing communal tension in the city. Integration, the film seems to suggest, can be accomplished *within* the family.[35] In the domestic space, Shekhar does not have to undergo any sort of transformation to prove his secularism. In any case, his 'religion' is not central to his identity. Also, by virtue of being the breadwinner, there are other conventional asymmetries in relation to male and female roles that he need never challenge. It is crucial to the narrative that the couple have children, for the film's logic suggests that it is the urbanized nuclear family which can solve the problem of communalism. This problem, indicates the film, is one of senseless hatred. Communalism is imaged here, as in some analytical accounts of recent events in India, as the resurgence of ancient hates, primordial hostilities. Thus it becomes a *residue*, a mark of the non-modern, or backwardness,[36] and, as I have suggested earlier, the anti-national comes to be staged as community (or caste, for that matter). Secularism or nationalism, therefore, appears as the 'other' of communalism;[37] however, in the 1990s, in a historical space where the privatization of

---

[35] In an interview, Maniratnam says: 'The family is the most invincible institution of our country. We lead our entire lives in the family's folds.' *Times of India* (2 April 1995).

[36] This depiction makes invisible the large-scale participation of the 'modern' middle class in the Bombay riots.

[37] For a useful discussion of this process in the colonial period, see Gyanendra Pandey, *The Construction of Communalism in Colonial North India* (Delhi: OUP, 1990), especially chapter 7, 'Nationalism versus Communalism'.

secularism seems to be taking place, this nationalism need not be part of a political agenda.[38] As *Roja* demonstrated, the middle-class attempt to delink itself from the state results in a transfer of functions to that class. The efforts of the new citizen will accomplish what state policy cannot, what indeed it has worked against; it is not only state economic enterprise that needs to be privatized, but also the solution to 'cultural' questions such as that of communalism. For if the problem is diagnosed as one of hatred, the solution has to be located in the possibility of love. Humanism, too, becomes a question of good individuals, happy families. And love in its modern form, as *Bombay* shows, achieves its most exalted and exemplary expression in romantic love, the love between individuals. It might, then, be worth asking whether the demand for banning *Bombay*, on the basis that it offends Muslim sentiments, was simply an expression of 'fundamentalism' or of Muslim patriarchal attitudes. Was it perhaps an indication that the liberal analysis and solution (communalism is caused by 'hatred' and can be cured by 'love') is unacceptable—as inaccurate, simplistic and patronising—to those who comprise the majority amongst the victims of communal violence?[39] Could it point to the need to rethink whose tolerance the dominant notion of secularism embodies, and whether 'love' and 'tolerance' can be recommended in equal measure to both the majority and minority communities?

It is the burden of both *Roja* and *Bombay* to create the contemporary convergences between the *human*, the *secular* and the *nationalist* and to dramatize the condensation of these characteristics in the Hindu male who has discarded marks of caste and community. The question of the nation is posed in these films through the depiction of

---

[38] The new nationalism is of necessity detached from anti-imperialism, the differences between the BJP and the RSS over the *swadeshi* campaign notwithstanding. Nationalism, then, becomes a purely internal question, to be asserted against non-Hindu. I use the word privatization here to invoke also the current changes in the Indian economy regarding the transformation of the public sector.

[39] I use the word 'patronising' to indicate the tone of those, like Shekhar in *Bombay*, who exempt themselves from communalism by their modernity. Reduced to hatred, communalism becomes an emotion reserved for the non-modern and the irrational.

the Kashmir situation on the one hand and the Bombay riots on the other. In both, the modalities of the question's 'framing' collapse any challenge to the national-modern, or the post-national-modern, into a simple assertion of religious identity. Simultaneously with the gradual erosion of the nation's economic sovereignty and the ongoing process of market consolidation, an earlier anti-colonial nationalism turns into one for whom the 'enemy' is within and needs to be either transformed or expelled. The figure of woman, indeed the agency of women, I have been suggesting, is central to the formation of the new nationalism. If the changes taking place today are being crucially mediated by popular cinema, figures like Geeta, Roja and Shaila Banu are active mediators of such changes. Characterizing women in this fashion will allow us to form a perspective somewhat different from those analysts of Maniratnam's films who see these women simply as the hapless victims of Hindu patriarchy, Muslim patriarchy, sexism and male chauvinism.[40]

To my mind, the ground prepared for a feminist politics by the latter approach allows women to engage only in certain kinds of protest: in a peculiar coming together of filmic portrayal and filmic critical analysis, Shaila Banu *must* cast off her burqa to escape from Muslim patriarchy, reaffirming in the process the stereotype of what constitutes the oppression of the Muslim woman, and reaffirming that the Muslim community is both 'backward' and patriarchal. Roja too is not merely a victim of patriarchy but a key figure in its reconfiguration. I would argue, then, that a discussion of the narrative functions of characters like Geeta, Roja and Shaila Banu and of the centrality of

---

[40] Chakravarthy and Pandian ('More on *Roja*', pp. 642–4) see Roja's desire as repressed by the Hindu patriarchy whose numerous representatives include Rishi Kumar as well as state institutions. Swaminathan S. Anklesaria Aiyar, who hails *Bombay* as 'a passionate plea for humanity to rise above sectarian mayhem', denounces the Muslim groups seeking a ban on *Bombay* for their 'sexism' and 'male chauvinism'. He adds: 'The concept of women as independent human beings with a right to choose their husbands, jobs or religion is alien to traditionalists of both communities'. 'Objecting to "Bombay": Sexism More Than Communalism', *The Times of India* (15 April 1995).

romantic love in these films can reveal for feminism the gendering of the new 'Indian' as well as the complicity of 'women' in producing the exclusions of caste and community which enable the formation of the citizen-subject. A rethinking of feminist politics provoked by the questions raised by films like Maniratnam's might well have to proceed from a rethinking of those structuring terms of our daily experience as well as our politics: nationalism, humanism and secularism.

Hegemonic Spatial Strategies: The Nation-Space and Hindu Communalism in Twentieth-century India*

SATISH DESHPANDE

IN THIS ESSAY I attempt to explore the spatial strategies implicated in the hegemonic aspirations of Hindu communalism in India. More specifically, I try to identify the different ways in which 'Hindutva' seeks to redefine the nation-space—seeks, that is, to rearticulate the link between an imagined community and its territorial domain. Such rearticulations, I shall argue, aim to prise loose the nation-space from its moorings in alternative ideologies in order to relocate it within the framework of Hindu hegemony.

The following argument is divided into six sections: the first discusses the theoretical background and the specific utility of terms such

---

*This essay is part of an ongoing project on the relations among Hindutva, globalisation, and conceptions of the Indian nation. It was written for this volume, though its editors have graciously allowed the publication of a slightly shorter version in *Public Culture* (10: 2, 1998). Ancestor versions were presented at seminars in Mangalore and Hyderabad, and in the *Economic and Political Weekly*, 16 December 1995. I am grateful to respondents from the various audiences, and especially to Carol Breckenridge, Partha Chatterjee, Pradeep Jeganathan and Rama Malkote for encouragement and advice. Mary John has helped shape and refine the argument.

as 'spatial strategy' and 'nation-space'; the second provides an overview of contesting ideologies implicated in the emergence of the Indian nation-space; the third and fourth deal with the two major spatial ideologies that have shaped the history of the present, namely Savarkar's Hindutva and Nehruvian developmentalism; the fifth and longest section outlines the spatial strategies employed by contemporary Hindu communalism; the final section outlines the limitations of the preceding argument by mapping the roads not taken and ends with brief speculations on the mutual impact of globalisation and Hindutva as spatial strategies.

I

Space, Nation and Nation-Space in Contemporary Social Theory

Perhaps it is only by coincidence that recent social theory has simultaneously rediscovered the concepts of 'space' and 'nation'. Even so, this seems to offer rich theoretical possibilities, especially because the manner and context in which these concepts have been revived are particularly conducive for cross-cultivation. Contemporary social theory has begun to reconsider both space and nation in ways which attempt to transcend (or at least to sidestep) the traditional dichotomy between the material and the mental. Moreover, questions of power, domination, cultural difference, class and gender have been highlighted in both contexts. The way is thus cleared for exploring the spatial aspects of the nation—the imagined community considered as a nation-space—and the ways in which social groupings with hegemonic ambitions attempt to reshape and appropriate it.

It is a commonplace that an identifiable *territory* is a necessary (though not a sufficient) condition for the emergence of a strong sense of nation-ness. And though it was known that such a physical territory also functions at a meta-physical level as a collective representation, the full implications of this insight have become visible only recently. This is in large measure due to 'the reassertion of space in critical social theory' through the claim that space is not 'natural' but is *socially produced.*¹

Thus, contemporary social theory reminds us that nations inhabit a space that is simultaneously abstract (imagined, mental) and concrete (physical, geographical). These contrary aspects of the nation-space can be linked because of their common existence in (and only in) the social realm. But it is only when this potential linkage is *realized* through active social practices and processes that the nation-space can take shape. Nations are emergent phenomena: they become visible only when an ideological terrain and an identifiable territory can be cross-mapped on to each other to produce a sense of nation-ness shared by large numbers. Even after it has been successfully produced, the sense of nation-ness remains vulnerable to history and must be continually nurtured, partly through efforts to ensure that ideology and geography stay in synch.²

But recent theory also insists that both space and nation are implicated in power relations. The production of a sense of nation-ness clearly involves ideological and material contests. In a colonial context, for example, the contestants include not only nationalists and imperialists, but also the complex internal conflicts among different factions

---

¹ The phrase quoted forms the subtitle of Edward Soja, *Postmodern Geographies: The Reassertion of Space in Social Theory* (London: Verso, 1989); some other works that treat social space in innovative ways include Henri Lefebvre, *The Production of Space*, tr. D. Nicholson-Smith (Oxford: Blackwell, 1991); Pierre Bourdieu, *Distinction: A Social Critique of the Judgement of Taste*, tr. Richard Nice (Cambridge: Harvard University Press, 1984), especially part II, chs 2 & 3; Michel de Certeau, *The Practice of Everyday Life*, tr. Steven F. Randall (Berkeley: University of California Press, 1984), especially part III, chs VII–IX; Yi-Fu Tuan, *Space and Place: The Perspective of Experience* (Minneapolis: University of Minnesota Press, 1977); Robert David Sack, *Human Territoriality: Its Theory and History* (Cambridge: Cambridge University Press, 1986); and David Harvey, *The Postmodern Condition* (Oxford: Blackwell, 1989).

² For different perspectives on these and related issues, see, for example, Benedict Anderson, *Imagined Communities*, 2nd Edition (London: Verso, 1991), Anthony D. Smith, *The Ethnic Origins of Nations* (Oxford: Blackwell, 1986), especially chapter 8, and Immanuel Wallerstein and Etienne Balibar, *Race, Nation, Class: Ambiguous Identities* (London: Verso, 1991).

on either side, each with its own regional, class-based or ethnic constituency. With suitable inflections, the idea of the nation can thus be used as a weapon in a broader social struggle for hegemony. Similarly, social space is not merely an arena *in which* power relations 'happen', but also one of the means *with which* power is sought to be exercised. This is what gives meaning to the notion of spatial strategies.

SPATIAL STRATEGIES AND IDEOLOGICAL SUBJECTS

A spatial strategy not only unfolds *in* space, it is also *about*s pace—its appropriation, deployment or control. Such strategies are among those designed to support and maintain relations of power or of resistance. Considered as ideologies, spatial strategies can be seen as articulating the physical-material and mental-imaginative aspects of social space. In short, successful spatial strategies are able to link, in a durable and ideologically credible way, abstract (imagined) spaces to concrete (physical) places.

In one of his unpublished lectures, Michel Foucault offers some suggestive comments which, despite being fragmentary and inadequate, provide a useful starting point for theorizing the ideological practices that link abstract spaces to concrete places in politically productive ways.[3] Foucault's point of departure is the assertion that we live not in a 'homogeneous and empty space' but, on the contrary, 'inside a set of relations that delineates sites which are irreducible to one another'.[4] In justifying this assertion, he identifies two crucial kinds of sites: 'utopias' and 'heterotopias'.

Utopias are 'sites with no place' or 'fundamentally unreal spaces'.[5]

---

[3] I must clarify that my source here is the translated text of the notes which formed the basis of a lecture given by Foucault in 1967. This manuscript was 'not reviewed for publication by the author and [is] not part of the official corpus of his work'. Moreover, I am also taking considerable liberties with it. Thanks are due to Mary John for pointing out this essay.

[4] Michel Foucault, 'Of Other Spaces', unrevised text of a lecture given in March 1967, tr. Jay Miskowiec, in *Diacritics*, Spring 1986, p. 23.

[5] Foucault 1986, p. 24.

They are abstract spaces with no immediate or necessary reference to any concrete place. They may represent 'society itself in a perfected form' or else 'society turned upside down', but their relationship to concrete, physical places is indeterminate—they have, so to speak, no fixed address.

Heterotopias, on the other hand, are 'real places—places that do exist', that can be pointed out on a map, lived in, visited, or empirically experienced in an obvious fashion. But heterotopias are very special kinds of places because (and here I depart from Foucault's formulation) they mediate, in a mirror-like fashion, between utopias and ideological subjects. In other words, heterotopias enable—incite, compel, invite—people to see themselves reflected in some utopia. They are places which function as an ideological hinge, linking social subjects (people) with a possible-moral identity (utopia) that they could assume (inhabit).[6]

However, though heterotopias are real physical places, they are not products of nature: considerable ideological labour is needed to transform a given concrete site into a heterotopia. It is true that different places, due to their particular history, physical attributes or geographical location, are more or less suitable raw material for producing a heterotopia. Thus, the unique natural properties of a place do help, and may sometimes be a necessary ingredient; but they are never sufficient, always requiring additional efforts that consciously transform a mere place into a culturally meaningful, politically charged space.

One way of understanding spatial strategies is to think of them as ideological practices involved in the construction of heterotopias.

---

[6] Foucault's use of the mirror metaphor may be helpful in clarifying the relationship between the utopia and the heterotopia: 'The mirror is, after all, a utopia, since it is a placeless place. In the mirror, I see myself there where I am not, in an unreal, virtual space that opens up behind the surface . . . But it is also a heterotopia in so far as the mirror does exist in reality, where it exerts a sort of counteraction on the position that I occupy. . . . [I]t makes this place that I occupy at the moment when I look at myself in the glass at once absolutely real, connected with all the space that surrounds it, and absolutely unreal, since in order to be perceived it has to pass through this virtual point which is over there' (Foucault 1986, p. 24).

This is the sense in which spatial strategies attempt to tie an imagined space to a real place in such a way that these ties also bind people to particular identities, and to the political/practical consequences that they entail.

A concrete example may help, and there can be few better than Ayodhya, the small town in eastern Uttar Pradesh that is also among the most potent heterotopias in our recent history. Hardly an unreal place, Ayodhya has nevertheless acted as a mirror opening into the imagined space—the utopia—of Ramrajya, Hindutva, Hindu pride and so on. Seen from another angle, Ayodhya (or, more accurately, the Ram Janmabhoomi/Babri Masjid) as a heterotopian site has offered thousands of people (particularly young Hindu males from urban and semi-urban lower-middle-class backgrounds) a social identity as inhabitants of the utopia that it projects, namely the identity of the *kar sevak*. The transformation of this rural small town from merely another geographically specific place into a heterotopia was the result of a conscious spatial strategy—there was nothing 'natural' about it.

Although historically several other places have claimed the name, it seems reasonable to assume that this particular Ayodhya has always been roughly where it is today. It has been known for several centuries as the supposed birthplace of a mythological hero, who is also one of the principal deities in the Hindu pantheon. That a Hindu temple was supposed to have been destroyed here by a General representing a Muslim king—this too has been known for more than four and a half centuries. Thus, the 'natural endowments' of Ayodhya as a particular physical place have been the same for quite some time, but its successful transformation into a heterotopia is a very recent occurrence. This transformation has been effected by a spatial strategy that has, firstly, strengthened the link between the concrete place and the abstract, utopian space of Hindutva; and, secondly, forged a bond between the utopia and the people for whom it provides renewed sense of belonging, a bond in which the place-as-heterotopia acts as the glue.

This essay is an attempt to understand the spatial strategies of Hindutva that have had a significant impact on contemporary Indian society and politics. It tries to answer questions such as the following: What kinds of places has Hindutva successfully transformed into heterotopias? What specific strategies are behind this success? How do these strategies deal with their rivals—what kinds of contestation and struggle are spatial ideologies involved in? How do these ideologies overcome the refractory nature of the materials—both geographical and human—that they have to deal with? It should go without saying that I consider the effort to answer these questions to be part of the larger effort to fashion defensive and offensive counter-strategies.

II
The Emergence of the Indian Nation-Space

The French Marxist philosopher Henri Lefebvre has suggested that the spatiality of the nation-form originates neither in 'nature' nor in 'ideology' but in two specific 'moments'—a *market* (understood as 'a complex ensemble of commercial relations and communication networks') and *state violence* ('be it feudal, bourgeois, imperialist, or some other variety').[7] While it correctly identifies two crucial factors involved in shaping the nation-space, this is too bald and cryptic a suggestion to be helpful today.[8]

For 'the market' impacts upon the spatiality of the nation-form not directly but through complex mediations. Indeed, as Etienne Balibar has bluntly declared:

> It is quite impossible to 'deduce' the nation form from capitalist relations of production. Monetary circulation and the exploitation of wage labour do not logically entail a single determinate form of state. Moreover, the realization of space which is implied by accumulation—the world capitalist market—has within it an intrinsic tendency to transcend any national institutions that might be instituted by determinate fractions of social capital or imposed by 'extra-economic' means.[9]

'The state', too, can produce drastically different effects, whether

---

[7] Lefebvre 1991, p. 112, emphasis original.

[8] This work, hailed as a classic in the English-speaking West after its belated translation, proves a disappointment for those interested in the spatiality of the nation-form: the explicit discussion of this question is limited to one and a half pages (Lefebvre 1991, pp. 111–12).

[9] Wallerstein and Balibar 1991, p. 89.

intended or not, in different concrete historical instances. The complexity of the concrete forms of state and market, and their role in shaping nations is especially evident in the non-Western world colonized by the West.

Long before it adopted the garb of the modernist nation, 'India' first appeared on the Western world map as the fabled space of imperial desire. Imperialism, after all, is the spatial ideology *par excellence*. Predicated on the ability to fuse abstract spaces and concrete places into a political agenda, it is born (in the words of Edward Said) '[a]t the moment when a coincidence occurs between real control and power, the *idea* of what a given place was (could be, might become), and an *actual* place.'[10]

Imperialism, then, is the attempt to turn the colony into a particular kind of heterotopia, one designed to reflect the imperialist self in its own power and glory. Though they are no doubt also, as Foucault suggests, heterotopias of 'compensation' (for the messiness or the puny scale of the 'mother' country, for example), colonies are more often heterotopias of amplification and excess.[11] They are places that must act as a 'vent for surplus' not only in economic terms, but also for a surplus 'will to power' that overflows its spatial boundaries.

But the colony is also the site of a struggle, no matter how unequal, between colonizer and colonized.[12] For the same coincidence of idea,

---

[10] Edward Said, *Culture and Imperialism* (New York: Alfred Knopf, 1993), p. 78, emphasis added.

[11] Foucault 1986, p. 27. Foucault has rightly been questioned for his 'sanctioned ignorance' of the colonial enterprise: 'Foucault is a brilliant thinker of power-in-spacing, but the awareness of the topographical reinscription of imperialism does not inform his presuppositions', in Gayatri Chakravorty Spivak, *In Other Worlds: Essays in Cultural Politics* (New York: Routledge, 1988), p. 290. The text from which I have been quoting may in fact be the only place (though I seem to recall a passing reference in *Discipline and Punish* which I have been unable to re-locate) where Foucault deigns to mention the colony. But even here the examples are curiously idiosyncratic—seventeenth-century America and the 'extraordinary' Jesuit colonies of Paraguay—and strangely silent about what the word 'colony' has usually meant to vast parts of the globe.

[12] To say nothing of the struggles among the difference species of colonizers themselves—for example, between traders and missionaries, adventurers and administrators, or soldiers and civilians.

place and power provides ideological resources 'both for Westerners taking possession of land and, during decolonization, for resisting natives reclaiming it'.[13] Thus, imperialism and colonialism establish a spatial order and a territorial ideology that are then selectively utilized by an emergent nationalism to fashion its own spatial strategies.

The social history of the map provides an interesting illustration of the dual role of nationalism as both the antagonist and the inheritor of imperialism. If maps are associated with a morality, as Anthony Smith has suggested, then nationalism claims the imperial map as its legitimate legacy, but radically transforms the moral meaning of this map.[14] The first strategy of nationalism is almost invariably the invention of antiquity, the retroactive projection of a modern nation into an ancient past as timeless as it is perfect.[15] This implies the harnessing of time to inflect the meaning of space, investing the nationalist map—itself borrowed from imperialism—with a hoary history. With this moral repositioning, the colonial map can be simultaneously appropriated and abrogated, while colonialism itself is cut down to size as a recent and momentary aberration in a 'great and ancient tradition'.

In the construction of the nation as a heterotopian space, the historical (or more accurately 'historicised') map is followed by what Benedict Anderson has called the 'second avatar' of the map, the map-as-logo. Among the significant methods which enabled the linking of a particular physical geography to a specific imagined community as its homeland, the logo-map was given a major boost by new print technology which enabled its cheap mass production, allowing it to function as a 'pure sign' rather than as a 'compass to the world': 'Instantly recognizable, everywhere visible, the logo-map penetrated deep into the popular imagination, forming a powerful emblem for the anticolonial nationalisms being born.'[16]

More generally, nationalist spatial strategies attempted to translate the 'facts' of social geography into matters of patriotic faith and, ultimately, received experience. These included conscious efforts to

[13] Said 1993, p. 78.
[14] Smith 1986, p. 202.
[15] Ibid., p. 183.
[16] Anderson 1991, p. 173.

'historicise' or to anthropomorphise nature. The most obvious manifestation of this in the Indian case is the figure of 'Mother India'.[17] Through insistent and widely disseminated patriotic songs and writings, the physical features of the subcontinent—mountains, rivers, oceans and regions—were transformed into a common national heritage over which every Indian, even if s/he had never seen that particular part of the country, was invited to feel a sense of proprietary pride. India's national anthem, for example, is a typical nationalist device for converting geography into a deeply penetrative ideology.

However—and this point is crucial for the present discussion—such spatial strategies were hardly homogeneous or univocal, given that nationalism itself was not a monolithic entity. Two kinds of nationalism were particularly important in India, one based on religious-communal identities and one on a more explicitly modernistic ideology of development. These strands have not been mutually exclusive—indeed, at the level of political rhetoric, there was almost a significant overlap since each claimed (albeit with more or less stridency at different times) that it subsumed and superseded the other. Nevertheless, they represent distinct dialects within nationalist discourse deploying different spatial ideologies.

III

Savarkar's Hindutva: The Nation as Sacred Space

There was nothing inherent in nationalist spatial strategies that prevented their use by groups based on religious or regional identities. Indeed, there were areas in which religious groups—especially Hindus—were at a significant advantage, because they could build on the powerful base of sacred geographies. Given the absence of any *national* community that was supra- or non-religious, attempts to construct an 'imagined community' had to fall back on whatever existed in living memory that could be used to help concretise this new and unfamiliar

---

[17] Patricia Uberoi has alerted me to the fascinating variety of cartogenic (or map-like) ways in which Mother India has been represented in popular calendar art.

notion. Thus, even self-consciously non-communal nationalists could not afford to ignore the mnemonic aids and powerful, long-familiar metaphors offered by the popular sense of history and geography, a sense inevitably inflected by religion.[18]

Moreover, the concept as well as the concrete political identity of 'nationalism' was flexible enough to permit communalists not only to claim but also to sincerely believe that theirs was a truly nationalist rather than a sectarian group. Matters were further complicated by late-nineteenth-century religious revivalism, especially within Hinduism, which attempted with partial success to yoke together modernist ideals (science, rationality, technology, progress) and a reformed religious-spiritual creed that downplayed the more atavistic and contradictory aspects of religion (untouchability, the subordination of women, superstition or excessive ritualism). With the advent of this new 'improved' variety of religious identity it did not seem so self-evident, as it had before, that one had to *choose* between religion and spirituality on the one hand, and the ideals of modernism and science on the other.[19] It is in this context that we have to examine the co-implication of Savarkar's distinctly modernist Hindu communalism in the emergence of the Indian nation-space.[20]

'Hindutva is not a word but a history', declares Savarkar at the

[18] Jawaharlal Nehru is a good example, as several passages from his *An Autobiography* [1936] (Delhi: Oxford University Press, 1985) or *The Discovery of India* (New York: John Day, 1946) attest.

[19] Partha Chatterjee's well-known account in *Nationalist Thought and the Colonial World* (Delhi: Oxford University Press, 1986), for example, constructs the 'moment of departure' of Indian nationalist discourse in terms of the Bankim model: modern (Western) science and technology plus traditional (Indian) dharma and culture.

[20] I am deliberately avoiding an extended discussion of the various views on the nature and sources of communalism, and will provide only a minimalist working definition: for the purposes of this essay, communalism involves both (a) the pursuit of political goals through the open or hidden appeal to religious sentiments and/or identities; and (b) the exploitation of this sentiment to exclude other religious groups and to cultivate hostility towards them. Let me also make it clear that though I will discuss only Hindu communalism, this should not be taken to imply that I believe it to be the only kind existing. Finally, because it offers so striking an instance of a conscious spatial strategy, I am restricting myself here to a single work by a single author,

beginning of his self-consciously ideological tract, even as he proceeds to show how this history is closely and crucially intertwined with a *geography*.[21] He is very clear that the term which he did more than anyone else to popularize, and which is enjoying a major revival today—Hindutva, or 'Hindu-ness'—is not to be confused with Hindu*ism*, the latter being a 'sectarian' term, referring to the followers of the Hindu religion proper. Hindutva, on the other hand, includes members of other faiths (like Sikhism, Buddhism, or Jainism), though it cannot be accused of being over-generous in this regard.

Savarkar invokes the etymology of the word 'Hindu'—derived from the Sanskrit 'Sindhu', the name of the river, also known as the Indus, and also the word for ocean. He recounts a story in which Aryan tribes from Central Asia came to settle in the Indus basin, and subsequently spread out into the entire subcontinent while managing to retain their sense of nation-ness and cultural identity, until 'the valorous Prince of Ayodhya made triumphant entry in Ceylon and actually brought the whole land from the Himalayas to the seas under one sovereign sway'.[22]

This established the true geographical boundaries of the 'Sindhu' nation, from 'Atak to Cuttack', and from the 'Himalayas to the Cape' or, more classically, from 'Sindhu to Sindhu', or 'river (Indus) to (the two) oceans'. Savarkar takes great pains to stress these boundaries, and especially the versatility of the sanctified word *Sindhu*.[23] The reason for this excessive concern for these boundaries soon becomes obvious when his criteria for determining Hindutva are announced. These are

---

'Swatantraya Veer' ('Hindu Rashtra Darshan') of the *Sampurna Savarkar Wangmaya*, the collected works of Savarkar, published (and partially translated into English from the Marathi) by the Maharashtra Patrika Hindu Sabha in 1964. Unless otherwise specified, all subsequent quotations and page references are from the English translation in this edition, V.D. Savarkar, *Samagra Savarkar Wangmaya*, vol. 6 (Poona: Maharashtra Prantik Hindu Sabha, 1964).

[21] Savarkar 1964, pp. 2 ff.
[22] Ibid., pp. 7–8.
[23] 'The word Sindhu in Sanskrit does not only mean the Indus but also the sea—*samudrarashna* which girdles the southern peninsula—so that this one word sindhu points out almost all the frontiers of our land at a single stroke'. Savarkar 1964, p. 20.

stated as the three conditions of *pitrabhoo, jati* and *sanskriti*. The first insists that a 'Hindu' should be born within Hindustan and thus have a legitimate claim to this nation-space as the fatherland.[24] The second makes it obligatory for a Hindu to inherit Hindu 'blood' through natural parents.[25] But the most crucial interpretive move is in the third criterion, namely that of a shared culture or sanskriti. Savarkar very quickly shifts from the common meanings of culture to a very specific one, namely allegiance to a particular sacred geography. Thus, the final and ultimately all-important criterion for being a Hindu is that one's *punyabhoo* or holy land should coincide with the pitrabhoo so carefully demarcated earlier.

Savarkar's essentially territorial test for defining a 'Hindu' is thus based on the claim to a sacred geography. Among the three criteria that he proposes, it is clear that punyabhoo takes precedence over pitrabhoo and jati. In fact, it is easily demonstrated that the latter two criteria are neither necessary nor sufficient: the case of a hypothetical American who may become a Hindu[26] demonstrates that blood and fatherland are not essential; while the fate of the Christians and Muslims of India,[27] who are excluded despite their fulfilment of both these criteria, shows that they are certainly not sufficient. These instances

---

[24] It may be significant—though this must be examined further keeping in mind the vagaries of translation and the semantic context of the Marathi original, something which I have been unable to do as yet—that Savarkar appears to consistently prefer the term 'fatherland' to 'motherland' despite the continued (though sporadic) mention of the latter word.

[25] Unlike in the case of *pitrabhoo* and *matrabhoo*, Savarkar seems to have used some interpretive license here (and this is unlikely to be a matter of translation) for he uses the word 'blood' to mean *jati*, usually translated as caste. His argument is that 'Hindus' are all of one caste and (therefore) of one blood because of the frequency of *anuloma* and *pratiloma* (i.e. inter-caste) marriages over the centuries and even millennia. It is interesting to compare Savarkar's criteria with Schneider's comments on the parallels between kinship by blood and marriage *vs.* nationality by birth and naturalisation in David Schneider, 'Notes towards a theory of culture' in K. Basso and H. Selby (eds), *Meaning in Anthropology* (Albuquerque: University of New Mexico Press, 1976), pp. 215–16.

[26] Savarkar 1964, p. 54.

[27] Ibid., p. 72.

establish beyond doubt that the criterion of punyabhoo is both necessary and sufficient, making it the only relevant condition. This conclusion is further reinforced by the highly significant *exceptions* that Savarkar considers—the Sindhis, and emigrant Indians settled abroad. In the case of the former, textual interpretation is invoked to stress that *both* banks of the Indus are to be included within the borders of Hindustan, thereby conferring membership on the Sindhis. As for emigrants, they are to be considered Hindus no matter where they are because of their holy lands being in Hindustan.[28]

Theorists of human territoriality have suggested that it is a form of classification, a mode of communication, and a method of enforcing control.[29] Savarkar's definition of Hindutva includes all three features. As a spatial form of classification, it divides all those living in the Indian subcontinent into two clear camps, those who possess Hinduness or Hindutva and those who don't. Hindutva also functions as a mode of communication since 'it requires only a single marker or sign—the boundary', one moreover which 'combines direction in space and a statement about possession or exclusion'.[30] In the case of Hindutva, this boundary also acts as the means for legitimizing power over and control of the nation-space. Savarkar's claims amount to the assertion that only those marked by Hindutva have the moral-political right to constitute the nation, since their secular and religious-cultural interests are presumed to refer to the same geographical space.[31]

---

[28] This eagerness to include what are now called 'Non-Resident' Indians has been a continuous feature of the Hindu right and especially the Vishwa Hindu Parishad. See, for example, Peter Van der Veer, *Religious Nationalisms: Hindus and Muslims in India* (Delhi: Oxford University Press, 1996), p. 126.

[29] Sack 1986, pp. 21–6.

[30] Ibid., p. 32.

[31] While this is something that needs to be taken up in greater detail as a separate discussion, it may be worthwhile to note in passing that these spatial strategies raise doubts about the viability of Partha Chatterjee's distinction between the 'inner' and the 'outer' realms. He has suggested that this distinction, and its transposition into the spiritual/material dichotomy, was the characteristic feature of Indian nationalism. This enabled Indian nationalist discourse to acknowledge the undeniable dominance of the West in the outer/material realm, while simultaneously reserving the inner/spiritual domain as its '*sovereign territory*'. See Partha Chatterjee, *The Nation and its*

Considered at a more general level, the basic spatial strategy behind Savarkar's notion of Hindutva has for its central theme the redefining of the nation-space as a sacred space: the claim that the nation is, and ought to be, formed in the shape of a punyabhoo, a holy land. This serves to invest a geographical space—the actual physical extent of the Indian nation—with a religious essence (the unanalysable relation of sacredness) that 'outsiders' can never experience or comprehend, and which forever and completely defines 'insiders'.

It is important to note that the basic premises of the punyabhoo model continue to be relevant today in a variety of contexts that go far beyond the narrowly communal. Thus, David Mandelbaum has argued that there exists a 'traditional basis for the larger national identification' in the shape of 'the idea, mainly engendered by Hindu religion but shared by those of other religions as well, that there is an entity of India to which all inhabitants belong. The Hindu epics and legends . . . teach that the stage for the gods was nothing less than the entire land and the land remains one religious setting for those who dwell in it. That sense was and is continually confirmed through pilgrimage.'[32]

Emphasizing the importance of pilgrimages in particular, Peter Van der Veer suggests that their significance may have increased in the colonial and postcolonial periods. Greater prosperity among the

---

Fragments: Colonial and Postcolonial Histories (Delhi: Oxford University Press, 1994), p. 6, emphasis added; see also Chatterjee 1986. However, such an analysis cannot accommodate Savarkar's spatial strategies, which do not necessarily restrict the sphere of nationalism or spirituality to the 'inner' realm. Moreover, this directly contradicts important nationalist-communalist initiatives (which I have been unable to discuss here) like that of B.G. Tilak, who politicized the 'Ganesh utsav' and transformed it from the household festival (which it traditionally was) into a public affair involving ten days of collective celebrations climaxed by an immersion procession. See Bernard Cohn, *An Anthropologist Among the Historians and Other Essays* (Delhi: Oxford University Press, 1987), pp. 125–6, for a brief discussion of Tilak, and Faisal Fatehali Devji, 'Gender and the Politics of Space: The Movement for Women's Reform, 1857–1900', in Zoya Hasan (ed.), *Forging Identities: Gender, Communities and the State* (New Delhi: Kali for Women, 1994), pp. 22–37, for a different view on the spatial dynamics of gender and Muslim religious identities in colonial India; see also part III below.

[32] Quoted in Van der Veer, 1996, p. 120.

landowning classes and the emergence of a secure urban elite went along with unprecedented improvements in the communication and transport infrastructure to increase the frequency and scope of pilgrimages. Moreover, 'Western discourse on the nation as a territorially based community colluded with religious discourse on sacred space' to influence the geographical dimension of the nation idea.[33]

It may be appropriate to conclude this section with a snippet of information: in the 1959 border negotiations with China, Jawaharlal Nehru argued that India's borders were not colonial creations but had been part of her 'culture and tradition for the past two thousand years or so', while a White Paper on this subject (prepared by the Foreign Ministry) 'invoked support from the Rig Veda, the *Mahabharata*, and the *Ramayana*'.[34]

IV

Modernist Geographies of Development: The Nehruvian Era

As recognized by many scholars, the mainstream of the Indian national movement led by the Congress included a broad spectrum of tendencies that based themselves on implicit or explicit appeals to Hindu religion.[35] These ranged from the militantly communal stance of a Tilak or a Savarkar to the much more complex but nevertheless recognizably

---

[33] Ibid., p. 122.

[34] G. Balachandran, 'Religion and Nationalism in Modern India', in Kaushik Basu and Sanjay Subrahmanyam (eds), *Unravelling the Nation: Sectarian Conflict and India's Secular Identity* (Delhi: Penguin Books, 1996), p. 116, citing Ainslee T. Embree, *Imagining India: Essays on Indian History* (Delhi: Oxford University Press, 1989), p. 16. Balachandran goes on to comment: 'This Bharat of the Brahmanical ideology' was not only "made congruent" with the 'India of the West's imagination, but also with the actual boundaries established at the end of Britain's nineteenth-century conquest of the subcontinent.'

[35] For example, Louis Dumont, 'Communalism and Nationalism', in *Homo Hierarchicus*, Revised English Edition (Chicago: University of Chicago Press [1964] 1980), Bipan Chandra, *Communalism in Modern India* (New Delhi: Vikas, 1984), pp. 47 ff., etc.

Hindu approach of Gandhi. Indeed, as Nehru notes in his autobiography, the explicitly secular tendency (as different from tendencies that believed in coalitional arrangements across communities, especially Hindu–Muslim unity) within the Congress was a relatively weak one, its main proponent being Nehru himself. Given these conditions, it is difficult to say what the specific course of our post-independence history would have been were it not for two decisive but contingent events.

The assassination of Mahatma Gandhi by Nathuram Godse and the latter's links with the RSS stigmatised the Hindu right and relegated it to the sidelines of national politics for more than a decade. Similarly, the sudden death of Sardar Vallabhbhai Patel in 1950 left the communal right within the Congress leaderless, and paved the way for the emergence of Nehru as the undisputed leader of the party, enabling him to play a decisive role in post-independence India.

The period from independence up to the mid-1960s—the Nehruvian era—has to be understood in the light of these events. If this era is now seen as the golden age of secularism, this is mainly because of the successful 'regionalizing' of communalism during this period, especially in the northern heartland and in the west. The 'golden age' of secularism was predicated not on the defeat of communalism, but rather its *repression* and *displacement* from the national public sphere.

If the nation-space in Savarkar's Hindutva was based on a sacred geography, the Nehruvian nation-space was shaped by an *economic geography*. In so far as the positive ideas of Nehruvian secularism had their roots in the Western model of a secular-modern nation and were insufficiently indigenised, they could only exist in the newly created national sphere—they did not strike roots at the regional level. This was in keeping with Nehru's essentially economistic understanding of communalism. Nehru believed that the legal guarantee of equality of citizenship regardless of religion, caste, creed or other social attributes would render communalism obsolete.[36] By refusing to guarantee this equality, the colonial state was keeping communalism alive in order to play off one community against another. A national state would

---

[36] Chatterjee, 1986, pp. 141–3, see also note 36.

remedy this, and thus end religious conflicts: 'Class conflicts there might well be, but not religious conflicts, except in so far as religion itself represented some vested interest'.[37]

The Nehruvian era amply demonstrates the centrality of the economy for the nationalism of the time. The major spatial strategy of this era is to foreground the economy—the nation is figured primarily as an economic space. It is this economic geography that the post-independence generation has grown up with. Powerfully disseminated through schools and all the state media, the nation becomes a space of production, and is imagined via economic associations. Places are named, so to speak, economically: Kodarma is 'mica', Ankleshwar is 'petroleum', Rourkela is 'steel', Bhakra Nangal is 'power', Coimbatore is 'textiles', and so on. These 'sites of development' were the principal heterotopias fashioned by the Nehruvian regime. They invited the citizen of the new nation to see themselves reflected in the mirror of technological progress and development, and to identify themselves as fellow travellers on the journey towards this common goal. The telos of development is thus not unlike that of the pilgrimage, and indeed, the comparison was often explicitly invoked.

When compared to the sacred geography of Hindutva, this spatial vision appears to be remarkably inclusive, even if ideologically naive in its substitution of socio-economic for religious-cultural identities. But closer scrutiny proves that exclusions are being practised here as well, except that they operate along very different axes.[38] Though it is yet to be written, a new spatial history of Nehruvian developmentalism—which goes beyond the naivete of treating 'regional imbalances' as merely another failure of plan implementation—will no doubt uncover the multidimensional relations of domination established along the inter-regional, rural-urban, and city-megacity axes. In the most obvious case, this spatial logic is surely at least partly responsible for a variety of contemporary regional-ethnic movements, from those in the North-East to Punjab, Kashmir, Jharkhand, and Uttarakhand. However, the precise ways in which this causality works may not be obvious, as the instructive contrast between Punjab and Jharkhand

[37] Jawaharlal Nehru, quoted in Chatterjee, 1986, p. 141.
[38] I thank Partha Chatterjee for reminding me of this.

indicates. If the former demonstrates the discontents that successful development can produce, the latter, as the locus *par excellence* of the Nehru–Mahalanobis model of development based on heavy industries, illustrates the axiom that 'development' need not erase the backwardness of the region where it occurs. Jharkhand contains five major steel plants or virtually all of India's steel industry; most of the major coal, iron ore and mica mines; and several large heavy engineering and chemical plants. Also located here is the nation's largest integrated river valley project for hydroelectric power-generation and irrigation. (All this does not even begin to account for the varied forest-based products of the region.) Yet Jharkhand and its original inhabitants remain backward and extremely poor.

While hindsight may have exposed it as (at worst) a fraud or (at best) an illusion, we still need to ask how Nehruvian developmentalism managed to seem so inclusive to so many for so long. Despite their apparently self-evident status, it may still be useful to focus attention on 'development' and 'nation' as the two main planks on which the hegemonic consensus of this era was erected.[39] More precisely, Nehruvian hegemony was the product of the synergistic union of these ideas—their ideological 'cementing'—by the nationalist movement in India during the first half of the twentieth century. The interweaving of 'development' and 'nation' produced a strong and durable ideological fabric, one side of which might be called 'the developing nation' and the other 'national development'. This pair worked to deflect the scepticism generated by either concept towards the other: questions of national identity were referred to 'development', and doubts about the development process were referred to 'the nation'.

Given that in India the nation was visualized specifically as a community of patriotic producers, the Nehruvian nation-space could identify as 'other' only the shirker—i.e. the person who refused to participate in the collective task of 'nation building'.[40] It is in this sense

---

[39] I have attempted to explore this theme elsewhere: Satish Deshpande, 'Ethnos, Economy and the Postcolonial Nation', a paper presented at the international conference on 'Democracy, Ethnicity and Development in South and South-East Asia', International Center for Ethnic Studies, Colombo, Sri Lanka, August 1993.

[40] See Satish Deshpande, 'Imagined Economics: Styles of Nation Building in

that the Nehruvian nation-space seems to be inclusive, because the 'other' has no particular *cultural* identity, except the generic one of the anti- or non-modernist. By contrast, Hindutva claimed a nation-space where the major axis of exclusion is cultural—the 'others' who arouse anxiety are indelibly marked by an essential cultural difference.

However, the other side of the apparent inclusiveness of the Nehruvian nation-space was an elitism that operated in an universalistic (rather than particularistic) mode. If the 'other' was culturally unmarked, so was the dominant group.[41] Thus, the Nehruvian era created and privileged a pan-Indian elite that could, by and large, afford to cut loose its regional moornings. Not only did this elite seem to be 'placeless', it also appeared to be 'caste-less' and 'class-less': a truly secular, modern elite. It spoke in the modernist idiom of secular nationalism, scientific technology and economic development; by adopting this idiom, the elite was able to render invisible its own ascriptive markers. The fact that it was almost exclusively upper-caste and middle-class, and that it came from a very select cultural background and a specific set of regions could become 'transparent'—and thus be made to vanish. Consisting of the rising technocracy, the professional-managerial class, intellectuals and top bureaucrats, this was an elite which thought of itself in purely 'national' terms, whose native habitat was the deterritorialized space called New Delhi.[42]

The Chinese war marked the beginning of the end of the Nehruvian

---

Twentieth-century India' in *Journal of Arts and Ideas*, December 1993, nos. 25–6, pp. 5–35, for an extended treatment of this and related themes concerning the principal ideological models of the economy in twentieth-century India.

[41] It now seems to me that a more accurate description of this situation might be that those who are labelled as 'anti-development' are made to carry the burden of an 'excessive' cultural identity, while the modernist forces lay claim to a more culturally abstract (and in this sense understated) identity. But this line of argument needs to be considered more carefully in the complex context of an identity politics 'before its time', i.e. during the Nehru era. In a certain sense, contemporary anti-developmentalist and anti-modernist positions (Ashis Nandy's would be the best known in India) can be seen as trying to self-consciously reclaim this 'excessively cultural' (or essentialist) identity and invest it with a positive critical-moral charge.

[42] As Sudipta Kaviraj has sarcastically observed, one of the consequences of the Nehru era is the situation where 'it seems only those people who are unable to speak

era; it not only discredited Nehru as a statesman, but also re-legitimized the jingoistic, Partition-era rhetoric of the Hindu right. The long-simmering discontent among the marginalised power brokers and regional elites surfaced with Nehru's death, which also coincided with a break in the process of planned development brought about by war, drought and an economic crisis. Indira Gandhi could take control of the Congress only by splitting it, and her reign inevitably marked the advent of the era of electoral arithmetic based on vote banks and an implicit communal logic.

The inclusive spatial sense of Nehruvian developmentalism was overtaken by an anxiety about the vulnerability of the borders of the nation. At the same time, the ideological privileges bestowed on 'national' development projects could no longer be maintained. They had to negotiate with the more immediate and localized sense of social space in the form of several 'sons of the soil' (especially around public-sector jobs), as well as movements projecting assertive regional identities that refused any longer to dissolve easily into the national. As the hegemony of Nehruvianism crumbled, the nation-space became increasingly vulnerable to contestations, especially since neither the official notion of secularism nor the Nehruvian vision of the national community had strong local roots. With the dream of egalitarian economic development becoming more and more implausible, new ways of visualizing the nation-space began to compete for control of the ideological high ground within civil society.

V

Contemporary Hindutva and Its Heterotopias[43]

A first approximation of the overall spatial character of Hindutva is that it is an attempt to reverse the spatial logic of Nehruvianism in

---

any Indian language are the real repositories of Indian nationalism', in Sudipta Kaviraj, 'Capitalism and the Cultural Process', in *Journal of Arts and Ideas*, May 1990, n. 19, p. 69.

[43] Unlike in the previous section, where I was referring to the term that Savarkar employed (which is why I had retained his capitalization of 'Hindutva'), in this section

order to return to Savarkar's vision of the nation-space. If Nehru claimed that dams and steel plants were the temples of modern India, Hindutva stands him on his head and insists that temples are to contemporary (post-modern?) India what steel plants and dams were to modern (Nehruvian) India.

The socio-spatial dimensions of communalism as a process of 'competitive desecularization'[44] involve an effort to re-sacralize the nation-space. Desecularization is directly dependent upon the strategic deployment of essentialism. It is in the name of religious essences—un-analysable, un-contestable truths that are self-evident to the faithful—that the 'flattening effect' of an even-handed secularism is denounced. Against this drab and debilitating anonymity, communalism asserts the privileges of non-negotiable, uniquely different identities. Where the heterotopia of the steel plant or the hydroelectric project is unable or unwilling to accord much importance to cultural distinctions, Hindutva's new heterotopias are designed to serve precisely as markers of irreducible cultural difference.

Hindutva may be seen as exploiting the ideological vulnerability of the 'placeless' universalism of the Nehruvian nation-space, or its

---

I am using the lower-case term 'hindutva' in a contemporary and rather broad sense as an abbreviation for both the general ideology associated with, and the socio-political movement led by, the neo-Hindu right-wing grouping crystallized around the so-called 'Sangh Parivar'. Compare Tapan Basu, Pradip Datta, Sumit Sarkar, Tanika Sarkar, Sambudha Sen, *Khaki Shorts Saffron Flags*, Tracts for the Times, n. 1 (New Delhi: Orient Longman, 1993), p. 1, fn. This is obviously an imprecise definition in that it does not recognize the many distinct (and sometimes contrary) tendencies contained within the same overall phenomenon. However, I believe that it will surface for the purpose of this essay. Moreover, when speaking of the overall spatial character and the particular spatial strategies adopted by 'hindutva', I am speaking of the ideological effects pertaining to social space that are being produced through the logic of hindutva as a socio-political force. I do not mean to imply, when referring to these ideological effects, that they are necessarily intended or consciously strategised by identifiable individuals or groups—but I don't rule out this possibility either. In short, while the coherence of Hindutva is to be sought in terms of *effects* rather than *intentions*, the co-presence of both is a matter for empirical investigation rather than theoretical prejudice.

[44] Achin Vanaik, *India: The Painful Transition* (London: Verso, 1993).

failure to articulate abstract space to more personalized concrete places: heterotopias like the steel plant could not project a sufficiently *intimate* relationship with particular individuals. The overall strategy of the Hindu right today thus involves an effort to rekindle a personalized commitment to particular places that are nevertheless embedded within the abstract social space of Hindutva.

Why has Hindutva rejuvenated itself during the 1980s and 1990s in particular? Part of the negative side of the explanation, as suggested in the previous section, is to be found in the erosion of the foundations of Nehruvianism. Perhaps one of the reasons on the positive side has to do with the creation and development of the communications network. Initially established as part of the Nehruvian scheme to spread the message of national development, radio and especially television have undergone radical changes in the decades since Nehru. The dramatic expansion of television broadcasting in the 1980s (with the 1982 Asian Games held in Delhi as the springboard) created for the first time in Indian history a national network organized around a medium more powerful than either print or radio.[45]

Frederik Barth has suggested that culturally defined groups—like ethnic or religious groups—also constitute a 'field of communication'.[46] The expansion of television and especially the historic *Ramayana* tele-serial can be said to have achieved this for the Hindu right. While this was hardly a conspiracy, the specific consequences of this tele-serial, which invited a vast hitherto un-addressed audience to enter into a particular sort of 'narrative contract'[47] with Hindutva, cannot be exaggerated. The religious teleserials of the 1980s prepared the ground for

---

[45] For suggestive discussion of this crucial episode in the cultural politics of contemporary India, see Ashish Rajadhyaksha, 'Beaming Messages to the Nation', in *Journal of Arts and Ideas*, May 1990, n. 19, pp. 33–53, and Arvind Rajagopal, 'The Rise of National Programming: The Case of Indian Television', in *Media, Culture, and Society*, January 1993.

[46] Frederik Barth, 'Introduction', in Frederik Barth (ed.), *Ethnic Groups and Boundaries: The Social Organization of Cultural Difference* (London: George Allen & Unwin, 1969).

[47] Sudipta Kaviraj, 'The Imaginary Institution of India', in Partha Chatterjee and G. Pandey (eds), *Subaltern Studies VII* (Delhi: Oxford University Press, 1992).

the Hindutva movement, as its leaders have themselves acknowledged,[48] by constructing a new, potent and abstract social-space mediated by the television screen, which could be readily cross-mapped on to Savarkar's punyabhoo model of the nation-space.

These rather cryptic assertions can be best clarified through a more concrete discussion of the specific spatial strategies of Hindutva. I would like to suggest that there are at least three distinct kinds of heterotopias that Hindutva has attempted to construct in our recent history: those centred on places, areas and routes.

PLACES OF ESSENCE: SACRED SITES

The strategy based on the site involves two facets. First, a chosen place, spot or site is invested with some unique particularity, or if it already has some such claims, then these claims are refined, amplified and particularized; the general objective is to (re)construct the site as the unique bearer of a singular essence. However—and this is the second aspect of the strategy—the criterion of selection is that the spot must implicate the 'other' deeply enough to preclude easy extrication. The combined result is an inexorably zero-sum logic that (if successfully implemented) places Hindutva in a win-win position *vis-à-vis* its (almost always Muslim) enemy: if they surrender the spot, victory is declared and celebrated as the defeat of the Muslim; if they don't give it up, then this is evidence of Muslim fanaticism, which in turn justifies escalating the conflict.

The site-based strategy is best exemplified by the campaign for the 'liberation' of the Babri Masjid-Ram Janmabhoomi in Ayodhya (as briefly discussed in Section I above). By declaring it to be the one-and-only brithplace of Ram, the Janmabhoomi is invested with a sacred essence that appears to be self-evidently non-negotiable.[49] Since a masjid shares the very same spot, it again seems obvious that the masjid must go, particularly since it is alleged to have been built after the

---

[48] Arvind Rajagopal, 'Ram Janmabhoomi, Consumer Identity and Image-Based Politics', in *Economic and Political Weekly*, v. XXIX, 2 July 1994, n. 27, pp. 1659–68.

[49] Arvind Rajagopal has suggested that the theme of a birthplace has special spatial and psychological significance (Rajagopal, 1994, p. 1662).

destruction of a temple, even if this took place four and a half centuries ago. The whole point is to construct a site of confrontation where faith meets faith in a fight to the finish. The Janmabhoomi controversy (and the numberless mosque/temples in Kashi, Mathura and elsewhere that are said to be awaiting liberation) emerge as answers to the question: Where (and how) can temple-construction be made indistinguishable from mosque-demolition? It is pertinent to note, however, that within the implacable logic of '*Mandir wahin banayenge*', construction has always been subordinated to demolition.[50] This is amply borne out by the manner in which the campaigns to 'reclaim' mosques in Kashi and Mathura are periodically heated up while the project of building the temple at the Babri Masjid site is allowed to go cold.

Although it invokes unique essences, there is nothing essential about the site-based strategy itself—its strategic-instrumental aspects can be readily analysed. However, the more successful the strategy, the more it seems to naturalize itself, making it harder to produce persuasive analyses. Or, to put it simply, the success of the strategy sacralises the subject at least partially, creating doubts about the limitations and biases of an atheistic perspective on a theistic experience or phenomenon.[51] Let me, therefore, briefly discuss the flag-hoisting controversy at Hubli—a less successful and less familiar example of the site-based strategy, and also one where I can coincidentally claim the status of an 'honorary' insider.[52]

---

[50] This was a popular slogan of the BJP-VHP movement, which its leaders (especially the hard-liners like Vinay Katiyar, Murli Manohar Joshi or Sadhvi Rithambhara) were always getting crowds to repeat at public meetings, with the characteristic emphasis on the middle word: 'Mandir *wahin* banayenge'. ('We're going to build a temple *right there*'.) In a context where several compromise solutions for building a temple without demolishing the mosque were being mooted, this adamant insistence on that very spot was a pivotal aspect of the Hindutva campaign. The point is that it was precisely such an 'unreasonable' insistence on those few square metres of land being the exact birthplace of Ram hundreds and thousands of years ago—this refusal to budge 'even one inch'—that was worn as a badge of honour by the movement.

[51] For example, I wonder whether many 'otherwise reasonable' people I know well—who refused to object to any aspect of the Janmabhoomi agitation except the fact and/or the manner of the demolition itself—would be convinced by my account.

[52] Hubli is in northern Karnataka, about 100 kms south of the Maharashtra border;

The Idgah Maidan is a roughly triangular piece of land about half the size of a football field in what has now become central or 'downtown' Hubli. In 1922, it was located on the outskirts of the city, and the British municipal administration leased it, for a period of 999 years at a nominal rent of one rupee per annum, to a Muslim cultural organization, the Anjuman-e-Islam, Hubli. However, the historical evidence (which is undisputed, though its precise legal implications are contested) suggests that the lease merely formalized what was established usage, the area having been associated with Muslim organizations and activities (including especially the Id prayers) for about two centuries or more. During the 1970s, with the real-estate value of the land having increased dramatically, the Anjuman's attempt to build a school-cum-commercial complex on one part of the plot was challenged in court by 'public spirited individuals' and a stay order has been in force, the matter being currently in the Supreme Court.

Against this background, attempts were begun by Hindu communal interests in the 1990s to recruit this issue for the Hindutva campaign. Partly inspired by the example of BJP minister Murli Manohar Joshi's symbolic hoisting of the Indian tricolour in Srinagar, local affiliates and allies of the VHP, RSS, BJP and Shiv Sena formed front organizations (such as the Rashtra Dhwaja Gaurava Samrakshana Samiti—or Society to Defend the Honour of the National Flag) and launched an agitation demanding the right to hoist the national flag at the Idgah Maidan on Independence Day and Republic Day. Since the unconcealed intent of this agitation was to undermine the Anjuman's right to the land, the organization refused to allow the flag-hoisting. Largely

---

it was formerly part of the Bombay Presidency. The twin cities of Hubli-Dharwad form the third-largest urban conglomeration in Karnataka (almost the same size as Mysore, but much smaller than Bangalore) with an area of about 200 square kilometres and a population of about 650,000 according to the 1991 census. During the last decade, it has earned a place on the national map of communal violence, with Hindu-Muslim 'riots' taking place almost every year. It is also the town in which my parents grew up and currently live, and the town that comes closest to being my own home town: although I have never been a resident, I have visited it regularly throughout my life.

Hegemonic Spatial Strategies 193

because of their fear of law-and-order problems, the courts have always refused permission to hoist the flag on the maidan. The mass campaign by the Hindutva organizations to hoist the flag in defiance of court orders has resulted in mob violence, repeated imposition of curfew and police actions—including shootings in which at least five persons have died and dozens been injured since 1993. During 1995–6 the Janata Dal government in Karnataka (then headed by Deve Gowda, who later became prime minister of India) claimed to have 'solved' the problem, persuading the Anjuman itself to organize a largely state-sponsored ceremony to hoist the flag on the national anniversaries (26 January and 15 August).[53]

In terms of the present argument, therefore, the Idgah Maidan campaign represents a variation on the Ayodhya strategy. It attempts to shift from a religious to a secular-nationalist idiom of contestation, but the overall logic is the same: an unreasonable insistence on a particular site; the blocking of all negotiations and compromises; and a systematic effort to trap the adversary in a lose-lose situation—allow flag-hoisting and risk losing the land, or disallow it and jeopardize your nationalist credentials. However, it is the *differences* between Ayodhya and Hubli that are instructive, especially in their ability to illuminate the process by which a particular site is (so to speak) 're-placed' as a heterotopia.

---

[53] As an illustration of the larger argument, what follows can only be a poor substitute for a proper study of the 'visual-spatial politics' of the Idgah Maidan, a project I plan to undertake separately. Apart from my own preliminary inquiries, I have relied on the following documentary sources: People's Democratic Forum (PDF), *Flag Without Tears: A Report on the Hubli Idga Maidan Issue* (Bangalore, December 1994); Sanjeev Kulkarni, *Idga Maidandalli Dhwajarohanada Vivada: Ondu Vishleshane* (Flag Hoisting Controversy at Idgah Maidan: An Analysis) (Dharwad: Janatantra Samaj [Citizens for Democracy], August 1994); and Karnataka High Court, Judgment delivered by Justice R.V. Vasanthakumar, in the Regular Second Appeal nos. 754/82 C/W. 1 of 1983, between Anjuman-e-Islam, Hubli, and the Karnatak Board of Wakfs (Appellants); and B.S. Shettar and 92 others, Hubli-Dharwad Municipal Corporation, and State of Karnataka (Respondents), delivered 18 June 1992. I am indebted to Dr Sanjeev Kulkarni in Dharwad, Ms. Chandrika Naik of the *Indian Express*, Hubli, and Ms. Sudha Sitaraman of the PDF, Bangalore, who (besides providing access to the documentary sources cited above) gave generously of their time and expertise in helping to deepen my understanding of the issue.

While it is situated within the overall framework of Hindutva, the Idgah Maidan campaign depended—or so I would like to suggest—on two specific types of shared experiences. One is the concrete, experiential recognition of the Maidan as a *public* space, and the other is the *visual-symbolic* impact of its location.

The open space that comprises the Idgah Maidan has always been used—and used intensively—by the general public. I remember it from my childhood as the preferred parking space for the carts and bullocks of vegetable farmers from nearby villages; light trucks and tractor trailers have joined them in the last ten to fifteen years. There have always been immovable groups of cattle and the vendors commonly found in such places, selling everything from cucumbers to combs. One corner of the Maidan has long been used as a public urinal. On any given day, the centre might be occupied by large family groups from the village squatting in the dust to eat their packed lunches; rope markers braiding long strands of coir, twine or nylon; or a small travelling amusement park for children with a giant wheel, swings and merry-go-round. There are even stories (whose accuracy I have not checked) of nationalist leaders (including Gandhi, Nehru and, more plausibly, Tilak) having addressed public meetings there.

The point I am making is that such a massive accumulation of popular memory of the Maidan as a public, 'non-exclusive' space (except for the two days in the year that Id prayers are offered) affords an excellent point of purchase for the Hindutva strategy of questioning 'Muslim' rights to the land. The success of this strategy depends on rendering ideologically invisible the countless other instances of encroachment of public space by all sorts of commercial establishments, individuals and groups that can be observed within walking distance of the Maidan. 'Muslims pampered by the government' can thus be made to bear the burden of the genuine frustration and anger that people feel at the vanishing of urban commons and open spaces.

The other crucial aspect—and this is perhaps what precipitated the issue in the first place—is the visual affront to the Hindutva sensibility of a large and imposing 'Muslim' building on the Maidan. For it was in 1972 that the Maidan first became controversial, with the launching of a successful 'public interest' litigation against the Anjuman's plan to build a school-cum-commercial complex at one end of the Maidan.[54] In order to appreciate this point it is necessary to understand the contemporary location of the Maidan in the social field of vision.

With the growth and development of the city, the Idgah Maidan now occupies the very heart of the city, adjacent to Traffic Island, which is the arterial junction of the main streets that lead on to highways headed for Bangalore, Hyderabad and Pune/Bombay. In the centre of the roundabout is a large equestrian statue of Rani Channamma, celebrated martyr of armed resistance to the British. (The regent/queen of Kittur, a small principality about 50 kms north of Hubli, she is to Karnataka what the Rani of Jhansi is to north India.) Along the base of this plot of land, which resembles a triangle with its apex lopped off, is a large shopping complex dominated by the biggest of the many Kamat restaurants in the city. (Incidentally, this well-known chain and its founder, Rangappa Kamat, began their careers in Hubli, which is still the business's headquarters.) Along one side of the triangle is a series of new multistoreyed commercial complexes housing the offices of multinational and large Indian firms, upscale shops and arcades. Along the other are local courts, the office of the Assistant Commissioner of Police, and the offices of the Hubli–Dharwad Municipal Corporation.[55]

Given the centrality—in every sense of the word—of the Idgah Maidan, the prospect of a prominent visual mark of Muslim presence (in the form of the proposed building) cannot be entertained within the Hindutva worldview. The flag-hoisting campaign was the logical extension of the drive to contain, and if possible erase, this sign of Muslim presence in the heart of the city, sharing social space with all

---

[54] Karnataka High Court 1983, p. 6.

[55] Long after this description was written, I discovered to my amazement that I had failed to mention a large, much-frequented Sai Baba temple sandwiched between the municipal courts and the Assistant Commissioner of Police. While this oversight surely indicates my own biases, it also reinforces the general point that even such undeniably physical realities as buildings and landscapes are located (and therefore seen or not seen in particular ways) within a socially conditioned field of vision.

the other visual markers of (Hindu) power, wealth and domination. Such antipathy to the visual traces of contemporary Muslim presence—especially if they seem assertive, prosperous, or more generally fail to display marks of subordination—are not unusual in a communalised society.[56] Once again, this is not a situation unique to Hubli but is common to numerous Indian cities and towns with significant Muslim populations.

While these two features, namely, the displaced anger of the urban middle classes at shrinking public spaces, and the fear that the ocular hierarchies proper to a Hindu-dominated social space might be disturbed, enabled the conversion of Idgah Maidan into a heterotopia, perhaps they also restricted its scope and strength in comparison to Ayodhya. A probable explanation is that, first, the Maidan's claim to being a site of unique essence was much weaker; and second, that this essence was not abstract—and therefore not 'portable'—enough. Although it was provoked by fears and frustrations common to other locations, the Maidan campaign had no effective way of accessing

[56] Thus, for example, Ratna Naidu describes her experience of going to Bidar for fieldwork shortly after a communal riot there: 'The symbols of culture associated with an ethnic enemy evoke in us a psychic event . . . rather than realistic recognition. I recall the uncanny fear which I experienced when the bus speeding me to fieldwork (in Bidar) suddenly took a turn to reveal a skyline studded with the beautiful domes of Islamic culture . . . Later introspection made me realize that the absurd fear was that of a Hindu (even educated and cosmopolitan), on the eve of close interaction with an isolated *Muslim*-dominated small town. I have tried to analyse the fear and am certain that it was an instinctive reaction to the architectural character of the city skyline': Ratna Naidu, *The Communal Edge to Plural Societies: India and Malaysia* (Delhi: Institute of Economic Growth and Vikas Publishing House, 1980), p. 149, emphasis in the original. And in his study of the growth of communalism in rural Marathwada, Thomas Blom Hansen reports on the Shiv Sena-led unemployed youth of large semi-urban villages agitating against Muslim encroachments on public space; the explicit aims of the Sena are to 'scale down the "undue visibility" of the Muslims, and it wanted, plain and simple, the business opportunities at the bus-stand for the Hindu youth.' This is amplified by an on-the-spot conversation with a respondent who points out to Hansen the visual offensiveness of Muslim structures. See Thomas Blom Hansen, 'The Vernacularisation of Hindutva: The BJP and Shiv Sena in Rural Maharashtra', in *Contributions to Indian Sociology*, July–December 1996, v. 30(2), p. 192.

these shared experiences, and worked well only with those with some first-hand experience of the site. As an essence, 'the birth place of Ram' was powerful and abstract enough to attract huge numbers of kar sevaks who had never been to Ayodhya before. However, the demand to hoist the national flag at the Idgah Maidan, though designed to achieve the same broad objectives as the Ayodhya campaign, could not sustain for long the commitment of armies of outsiders who did not have a gut-level understanding of the 'meaning' of Idgah Maidan. Of course, the manifest cynicism and hypocrisy of such a demand emanating from organizations (like the Rashtriya Swayamsevak Sangh or RSS), which themselves have refused to recognize or respect the national flag in the past, may also have helped discredit the campaign.

It is in this sense that the less successful instance of the site-based strategy offers a better view of its mechanisms. Perhaps the Hubli campaign erred in opting for a site-based strategy rather than a more modest neighbourhood-based one; or perhaps it simply illustrates the relative ideological efficacy of religious and national symbols today.

AREAS OF INTIMACY: LOCALITIES AND NEIGHBOURHOODS

Unlike the site-based strategy which involves an abstract, universal essence embedded in the site, the spatial strategy based on the *neighbourhood* emphasizes the concrete intimacy that everyday familiarity with a given locale makes possible. The status of Ayodhya as site-of-essence (*the* birthplace of Ram) is an abstract and universal one; its sacredness is intended to interpellate all Hindus equally—those who happen to reside in Ayodhya are not necessarily privileged over those living elsewhere. (Indeed, it is precisely because of this universalized relationship that armies of the faithful who are themselves from elsewhere can invade the site to 'reclaim' it.) Moreover, site-based campaigns necessarily acquire an occasion-specific, do-or-die character that is the very antithesis of the quotidian. They take the form of heroic struggles conducted in short spasms of 'revolutionary' or 'sacred' time, during which the profane logic of everyday life is swept aside, albeit temporarily.

By contrast, spatial strategies based on the neighbourhood build on the sedimented banalities of 'neighbourliness'—the long-term, 'live-in' intimacy of residential relationships among persons and families, and between them and their local environment. Such strategies are at home in the *longue durée* of the quotidian, and seek to recruit mundane, everyday experiences for the cause. The ideological forms of address that they typically employ are designed to hail those who inhabit the space that is to be turned into a heterotopia. In keeping with this philosophy, the prominent ideologue and general secretary of the Bharatiya Janata Party, K.N. Govindacharya, emphasizes the need for 'more and more interaction, in an open and cordial atmosphere, between all the people, Hindus and Muslims, *residing in a particular locality*. This dialogue must take place between *the people of the locality themselves*, directly, not through the self-proclaimed political leaders of one community or the other . . .'[57]

Localities and neighbourhoods constitute the home ground of Hindutva, the places where it leads an everyday and not an episodic existence. A strong case can be made for them as the privileged loci for the consolidation, validation and reproduction of the communal worldview. They are spaces where ideology cements itself into the everyday lives of ordinary people, is invested with experiential truth-value, and thus acquires the status of self-evident 'common sense'.[58]

It is understandable that incidents and places involving large-scale communal *violence* should receive considerable attention from the state and the media as well as activists and scholars—indeed, this essay

---

[57] K.N. Govindacharya, *Ayodha and the Future India*, extracted in *Blitz* Weekly, 3 December 1993, p. 22, emphasis added. Indeed, it seems he is almost obsessed with the locality and neighbourhood as the proper sphere for political negotiation in his book (extensively extracted in *Blitz* as part of an anniversary issue commemorating the destruction of the Babri Masjid). However, Partha Chatterjee has suggested to me that this emphasis on locality may also be a strategy designed to 'denationalize' the communal question so as to disengage it from the state and the larger public sphere, where Hindu communalism has thought of itself as disadvantaged.

[58] Compare Veena Das, 'The Spatialization of Violence: Case Study of a Communal Riot', in Basu and Subrahmanyam 1996, p. 202, and also the conclusion of her essay with this and subsequent paragraphs.

is itself no exception. Nevertheless, it is a matter of regret that we know comparatively little about communalism when it is peaceably at home, so to speak, rather than out in the street killing and burning. For it is only by recognizing the *continuities* between its normal and pathological forms that we can hope to produce a better understanding of communalism as a living phenomenon with deep social roots.[59] However, some recent studies (though mostly conducted in the shadow of communal violence) do seem to have begun the move towards producing thicker and more or less self-consciously spatialised descriptions of the neighbourhood as a key site for studying communalism.[60]

In speaking of the territoriality of peasant uprisings during the colonial period, Ranajit Guha invokes the earlier anthropological discussions on *consanguinity* and *contiguity*.[61] Contemporary Hindu

[59] In a well-known essay, Gyanendra Pandey has complained: 'The history of violence is written up in the historiography of modern India as aberration and absence. *Aberration* in the sense that violence is treated as something removed from the general run of Indian history, its distorted form . . . not the "real" history of India at all. *Absence*—and here the point applies more emphatically to a field wider than Indian history—because historical discourse has experienced very great difficulty in capturing and re-presenting the moment of violence. The "history" of violence is, therefore, almost always about context—about everything that happens around violence,' in Gyanendra Pandey, 'In Defence of the Fragment: Writing About Hindu-Muslim Riots in India Today', in *Economic and Political Weekly*, Annual Number, March 1991, vol. XXVI, nos. 11–12, p. 559, emphasis original. It should be clear from my argument, however, that the attention to context (and specifically the spatial context of the neighbourhood) that I am advocating is predicated precisely on *denying* an aberrational status to communal violence, and on stressing its *presence*, albeit at one end of a continuum whose other end is 'everyday life'.

[60] The subsequent account relies largely on the following studies: Gerard Heuze, 'Cultural Populism: The Appeal of Shiv Sena', in Sujata Patel and Alice Thorner (eds), *Bombay: Metaphor for Modern India* (Bombay: Oxford University Press, 1996), pp. 223–7, and Kalpana Sharma, 'Chronicle of a Riot Foretold', in Patel and Thorner, 1996, pp. 268–86 for Bombay; Hansen, 1996 for Marathwada, Veena Das, 1996 for Delhi; and Uma Chakravarti, Prem Chowdhury, Pradip Dutta, Zoya Hasan, Kumkum Sangari and Tanika Sarkar, 'Khurja Riots, 1990–91: Understanding the Conjuncture', in *Economic and Political Weekly*, 1992, vol. 27(18), pp. 951–65 for Khurja.

[61] Ranajit Guha, *Elementary Aspects of Peasant Insurgency in Colonial India* (Delhi: Oxford University Press, 1983), pp. 279 ff.

communalism and its embeddedness in neighbourhoods also seem to involve the intersection of these (or closely analogous) notions, namely those of cultural kinship ('our people') and residential belonging ('our area').[62] This is hardly surprising, given that major communal organizations have all tried (in different styles and with varying degrees of emphasis) to leverage their cause on the fulcrum of the *family*, an institution defined more than any other by the interlocking ties of blood and residence. However, a more detailed study of this aspect of communalism may help to clarify the ways in which both consanguinity and contiguity are not *given* as 'primordial' categories, but are rather painstakingly *constructed* and reconstructed, even though they are not infinitely malleable.

The Bombay-based Shiv Sena, for example, has established itself by cultivating families and involving them in its activities.[63] This emphasis has blended very well with the Sena's reliance on neighbourhood-level organization through its *shakhas* and *gata-shakhas* (sub-shakhas). As a result, middle- and lower-level Sena functionaries like the shakha and *gata pramukhs* are solidly entrenched in lower-middle-class and poorer neighbourhoods. As people who deal with everyday local issues

---

[62] In this connection, it may be useful to examine the vernacular vocabularies of territoriality which have accompanied urban communalism. The English words 'area' and 'society' or 'colony' (from housing society/colony), for example, seem to have joined older terms like *mohalla, para, gali, chawl, ilaka, oni*, and so on.

[63] It has to be remembered, however, that the Shiv Sena did not embark upon its political career as a specifically *communal* organization, but acquired/claimed this identity only in the late 1980s and especially the 1990s. Also, the initial spread of the organisation was more haphazard than planned, as admitted by Thackeray himself. Dipankar Gupta, *Nativism in a Metropolis: Shiv Sena in Bombay* (Delhi: Manohar, 1982), pp. 72–4. But by following its 'natural' trajectory, the Sena found itself concentrated in certain kinds of neighbourhoods and among certain types of families. As Gerard Heuze notes: 'Within the *shakhas*, posts of responsibility are very often entrusted to a group of brothers, or brothers and uncle, sometimes sons and father. The *shakha* being considered as a new family, or as an extension of the family, is thus not just a simple metaphor.' Heuze 1996, p. 218. While this is hardly atypical of other Indian political organizations, the important difference is that in the Shiv Sena this is explicitly encouraged and defended as 'perfectly natural and positive'.

ranging from 'husband wife problems to leaking pipes', they are well known to and know well the residents of their neighbourhoods.[64] The Sena has, of course, borrowed this overall strategy from the RSS, which first pioneered it. As is well known, the traditional habitats of the RSS and the social geography of the urban middle- and lower-middle classes are closely intertwined.[65] And as Tanika Sarkar in her valuable study of the Rashtra Sevika Samiti has found, the women's wing of the RSS places even more emphasis than its male counterpart on low-key but unrelenting ideological work in the immediate social vicinity of its cadres: the intimate and intensely particular spaces of domesticity and the family.[66]

The full implications of the neighbourhood as a heterotopia emerge in the context of their actual mobilization for some larger-than-everyday activity or campaign, often related to or resulting in communal violence. The Shiv Sena and RSS-sponsored *mahaarti* has emerged as an important example in the context of the countrywide spell of anti-Muslim violence following the destruction of the Babri Masjid in December 1992. While both organizations have been involved in reinventing and politicizing Hindu festivals, the mahaarti is a recent development designed to 'recapture the streets for Hindus'.[67] It is said to have had a direct role in the instigation of violence against Muslims in

---

[64] Gupta 1982, pp. 75–80, 89–90.

[65] Basu *et al.*, 1993.

[66] Tanika Sarkar, 'Women as Communal Subject: Rashtrasevika Samiti and Ram Janmabhoomi Movement', in *Economic and Political Weekly*, 31 August 1991, v. 26, n. 35.

[67] Kalpana Sharma, a Bombay-based journalist, notes that the mahaarti was launched on 11 December (during a lull in the communal disturbances following 2 December), in a temple (Gol Deval) strategically located between Muslim-dominated and Sena-BJP dominated localities. As she points out: 'A *maha-arti* is not an everyday Hindu ritual and even when one is held, it does not take place on the street outside a temple. Yet the Shiv Sena decided to make an issue of the fact that the Muslims have to spill out on the street during prayers on Friday because their mosques are too small to accommodate the entire congregation. Their leadership was quoted as saying that this would help recapture the streets for Hindus and end the policy of appeasement of the Muslim minority.' Sharma 1995, p. 278.

Bombay, and in the widening of the support base for such violence in middle-class localities.[68] Also relevant in this context is the neighbourhood-based organization of what might be called 'exchange violence'. This involves an explicitly planned strategy whereby the residents of neighbourhood A will, in connivance with the Hindus of neighbourhood B, attack Muslims of the latter locality in return for similar attacks on Muslims in their own locality by Hindus of neighbourhood B.[69] Occupying the other end of the spectrum, but also based on the locality, is the phenomenon of violence born of contiguity, where members of the majority practice 'ethnic cleansing' against their own minority-community neighbours.[70]

While it is broadly true to say that '[p]opular vision centred on space is usually both defensive and decentralized ... The street, or a small part of the street, sometimes the slum or the mohalla, are the common notions of popular space',[71] such a view underestimates the extent to which this apparent limitation can be converted into a source of strength. In the last analysis, the significance of the locality as a heterotopia is not really in terms of what it is able to achieve within its own spatial limits, but rather in the possibilities it creates for inserting such localities into a larger grid of ideological dissemination and political action. Thus, the neighbourhood acts as a sort of relay which, though it is crucially dependent on its particular location in social space, can nevertheless provide the ideological context for the production and reproduction of worldviews, as well as properly indoctrinated workers for the Hindutva cause. Localities and neighbourhoods form

---

[68] Sharma 1995, p. 283; Heuze 1995, p. 242.

[69] Such instances have been reported in several major communal riots, but the most recent (and relatively well-documented) instance is once again in Bombay. Evidence for this emerged in the hearing of the Sri Krishna Commission, especially during the examination of the zealous Shiv Sena MLA (now an MP), Madhukar Sarpotdar. (The hearings were reported by the daily press, but extensive accounts can also be found in the fortnightly *Frontline*.)

[70] Detailed accounts of such instances are to be found in Veena Das's attempts to explore the spatialisation of violence in the anti-Sikh riots of Delhi following Indira Gandhi's assassination in 1984, and in the study of the Khurja riots. See Das, 1996; Chakravarti *et al*., 1992.

[71] Heuze 1995, p. 244.

part of the conditions of possibility for spatial strategies based on the site and the route. Simply put, these quotidian spaces represent the 'before' and 'after' of the subaltern crowds recruited for the specific, more or less short-lived campaigns of/for Hindutva.

ROUTES OF SYNERGY: PROCESSION AND PILGRIMAGES

Spatial strategies based on pilgrimages and processions bring together and set in motion the adamantly zero-sum logic provided by sites-of-essence and the masses of committed agents produced within areas-of-intimacy. The forte of such strategies is thus their *dynamism*, which serves to vastly amplify the political-ideological impact of Hindutva.

The pilgrimage has been an integral part of the world of the faithful since ancient times, and may always have involved questions of hegemony, power and territorial control.[72] Its redeployment as an explicitly political spatial strategy involving a ritualized mass journey is also well known in recent history, as shown by the widely different examples of Mao Zedong, Mahatma Gandhi and Martin Luther King. But its repeated and effective use in current Indian politics has been a characteristic of the Sangh Parivar, the loosely linked set of organizations under the umbrella of the RSS.

The first of these political pilgrimages was the *ekatmata yajna* organized by the Vishwa Hindu Parishad (VHP) in 1983, which comprised three main yatras criss-crossing the country from Hardwar to Kanyakumari, Kathmandu to Rameshwaram and Gangasagar to Somnath. With its 47 subsidiary yatras, this 'yajna' is claimed to have reached 60 million people in India, not to speak of the international participation from Hindu communities in Nepal, Bhutan, Myanmar, Bangladesh, Pakistan and Mauritius, who sent 'holy water' from their local rivers. The yajna and its cross-country processions are said to have 'garnered enormous publicity and enabled the VHP to start local branches in all parts of the country'.[73] This was followed, of course, by the much more overtly politicized yatras—Advani's *rathyatra* to Ayodhya, which

---

[72] See also the discussion above at the end of the section on Savarkar's Hindutva.
[73] Van der Veer 1996, pp. 124–6.

dragged a trail of communal violence in its wake; Joshi's Kanyakumari to Kashmir yatra culminating in the farcical hoisting of the national flag in Srinagar; and the recent (less successful) *jan aadesh yatra*.

The pilgrimage-based strategy attempts to string together and multiply the effect of many particular places by joining them into the 'route' of a goal-directed journey. This 'dotted line effect' gets the best of two worlds. Each 'dot' along the way remains a small town and yet can participate in something on a 'national' scale. Thus, it takes advantage of the strong sense of involvement, identification and popular energy that can be generated in a localized setting, but without sacrificing the ideological economies of scale. The concept of a yatra also enables the invocation of a certain spatial sense of the power and persuasive sweep of an ideology.

A more frequently used and much more powerful spatial strategy is that based on a localized mass procession. Usually operating on a citywide scale, the procession exemplifies the synergistic fusion of both site and neighbourhood-based strategies. The inflexible stand on the site is reproduced in the refusal to negotiate the route or destination of the procession, which is chosen with political objectives in mind; and neighbourhood-based groups act as the mass base providing the well-prepared crowds which will actually form the procession. And unlike the everyday routine of neighbourhood groups or the episodic nature of site-based campaigns, the procession can be both institutionally regularized and made more or less predictable while also providing a theatre for intensely concentrated, 'spontaneous' outbursts of political energy, often leading to violence. In the procession, both site-based and neighbourhood-based strategies can hope to overcome their limitations: the former can become more flexible and regulated, while the latter can transcend its local ambit and become mobile.

As part of her larger project on the new predicaments facing old cities, Ratna Naidu has conducted what is perhaps the most detailed study of its kind, mapping the evolution and the spatial-political impact of processions in the city of Hyderabad.[74] The city has three

[74] Naidu 1990.

traditional processions associated with religious festivals: the *Ganesh Utsav* procession dates from the turn of the century; the *Bibi ka Alam julus*, part of Muharram, the Muslim festival of mourning, originates in the Qutub Shahi period (1591–1687); and the *Bonalu* festival procession, involving incarnations of Kali worshipped by lower-caste Hindus (with mostly women processionists), is by far the oldest as it is associated with the indigenous population of the area. However, the use of processions as a political device is, of course, very recent, having begun only in the late 1970s. Ratna Naidu outlines the transformations:

> While the Muharram procession seems to have retained its original character, the Ganesh and Bonalu processions have undergone considerable changes over the past nine years . . . Before 1978, all Hindu processions were local and small in size. There were only three major Ganesh processions, and even these were local, with their termination points at a nearby pond, well or river . . . In 1978 this pattern changed to some extent, and in 1980 it changed completely . . . During the 1980 Ganesh festival, the [Ganesh Utsav] Samiti, whose other active participants were the Vishwa Hindu Parishad, the Hindu Raksha Samiti, the RSS activists and some of the local businessmen, took up the task of bringing together all the old city processions to form a single, monolithic procession.[75]

The major changes in the Hindu (i.e. the Ganesh and Bonalu) processions have been in their size and character. They have become incomparably larger, in terms of the number of 'tributary' processions, the length of the routes and the numbers of processionists. For example, the 1984 Ganesh procession involved no less than 151 sub-processions which joined around Charminar to form one mammoth procession, and then proceeded through the centre of the city of the Husain Sagar lake—renamed Vinayak Sagar for the day!—about eight kilometres away. And the Bonalu procession of the same year involved 35 subsidiaries. These changes in size are also related to the change in the nature of processions. From small, local religious-cultural events they have now become prominent political theatres for demonstrating strength and exerting aggressive pressure on opponents, particularly

[75] Ibid., pp. 128–9.

the Muslim community. Thus, routes have been changed to pass through Muslim localities and by major mosques, ensuring that the potential for provocation is maximized.[76]

A new *Pankha* procession seems to have been launched by Muslim communal organizations during the 1980s in response to the provocations of the reorganized Ganesh and Bonalu processions, and has also resulted in violent conflicts. But the institutionalized and vastly superior ability to generate violence via the Hindu processions is reflected in the way that respondents have answered the survey questions on this subject:[77] 89 per cent of the Muslim respondents emphatically support a government ban on all processions, while the figure for both Hindus and scheduled castes/tribes is 53 per cent. Only 8 per cent of Muslims are indifferent to this question compared to 17 per cent of Hindus and 14 per cent of SC/STs. 29 per cent of Hindus and 22 per cent of the SC/ST respondents oppose a ban on the grounds that it would restrict religious freedom, while the figure for Muslims—commonly projected as fanatical—is only 8 per cent. Perhaps the most telling figures are those on participation in processions: a mere 6 per cent of Muslims say that they participate in the processions organised by their community, compared to 32 per cent of Hindus and 49 per cent of the SC/STs.[78]

Hyderabad is not an exception—the systematic use of processions by Hindu communalists has long been an established feature of the Indian political scene. The reports of several commissions of enquiry, set up to look into incidents of communal violence, provide a depressingly detailed testimony on their repeated and varied use all over

---

[76] Despite their regulation, loudspeakers are used to hurl abusive and insulting slogans and to whip up mass hysteria. (In the 1984 Ganesh procession, the police confiscated 300 unlicensed public address systems.) The Bonalu procession, in which men now outnumber women, has resulted in major riots in 1981 (the first time it was reorganized on the model of the 1980 Ganesh procession) and 1984. The Ganesh procession has provoked at least half a dozen riots since 1980.

[77] To begin with, Naidu reveals that some of the investigators in her study, 'who are old city residents and participate in the Ganesh procession, say that they always carry a knife during the procession—a telling commentary on what the culture of religious processions has deteriorated into.' Naidu, 1990, p. 134.

[78] Naidu 1990, p. 135, Table 7.5.

India, especially in the north. Thus, for example, the Justice D.P. Madon Committee Report traces the history of the Shiv Jayanti procession (which commemorates Shivaji's birthday—strictly speaking, not a religious festival) in Bhiwandi over four successive years, describing in minute detail the fashioning of the procession into an incendiary device.[79] And, as if to prove that the procession-based strategy is an abstract conceptual scheme immune to particularities, the Justice Jaganmohan Reddy Committee Report records the circumstances in which a 'procession' of cows was instrumental in igniting the notorious Ahmedabad riots of 1969.[80]

As a spectacular and often terrifying demonstration of strength, the spatial strategy based on the procession is in a class of its own. It offers the cover of large numbers and a semi-religious occasion for premeditated attempts to attach the person and property of adversaries. At the same time, as an institutionalized and regular annual event it tacitly offers hospitality and encouragement for entirely unplanned 'spontaneous' violence that can then be piously disowned by the large organizations responsible for the procession. If neighbourhood strategies can sometimes be defensive, the procession is unmistakably offensive in orientation.

VI

Conclusion: The Roads Not Taken

The preceding argument tries to make a case for studying the spatial aspects of Hindutva in terms of the heterotopias it attempts to

---

[79] Justice D.P. Madon, *Report of the Commission of Inquiry into the Communal Disturbances at Bhiwandi, Jalgaon and Mahad in May 1970*, vols I–VII (Bombay: Government of Maharashtra Home Department, Special, 1974).

[80] Justice Jaganmohan Reddy, *Report: Inquiry into the Communal Disturbances at Ahmedabad and Other Places in Gujarat on and after 18th September 1969*, Justice Jaganmohan Reddy Commission of Enquiry (Ahmedabad: Government of Gujarat Home Department, 1970). This, of course, is not an exceptional event, since the cow has often served as a symbolic rallying point in Hindu-Muslim conflict in the subcontinent. See for example Yang, 1980, and Sandria Freitag, 'Sacred Symbol as Mobilizing Ideology: The North Indian Search for a "Hindu" Community', in *Comparative Studies in Society and History*, October 1980, v. 22(4), pp. 597–625.

construct. This way of approaching communalism may offer an empirically-grounded method to analyse the micro-macro links, the ideological synergies and the scale effects involved in the production and repro-duction of the Hindutva worldview.

But in order to attain the objectives outlined at the beginning of this essay—especially that of fashioning counter-strategies—this perspective has to be complemented in several ways. For communalism is not the only force attempting to reshape the nation-space; several others are also at work altering the socio-spatial profile of the nation, and it is the '*net effect*' of these forces that will be decisive. Apart from communalism, there are at least five others that seem to be crucial: the New Economic Policy in place since 1991; the range of processes loosely termed 'globalisation'; the recent continuing realignments along the caste–ethnicity axes; the emergence of the 'new middle classes' with a transformed socio-political profile; and, as something arising out of but not limited to the combined effect of the first five, a new regionalization of the Indian nation-space. As an illustration of what might be meant by 'net effect', here are some preliminary speculations on the probable mutual interactions among globalisation and Hindutva.

GLOBALISATION AND HINDUTVA

Among the most powerful competitors of Hindutva for the status of major engine of contemporary social change is 'globalisation'. At first glance, globalisation appears to be a contrary tendency—it seems to undermine the particularity of places, subordinating them to a universalized logic. The orientalist version of this tendency has been labelled 'moral commensuration', a practice whereby Western metropolitan places are assigned 'a kind of export value: whatever is good or bad about places at home is shipped out and assigned comparable virtue or vice abroad'.[81] However, the contemporary equivalent for globalisation seems (usually, but not always) to move in the reverse direction: non-Western (Third World) places are compared to some Western

[81] Said, 1993, p. 79.

norm-place, and are thus assigned a new ideological value.[82] In effect, this kind of moral commensuration 'equalizes' places and seeks to underplay differences rather than to accentuate them.

More generally, theoretical prognoses of the development of capitalism from Marx onwards have pointed to the universalising tendencies of capital. In spatial terms, this expresses itself in the process of deterritorialization, the uprooting and enforced 'portability' of all forms of social life captured by capital, or 'the disembedding of social relations'. This is the process rendered familiar by the literature on the 'restructuring of capital', 'flexible accumulation' and 'post-Fordism'.[83] Industries turn nomadic in the search for the most profitable location; production processes are broken up and subcontracted globally; innovations in telecommunications enable certain industries (like computer software) to engage in 'space-less' production—i.e. without a single, specific spatial location in the conventional sense. (Satellite links enable software engineers located in far-flung corners of the globe to participate simultaneously in production, while the product itself exists only in the 'cyberspace' of electronic storage devices.) The basic outcome of such a conquest of space is a profound indifference towards its specificities. Thus, the spatial consequences of the economic logic of contemporary capitalism include the dilution of nation-specific production into a more anonymous globalised process.[84]

However, recent research has also demonstrated that the alleged conquest of space is far from complete and is in any case a rather uneven and contradictory process. These researches build on the insight reported more than two decades ago, namely that although modern societies are defined by processes of deterriorialization, '*what they*

---

[82] As an example, one can cite a well-known series of advertisements for the Tata group of companies which is built around the strategy of comparing places and things Indian to their global counterparts: Bombay is compared to Beijing or New York, an Indian steel plant is compared to a German one, and so on. This is the opposite of the essentialisation that is an integral part of the spatial strategy of Hindutva.

[83] For an overview of the literature see Harvey, 1989, especially part II, chs 7–11: 'the political-economic transformation of late twentieth century capitalism'.

[84] Deshpande, 'Imagined Economics'.

deterritorialize with one hand, they reterritorialize with the other.[85] The process of reterritorialization takes many forms, but two are especially common. First, there is the simple refusal of archaic territorial entities to go away, and, indeed, an increase in their mass appeal. An excellent example is the nation, which, in defiance of widespread expectations regarding the erosion of national identities, continues to command the often fanatical loyalty of large numbers. The second, more complex form of reterritorialization can be considered to be an integral part of the process of globalisation itself, namely the cultivation and deepening of spatial specificity, but within a framework where this is subordinated to the overall logic of globalisation. Obvious examples are the tourism industry or the media, which foster and even invent specificity as 'authentic exoticism', but only in order to offer up these exotica in a domesticated, pre-packaged form to the global consumers of cultural difference such as affluent tourists, cinema or television audiences.[86]

This latter tendency has caught the attention of social researchers trying to account for the striking fact that globalisation is *accompanied by* the growth of particularistic cultural identities of all kinds. Across the globe today, what may be termed 'essentialist' cultural identities—based on religion, ethnicity, nationality, language, or region—are enjoying an unprecedented revival even as the processes of globalisation are simultaneously intensified. It has been tempting, therefore, to speculate on a possible causal link between the two processes, in the form of the broad thesis that globalisation produces a sort of 'identity anxiety' that individuals and groups seek to redress through the reassertion of particularistic identities. Economic globalism produces—indeed, even requires—cultural parochialism as its own antidote and precondition. Religion is particularly relevant in this context, as

---

[85] Gilles Deleuze and Felix Guattari, *Anti-Oedipus: Capitalism and Schizophrenia* (New York: Viking Press [1972] 1977), p. 257, original emphasis.

[86] For a rich variety of perspectives on this set of issues, see the articles in the volume edited by Mike Featherstone, *Global Culture: Nationalism, Globalization and Modernity* (London: Sage, 1990), especially those by Robertson, Wallerstein, Smith, Arnason, Hannerz, Appadurai, and Beyer.

demonstrated by the remarkable revitalization of Catholic, Protestant, Jewish, Islamic, Hindu and Buddhist fundamentalisms of various kinds in widely differing local milieux.[87]

In the context, it is clear that globalisation and Hindutva impact on each other in contradictory as well as complementary ways (not to speak of ways that may go beyond this dichotomy), making it difficult to hold on to any unidimensional conception of their reciprocal involvement. One important aspect of this mutual impact is the globalisation of Hindutva itself, that is, the globalisation of its congregations and constituencies. The emergence of what might be called 'non-resident *Hindutva*' (especially in the USA and the UK) provides an obvious instance where the 'portability' *as well as* the 'changelessness' of its essence are simultaneously highlighted. Today, when the world is witness to more and more such ongoing negotiations (involving both collusions and collisions) between the local and the globalised faces of ethnicity, the net impact is too complex to predict.[88]

If regions are the product of historically contingent, multi-dimensional 'coherences' that make a particular geo-social space stand out in relief (while simultaneously blurring others), then it is clear that communalism, globalisation and the other forces listed above are, individually and jointly, rearranging the regional map of India. In the contest for spatial hegemony, these forces will interact with each other in complex ways, as will the regions they create. By concentrating solely on communalism, and that too on its more micro-level effects, this essay has obviously presented a one-sided picture that may be significantly modified when the overall effect of the other forces is also factored in. But it is equally obvious that some such partial starting point is needed precisely in order to anchor the more complex dynamics of the multidimensional analysis, which, I hope, would form future instalments of a larger project.

---

[87] Peter F. Beyer, 'Privatization and the Public Influence of Religion in Global Society', in Featherstone, 1990, pp. 373–96.

[88] Arjun Appadurai, 'Disjuncture and Difference in the Global Cultural Economy', in Featherstone, 1990, pp. 293–310.

Constituting Nation, Contesting Nationalism: The Southern Tamil (Woman) and Separatist Tamil Nationalism in Sri Lanka*

QADRI ISMAIL

> How could someone ... make a final home in [any] classification without suffering claustrophobia?
>
> —Denise Riley, *Am I That* Name?

> The ordinary apparatus of historiography ... [d]esigned for big events and institutions, is most at ease when made to operate on those larger phenomena which visibly stick out of the debris of the past ... A critical historiography can make up for this lacuna by bending closer to the ground in order to pick up the traces of a subaltern life in its passage through time.
>
> —Ranajit Guha, 'Chandra's Death'

*This paper is part of a larger study of the failure of nationalism to offer its subjects (nationals) adequate and unoppressive community; and of the necessity to (re)write the history of nationalism accordingly. Early versions of it were read at the 5th Bi-Annual Subaltern Studies Conference, Colombo, the Southern Asian Institute, Columbia University, and the South Asia Workshop, University of Chicago. My thanks to those who made this possible, particularly Kumari Jayawardena and Phil Oldenburg, and to all who commented on it at those venues, particularly Mala de Alwis, Arjun Appadurai, Partha Chatterjee, Jean Howard, Chandan Reddy and David

Introduction: Nine Claims About Nationalism

CONSIDER A NATIONALISM which is unwilling to countenance the obstacles imposed upon it by a state that it finds oppressive, foreign and/or inorganic; and which is unprepared to further compromise with that state or unconvinced of such possibility; and which is unable to conceive of an alternative. When such a nationalism declares itself in pursuit of a distinct, exclusive and organic state for its nation, it must know its limits. Such a nationalism must moreover clarify, mostly—but not exclusively—to itself, the geographic boundaries of the envisaged country, the political boundaries of the proposed state, and the social boundaries of the nation that is sought to be mobilized to achieve this state. Clarity being a logical, not a chronological, imperative, the project of nationalism cannot begin without it.[1] (Of course, these events, these delimitations, do not happen in isolation; the demarcation of one boundary will affect another; the geographical, the political and the social can be considered separate only for analytic purposes.) Such a project must specify where its territory begins and/or ends; where, for instance, its customs and immigration posts would be sited, even if these sites turn out to be negotiable. Equally critical is a specification of nationalism's political boundaries: what it is and isn't prepared to do—its ideology—and its expectations of, promises and guarantees to, its presumed subjects, or *nationals*; otherwise, interpellation of these subjects cannot happen. Cardinally necessary, therefore, before commencement of the nationalist project, is a specification of the basic constituent of the nation—what I term the 'national'.[2]

Scott. It is, however, most intimately the result of many conversations with Sanjay Krishnan, Milind Wakankar and, especially, Pradeep Jeganathan.

[1] This is true of both the post-colonial ('separatist') nationalism discussed here, and of anti-colonial nationalism, though not quite in the same manner. In the latter case, for instance, locating the boundary of the envisaged (decolonized) country does not present a problem for nationalism: the boundary of the post-colonial country (to be) is always seen to coincide with the borders of the colonial state.

[2] My understanding of this term is different from its common sense, as interchangeable with citizen; the necessity for such a term and its refashioning is explained later. For now, 'national' can be taken to be a 'member' of the nation.

This essay looks at the logic by, and pressures, contradictions and conditions under, which nationalism specifies the nation and the national; it investigates the logic of nation-constitution, and the consequences of that logic. A fresh examination of this phenomenon is necessary in part because, while it is now a commonplace in the literature that nationalism binds disparate groups together to constitute, 'invent', or 'imagine' a nation as community, it is also assumed that the boundaries of a nation, once so constituted, invented or imagined, remain unchanged, and that the *national* is a stable, unchanging category.[3] Such a position removes from discussion the possibility—advanced most compellingly in the work of Partha Chatterjee and Ranajit Guha—of reading nation and nationalism dynamically; or, in Anderson's terms, as being constantly re-imagined. Guha has also made the case for seeing 'nationalism itself as a tissue of contradictions, with its emancipatory and unifying urge resisted and modified significantly by the disciplinary and divisive forces of social conservation.'[4] While it is not social conservatism, so much as the inherently hierarchical and exclusionary impulse of nationalism that is examined in this study, it too will conclude that nationalism is a conservative ideology and politics.

This essay makes nine claims that I contend are essential for furthering our understanding of its subject: nation, nationalism, the dynamic nexus between the two, and the production, by this very dynamic, of spaces that raise the possibility of subverting nationalism and of imagining more enabling forms of community. Some of these claims, as the reader will notice, are not new; indeed they may be, in Eve Sedgwick's phrase, 'imbecilically self-evident';[5] but they require to be reiterated nevertheless, until they become, again to take a term from

---

[3] This position is shared by what might be termed the Eurocentric tendency on nationalism: the influential work of Bendict Anderson, Ernest Gellner and Eric Hobsbawm.

[4] Ranajit Guha, 'Discipline and Mobilize', in Partha Chatterjee and Gyanendra Pandey (eds), *Subaltern Studies VII* (New Delhi: Oxford University Press, 1992), p. 79.

[5] Eve Sedgwick, *Epistemology of the Closet* (Berkeley: University of California Press, 1990), p. 22.

Sedgwick, 'axiomatic'. Other claims are made, argued, explained, and canvassed for in the belief that they too should become axiomatic in the discussion on nationalism.

The *first* claim was intimated above and will be substantiated later: that, partly due to its profound and structural dependence on nostalgia, *it is no longer possible to speak of nationalism, in any of its manifestations, as anything but a conservative ideology and politics.*[6] The *second* is that *nationalism cannot and does not take its subjects for granted.* Not in the sense that it cannot be certain of the political allegiance, or affiliation, of every national (though correct, it is not my concern here);[7] but in the sense that those social groups that will make the nation are not given, they cannot (all) be known a priori. Or, as Etienne Balibar put it, 'The fundamental problem is . . . to produce the people.'[8] The logical, and the political, necessity for this is easily apparent: as suggested earlier, nationalism cannot mobilize groups, especially in a separatist instance as considered here, without specifying them (specification being another way of identifying a boundary or limit). If that is a relatively uncontroversial statement, the *third* claim is perhaps not; it will take some work to establish, but should be stated now: *the constitution and therefore appearance of a nation changes from conjuncture to conjuncture.* In other words (i) not every group that might conceivably be specified as a constituent of the nation is always thus identified; and (ii) every group thus identified will not necessarily always occupy the same position within the vertical structure of the nation. Those social groups in dominant positions within the nation at certain moments

---

[6] This implies that it once was possible to see nationalism as progressive, liberatory, or even heroic; and that may indeed have been the case. But, making such a judgement would necessarily entail a prior consideration of other questions—broadly speaking, concerning reading, delimiting and adjudicating the past—addressing which would be beyond the scope of this paper.

[7] For an excellent study of the use of coercion—in this instance, caste sanctions in early-twentieth-century India—to ensure nationalist allegiance and mobilization, see Guha (1992).

[8] Etienne Balibar, 'The Nation Form: History & Ideology', in Etienne Balibar and Immanuel Wallerstein, *Race, Nation, Class: Ambiguous Identities* (New York: Verso, 1991), p. 93.

will not necessarily dominate always, and the situations of groups marginalized, subordinated—even expelled—by nationalism in other conjunctures are not immutably fixed either. A subordinated group at one moment could be the dominant one at another, and vice versa; even expulsion from the project of nationalism is not necessarily a permanent condition. Another way of saying the above is that a variety of social groups—sometimes predictable ones, sometimes unexpected ones—are available for appropriation and/or expulsion by nationalism;[9] the logic underlying such demarcation, as will be clear, is not ethical but political—what the conjuncture makes possible.

If the appearance of the nation changes with conjuncture, then it must follow that the *nation be read situationally and dynamically*. Dynamically, because nation cannot be understood in and of itself, but only grasped as that *unit which nationalism seeks to define and mobilize*—indeed, it is that unit which nationalism *defines by mobilizing*, and vice versa. (Mobilization not being a call to arms, but a phenomenon akin to, though not homologous with, interpellation.) Consequently, the constitution of the nation will change, as the immediate goals of nationalism change, from conjuncture to conjuncture. And I hold that nation must be read situationally, or conjuncturally in the strict Althusserian sense, because what appears as 'nation' I understand to be constituted by overdetermined contradictions. Which is why the appearance of the nation will change with every change in the conjuncture—taking the face of the dominant social groups, or forces, in these overdetermined contradictions.

This essay investigates the appearance of the Sri Lankan Tamil nation at three pivotal conjunctures and attempts to unravel the logic by which 'separatist' Tamil nationalism constitutes its nation.[10] *Inherent in this logic*—in this process of incorporation, subordination and

---

[9] On the incorporation of groups migrating from Southern India during the colonial period into the Sinhala nation, which sees itself as the unchanged product of Northern Indian immigration two thousand years before, see Senaka Bandaranaike, 'The Peopling of Sri Lanka: The National Question and Some Problems of History and Ethnicity', in Charles Abeyesekera and Newton Gunasinghe (eds), *Facets of Ethnicity in Sri Lanka* (Colombo: Social Scientists Association, 1987).

[10] The terms 'Tamil nationalism', and 'Tamil separatism' are used interchangeably

expulsion of social groups—*is the possibility of nationalism's own subversion*—this being my *fourth* claim. This essay identifies, with respect to Tamil nationalism, one such possibility, one such space (without denying the possibility of others). In this instance, the intersection of gender, nation and region/habitation produces a space shorn of political identity, a space outside (national) community; a not altogether stable space that, as we shall see, demands identity and identification with a politics and a potential community outside the grasp of nationalism. In such expulsions, or epidermal locales that nationalism must produce in order to be, lies the possibility of other, more enabling, or 'operable' notions of community. Demonstrating such possibility, and thus telling a different story about (the history of) nationalism, I take to be among the more pressing obligations of the (South Asian) cultural critic.

Renarrativizing history with this end—or perhaps beginning—is not, as we know, a particularly novel endeavour. An analogous urgency compels much, if not in a certain sense all, feminism. To cite but one recent instance, Jacqui Alexander has written, in an important paper, of a 'move on the part of . . . the contemporary women's movement in the Bahamas to *choose from particular feminist genealogies, particular histories of struggle*,'[11] as one of the strategies necessary to contest the Bahamian nation-state's appropriation, and attempts at co-optation, of the women's movement. She emphasizes the possibility, correctly in my view, that such renarrativizations have the '*potential* of undoing the nation entirely'[12] though not of course apart from other efforts across the political spectrum. However, as Alexander takes

---

in this paper. When Tamil nationalism is discussed in its earlier, non-separatist incarnation, that is made clear. Describing the phenomenon by the term 'separatist', of course, makes one somewhat complicitous with the terms offered by Sinhala nationalism, which insists upon the ancient and eternal unity of the country Sri Lanka. But, I prefer it to the one offered by (LTTE) Tamil nationalism: liberation.

[11] Jacqui Alexander, 'Erotic Autonomy as a Politics of Decolonization: An Anatomy of Feminist and State Practices in the Bahamas Tourist Industry', in Jacqui Alexander and Chandra Mohanty (eds), *Feminist Genealogies, Colonial Legacies, Democratic Futures* (New York: Routledge, 1997), p. 63 (emphasis added).

[12] Alexander 1997, p. 64, emphasis added.

pains to point out, the consequences of such undoing by no means follow inevitably from challenging history. Such work requires caution, because it deploys 'tools that might entrap, ensnare *or liberate*'.[13] A similar caution will be required when it comes to locating the subversive potential in the Southern Tamil women's stories read in this paper. But it is a caution that takes inspiration from the fact that such efforts at re-narrativizing history are not made in isolation.

The feminist critique of nationalism suggests, as does my own reading of the predicament of Southern Tamil women in post-1983 Sri Lanka, the, *fifth* claim: *women cannot find home in nation*. Sitralega Maunaguru is one of the many who have insisted that nationalism 'produces a construction of women which is subordinated to that of men.' While agreeing with her that this is 'an argument that must be re-made until it can be assumed'[14] or because axiomatic, I would also insist that it can and should be pushed one step further, to the conclusion that such a position logically implies: *from a feminist perspective, nationalism—to be precise, the nation—cannot be seen as providing enabling community.*

Implicit in claim five is the assumption of a bind between 'home' and 'nation'. It could be explicated as follows: the proposition and promise of nationalism is security (in the fullest sense of the term) in community; or, more precisely, in a single and superadequate community and communal identity, known as nation. For the national—or, more correctly, the subject sought to be interpellated as national—to be satisfied with a single and exclusive identity, the security promised by such identity must be more than adequate; it must be absolute. Such security is to be found, ideally at least, only at home: a space that provides not just physical security, but is also without claustrophobia and dysphoria.[15] Metaphorically speaking, nationalism promises to take

---

[13] Ibid.

[14] Sitralega Maunaguru, 'Gendering Tamil Nationalism: The Construction of "Woman" in Projects of Protest and Control', in Pradeep Jeganathan and Qadri Ismail (eds), *Unmaking the Nation: The Politics of Identity and History in Modern Sri Lanka* (Colombo: Social Scientists Association, 1995), p. 158.

[15] For the use of this term, see Judith Halberstam, 'Lesbian Masculinity, or Even Stone Britches Get the Blues', in *Women and Performance*, 8(2), 1996.

its nationals home, to end homelessness and homesickness, represents itself as the exclusive and ultimate cure for nostalgia.[16] However, this promise is one that cannot be kept; for, if that were to happen, if it actually delivered on its promise, nationalism would have exhausted its obligations and would find itself with nothing left to do. Thus my *sixth* claim: *nationalism cannot and does not keep its promises* (to its nationals).

Alfred J. Wilson has argued that it took decades before Sri Lankan Tamil nationalism resolved the problem of which social groups would constitute its nation. To Wilson, the immanent problem for Tamil nationalism arose as a consequence of regional difference: in the period 1920–31, largely due to the commissions and omissions of British colonialism, Tamil identity 'split' into three 'regional identities', which he calls, in keeping with the terminology of Tamil nationalism, 'Colombo', 'Jaffna', and 'Batticaloa' Tamil. (My terms Southern Northern and Eastern Tamil, respectively, are intended to be more inclusive.) In other words, *though always a unit, the Tamil nation was fractured by colonialism; the post-colonial task was to bring the parts together*, or reconstitute the nation, in Guha's phrase, 'as integer'. After much effort, the Tamil United Liberation Front (TULF) succeeded in this endeavour by the 1970s, largely due to 'Sinhala aggrandizement', says Wilson; but not all the parts were to be united: 'at the political level . . . "the Jaffna man" [*sic*] and the "Batticaloa man" . . . realized that their merging is essential for the protection of the Ceylon Tamil

---

[16] The literature on the question of home is, of course, quite extensive. I will mention here just one very thoughtful recent contribution, that of Rosemary George. She sees home not in the ideal sense looked at here—and offered by nationalism—but materially, as a place 'of violence and nurturing . . . a place to escape to and a place to escape from. Its importance lies in the fact that it is not equally available to all. Home is the desired place that is fought for and established as the exclusive domain of a few. It is not a neutral place. It is community. Communities are not counter-constructions but only extensions of home, providing the same comforts and terrors on a larger scale.' See Rosemary George, *The Politics of Home: Postcolonial Relocations and 20th Century Fiction* (Cambridge: Cambridge University Press, 1994), p. 9.

identity. In the process, it became necessary to write off "the Colombo man".'[17] The many erasures, elisions, and equivocations that enable this cold, calculated and calculating formulation are formidable. Most remarkably, Wilson's paper makes not a single reference to the (Sinhala) state-sponsored pogroms against Tamils, that increased in virulence from 1956 to 1983, and which had as primary target the presence of the Southern ('Colombo') Tamil in southern or the Sinhala-dominated parts of Sri Lanka.[18] These same pogroms—or, the victimhood of the *Southern* Tamil—renarrativized as genocide, are the main buttress upon which Tamil nationalism justifies its separatism. This erasure enables Wilson, too, to 'write off' Southern Tamils from not just the future, but even the present of Tamil nationalism. The elision from the passage ('Tamil speaking') Muslims and UpCountry Tamils is also noteworthy, given Tamil nationalism's occasional effects—echoed by Wilson earlier in his paper—to incorporate those two social groups within its project. The significance of these erasures and elisions will be addressed later, when I return to Wilson; the point to note now is that the following five groups, at the very least, could have been incorporated, and/or were available for incorporation, by separatist

---

[17] Alfred J. Wilson, 'The Colombo Man, the Jaffna Man, and the Batticaloa Man', in Chelvaduri Manogoran and Bryan P. Pfaffenberger (eds), *The Srilankan Tamils: Ethnicity and Identity* (Boulder: Westview Press, 1994), p.140, emphasis added. 'Ceylon', the British colonial name for the country, is often used in Tamil nationalist texts in the place of and in opposition to 'Sri Lanka'. This is justified on the grounds that, in the first republican constitution of 1972 where the name of the country was officially altered, the dominance of the Sinhala state over the Tamil nation was institutionalized. By continuing to use 'Ceylon', Tamil nationalism represents itself as resisting such domination. So doing, however, also betrays a colonialist nostalgia; for, 'Ceylon' was the name given the country by the British colonial power. Likewise, one cannot use 'Sri Lanka' to refer to the island (before 1972) without in some (minimal) way being complicitous with Sinhala nationalism. Sri Lanka is used throughout this paper not as an anti-Tamil nationalist (or pro-Sinhala nationalist) gesture, but for convenience.

[18] The best brief account of this history remains A. Sivanandan, 'Sri Lanka: Racism and the Politics of Underdevelopment', in *Race and Class*, 26(I), 1984. For a more comprehensive, and equally committed, account that brings the story upto 1990, see Rajan Hoole, *et al.*, *The Broken Palmyrah: The Tamil Crisis in Sri Lanka—An Inside Account* (Claremont: Sri Lanka Studies, 1990).

Tamil nationalism, as constituent of the Tamil nation: Northern, Eastern, UpCountry and Southern Tamils, and (Northern and Eastern) Muslims.

While a comprehensive account of Tamil nationalism would require the relation of all these groups to its project, the focus in this essay is with *the liminal—or, more properly, epidermal—status accorded to Southern Tamils by separatist Tamil nationalism.* That status, and the response of Southern Tamil women to it—to being marginalized, appropriated and, finally, expelled from the project of Tamil separatism, to being denied its protection or refused a home—is what I seek to investigate, expose and respond to here. In the course of this inquiry, it will be evident that a reassessment is necessary of the current condition of our knowledge of the categories nationalism, nation and state; and of the nexus between them. This should be apparent already of nation—if indeed its appearance does change, as I contend, with conjuncture. A complete re-assessment of the theory of nationalism is of course beyond the scope of a single essay; but—claim the *seventh—clarifications are necessary* (and will be offered when and where appropriate) *of the following terms,* much misunderstood, if not abused, in the literature: *nationalism, nation, nation-state, country, national, citizen.* The texts of nationalism themselves demand the distinctions.

The *eighth* claim of this essay, then, is about the necessity to pay closer attention than we have done so far to the very texts we read; to be more attentive readers. For it is there, in the act of reading, that one can fully grasp nationalism and its awesome narrative power, its reliance on the narrative form to buttress its hegemony, its ability to present its story *as the* truth, as incontrovertibly and uniquely true; and, consequently, it is also by reading that one can contest the story of nationalism, represented as self-evident, with other, less oppressive, more enabling ones. To put this differently: carefully *reading (the texts of) nationalism is an indispensable—a central, though not exclusive—component of the tasks of comprehending the phenomenon and of (re)writing its oppressive history.*

Of course, equally crucial is adopting what Edward Said[19] has

---

[19] Edward Said, *Culture and Imperialism* (New York: Knopf, 1993).

termed a 'contrapuntal' reading strategy: reading those texts, produced as a consequence of the logic of nationalism, that are not merely critical of but challenge the nationalist project, against the official story. These resistant texts are often singular—a term not to be confused with unique—in their narrative voice, as opposed to the aggregate voice assumed by nationalism. Reading carefully, therefore, also requires *vigilance of truth claims based on number*, and it requires patience, the search for meaning in unexpected—though not unpredictable—places, that don't 'visibly stick out of the debris of the past'. Reading carefully, in other words, would produce new writing, new histories that confront what John Mowitt has termed 'the apparent fixity of the present' and would expose the constructedness of what appears self-evidently true and fixed. The importance of such an effort, for those of us who hold, with Mowitt, that 'what we believe to have happened to us bears concretely on what we are prepared to do with ourselves,'[20] need hardly be laboured.

Having said all this, my *ninth* claim cannot be unexpected: that *the nation itself is inoperative, oppressive, disabling community*. To make that statement is not to say anything fundamentally new; it is only to (re)state, if somewhat bluntly, one of the foundational premises, and signal achievements, of *Subaltern Studies*, not to mention other Marxisms. Therefore, I will conclude this section of my essay with an invocation of an inexplicably forgotten but important Marxist intellectual whose work must be seen as part of the genealogy both of the Indian collective, and of other contemporary Marxist critiques of the nation as enabling community—Rosa Luxemburg. She wrote at the beginning of this century: 'the concept of the "nation" as a homogeneous social and political entity . . . is one of those categories of bourgeois ideology which Marxist theory submitted to a radical revision . . . In a class society, "*the nation*" as *a homogeneous social entity does not exist*. Rather, there exists within each nation, classes with antagonistic interests and "rights".'[21]

---

[20] John Mowitt, *Text: Genealogy of an Anti-Disciplinary Object* (Durham: Duke University Press, 1992), p. 2.

[21] Rosa Luxemburg, *The National Question: Selected Writings* (New York: Monthly Review, 1976), p. 135, emphasis added.

Constituting Nation, Contesting Nationalism 223

One would today supplement this statement by substituting the term 'social groups', for 'classes'; these groups to be understood as constituted on the axes of gender, 'ethnicity', region, caste, sexuality, etc. But Luxemburg's fundamental claim, the strength of which lies in it not being based on a false consciousness argument, cannot be faulted: that the nation is not an integer, but a gathering of *antagonistic* social groups that only *appear* to have a unity, or commonality; or, to be precise, that an apparent, or appearance of, unity is given these groups, under the name nation, by nationalism.

The premise that nation, state and country are distinct compels separatist Tamil nationalism. Its reading of post-independence events in the country Sri Lanka is based on the distinction, and on identifying a historical failure: of a nationalism that could properly be named Sri Lankan to occur, and of a community that could be called the Sri Lankan nation to inhabit the similarly named country. In its documents, country and nation are seen as failing to coincide. That is to say, *Tamil nationalism denies the existence—and, with hindsight, the very possibility—of a Sri Lankan nation*; the latter being, as it were, always already impossible. *Instead, two competing nationalisms, Sinhala and Tamil, which presume two distinct nations, are seen to inhabit one country, Sri Lanka.*

A differently inflected history of post-colonial Sri Lanka would not tell this story in terms of a lack. In such a reading, Sinhala nationalism would be seen to dominate, if not to have captured, the Sri Lankan state; consequently making it possible to call the Sri Lankan state a Sinhala one (and, as I shall explain later, to speak of a *Sinhala nation-state*). In this story, with the capture of the state, non-Sinhala Sri Lankan citizens were othered, minoritized,[22] even disenfranchised;[23]

---

[22] The process of minoritization, or minority production, had its origin in the colonial period. For a Tamil nationalist account of these events, see Satchi Ponnambalam, *Sri Lanka: The National Question and The Tamil Liberation Struggle* (London: Zed Books, 1983).

[23] I refer, of course, to the UpCountry ('Indian') Tamils. For a comprehensive

the post-colonial history of Sri Lanka is also the story of resistances (by the othered, minoritized) to this happening. Separatist Tamil nationalism, in this understanding, is one response among many conceivable to the Sinhala nationalist domination of Sri Lanka.

This essay discusses two responses, two resistances, two very different—in their politics—and unequal—in their narrative power—alternatives to the equation of Sinhala with Sri Lankan. One is organized, explicit, popular; the other, without an assured agenda, implicit, singular. The one responds to being minoritized by demanding majority status; the other attempts, if inchoately, to look outside this logic. The one, unabashedly nationalist; the other, seeking ways of being untrammelled by such a claustrophobic ideology and identity. The one insists upon and delimits the terms of its interpretation; the other leaves interpretation open. The one is unambiguous, certain, absolute; the other, uncertain, sometimes even confused, usually in need of explanation and clarification. The one assumes 'common being', the subsumption of difference, the adequacy of being within a single identity; the other raises the possibility of 'being in common', community without identity.[24] I locate these resistances in two very different kinds of texts: programmatic works of Tamil nationalism, and testimonies of (Southern) Tamil women refugees. The first set of texts enable the critic to approach the (Tamil) nation; the second, to tell another story and attempt to leave it behind.

The opening section of this essay examines three momentous Tamil nationalist documents, of three different conjunctures, that allow one to track the mutations in the appearance of the Tamil nation: the *Vadukkodai Resolution* (1976, hereafter VR), bearing the signature of the Tamil United Liberation Front (TULF), in which organised Tamil nationalism first demanded a separate state;[25] *Liberation Tigers*

---

account of their history in Sri Lanka, on which the literature is extensive, see S. Nadesan, *A History of the UpCountry Tamil People* (Colombo: Nandalla Publishers, 1993).

[24] The terms are from Jean-Luc Nancy, *The Inoperative Community* (Minneapolis: University of Minnesota Press, 1991).

[25] In 1972, around the time of the first republican Sri Lankan constitution that VR refers to as 'capping' Sinhala mistreatment of the Tamils, the Northern-based Federal Party (FP), the UpCountry-based Ceylon Workers' Congress (CWC) and the

and *Tamil Freedom Struggle* (1983, hereafter LTE), where the Liberation Tigers of Tamil Eelam (LTTE) announced 'to the world', soon after the pogrom of July 1983, that its (armed) struggle for a separate state challenged not only Sinhala nationalism, but also the Tamil nationalism of the (bourgeois, 'non-violent', collaborationist) TULF; and the *Thimpu Declaration* (1985, TD), issued by the TULF, LTTE and four other Tamil political parties which, in a moment of rare unity within the Tamil resistance, reiterated the demand for a separate state as the only possible solution to the oppression of the Tamil nation.

These texts virtually suggest themselves for a reading such as attempted here because *they mark crucial moments in the autobiography of Tamil nationalism.*[26] Other documents could have been selected from the same organizations, but these enable a better grasp of the phenomenon. They are products of, produce, and give the reader access to, different contradictions, different conjunctures in this story; they address different audiences, respond to different events in the history of Sinhala and Tamil nationalisms and of the country Sri Lanka. In so doing, however, in being produced and producing, in addressing and responding, these three texts also—as they must—specify or fix the nation; and thus enable the critic/reader to determine with some accuracy the constitution of the Tamil nation at different conjunctures.

The second section of this essay reads the testimonies of two women refugees, gendered responses to being Southern Tamil and *denationalized* at a specific and lasting moment in the history of Tamil separatism.

Southern-based Tamil Congress combined to form the Tamil United Front. The FP dominated this combine which, in 1976, reconstituted itself as the Tamil United *Liberation* Front. The CWC's commitment to this organization and politics was qualified. For an account of the continuities and discontinuities in Tamil politics in the post-colonial period that focusses on the FP's founder, Samuel James Chelvanayakam, see Alfred J. Wilson, *S.J.V. Chelvanayakam and the Crisis of Sri Lankan Tamil Nationalism, 1947–1977* (London: Hurst, 1994).

[26] To say that is not necessarily to also say that they mark important moments in the history of Sri Lanka. Chandra de Silva has written a history of Sri Lanka, by no means a Sinhala nationalist account, without a mention of any of these documents in *Sri Lanka: A History* (New Delhi: Vikas, 1987).

This nationalism, unwilling to acknowledge its own complicity in the expulsion of Southern Tamils from its project, unprepared to allow the stories of these women any meaning outside its frame of reference, can only see them as traitors.[27] The (feminist) cultural critic, however, has a different charge. These women's narratives insist upon being read as contesting and destabilizing the nation and the project of (Tamil) nationalism; they must be responded to as such. Much excellent feminist work has been produced on the nexus between women and nation, on the unfair and unequal burdens placed upon women by nationalism; this section of my essay is in the spirit of extending that feminist critique.[28] I find that in these Southern Tamils' texts, in not just the predicament of these women but also in their understanding of and responses to it, lies the possibility of generating spaces, politics, community, outside the ubiquitous and claustrophobic presence of nationalism. Generated as they are by the very logic of nationalism, these narratives could be considered 'emergent', in Raymond Williams's sense, being both new and, however incipiently, oppositional. Their

---

[27] The figure of the traitor would be a most insightful one through which to read Tamil separatism; for, while the fate of the non-inhabitant Tamil, though understood, is left to be determined by others, determining that of the inhabitant Tamil 'traitor', LTTE nationalism takes upon itself. (The terms 'inhabitant' and 'non-inhabitant' will be clarified soon.) The latter category included informants, collaborators, political opponents and some of the most outstanding political products of post-colonial Sri Lanka—Rajani Thiranagama and K. Padmanabha, to name just two. The LTTE punishment for 'treachery' is, of course, death.

[28] A long bibliography is called for here; I will content myself by referring the reader to the work of Floya Anthias and Nira Yuval-Davis, Jean Howard and Anne McClintock, and the collections edited by Kumkum Sangari and Sudesh Vaid, Jacqui Alexander and Chandra Mohanty, and Andrew Parker, *et al.*, and the following: Floya Anthias and Nira Yuval-Davis, 'Introduction' in *Women-Nation-state* (London: Macmillan, 1989); Jean Howard and Phyllis Rackin, *Engendering a Nation: A Feminist Account of Shakespeare's English Histories* (New York: Routledge, 1997); Anne McClintock, *Imperial Leather: Race, Gender and Sexuality in the Colonial Contact* (New York: Routledge, 1994); Kumkum Sangari and Sudesh Vaid (eds), *Recasting Women: Essays in Indian Colonial History* (New Brunswick: Rutgers University Press, 1989), Alexander and Mohanty 1997; Andrew Parker *et al.*, *Nationalism and Sexualities* (New York: Routledge, 1992).

oppositional nature, of course, is both inherent and to be recognized as such, foregrounded and advanced by the Marxist-feminist critic. We refuse this charge, this call for collaboration, this duty, at our own peril.

Constituting the Nation: Documents of Tamil Nationalism

One of the signal achievements of Sri Lankan historiography has been its critique of Sinhala nationalism and of the Sinhala-dominated Sri Lankan state: I think here of the exemplary scholarship and commitment of Newton Gunasinghe, R.A.L.H. Gunawardana, Kumari Jayawardana and Gananath Obeyesekere. I cannot rehearse that critique of the criminal history of Sinhala nationalism, but only gesture towards an impressive body of work which this essay takes as given, as constituting the most persuasive account of post-colonial Sri Lankan history. That work has taken apart, in meticulous detail, Sinhala nationalism's fabrication of an ancient history for the Sinhala nation, demonstrated the modern provenance of these nationalist claims, and laid bare the classed and gendered interests at stake in their making. Most of all, their work has enabled a questioning of the exclusivist and oppressive Sri Lanka that is the legacy of Sinhala nationalism.

The story of separatist Tamil nationalism as response to oppressive Sinhala nationalism has been told, too.[29] This narrative posits Tamil nationalism to be determined purely by extrinsic (Sinhala nationalist) forces—a move which, ironically enough, discounts the agency of the very forces it supports—and leads logically to but one conclusion: the justification of separatism.[30] In this account, the Vadukkodai Resolution

---

[29] For the liberal version, see Alfred J. Wilson, *The Break-up of Sri Lanka: The Sinhalese-Tamil Conflict* (Honolulu: University of Hawaii Press, 1988) and Wilson 1994; for the leftist, Ponnambalam, 1983.

[30] With this discounting of agency comes a denial of responsibility. Wilson makes several statements to this effect: 'Mrs Bandaranaike ... was in the end *responsible* for the demand for a separate state' (1994, 123, emphasis added); and takes great pains to stress that Tamil nationalism was 'defensive', not 'aggressive'—thus making the Sinhala state solely responsible for the criminal record of Tamil separatism.

of 1976 marks a break in the long history of the Sri Lankan Tamil people. As said before, it is the first demand of organized Tamil nationalism for a separate state. Put differently, the conjuncture this text seeks to produce, or insists that its reader identify, is one in which the dominant, overdetermining contradiction in the country, Sri Lanka, *is seen to be* that between two nations, Sinhala and Tamil, or, the forces of Sinhala and Tamil nationalism.

This document, which Wilson calls 'historic and momentous', opens thus: 'throughout the centuries, from the dawn of history, the Sinhalese and Tamil nations have divided between them the possession of Ceylon . . . the Tamils *possessing* the Northern and Eastern districts.'[31] The necessity to distinguish between the terms country and nation—not as ontological phenomena, but as analytic categories—is, I hope, now clear. The very text of (Tamil) nationalism demands one, almost transparently so by the end of this story:

> the Tamil Kingdom was overthrown in war and conquered by the Portuguese in 1619 and from them by the Dutch and the British in turn independent of the Sinhalese Kingdoms . . . [The British] *joined under compulsion* the territories of the Tamil Kingdom to the territories of the Sinhalese Kingdoms for purposes of administrative convenience . . . [These] facts of history were completely overlooked and power was transferred to the Sinhalese nation over the entire country [at independence in 1948].[32]

This passage is typical of both the conservativeness, and of the profoundly nostalgic rhetoric of nationalism, where the avowed task of nationalism is to end nostalgia—redeem the loss, restore past greatness. All nationalisms, as we well know, seek to legitimize themselves by giving their nations an interminable past; by celebrating, as Benedict Anderson has pointed out, not their youth but their age. Tamil nationalism will not be an exception to this rule. Equally typical is the representation of this particular nation as possessing, or being bound, in and over time, to a particular territory; this crucial bind will be returned to.

---

[31] *Vadukkodai Resolution*, 1976, p. 1, emphasis added.
[32] Ibid.

Constituting Nation, Contesting Nationalism 229

The immediate necessity, without which this argument cannot move, is grasping the use of a notion of 'country' in the passage above. *'Ceylon', to VR, is a country*, a term deployed in three senses: the first, as a piece of land inhabited by two nations; the second, as a piece of land with many kingdoms (polities). These two senses, in which the island is referred to before British colonialism, are not mutually exclusive: while the social and political—the Tamil nation and kingdom—coincide in one case, and does not in the other—the Sinhala nation is divided into many kingdoms, *'country' in both these instances is land delimited only by sea, or nature*. The third sense, however, is different: *now, under British colonial rule, the geographical has coincided with the political; land is territory;* the island with two indigenous nations is governed by a single, clearly inorganic, colonial state (and, presumably, inorganic nation as well, though this question is not addressed).

One can see why Tamil separatism—not to mention those who would seek to understand it—must distinguish between country and nation (and state): it would, quite literally, be unable to make its case without so doing. This is a distinction that, if borne in mind, would also help the cultural critic avert confusion. Anderson, for instance, would have avoided much embarrassment if he had kept the categories separate. Towards the beginning of his hugely influential work, he states: 'nationalism has proved an uncomfortable *anomaly* for Marxist theory and, precisely for that reason, has been largely elided . . . How else to explain Marx's failure to explicate the crucial adjective . . . "The proletariat of each country much, of course, first of all settle matters with *its own* bourgeoisie".'[33]

. I have elsewhere commented upon the arrogance (a generalization about Marxism based on reading one sentence in Marx) and sheer ignorance (of Luxemburg, amongst others) of this formulation.[34] The point to be made here is that, in the passage above, *Marx speaks of a*

---

[33] Benedict Anderson, *Imagined Communities: Reflections on the Origin and Spread of Nationalism*, 2nd edn. (London: Verso, 1991), p. 4.

[34] See Qadri Ismail, 'Battling Against the Break: On Cricket, Nationalism and the Swashbuckling Sri Lankans', in *Social Text*, 50, 1997. This essay, by the way, also attempts to locate an emergent space outside the grasp of nationalism.

socialist revolution as happening within a country, not a nation. And, while it is true that he sometimes slips and substitutes the terms for each other, including in the sentence from the *Manifesto* previous to the one quoted by Anderson, he also uses the terms quite distinctly in his work. And, surely, it must have occurred to Anderson that the *Communist Manifesto* is just that, a call to arms, not the most obvious or exclusive text one might depend upon for theoretical insight? I cannot here provide a detailed reading of Marx's deployment of these two terms; but a close examination of works like *The Eighteenth Brumaire of Louis Bonaparte* would show that 'country' is seen as a geographical *and* political entity (land/territory plus state)—not as a product of nature; and that 'nation', of which Marx has a most complex if implicit understanding, is not seen as having a geographical or territorial dimension—or, more precisely, isn't grasped in these terms.

VR, one might therefore say, if somewhat mischieviously, has an almost Marxist understanding of the distinction. According to it, what happens in Sri Lanka following independence in 1948, is that, while the country does not change—geography and policy continue to coincide—one nation, the Sinhala, inherits the state. This powerful combine sees the Tamil not as a nation, but as a 'numerical minority'. The combine in question being that category much confused and abused in the literature, the (Sinhala) *nation-state*, which has to be seen as distinct from both 'nation' and 'state'. In other words, *the nation-state is to be understood as a purely conjunctural phenomenon and not as a permanent or static entity*; it can be said or seen to be only at those moments, either when the state acts on behalf of the nation, or the nation invokes the state; or, more exactly, its presence can be detected or read only in those acts where the interests of nation and state coincide.

VR, therefore, implies that the Tamil rebellion is against the Sinhala nation-state, against a (Sinhala nationalist) conception of country (Sri Lanka) in which the Tamil (nation) can only have minority—less than equal—status.[35] VR responds to this status with the idea of

---

[35] I am able to make this point because of Ayesha Jalal's revisionist reading of the figure of Jinnah in *The Sole Spokesman* (Cambridge: Cambridge University Press,

majority status and the *same concept* of country. The difference lying only in the substance of this new country—for, *to the extent that VR demarcates the future, its anticipated state, too, will consist of a majority and minorities*, with the proviso that, now, the majority will no longer be the Sinhala, but the Tamil nation. A singular failure of the political and *ethical* imagination could, and perhaps should, be noticed in the response of Tamil nationalism to the Sinhala; a failure that would have consequences—for Tamils and for others.[36] Or one might say, temperately, within the terms offered by Chatterjee's pathbreaking *Nationalist Thought and the Colonial World*, that Tamil nationalism 'reasons within . . . the very structure of power . . . [it] sought to repudiate;'[37] that while other responses to Sinhala nationalism could be conceived, Tamil nationalism did not think outside a logic that saw political significance in number.

If VR, then, seeks to create a new country, it does not do so without specifying geographic boundaries for it: 'the Northern and Eastern districts' of contemporary Ceylon. The basis of the right of the Tamil nation to this land is also explained: 'from the dawn of history', or always, the Tamil nation '*possessed*' the land. This seemingly casual choice of word contains a crucial assertion: the north and east of the

---

1985) and, following her work, of Aamir Mufti's excellent and provocative recasting of the story of Congress Indian nationalism in 'Secularism and Minority: Elements of a Critique', in *Social Text*, 45, 1995. Implicit in Wilson is a similar take: until the FP/TULF'S 'ideology of defensive nationalism', he argues, the Tamils 'had almost reconciled themselves to the role of a perpetual minority.'

[36] In the 1980s, Tamil separatism has been accused of treating the 'minorities' in its territory with the same genocidal impulse that it has accused the Sinhala state of treating the Tamil nation; see, for instance, Ram Manikkalingam, *Tigerism and Other Essays* (Colombo: Ethnic Studies Group, 1995).

[37] Partha Chatterjee, *Nationalist Thought and the Colonial World: A Derivative Discourse?* (Minneapolis: University of Minnesota, 1993 [1984], p. 38. This is not to argue, of course, that anti-colonial and post-colonial 'nationalist thought', or nationalism as ideology, are homologous. Chatterjee's argument is that anti-colonial nationalism accepts an essential difference between East and West; a difference produced, as we well know following the work of Edward Said in *Orientalism* (London: Routledge, 1978), by colonialism. That particular question, needless to say, does not arise with regard to post-colonial nationalism.

country Sri Lanka *belonged and belongs*, belongs today because it *always* belonged, to the Tamil nation; it is a possession—is so now and was so always. Implicitly, therefore, no one else can have a credible claim upon it. This argument has two consequences. First, that its converse is also true: since Tamils possess the Northeast, those possessing the Northeast are Tamil; others may live in the same land, but they do not and cannot *possess* it (not being of the majority nation). The next, in distinguishing between those who possess and others who merely live or reside in the land, creates two categories of person in the anticipated state it names Eelam: I term them (majority) *inhabitants*, those who can only, and will always, be Tamil—to whom, as it were, Tamilness has become a matter of habit, and (minority) *residents*, those who cannot be Tamil. The political consequences of this distinction will be evident soon; the analytic one, of course, is between one group, inhabitants, whose relation to a territory is assumed to be more organic, natural, binding, authorized, than the other, more transient, residents.[38] The second consequence is that those Tamils resident outside the Northeast are depicted as, somehow, *dispossessed* of Tamil nationality; they become outside, and outsiders—epidermal—to the Tamil nation; indeed, in a certain sense, diasporic. Not outside Tamilness, or of being Tamil—they are still liable to being counted by the census—but of Tamil nationality, of participation in the nation, of being national.[39]

---

[38] Alan Sinfield has also recognized the need for some distinction along these lines in 'Diaspora and Hybridity: Queer Identities and the Ethnicity Model', in *Textual Practice* 10(2), 1996, p. 273. ' "citizen" has never meant "inhabitant". It always counterposes some others who are present but not full citizens—at best, visitors, but usually also racial, ethnic and sexual minorities, slaves, criminals, the lower classes, women, children, the elderly. In our Enlightenment inheritance, the nation is an unstable construct, and ideas of citizenship are deployed, typically, in a hegemonic process whereby outsiders are stigmatized and potential deviants jostled into place.' Sinfield, of course, uses 'inhabitant' in its everyday sense; and, in any event, doesn't take care to distinguish between a category implying a nexus to the state, and one implying a nexus to the nation.

[39] Thus a Tamil, in my understanding, is a census category; something possible, of course, only if the categorized assents to such categorization (interpellation). It must be stressed that without the assent of the categorized, this process, of identification of

All of which is to point out that VR distinguishes between, in fact creates, two categories of Tamil: those I term *national* and, in the absence of a better word, *non-national*.⁴⁰ In this conjuncture, of 1976—and the same does not hold in all—the Tamil national is an inhabitant of, possesses and is possessed by, the territory that is and will be Eelam.

The necessity for such a term, 'national', does not emerge from VR alone. If available earlier it could, for instance, have rescued Eric Hobsbawm from this clumsy formulation: 'the political duty of Ruritanians to the polity which encompasses and represents the Ruritanian nation, override all other public obligations, and in extreme cases . . . all other obligations . . .'⁴¹ 'Ruritanian', as used by Hobsbawm, refers to the basic constituent unit of nation—and is roughly equivalent to 'national'. What the passage indicates is that such a term is required, though not in quite the same sense as deployed by Hobsbawm. In my usage, 'national' does not refer to a person but is to be understood as a coding of being offered by nationalism to those it interpellates;⁴² such being

---

'ethnicity', cannot work. The special significance of acquiescence to interpellation, or performing one's identity, in the Sri Lankan Tamil situation is discussed in detail in the next section of this paper. But it should be mentioned here, that looking at performance, rather than the census, presents another way of comprehending or identifying Tamilness. In this understanding, Tamilness is to be grasped as a 'set of signifying practices'; needless to add, such a method is available only to the anthropologist. For an important study of Tamilness in Southern Sri Lanka in the post-1983 conjuncture, see Pradeep Jeganathan's 'In the Shadow of Violence: Tamilness and the Anthropology of Identity in Southern Sri Lanka', in Tessa Bartholemeusz and Chandra DeSilva (eds), *The Near Other, the Far Other and the Other's Other: Buddhism & Identity in Sri Lanka* (forthcoming). He argues, persuasively, that Southern Tamilness in post-1983 Sri Lanka is to be identified by the practice of the 'tactics of anticipation' of violence; of course, Southern Tamilness in other conjunctures would differ.

⁴⁰ A more precise wording would be 'nationalized' and 'denationalized' Tamils; but that is an even less elegant formulation than the above.

⁴¹ Eric Hobsbawm, *Nations and Nationalism since 1780* (Cambridge: Cambridge University Press, 1990), p. 9.

⁴² Cf Gayatri Spivak, *Outside in the Teaching Machine* (New York: Routledge, 1993), p. 231. ' "Agent" and "subject" are different codings of something we call "being".' Implicit here, of course, is a critique of the Althusserian notion of subject as a category 'without history'.

implies a fundamental, almost always exclusive, as Hobsbawm notes, allegiance to nation (as superadequate community and identity). This category is to be contrasted with *citizen*—which implies a nexus to the state and could be understood, in this context, as a coding of being offered by the state. To illustrate the difference: a Sri Lankan Tamil would, by virtue of being a Sri Lankan citizen, be entitled to certain benefits of the state, like a passport, constitutionally guaranteed rights, etc. *The national, however, has duties, not rights*—including those outlined by Hobsbawm above. This same Tamil would, *if interpellated as a national*, have certain demands made of him/her by nationalism. In other words, *'national' cannot be confused with 'citizen'*; equally importantly, I hope, the preceding discussion has demonstrated the necessity for the distinction—without which the debate on nationalism lacks analytic clarity. A similar argument, of course, would hold for the other distinctions and clarifications offered here—between nation, state and country.

In the conjuncture of VR, as stated above, it is the Northeastern inhabitant Tamil that is sought to be interpellated as national by Tamil nationalism, which has, as its *immediate* end, the achievement of a separate state. The necessity for this end is justified on a variety of grounds. We remember that the Tamils were always a nation, from 'the dawn of history', and never consented to being colonized, by the Portuguese, Dutch and/or British; or, subsequently, to being ruled by the Sinhalese. In the post-colonial period, the Tamils were the victims of 'aggressive Sinhala nationalism'. This aggression is listed, a series of deeds familiar to anyone familiar with post-colonial Sri Lanka: the disenfranchisement of UpCountry Tamils, state-aided mass colonization of the Northeast (the Tamil 'homeland') by Sinhala settlers, the replacement of English with Sinhala only—as opposed to Sinhala and Tamil—as the official language of the country, and other similar, if less consequential, deeds. 'Capping it all', states this document, was the new constitution of 1972, which deprived 'the Tamils of even the remnants of safeguards they had under the earlier constitution.' As we shall see, by the moment of the next document under scrutiny, 1983, the chargesheet against Sinhala nationalism would be even more damning. And, keeping that in mind, two points should be noted of VR. First, it makes no specific mention, six years later, of something that would be highlighted in LTF—a policy of the Sinhala state termed 'standardization', instituted in 1970, consequent to which the intake of Tamil language students into Sri Lankan universities, especially the science faculties, dropped drastically. Second, the only 'genocide' this text refers to is 'cultural'—justified on the grounds that the Sinhala state systematically denied Tamils 'opportunities of developing their language and culture.' In LTF, which appeared soon after the pogrom of 1983, these same deeds, this same history, is renarrativized; much is made there of the Sinhala state's physical genocidal ambitions. This point cannot be underscored too much: that *nationalism continually renarrativizes the past in order to serve its present*; another reason why its documents must be read very closely.

But in 1972, states VR, the Tamil people, through their representatives, continued to agitate to 'win their rights . . . without jeopardizing the unity of the country.' Their 'last attempt' on this score was to amend the first republican constitution of that same year, but their pleas were 'callously ignored'. Consequently, VR claims that, 'restoration and reconstitution of the Free, Sovereign, Secular, Socialist State of TAMIL EELAM *based on the right of self-determination inherent to every nation* was inevitable in order to safeguard the very existence of the Tamil Nation in this Country.'[43] This is a classic instance of nationalist nostalgia, of the dilemma facing every nationalism in search of a state that seeks simultaneously to draw its poetry from the past *and* the future, that seeks to justify the future in terms of the past. These nationalisms, as J.M. Fritzman put it, anticipate a state 'in which the future would retroactively constitute the past, and make meaningful the present.'[44] For, the entity whose 'restoration and reconstitution' could credibly be demanded given the previous argument is not the

---

[43] VR 1976, p. 6, emphasis added.

[44] J.M. Fritzman, 'The Future of Nostalgia and the Time of the Sublime', in *Clio*, 23(2), 1993, p. 169.

'Secular, Socialist, State of Tamil Eelam'—which could not have existed in the past, since socialism happened after the conquest of this state by the colonial powers, and is, in any event, explicitly anticipated in this text—but the Tamil Kingdom. However, the liberatory, fraternal rhetoric of nationalism does not allow for the restoration of kingdoms, even if they are to be reconstituted. So this text, in effect, calls for the restoration of something that wasn't; which, therefore, cannot be reconstituted.

Two other points that emerge from the passage demand notice, if not emphasis. First, that carefully worked out in it—and almost as an object lesson to the legions of scholars, many distinguished, who have confused the two—is another distinction, between nation and state. At an initial glance, this passage is stating the banal: it asserts the right of every nation to a state. But this could be phrased differently: that, in VR, *separatist Tamil nationalism presumes a nation and anticipates a state*. That it must do so is almost obvious, for the explicit end of this document is to mobilize the nation towards the state; it being in the state that the promise of nationalism, security, can be most confidently guaranteed. But, in so doing, it reminds us that *one can—and sometimes cannot not—speak of nation without or before the state*; and that the two are distinct categories. Otherwise, if one confuses nation with state, one would have, as in the Tamil instance in 1976 where the state has a purely anticipatory being, nationalism without nation—surely a logical impossibility and analytic absurdity.[45] This point would

---

[45] Nevertheless, the literature teems with confusion, and I'll cite but two symptomatic instances. Homi Bhabha wrote in his 'Introduction' to *Nation and Narration* (New York: Routledge, 1990): 'Amidst these exorbitant images of the nation-space in its transnational dimension there are *those who have not yet found their nation:* amongst them the Palestinians and the Black South Africans' (p. 7, emphasis added). At that writing, the Palestinians and 'Black South Africans'—a formulation, by the way, ignorant of the inclusive rhetoric of the African National Congress—had yet to have any control over their own affairs in the form of a state—which is what, if anything, they had 'not yet found'. However, it does not follow from this that they therefore lacked a nation; since these two peoples had *national*liberation organisations, and nationalisms, these nationalisms must have presumed a community that one cannot but understand as nation. According to Bhabha's (at best sloppy) phrasing, though, the Palestinians and Black South Africans would appear to be images! From a very different site, the

perhaps be easier to make if one thought of organized Tamil nationalism before 1976. The stated goal of the Federal Party (FP), the main precursor to the TULF, was not a separate state but a federal unit. The former was not even on the FP's agenda; still, it was a party organized upon explicitly and recognizably nationalist lines, and therefore must have, logically, presumed a nation.

Second, that VR takes—and can take—for granted that '*every nation*' has an 'inherent' right of self-determination; this is asserted—it is not sought to be proved or argued, because such a demonstration is no longer necessary. What this shows is that, at the level of what Chatterjee calls the 'problematic' of nationalist thought, or that which has to be justified, *post-colonial nationalism can assume or take for granted the 'right' of the nation as such to self-determination.* Such nationalisms appear at a time when, as Anderson put it, 'nation-ness' has become 'the most universally legitimate value in . . . political life;'[46] these nationalisms can take for granted the consequences of victory in India, Algeria, Vietnam. In contrast, anti-colonial nationalism had to make the general case of self-determination *in every instance*. Post-colonial nationalism benefitted from the victories of decolonization; its task was/is only to justify the entitlement of a *particular* nation to a state; thus, VR will (only) attempt to substantiate that the Tamils are a nation. This is all it has to do, to prove, in a post-colonial conjuncture; it can assume that, with successful proof or demonstration, the right to a separate state must and will be granted.[47]

---

imperative to counter Eurocentrism led the usually careful Samir Amin to write that all nations are not bourgeois/modern phenomena and that, therefore, one could 'talk of an Egyptian nation throughout history' (21). The fact, of course, that there has been a strong state in that part of the earth now known—to non-Arab outsiders—as Egypt does not mean that its inhabitants a nation made. Among other things, a necessary feature of nationalism as ideology is a representation of the nation as an egalitarian/fraternal community—surely not to be found, in even as great a civilization as Egypt, before the modern period.

[46] Anderson 1991, p.3.

[47] Needless to say, the predictable response of Sinhala nationalism to this has been to deny the Tamil nationalist claim to 'nation-status', and to insist, instead, on minority status. A typical, recent instance of this is to be found in Shantha Hennanayake, 'The Muslims in the Ethno-Nationalist Conflict in Sri Lanka', in Mahindra Werake

The resolution does not explicitly specify those who would enjoy this right, or the exact contours of this Tamil nation; nationalism, after all, does not and cannot openly admit to its exclusions and/or expulsions. VR does, however, allow the reader to figure these contours out when it delineates what makes the Tamils a nation:

> by virtue of their great language, their religions, their separate culture and heritage, their history of independent existence as a separate state over a distinct territory for several centuries till they were conquered by . . . the European invaders and *above all by their will to exist as a separate entity ruling themselves in their own territory* [the Tamils] are a nation distinct and apart from the Sinhalese . . .[48]

One might note in passing that, while the distinction is clearly maintained earlier, nation and state are confused here: one of the distinguishing features that make the Tamils a nation is that this people once had their own state. (Which, logically, may buttress their claim to restore that state; but cannot relate to their claims to be a nation.) More noteworthy is the distinction the text makes—almost despite itself—between what constituted the Tamil nation in the past, and in the contemporary moment. The Tamils of Ceylon share a language, culture, heritage, history and possess a territory; this is what made the Tamils a nation—in the past. What, 'above all', makes them a nation *today*, at the time of this Resolution, are these constative characteristics together with their 'will to exist as a separate entity'; and, presumably, their (nostalgic) will to restore (and reconstitute) their past greatness.

---

and P.V.J. Jayasekera (eds), *Security Dilemma of a Small State, Part Two: Internal Crisis and External Intervention in Sri Lanka* (New Delhi: South Asian Pub., 1995). 'In real politic [*sic*] of any state majority minority divisions are a fact of life. Unacceptance of this is bound to create problems as has been clearly evident by the unwillingness of Tamil political leaders to accept the political ethnic minority status in Sri Lanka' (p. 188). This is a horrific statement: material acts of the Sinhala state—including mass murder, if not genocide—are here reduced to 'problems', *brought upon themselves* by the Tamils, who stand accused only of the crime of refusing to accept Sinhala hegemony.

[48] VR, 1976, p. 6, emphasis added.

In other words, VR insists upon being read as marking the rupture of Tamil with Sinhala nationalism: until this point, according to the autobiography of Tamil nationalism, the two could have been accommodated within one country, one (bi-national) state; but not any more. The Tamil nation, and therefore Tamil national *circa* 1976, is to be determined now by a performative act, by a political will or commitment to a separate state.[49]

How this performance—akin to acquiescing to interpellation and, strictly speaking, non-agential—could be identified is also carefully specified by the text.[50] In so doing, this text denationalizes a section of the Tamil population.[51] For, it follows from the above that those Tamils not possessed of such will would be non-national: Tamil, but not of the nation. This category of Tamil, though not named, is directly addressed by the text: 'the State of TAMIL EELAM shall consist of the people of the Northern and Eastern provinces and shall also ensure full and equal rights of citizenship . . . to all Tamil-speaking people living in any part of Ceylon.'[52]

This passage returns to the distinction between state and nation

---

[49] The terms 'performative' and 'constative' are from Jacques Derrida.

[50] As is well known, Althusserian Marxism cannot account for multiple interpellation and one of its consequences—resistance to interpellation; and it does not enable a reading of subject-constitution and its consequences from the perspective of the subject(ed), rather than that of ideology. I find, and argue later, that a notion of 'performitivity' is a most useful way of thus supplementing Althusser. An instance of resistance to interpellation is to be noticed in the Tamil women's testimony examined in the next section of this paper. My own understanding of the performance of identity is inspired by a critical reading of Judith Butler's deservedly influential work, *Bodies That Matter: On the Discursive Limits of Sex* (New York: Routledge, 1993).

[51] As Wilson 1994 indicates, as ideology, the nationalism of the Federal Party encompassed *all* Tamils in Sri Lanka, including the UpCountry, whose claims and interests it sought to represent. In other words, until the separatist demand, all Tamils in Sri Lanka—indeed all Tamil speakers, a category that included Muslims—were considered within the Tamil nation. It was the introduction of the autonomous, as opposed to the federal, state as the most pressing goal of this nationalism that made habitation determine nationality.

[52] VR, 1976, p. 7.

and, therefore, between citizen and national. That is to say, VR admits to a category of Tamils outside the nation—whom I have termed non-national Tamils—who would be accommodated within the (anticipated) state. Otherwise, there would be no need to distinguish, above, between 'the people of the Northern and Eastern Province' (inhabitant, national, possessing territory) and 'all Tamil-speaking people living in any part of Ceylon' (non-inhabitant, non-national, dispossessed). Thus, to reiterate the point, Tamil national here equals Tamil inhabitant of the Northeast—only this category possesses the land and therefore the will, and will be invited/mobilized to make the state.[53] Put differently, *habitation alone guarantees interpellation and determines (Tamil) national status in the conjuncture of 1976.*

But, as indicated above, VR does not only address Tamil nationals. It also—in an uncharitable reading—displays an anxiety, if not guilt, about those Tamils it denationalizes; or—in a generous reading—seeks to accommodate non-national Tamils, if only in a subordinated fashion, within its project. For, while these Tamils—Southern by definition, since this category consists exclusively of non-inhabitants—are denationalized, they are promised accommodation in the anticipated state; they are invited to enjoy the benefits of citizenship. In other words, *at the conjuncture of VR, where habitation determines nationality, Tamil nationalism sees the Southern Tamil as non-national, but as potential citizen*; this category of Tamil is outside the nation, but inside the anticipated state.[54]

A similar status is accorded to both UpCountry Tamils and Northeastern Muslims, too, since they fall under the category 'Tamil-speaking people living in any part of Ceylon'; but not without qualification.

---

[53] It should be noted that all inhabitants and therefore national Tamils are *assumed* here to possess this will: it is taken for granted and does not have to be demonstrated, because this is Tamil nationalism at its most self-confident—it sees the future as infinite possibility.

[54] Thus, I cannot agree with Wilson's belief that, with VR, 'for the first time the [Northeastern] Ceylon Tamils had decided to sever their links with the Ceylon Tamils living outside the envisaged new state.' This did not happen till another conjuncture. (Wilson, 1988, p. 89).

The formula 'Tamil-speaking people' has a history that I cannot discuss here. As those familiar with the Sri Lankan debate know, it is an attempt to resolve another contradiction between residence and Tamil separatism. The presence of Muslims within the Northeast and the 'Tamilness' of the UpCountry Tamils have always presented problems for Tamil nationalism.[55] These problems are sought to be resolved with the promise of citizenship. To discuss the Muslims first: they are, by implication, residents, not inhabitants, of the Northeast: they are not said to share the same history, inhabit the former kingdoms, and so on. Therefore, they are not sought to be mobilized by Tamil separatism. That is, Muslims are subordinated by this document, though in an intriguing fashion: they are sought to be nationalized, incorporated within the 'Tamil-speaking people'; but this *people* has an (unspecified) history different from the detailed history of the Tamil *nation*—a move that denationalizes the Muslims at the same time as it attempts incorporation.[56] This move, therefore, effectively makes the Muslims a minority in the anticipated new state/country.

As for the UpCountry Tamils, while they too are implicitly offered citizenship, their special status is explicitly addressed by VR, which takes 'note of the reservations in relation to its commitment to the setting up of a separate state of TAMIL EELAM expressed by the Ceylon Workers' Congress, as a Trade Union of the Plantation Workers, the majority of whom live and work outside the Northern and Eastern areas.'[57] The exact reservations of the organization of the 'plantation workers'—a phraseology that avoids distinguishing between categories

[55] On the Muslim question with regard to Tamil nationalism, see Sivathamby. On the UpCountry Tamil, see Nadesan, *A History of UpCountry Tamil People* (Colombo: Nandalala, 1993).

[56] An uncharitable reading of this contradictory move would be that the Muslims are invited by VR to become Tamil, to deny their difference. This, certainly, is how they came to be seen in the late 1980s by the LTTE, as 'traitors'—those who denied or rejected their Tamilness—a labelling that justified their extermination and/or expulsion from the Northeast at LTTE hands. In so far as a continuity can be posited between the politics and ideology of the LTTE and the TULF, one could read VR as laying the (theoretical) basis for this happening.

[57] VR, 1976, p. 6.

of Tamils (on regional grounds) even while so doing (on ostensibly occupational criteria)—are not specified; but, clearly, they are related to the question of habitation. It is here that the failure in imagination of Tamil separatism at the conjuncture of VR, its inability to think beyond the equation of habitation and nationality, its inadequacy as a response to Sinhala nationalism, is most stunningly apparent. Within the narrative of Tamil nationalism, its adoption of separatism was unavoidable given its treatment at the hands of the Sinhala state; Wilson adopts this view, as do many other Tamil academics; and so, of course, does the LTTE. But, surely, other responses are conceivable: coalition with organized Muslim, UpCountry Tamil and antinationalist Sinhala groups on a liberal or pinko *Sri Lankan nationalist* platform; or a Marxist response—as would be advocated later, in different ways, by the Eelam People's Revolutionary Liberation Front (EPRLF) and the People's Liberation Organization of Tamileelam (PLOT). There was, and this should be stressed, nothing inevitable about the necessity for separatism; nothing inevitably necessary about the dismissal of UpCountry and Southern Tamils from the protective umbrella of Tamil nationalism. And what is striking about this, when seen through the position of the UpCountry Tamils, is that even their organized presence within the TULF could not produce an alternative politics. The FP-dominated TULF could not produce a more adequate political response to the very specific situation of the UpCountry Tamils—most of whom were still disenfranchised, without Sri Lankan citizenship, at this point—apart from a promise of inclusion in an uncertain future state. These exclusions—especially, the expulsion of Southern Tamils—would in time return to haunt the project of Tamil separatism, enable the possibility of its undermining.

A final point must be made about VR, and its guarantee that 'the state of TAMIL EELAM shall consist of the *people* of the Northern and Eastern provinces.' Since the residents of the Northeast consisted not only of Muslims but of Sinhalese, too, this text, though it does not directly address them, implicitly promises them citizenship, and therefore security; despite its complaint against discrimination at the hands of the Sinhala nation-state, Tamil nationalism in 1976 promises, if implicitly, not to discriminate—or seek vengeance—against the Sinhalese in 'its own' territory. Given what we shall find with the LTTE, in word and deed, the inclusive rhetoric of the TULF deserves some notice.

VR, then, is the product of many contradictions that the text attempts to contain; some—like the questions of the Southern and UpCountry Tamils and of the Muslims, of the contradiction between habitation and nationality—are active, visible and leave their mark upon the text; others—particularly, questions of gender and caste—do not do so explicitly, and must be read as repressed. That is to say, the nationalist text itself reveals but a partial picture of the conjuncture it is made by and seeks, in turn, to make, to give shape and meaning to. Thus, the contrapuntal reading strategy advocated in this paper necessitates paying close attention to both the documents of nationalism, as well as to other documents, stories, etc. on and against nationalism; without the latter, the phenomenon cannot be fully comprehended, leave alone adequately contested. For, nationalism cannot be taken at its word.

What VR does affirm, as implied before, is that the primary, antagonistic, *overdetermining* contradiction that marks it as the rupture between the Sinhala nation-state and Tamil nationalism; or, to be precise, this is how VR would insist upon being read. It also carriers evidence of another contradiction, within Tamil nationalism, that had been active for some years—and would soon become antagonistic and lead to another rupture. Not coincidentally, it appears in the very last clause of VR: 'this Convention calls upon the Tamil Nation in general and *the Tamil youth in particular* to come forward to throw themselves fully in the sacred fight for freedom and to flinch not till the goal . . . of TAMIL EELAM is reached.'[58] Why this emphasis on and address to the youth 'in particular'? What does it do, or try to do? What political purchase might it bring the TULF? What more does it tell us about the

[58] VR, 1976, p. 8, emphasis added.

conjuncture of VR? In the 1970s, as many writers on the subject, including Wilson, have explained, young Tamil men operating inside and outside the TULF's youth wing became the most visible manifestations of Tamil nationalist opposition to the Sinhala state. By 1976, two groups committed to violent resistance—implicitly opposed to the TULF's 'Gandhian' or 'non-violent' beliefs—were already in existence: the LTTE and the Tamil Eelam Liberation Organization (TELO). As early as 1974, Tamil militants had killed Jaffna's 'collaborationist' mayor, Alfred Duraiappah. (Velupillai Prabakaran has claimed to have carried out the execution himself.)[59] The TULF, therefore, had to be wary of this presence, of this challenge to its legitimacy and effectivity—and therefore its dominance within Tamil nationalism—even if members of the same youth groups often collaborated with the TULF. What the clause signifies, then, is the existence of a contradiction between two generations of Tamil nationalist men; a contradiction, as we shall soon see, overdetermined by caste and class. It signifies also an attempt to contain this contradiction: to keep the younger, more militant, petty-bourgeois, karaiyar caste men within TULF ideology and politics and, therefore, under bourgeois, vellala hegemony. (We know this not from VR, where the questions of caste and class are not raised, but from LTF, the next text to be discussed, where they are. In other words, a contrapuntal reading practice requires the reading not only of different forms or genres of texts against each other, but even the contrasting of documents of a similar texture.)

If non-antagonistic in 1976, this contradiction between the forces dominant within Tamil nationalism had clearly become antagonistic by the conjuncture of post-pogrom 1983, the date of publication of *Liberation Tigers and Tamil Freedom Struggle* (LTF). The closest thing to a manifesto ever written by the LTTE, it was published within weeks of the July 1983 anti-Tamil pogrom. It is a classic instance—because typical, not because profound—of Chatterjee's characterization of 'nationalist thought':

---

[59] The most comprehensive, though uncritical, account of the rise of the LTTE is M.R. Narayan Swamy, *Tigers of Lanka* (New Delhi: Konark, 1994). His access to information on the first half of the 1970s, however, isn't as good as his later sources.

its voice, now impassioned, now faltering, betrays the pressures of having to state its case against formidable opposition . . . Pitting itself against the reality of colonial rule . . . nationalism seeks to assert the feasibility of entirely new political possibilities . . . Only a vulgar reductionist can insist that these new possibilities simply 'emerge' out of a social structure or out of the supposedly objective workings of a world-historical process, that they do not need to be thought out, formulated, propagated and defended in the battlefield of politics . . . [I]t is precisely in the innovative thinking out of political possibilities and the defence of their historical feasibility that the unity is established between nationalist thought and nationalist politics.[60]

The 'formidable opposition' faced by Tamil separatism, of course, is the post-colonial Sinhala nation-state, not colonial rule. Still, ideologically, *at the level of what Chatterjee has termed the 'problematic', even if what is to be justified is different, anti-colonial and post-colonial nationalisms share a structural similarity: what gets justified must be 'thought out, formulated, propagated and defended' in the face of severe, almost overwhelming opposition.* These nationalisms—anti- and post-colonial must, therefore be distinguished, at least in this regard, from early northern European nationalisms, which are not the products of a similar history and did not require an articulation of their projects against 'formidable opposition' (another reason why such nationalisms cannot be considered 'modular', in Anderson's sense, of the northern European exemplar).[61]

It is not, however, the forbidding presence of the Sinhala state alone, accused here of genocide, that makes the voice of this text falter. LTF has to make its case against both the Sinhala state *and* what it sees as the limitations, compromises, inadequacies and irredeemable failures of the TULF while simultaneously presenting itself as being in seamless continuity with the spirit of VR. For, without a radical critique of the TULF, the LTTE would be hard-pressed to justify its own existence; but, making such a critique would leave itself open to the charge

---

[60] Chatterjee 1986, p. 40.

[61] This case with regard to anti-colonial nationalism has, of course, been established by Chatterjee.

of 'blaming the victim'—a charge the LTTE had to be especially sensitive to in August 1983, in the wake of the pogrom against Tamils all over Sri Lanka. One way of getting around this charge would have been to support the aims and the ideology of the TULF, while exposing the tangible inefficacy of its 'non-violent' *methods*; such a strategy would place the blame for the failure of the TULF squarely upon the shoulders of the Sinhala state. This course—charted, most notably, by TELO—would bring with it its own pitfalls: it would necessitate maintaining the TULF as allies, even if only in a junior capacity. But it was control—not dominance—of the Tamil resistance that the LTTE sought in 1983. This required supplanting, not sidelining, the TULF—ideologically, as well as in terms of the mode of resistance. The history of national liberation has made available just two ideological alternatives to the bourgeois-liberal variety: religion-based ('fundamentalist') and Marxist-inspired nationalisms. It is, without doubt, possible to argue that other alternatives, other responses to specific situations, can be thought out; the LTTE settled for being a vanguardist party on the Leninist model.[62]

If an innovative resolution of the dilemma of how to creatively distance from the TULF, resorting to Marxism, as we know, presents a formidable ideological quandary to a *national* liberation movement. The commitment of such a movement to the nation as the basic unit of social organization and mobilization, and the nationalist component of its ideology, would seem to necessitate an invitation at least on paper to all those who could be nationals—all those identified as Tamil by the census—to be mobilized as part of the struggle. As Mao pointed out, the objective in these instances is to unite the many and divide the

---

[62] Part of the explanation for this response to Sinhala nationalism—which draws its inspiration and sustenance from a certain reading of Buddhism (See R.A.L.H. Gunawardena, 'The People of the Lion: Sinhala Consciousness in History and Historiography', in Charles Abeyesekera and Newton Gunasinghe (eds), *Facets of Ethnicity in Sri Lanka* (Colombo: Social Scientists Association, 1987); and Gananath Obeyesekere, *A Meditation on Conscience* (Colombo: Social Scientists Association, 1988)—no doubt lies in the fact that Tamil nationalism, in Sri Lanka and India, has always been secular.

Constituting Nation, Contesting Nationalism 247

few. If this is not possible—and, as we saw in VR with regard to Southern Tamils, it isn't always—then good or cunning nationalist strategy demands that one tries one's best to neutralize those groups that cannot be incorporated, invited or interpellated. But the imperative of Marxism is to define one's project *in opposition* to social groups that may otherwise get identified as part of the nation, or nationalist project. *Marxism, to be both crude and brief, makes enemies of social groups that nationalism would rather see as allies, if not friends.* This, by the way, is why the two philosophies—as Luxemburg understood and argued, alone and bravely, against Lenin and so much other opposition in the Second International—if not mutually contradictory (in the common sense of the term) on the theoretical plane, certainly suggest incompatible programmes—they sit uneasily together at the political plane. (To say which is not to make the same argument, as Anderson unfathomably does, that a theoretical *Marxist understanding* of nationalism is not possible.) Consequently, the ideological contradiction facing a group trying to be both Marxist and nationalist can only get resolved in one of two possible ways: the movement's nationalism gets emphasized at the expense of its professed Marxism or, much less oftener, its nationalism is devitalized.[63]

Recognizing, if not admitting, the necessity to distinguish itself

---

[63] The most exhilarating, explicitly stagist, theoretical exposition of the latter possibility is to be found in Frantz Fanon, *The Wretched of the Earth* (New York: Grove, 1991), p. 963. This work does not collapse under the strain of making nationalism compatible with Marxism because it advocates a revolutionary programme and party that would 'use' the bourgeoisie to lead the struggle to achieve the state for the colonized nation, a practice that would require mobilization of the widest possible section of the populace; then, upon successful capture of the state and eviction of the colonial ruler, this programme demands shunting aside the bourgeoisie *immediately* thereafter. This text, in other words, holds that, in the colonial context, the nationals of every country must first settle matters with their own colonial regime before the proletariat of the same country settles matters with its bourgeoisie. This commitment to Marxism in Fanon—a commitment, by the way, either unnoticed or ignored by his liberal postcolonialist celebrators like Bhabha—and his subject-position, his being a Martinican in the Algerian struggle, a nationalist fighting to liberate another's nation, prevents his commitment to nationalism from being nostalgic, from being based upon resurrecting

from the TULF, LTF opens by invoking Lenin: 'the Marxist-Leninist theoretical and political framework recognizes that the national liberation struggle of *any* oppressed nation is progressive in essence . . . [and] upholds the universal socialist principle of the fundamental right of a nation to secede and form a state of its own, a principle aimed to protect a small nation from the oppression generating from the national chauvinism of a big nation.'[64] At first glance, there is no difference between the right asserted here, and in VR. The difference lies in the basis of this right: if VR echoes Renan and Jefferson, Lenin is the guiding spirit here. Why? What purchase and possible political advance does this grant the LTTE? It is tempting, given the subsequent history of the LTTE, its physical elimination of the Marxist Tamil resistance to the Sinhala state, to dismiss this as mere rhetoric; to label it, in Lenin's phrase, 'Socialism in words, chauvinism in deeds.'[65] But one must remember that, though written in English and ostensibly addressed

---

ancient glories, from being anything but strategic. (Thus the importance of the chapter, 'The Pitfalls of National Consciousness'.) Fanon, in other words, recognized that nationalism was not a transformative politics; thus the requirement of Marxism, coded in his work as 'liberation', to prevent the otherwise inevitable bourgeois domination of the newly decolonized entity. His two-stage theory of national liberation, of course, makes Fanon the grand theorist of 'third world' nationalism. His work exposes the sanctioned, Eurocentric, ignorance at the heart of formulations like the following: 'nationalism has never produced its own grand thinkers' (Anderson, 1991, p. 5); 'no serious historian of nations and nationalism can be a committed political nationalist' (Hobsbawm, 1990, p. 12). Anderson's formulation is persuasive about the West, where nationalisms, and therefore nations, emerged in conflict and competition against one another. In a third-world, or more properly anti-colonial, conjuncture, where the success or failure of one nationalism had serious consequences for the fate of others, conditions were different. In that situation, at the moment of decolonization, one could be, and *many were, nationalists in principle, and stood for the right to self-determination of every colonized nation*: thus Fanon, Nehru, Sukarno, Senghor . . . the list is long.

[64] *Liberation Tigers Tamil Freedom Fighters (LTF)*, 1983, p. 3, emphasis added.

[65] V.I. Lenin, *State and Revolution* (New York: International Publishers, 1994 [1918]), p. 5. This footnote is inadequate to its purpose, but all I can do in this paper is not to write out of the story of Tamil resistance its Marxist component: PLOT, and

Constituting Nation, Contesting Nationalism 249

to the 'progressive world', the primary audience/addressee of this text is local, Tamil. This audience has to be convinced of the superiority of the commitment, promise and project of the LTTE over that of the TULF (not to mention the other militant groups); not only must its support be taken *away* from the TULF, segments of this audience must also be interpellated and mobilized as fighters *for* the LTTE.

It is to this end that the argument about genocide, and the critique of the TULF in the Marxist-Leninist idiom, is put most effectively to work. One might see the TULF, in LTF, as being taken out of the nation and, as it were, put in its class (and caste):

> National oppression showed its intensity in the economic strangulation of the Tamil Eelam nation . . . The most tragic fact is that while the Tamil nation gradually deteriorated into economic backwardness wasting its potential productive labor, the Tamil capitalists, encouraged and aided by the Sinhala ruling class, invested in . . . South[ern, Sinhala-dominated, Sri Lanka]; a brutal fact [that] illustrates the class collaboration and class interests of the Tamil bourgeoisie.[66]

The rhetoric here is tough: the Tamil bourgeoisie is called 'brutal', almost explicitly equated with the genocidal Sinhala state for its complicity with the 'economic strangulation' of the Tamil nation. Indeed, this bourgeoisie is accused of enjoying the fruits of the 'strangulation'

---

more importantly, EPRLF. Their role has to be described and evaluated more comprehensively elsewhere; but this much at least must be said here: these two, admittedly less than perfect, but nevertheless heroic, groups stood, and fought in different ways, in alliance with like-minded organizations outside the Northeast, for a Marxist vision of Sri Lanka. Their 'defeat' can, of course, only be explained with reference to the conjuncture—and their own mistakes; but often left out of contemporary accounts of Tamil nationalism is both the contribution of these groups, and the fact that their leadership and cadre were systematically eliminated by the LTTE—often in collusion with the Indian, and sometimes with the Sri Lankan, states. If such a writing out is to be expected in the work of the Tamil right, who can only see these groups as traitors, it is disturbing when encountered in the narratives of those not identified with the right, like Valentine Daniel's *Charred Lullabies: Chapters in an Anthropography of Violence* (Princeton: Princeton University Press, 1996).

[66] *Liberation Tigers Tamil Freedom Fighters*, 1983, p. 14.

of the rest of the Tamil nation, a process that began in the colonial period:

> The Tamil social formation was constituted by a unique socio-economic organization, in which feudal elements and caste system were tightly interwoven to form the foundation of this complex society. The notorious system of caste stratification bestows, by right of birth, power and status to the high-caste Tamils, the minority of whom (landowners and business elites) owned the means of production and exploited the rest . . . Privileged by caste, provided with better educational facilities created by foreign missionaries, a section of the high-caste Tamils adopted the English educational system . . . The English imperial masters encouraged these Tamils . . .[67]

The upper-caste Tamil bourgeoisie, in other words, dominated Tamil politics merely in order to continue preserving its privilege. This caste-class is identified with the FP, precursor of the TULF, and is called, 'a nationalist party founded on a conservative ideology with bourgeois class elements and interests dominating the leadership.'[68] Consequently, it is only to be expected that the FP too will be termed 'collaborationist'— and it is, for the sin of continuing to attempt wresting concessions from an oppressive state despite a track record of failure upon failure. By the time one gets to the TULF in this narrative, a more straightforwardly dismissive adjective is necessary, and is available, to describe the politics of a group that continues to collaborate despite an experience that should have dictated otherwise: 'reactionary'.

It is instructive to note that, even in this relatively early text, one of the most significant bases upon which LTF distinguishes itself from VR is in terms promising to keep its promises. The TULF, it states, received at the election of 1977, from 'the people of Tamil Eelam', an 'authentic, *irreversible* mandate . . . to establish an independent, sovereign, socialist state of Tamil Eelam.'[69] This document, by the way, desires that such a state be 'established'; this is in contrast with VR, which

---

[67] Ibid., p. 7.
[68] Ibid., p. 14.
[69] Ibid., p. 29, emphasis added.

wanted it 'restored'. However, if LTF is sensitive to socialism as a state yet to be, and to monarchy as incompatible with such an enterprise, it cannot escape the nostalgia one found in VR. LTF, too, seeks to legitimize its present claims with at least a partial claim upon the past:

> When the Portuguese first landed . . . they found two ancient kingdoms . . . two distinct social systems with different cultures, constituting themselves as *separate nations of people ruled by their own kings* with independent state structures . . . The Portuguese, and the Dutch who came after them, governed the Tamil nation as a separate kingdom without violating its territorial integrity until the British, in 1833, brought a unified state structure amalgamating the two nations . . . *This forceful annexation* and amalgamation of two separate kingdoms, of two nations of people . . . was the *root cause of the present Tamil-Sinhala antagonism.*[70]

The prime purpose of this passage—the significance of which will be evident soon—is to establish the Tamil nation as being 'historically constituted'. This cannot, as argued before, be done without recourse to the nostalgic—even if that on display here is mild in comparison with VR's. The point being that nostalgia—looking back, seeking to resurrect lost community—is a condition no nationalism can escape.

But LTF will relentlessly seek its poetry largely from the future. Thus, it will represent the TULF as of the past, as seeking 'a collaboration strategy to placate the Sinhala leaders'; thus, the TULF only succeeded in deceiving the Tamil people and are called 'impotent'. In contrast, the 'militant Tamil youths' are of the future, '*unappeasable, irreconcilable and committed to the core* to the goal of an independent, socialist Tamil Eelam.'[71] The entirety of subsequent LTTE politics is summed up in that passage: Eelam or death. To be potent is to be irreconcilably committed to the end; any compromise causes impotence, death. This is a politics of frightening simplicity, a frighteningly simple masculinist politics; a politics that, in turn, dictated a sentence of death to all—including, eventually, the leadership of the TULF—that stood in its path; a politics the criminality of which can be seen

---

[70] Ibid., p. 6, emphasis added.
[71] Ibid., p. 29, emphasis added.

precisely in such acts as the killings of TULF leaders. For, the question arises: what *political* purchase, if any, can be found in the elimination of those deemed impotent?

Such deeds are carried out, of course, in the name of the people; and the invocation of the Tamil people—not to be confused, as we shall see, with nation—must be noted: they voted for a separate state, and this desire *must* be granted, worked for unappeasably, because mandates are 'irreversible'. LTE, actually, has no option but to present itself as inflexible; otherwise, it would have no case, or cause; otherwise, if it too will be flexible or appeasable, it cannot present itself as different from the collaborationist TULF. But the passage also indicates that *the people cannot change their minds*; once a mandate is granted, it cannot be revoked. Statements like this are more than mere rhetoric; they impose their own logic on (LTTE) politics: the unappeasable fighters of LTTE will not let the people reconsider; they will, instead, make the people into a nation and take the nation to the new country named Eelam. Here lies the element of continuity with VR: a continuity of purpose and promise.

But to whom is this promise made? To the Tamil 'people', the voters of 1977, who mandated the TULF and would like to see the promise kept? Or, to a Tamil nation different in constitution from both the people who voted and the Tamil nation in a previous conjuncture? Put differently: who qualifies as a Tamil national, to LTE, in this post-pogrom conjuncture? Like VR, LTF does not define the unit sought to be interpellated and mobilized; unlike VR, it refuses to do so explicitly: 'The Tamil nation is a historically constituted social formation possessing all the basic elements that are usually assembled to define a concrete characterization of a nation. Yet a definition as to what constitutes a nation is theoretically unnecessary since we can precisely formulate our issue within the Leninist conceptual framework of the self-determination of nations.'[72] Together with the invocation of Lenin before, this illustrates again the post-colonial inheritance from the anti-colonial struggle: now, the 'right' to secede can be taken for

[72] Ibid., p. 36.

granted; indeed, in LTF, 'nation-ness' is taken to be so legitimate as not to require theoretical definition and justification. Lenin settled the argument early in the twentieth century, and that is the end of the matter.

One could quarrel with this reading of Lenin. It could be argued, for instance, that all there is in Lenin is a *pragmatic* response to a problem that is fundamentally *theoretical* in nature; that, apart from a few suggestions about the role of the market (capitalism) and language (print)—yes, this does remind one of Anderson's argument—Lenin offered no carefully elaborated Marxist take on nationalism; or that, if he did, he saw nationalism as a non-transformative means, not an end. But a careful reading of Lenin on nationalism is beyond the scope of this paper; what needs to be said is that he left the theoretical work of explaining nationalism to Joseph Stalin. The famous definition that resulted is both perfectly positive and notoriously normative: 'A nation is a historically constituted, stable community of people, formed on the basis of a common language, territory, economic life, and psychological make-up manifested in a common culture.'[73] This could be deemed non-Marxist because it dehistoricizes the category (a most ironic happening, since the category itself is supposed to be 'historically constituted'); but it is not my purpose here to quarrel with Stalin. My point is that the recurrence of the phrase 'historically constituted' in LTF strongly suggests that the 'basic elements' it had in mind were, indeed, Stalin's. Given Stalin's strict criteria, however, one can understand LTF's reluctance to name the elements and thus proceed to demonstrate that the Tamil is entitled to nation-status (without which, given its Leninism, it cannot claim the right to self-determination). After all, as discussed before, the acknowledged existence in LTF of UpCountry and Southern Tamils (no common territory), not to mention the Tamil-speaking Muslims (no common 'psychological make-up'), would derail any such attempt. All this does not mean that the Tamils do not a nation make; but that positive

---

[73] Joseph Stalin, 'Marxism and the National Question' in *Selections from Lenin and Stalin: A National Colonial Question* (Calcutta: Calcutta Book House, 1970), p. 69.

definitions of the term—as just about every recent scholar writing on the subject has pointed out—cannot hold. In other words, LTF implicitly refutes Stalin. Within the Marxist story, this is not an insignificant happening: Stalin's, as Tom Nairn has noted, was 'the most influential single theory of political nationalism' produced by Marxism.[74]

If positive criteria are decried, how, then, does LTF determine and demarcate its nation? Not, as in VR, with a turn to Renan and an invocation of national 'will'; but with an innovative, if implicit, invocation of Lenin and a renarration of history. Recall that, to LTF, Leninism justifies the right not of any and every nation to secede—but only that of 'oppressed' nations. LTF, in order to be convincingly Leninist, must prove the fact of oppression. Indeed, it predictably lists many of the same juridical and extra-juridical 'oppressive' acts of the Sinhala state as does VR; but its emphasis differs. Appearing as it does after the pogrom of July 1983, LTF has plausibly available to it the word 'genocide', which it employs purposefully. Recall that, in VR, the only genocide identified was 'cultural'; in LTF, the past, the same events referred to by VR, is renarrativized, to logically culminate in physical genocide.

Such renarrativization is not an inconsequential happening; and should provide for a moment of sober reflection upon the nexus between 'event', narrative and nationalism; upon, more particularly, nationalism's capacity to, if not dependence upon, renarrativizing events, as the conjuncture dictates, to ensure continuance of its hegemony over its nationals. For, if arguments about nationalism's 'inventions of tradition' and of glorious pasts for its nations have by now become commonplace, the literature has yet to investigate nationalism's narrative power, to question its invention—in the strict sense—of powerfully charged terms like 'oppression'. Indeed, the debate on this question has been monopolized by the position that deems 'oppression' to be a matter of prediscursive fact, rather than ideological interpretation,

---

[74] Tom Nairn, *The Break-up of Britain: Crisis and Neo-nationalism* (London: Verso, 1991, 2nd edn).

which therefore does not require critical scrutiny. Since this is an emotionally powerful and seemingly incontrovertible argument—the resort to 'oppression' to justify a (nationalist) political practice that may otherwise appear difficult to defend, a justification to be seen not just in a section of the Sri Lankan debate but also characterizing a certain kind of (contemporary) Marxism—it demands comment. A typical recent instance of such a position is to be found in an article by David Lloyd, a critic, I would have thought on the evidence of his other work, who should surely know better.

Lloyd makes a case against what he calls the 'anti-nationalist prejudice' prevalent in Western leftist circles.[75] His ultimate defence of nationalism is on 'pragmatic grounds', that it enables a maintenance of difference, provides for a 'minimal defence against [the] homogenization' wrought by transnational capitalism.[76] A defence of what, exactly, we are not told. In any event, it has been convincingly demonstrated, most notably by Chatterjee and Dipesh Chakrabarty, that capital in fact does not, and *cannot*, homogenize; that its cultural logic isn't universal; that, while the market does 'nestle everywhere, settle everywhere, make connections everywhere,' *all* 'that is solid' does *not* 'melt into air'. However, the most remarkable aspect of Lloyd's argument is the admission that nationalism compresses difference: 'what nationalism achieves is a vertical integration based on political solidarity against a common enemy rather than a horizontal integration based on class antagonisms . . . [S]uch solidarity is not based merely in ideological manipulation of the masses but to some extent at least in the common experience of domination (I speak here, of course, of insurgent nationalisms . . .).'[77]

---

[75] David Lloyd, 'Nationalism Against the State: Towards a Critique of the Anti-Nationalist Prejudice', in Timothy P. Foleis, *et al.*, *Gender and Colonialism* (Galway: Galway University Press, 1995). Lloyd locates this tendency in the work of Anderson, Gellner and Hobsbawm. It is worthy of note that he does not find, or at any rate mention, evidence of such a 'prejudice' outside the Western academy.

[76] Lloyd 1995, p. 276.

[77] Ibid., p. 77.

This incredible defence of an avowedly hierarchical ideology, I will not waste time on. Though it should be pointed out that, at the very least, positions like that of Lloyd represent a serious abdication of intellectual and political responsibility: for, surely, *one cannot and should not defend an ideology one admits to be seriously flawed—on any grounds, leave alone those that there exists no alternative.* For surely it is among the tasks of the committed intellectual to work, directly or indirectly, whether by the production of critique or the articulation of programmes towards the enabling of such alternatives; and not to refuse to think, on 'pragmatic' or any other grounds. And, as I claim later in this essay, such alternatives can be found—if looked for carefully, usually in forgotten, or silenced, or unrepresentable realms, in the 'debris' of history. As we shall see with the Southern Tamil women, when found, and when nationalism is, in turn, scrutinized from such a perspective, the 'experience', of domination or oppression, even in 'insurgent' situations, would be found, contra Lloyd, not to have been endured 'commonly', or evenly—though an argument is certainly produced, by nationalism, to that effect.

In any event, as Joan Scott has pointed out, experience is not self-evident or transparent. And I suppose it should be underlined that *I do not seek to deny certain happenings in the history of the post-colonial Sri Lankan state, that constitute what I have termed its criminal record, that I would deem oppressive of Sri Lankan Tamils*, though not necessarily oppressive of all of them commonly or equally. What must be insisted upon is that the meaning of these happenings—in so far as, of course, the two could be distinguished—are never self-evident, but produced; and produced, as always, within ideology. Therefore, the critic must notice in the response of LTF to the 'same' events understood by VR as 'discrimination', *a re-narrativization, a production of new meaning, indeed the production of a new event and consequently a new and different experience.*[78] The Tamil people are being presented in LTF with nothing less than a new history—not an entirely original

---

[78] For those interested in a TULF narrative, among the most comprehensive early documents is the memorandum to the International Commission of Jurists, dated 4th September 1973, which bears the signature of Chelvanayagam.

one, but significantly so; a history that, if the LTTE goal of establishing a state for itself became successful, would make the future, to recall Fritzman, 'retroactively constitute the past'. My point being this; an obvious, or natural, or self-evident, or indisputable continuity does not exist between the two attacks on Tamil civilians by organized Sinhala mobs in 1958 and in 1983—two very different conjunctures in which the goals of both Sinhala and Tamil nationalism differed. It is LTF that effects narrative continuity between the two attacks, turning the 'riot' of 1976 to the 'genocidal riot' of 1983. The Tamil masses may, or may not, be being crudely manipulated here, by having interpretation thrust upon them; but the past is certainly being reconstructed, to suit the present conjuncture—such revisions being one of the many necessary means by which nationalism perpetuates itself.

Nationalism, and here it is no different from disciplinary history, continuously renarrativizes the past to suit the present. It is intimately dependent upon narrativization—the successful representation of a story or interpretation as truth without author—to establish its authority, if not hegemony. Not to see this is to refuse to see nationalism as ideology, but to situate it, as does Anderson, as sociological—or, more exactly, anthropological—fact; not to see this is to deny the possibility of resisting interpellation and of envisioning 'operative' or enabling community.

It is precisely in order to ensure interpellation of its potential subjects that LTF cannot locate the moment of rupture between Sinhala and Tamil nationalisms at a juridical event (unlike VR, which places its accent on the constitutional changes enacted in 1972). Rather, as indicated above, the text of 1983 places the break further back, at the first major Sinhala state-sponsored attack against Tamil civilians, in 1958. This makes perfect sense given the LTTE's revisionist narrative strategy; for, if genocide is the willed-for end of the Sinhala state's actions against the Tamils, it must have also been the willed-for beginning. If, as Margaret Atwood once said, 'All history is written backwards',[79] then it must, for the sake of conviction, coherence and consistency, be so narrated from whatever point is chosen as the end

---

[79] Margaret Atwood, *The Rubber Bride* (New York: Bantam, 1995), p. 123.

of the story to whatever could constitute its beginning. Continuity, of course, being among the requirements of the narrative form itself: it enables the representation of events not merely in sequence, but as causally—meaningfully—linked;[80] it turns discrete, perhaps discontinuous, events into an *experience through time*—for, without being aggregated, the separate assaults on Tamils in 1958 and 1983 would not and cannot make genocide. Therefore, LTF calls the 1958 attacks on Tamils—the product of a conjuncture at which Sinhala hegemony over the Sri Lankan state was being accomplished, and therefore not necessarily continuous with the attacks of the late 1970s and early 1980s, or the 1983 pogrom—a 'great betrayal' . . . 'by the Sinhala national bourgeoisie [. . .It] blew up all hopes of national harmony and *relations between the two nations became hostile* . . . This communal fury that ravaged the island stained the pages of Ceylon's history with blood. The horror and savagery perpetrated against the innocent Tamils are indescribable.'[81]

'All hope' was lost then; not after 1983, or even 1972, but way back in 1958. Indeed, such hope for national reconciliation was 'blown up', 'exploded'—smashed into little pieces that cannot be put together again by bourgeois compromise—by the fury and savagery of the Sinhala nation-state. Consequently, it is only to be expected that LTF could have no time for those (the TULF and its class-caste) who would collaborate with such a state; and, that its own narrative of these events would be summarized thus: '*This oppression has a continuous history of 35 years and a genocidal intent* involving a calculated plan aiming at the gradual and systematic destruction of the essential foundations of the Tamil-speaking nation: on language, on education, on culture, on religious and political institutions, on traditional lands and on the economy, that jeopardized the very existence of the Tamils and made unitary life intolerable and impossible.'[82]

---

[80] For a fine summary article on narrative, see Hayden White, 'The Value of Narrativity in the Representation of Reality', in W.J.T. Mitchell (ed.), *On Narrative* (Chicago: University of Chicago Press, 1981).

[81] *Liberation Tigers Tamil Freedom Fighters*, 1983, p. 17, emphasis added.

[82] Ibid., p. 8, emphasis added.

A sleight of hand must be noted here: the target of 'systematic destruction' is named as 'the Tamil-speaking nation'; actually, the 1983 pogrom, or its precursors, did not target a component of this group, Muslims. But the importance of this passage lies in its inclusive nature: Muslims and all Tamils—Northeastern, UpCountry, Southern— are represented as targets and victims of the Sinhala state's genocidal policy. Consequently, *in LTF, all Tamil speakers are Tamil nationals; there is no distinction made between citizen and national, no contradiction apparent between habitation and nationality in this text and conjuncture: in 1983, the nation is all the (census category) people.* This would change, and change quickly; habitation in the Northeast would make its exclusionary demand again—and do so with seeming permanence, this time; but, at the immediate post-pogrom conjuncture, the only contradiction this text admits to is one between the Sinhala and Tamil *nations*—consequent to which 'unitary life' has become both 'intolerable and impossible'. VR, one might remember, saw the Tamil *nation* in contradiction with the Sinhala *state*—the agent responsible for juridical acts of discrimination. LTF, in contrast, while calling the 'Sinhala ruling regimes' responsible for 'inspiring and master-minding' the pogroms, takes pains to accuse Sinhala 'hooligans and vandals' of at least equal complicity in 'sadistic orgies of arson, rape and mass murders';[83] and, as one recalls, locates after 1958 the fact that 'relations between the two *nations* became hostile'. *The Sinhala nation as a whole is blamed by LTF for the repression, for the genocide, of the Tamils.* Consequently, it is not unexpected that this text would have nothing to say of Sinhalese resident in the Northeast—unlike VR, which anticipated a Sinhalese presence in the anticipated new state of Eelam. LTF's textual erasure prefigured a physical one. In the years to come, the LTTE took the homogenizing logic of nationalism to its proper, if perverse, conclusion: what was excluded on paper was excluded in fact—it systematically targeted and exterminated peasant Sinhala presence in the Northeast. The aim, quite simply, was for a homogeneous nation-state: for one nation, one group of nationals alone, to inhabit the country, the territory of the battled-for state.

[83] Ibid., p. 14.

How does one account for this change from VR to LTF, this change in the constitution of the Tamil nation and of the anticipated Tamil state, this change in the definition of Tamil national, from one conjuncture to another? As said above, part of the story is the struggle for hegemony within Tamil nationalism, between those interests represented by the militant, petty-bourgeois Karaiyar caste young men, and the dominant interests they sought to displace and replace, represented by the older, bourgeois, parliamentary-oriented, Vellala caste politicians. This required, on the part of the LTTE, a representation of itself as the representative, if not as the only available and feasible guardian, of all Tamils—and a consequent painting of the TULF as impotent betrayers of the people's trust. Thus the invocation, indeed the imperative, to renarrativize the past as genocide: those sought to be interpellated by the LTTE had to be persuaded of the necessity for a new organization and a new politics—not merely to defend their interests but, now, to preserve their very lives. Without the possibility of genocide, such an argument would lose much of its force. With such a possibility, if the Tamil people were indeed facing genocide, sticking to parliamentary modes of resistance would be a response equivalent to suicide. Thus the need to resort to violence, if only for the minimal purposes of self-defence. Faced with genocide, even bourgeois Tamils would see the necessity to discard their 'natural' allies, the TULF, and not just support the LTTE instead, but also abdicate to them the responsibility of guarding the nation, of being its guardians.

Marx says in *The Eighteenth Brumaire* that 'whomever one seeks to persuade, one acknowledges as master of the situation.'[84] At this conjuncture, in the wake of the pogrom, the Tamil people were, indeed, and if only for a moment, 'masters' of their own fate. Not in the sense that they had agency; but that, like in 1972, they were being appealed to, they were admitted as a factor in the equation. (By 1985, as we shall see, this would no longer be the case.) For, without them being persuaded about the superiority of one politics over another, of one organization over another, the battle for hegemony within Tamil nationalism

---

[84] Karl Marx, *The Eighteenth Brumaire of Napoleon Bonaparte* (Moscow: Progress Publishers, 1977 [1852]), p. 74.

could not be resolved. History had to be re-narrativized, not in order to manipulate the masses, but—and the difference is acute—as an instrument of hegemony.[85] So the LTTE appealed to all the people, represented all Tamils as nationals, because, even though it (knew it) would fail to persuade every single one, all of them were its constituency. At the level of interest, of survival, of the future, the immediate post-pogrom conjuncture had to be produced as one in which there was perfect coincidence between people and activist; which reminds one of the famous passage from *The German Ideology:* 'For each new class which puts itself in the place of one ruling before it is compelled, merely in order to carry though its aim, to represent its interests as the common interest of all the members of society . . . to give its ideas the form of universality.'[86] Though not a class in the strict sense, the LTTE's representation of coincidence of interest worked. Faced with profound dysphoria in the aftermath of the pogrom, the Tamil people, at least those of them who did not, or could not, find succour in emigration, or otherwise shedding their *Sri Lankan* Tamilness, were looking for protection, for guarantees of security, for guardians.

But nationalism is both ideology and praxis; so it must also be noted that, politics being the craft of the possible, representing all Tamils as nationals was possible at this conjuncture. It was possible, following the horrors of July 1983, for Tamil nationalism to envisage without embarrassment a mass exodus of Tamils from other parts of Sri Lanka to the Northeast, the demarcated territory of the anticipated new state. To encourage such a possibility, and to do so credibly, Tamil nationalism's definition of nationality had to be inclusive, open. In other words, Tamil nationality at this conjuncture was determined by habitation, but habitation was represented as open, navigational, determined by a future happening, not present habit. The LTTE's programme was also helped by the fact that, at this point, it had not broken any promises; being relatively new to Tamil politics, it had not even been in

---

[85] My understanding of hegemony is derived not so much from Gramsci as from Guha's recasting of Gramsci.

[86] Karl Marx, *The German Ideology* (New York: International Pub, 1993 [1894]), p. 65.

a position to do so. Thus, in a sense, it could ask its nationals to come home (the Northeast), so that they could be taken home (the new and separate state).

Despite the continuities, the texture of the promises of VR and LTF is significantly different. If the TULF presented itself as being in seamless continuity with the nation, the LTTE had no illusion about its vanguardist role. Though all Tamils were affected by 'the genocidal violence of the oppressor', LTF does not expect all Tamils to respond violently; unlike VR, this text does not even call upon all Tamils to join in the struggle. The 'Tamil youth'—read young men—'were the immediate targets and victims of the racist policies of successive Sinhala governments.'[87] They were the primary victims of a 'notoriously discriminatory selective device called "standardization" . . . [which] dramatically reduced the number of Tamil students'[88] getting admissions to the university; recall that standardization is not even mentioned in VR. It was these young men alone, who: 'Angered by the imposition of an alien language, frustrated without the possibility of higher education, plunged into the despair of an unemployed existence . . . grew militant with an iron determination to fight back the national oppression.'[89] Narayan Swamy, amongst others, has pointed out that, while the vast majority of the pre- and immediate post-1983 generations of Tamil nationalist guerillas have been young men, very few of them were disgruntled students. Be that as it may, the argument above is consistent with Tamil separatism's general tendency to describe its politics as purely a response to the actions of the Sinhala state. With the proviso that, of course, LTF at this conjuncture had also to present itself as the sole and much needed alternative to, if not replacement of, the TULF. The final, clinching argument that could be made in this regard is that it was the youth, not the older generation, that originally demanded Eelam; that the TULF's promise of 1976 was made under duress, without conviction; that the TULF broke its promise because it never meant to keep it:

[87] *Liberation Tigers and Tamil Freedom Fighters*, 1983, p. 23.
[88] Ibid., 1983, p. 13.
[89] Ibid.

The most crucial factor that propelled the Tamil United Front to move rapidly towards the secessionist path was the increasing impatience, militancy and rebelliousness of the revolutionary youth . . . [whose] organized forms of revolutionary resistance in the later stages became a frightening political reality to both the peace-loving conservative Tamil leadership and to the oppressive Sinhala regimes . . . The only alternative left to the Tamils under the conditions of mounting national oppression, the youth rightly perceived, was none other than a revolutionary armed struggle for the total independence of their nation. Therefore, the radical Tamil youth, while making impassioned demands pressuring the old generation . . . to advocate secession, resorted to revolutionary violence to express their militant stand.[90]

According to this revised story, the TULF actually followed in the wake of the 'unappeasable, irreconcilable' youth. Now, LTF proclaims, the duty, nay the only choice, left facing the entire Tamil nation is to follow suit.

By the conjuncture of July 1985, the moment of the last official document of Tamil nationalism to be discussed here, the *Thimpu Declaration* (TD), the LTTE was on the verge of becoming the predominant force within the Tamil resistance. TD, however, marks a prior moment, a rare moment within the story of Tamil resistance, reminiscent of the formation of the Tamil United Front in 1972, one of unity. TD was signed by all the major Tamil political organizations of the time, including the TULF and LTTE, and was presented to the Sri Lankan government during peace talks held in Bhutan.[91] These talks came

[90] Ibid., p. 23.
[91] TD was named such by the Tamil groups themselves, after the Bhutanese capital, Thimpu, in which the negotiations were held, in 1985. That year, by the way, was a momentous one in the history of Tamil separatism; and its importance has not tended to be recognized in the literature, including Narayan Swamy. Two events immediately prior to TD need mention here. *One*: during the ceasefire that preceded the peace talks that produced the Declaration, the Sri Lankan military was restricted to its barracks

after the failure of year-long negotiations between the TULF and the Sri Lankan government in 1984; TD emerged most immediately from the failure of the Thimpu talks, the first occasion that the Sri Lankan government publicly met with the militant Tamil resistance. At this conjuncture, from a Tamil nationalist perspective, the prospect of a non-violent, negotiated resolution of the problems presented the Tamil people by the Sinhala state appeared bleak, because Sinhala nationalism refused to relinquish its hegemony over the Sri Lankan state. Consequently, Eelam had never looked more possible; indeed, to some it appeared both inevitable and imminent.

The Declaration, a brief but nevertheless remarkably comprehensive and adequate document, reflects such a sensibility. This is how it begins:

> It is our considered view that any meaningful solution to the Tamil national question must be based on the following four cardinal principles:
> 1. recognition of the Tamils of Ceylon as a nation.
> 2. recognition of the existence of an identified homeland for the Tamils in Ceylon.
> 3. recognition of the right of self-determination of the Tamil nation.
> 4. recognition of the right of citizenship and fundamental rights of all Tamils in Ceylon.
>
> Different countries have fashioned different systems of government to ensure these principles. We have demanded and struggled for an independent Tamil state as the answer to this problem arising out of the denial of these basic rights of our people.[92]

One should notice in passing that the distinction between 'country' and 'state' is maintained here, as it is—and must be—in all texts of

---

and the LTTE took effective military control, for the first time, of the Jaffna peninsula—control it would not relinquish to Sri Lankan forces for a whole decade. *Two*: in April 1985, for the first time in post-colonial Sri Lankan history, Tamil and Muslim *civilians* in southern parts of the Northeast, clashed violently, destroying each others' life and property.

[92] N. Seevaratnam, *The Tamil National Question and the Indo-Lanka Accord* (New Delhi: Konark, 1989), p. 137.

Tamil separatism. And it must also be noted, if not stressed, that TD seeks to speak for the Tamil, not the *Tamil-speaking*, people and/or nation. At the conjuncture of 1985, therefore, Tamil nationalism no longer seeks to represent Northeastern Muslims who—like Southern and UpCountry Tamils, as we shall see—considered nationals in LTF, have now been rendered non-national. Indeed, TD fails even to admit their presence in the 'identified [now exclusively Tamil] homeland,' which is said to belong solely to the 'Tamils in Ceylon'. In later years, like the fate of the Sinhala residents of Northeastern Sri Lanka foreshadowed in LTF, LTTE cadre would attempt to 'prove' this textual elimination by exterminating and/or forcibly evicting Northeastern Muslims from their 'homeland'.

The *Thimpu Declaration*, in other words, reads almost as an announcement of a parting of the ways—and not, as in VR certainly, and LTF to a lesser extent, as merely a threat to do so. Its tone, its form, are radically different from VR and LTF; in the conjuncture of 1985, it is no longer necessary for a narrative of oppression that would justify the separatist demand. That is taken as given, known, unnecessary of repetition. The tone here is assertive, confident—of, among other things, the interpellated national—and, therefore, anticipatory of Eelam in ways not found in, or available to, VR and LTF. There, the national is appealed to, those texts seek to produce interpellation; this assumes it to have happened.

But my primary concern, here as with the previous texts, is: what constitutes the Tamil nation, and national, at this moment? TD has a carefully prepared answer. The Tamil 'people', it states, have been denied 'basic rights', been oppressed by the Sinhala state. However, it should be noted that it is not these same *people* in whose name the right to and struggle for self-determination is being asserted; it is the *nation* that demands this right. There is, once again, a lack of fit between people (census category) and nation. If LTF sought to resolve this contradiction by seeking to interpellate all the people into the nation, not so TD; here, the nation is said to be formed by the 'Tamils *of* Ceylon'—as distinct from the 'Tamils *in* Ceylon'.

These shifts in pronoun are not products of chance. Like with VR, the Tamil national in TD is defined as 'of' the country; as, since we have read VR—and we must know VR to know this—a Northeastern inhabitant. The Tamil people, in contrast, are those Tamils resident elsewhere in Ceylon, the country. These people, these non-national Tamils, can, however, become national—a mere shift in residence, it is implied, would suffice. After all, the 'identified homeland'—and, again, note the lack of necessity to specify its boundaries, this too is known—is for *all* the Tamils *in* Ceylon. I do not seek, with this kind of close textual analysis, to split hairs; these are matters, quite literally, of life and death. For, what ultimately distinguishes TD, and its conjuncture, from the two others discussed before, is the declaration's final clause: this anticipates a category of Tamils that cannot be accommodated by Tamil nationalism. Put differently, even though, unlike VR but like LTF, Tamil nationality may appear to be flexible, open, at this conjuncture, this 'flexibility'—and in this respect TD differs from LTF—is purchased at a terrible price.

TD asserts the Tamil nation's right to establish a state distinct from, and in contradistinction to, the Sinhala; a state in which Tamil Sri Lankans would presumably enjoy citizenship. This new and separate state named Eelam is demanded because the other, the Sri Lankan, has been and is discriminatory and/or oppressive, has denied the Tamils 'basic rights'. *Implicit here is the understanding that the Sri Lankan state would continue to deny Tamils those rights—otherwise, the demand for a separate Tamil Eelam would be unnecessary.* Nevertheless, despite its own fundamental critique of the Sri Lankan state, TD calls upon that discriminatory state to recognize 'the right of citizenship and fundamental rights of all Tamils in' that state; whereas, surely, logic alone would dictate that this cannot happen, or be expected. In other words, *TD, unlike VR and LTF, does not seek to represent all Tamils; indeed, unlike VR, which invites all the Tamil people into the state, and LTF, which invites them into the nation, TD (alone) explicitly anticipates a category of Tamil that would be left out of both nation and state, that would remain in Sri Lanka upon the establishment of Eelam:* these being, as should be obvious by now, those resident outside the Northeast—Southern and UpCountry Tamils, of the 'people', but not of the 'nation'. These Tamils are left, if one reads TD alone, to be discriminated against; if one reads TD after LTF, as one must, they are expelled *from the project of Tamil separatism and left to the mercy of a state deemed to have* genocidal *designs upon these same Tamils.*

I am not alone in noticing this. The significance of the Wilson statement of 1994, which I quote here at greater length, should now be easily apparent: '... at the political level, the concept of "the Jaffna [Tamil] man" and the "Batticaloa [Tamil] man" is no longer of relevance ... [Wilson is writing of the mid-1970s.] The two identities have realized that their merging is essential for the protection of the Ceylon Tamil identity. In the process *it has become necessary to* write off *the "Colombo [read Southern Tamil] man"*. The "Colombo man" has one of two alternatives, either to remain in Colombo and survive, facing all the uncertainties of an unpredictable future, or return to the homeland and start life anew.'[93]

Though I would date the move a decade or so later, somewhere between 1983 and 1985,[94] I agree, of course, with Wilson that Tamil separatism 'wrote off' Southern—and UpCountry—Tamils from inclusion in its project: they are invited to join the nation—to change residence, become inhabitants of the Northeast and therefore Tamil nationals. But, so doing, at the risk of stating the obvious, would make those Tamils no longer Southern or UpCountry, but Northeastern. My disagreement lies with his assertion that these Tamils were left to an 'unpredictable future'; because Tamil separatism after LTF, or the 1983 pogrom, is predicated on the belief that the only alternative to separation is genocide. Indeed, *Tamil separatism after 1985 is predicated on requiring, acknowledging and accepting the genocide of Southern and UpCountry Tamils in order to enable its own survival and continuance.* I said at the outset that my particular concern in this paper is with the

---

[93] Wilson 1994, p. 140, emphasis added.

[94] It is difficult, perhaps impossible, to date such happenings precisely: changes in conjuncture do not occur in any predictable fashion, or in regular intervals of time. From the Southern Tamil perspective, for instance, the immediate post-pogrom conjuncture, located in LTF, proved to be brief. The next, being expelled from the Tamil nation, located in TD, has been lasting.

place accorded Southern Tamils by the project of separatist nationalism. As we now know, after 1985, the Southern Tamil is no longer liminal or epidermal, *but outside*, expelled by and from this project. Outside, however, in a constitutive way: as a necessary outside, needed for the separatist project to both justify and impel itself; thus my contention that, *after the conjuncture of 1983, the Southern Tamil becomes the* designated genocidee *of separatist Tamil nationalism*. Given its willingness to sacrifice a part of its population in order to save the 'whole', and given its record of criminal practices directed at all the peoples of Sri Lanka, *contemporary Tamil separatism cannot be considered a defensive, emancipatory or, for that matter, in any way an ethical project*.

Contesting Nationalism: Narratives of Southern Tamil Women

Four years after the pogrom of 1983, Valli Kanapathipillai interviewed many Southern Tamil survivors living around Colombo and related the stories of a few. These survivors' testimonies come to us via the sociologist; their voices are mediated by her understanding of their significance; therefore, we have to keep in mind that her emphases may not be their's. Still, it is not impossible, despite the palimpsest character of this text, to make other interpretations, find other significances in the predicament of these women.

The strength of Kanapathipillai's analysis lies in her insistence that every incidence of violence has a 'local' dimension distinct from the 'national'; however, she eventually subsumes the local into the national. The meaning of the local is ultimately established in extra-local terms: 'local-level events . . . are grafted on to national events by reasons of continuity.'[95] This formulation, actually, succumbs to the more powerful lure of the readily available national(ist) explanation of these same events; the 'grafting'—an accurate term the implications of which are not investigated—spoken of is done by nationalism itself

---

[95] Valli Kanapathipillai, 'July 1983: The Survivor's Experience', in Veena Das (ed.), *Communities, Riots and Survivors in South Asia* (Delhi: Oxford University Press, 1992), p. 327.

which, as argued earlier, presents these events as genocide.[96] In Kanapathipillai's account, the survivors emerge as victims, ultimately, not of local or neighbourhood conflicts, but of a 'larger' or more impressive history—the criminal post-colonial history of the Sri Lankan (Sinhala) nation-state. The 'riots of 1983', she writes, 'brought home' to Southern Tamils 'the painful fact that regardless of their political ideology they were identified as Tamils and not Sri Lankans.'[97] One aspect of this statement cannot be quarrelled with: that 'being' Tamil expresses not an essence, but an ideological commitment—in this situation, of rampant Sinhala nationalism, to be understood in opposition to (a commitment to) being Sri Lankan. But the statement is made without qualification, without admitting the possibility of locating significance in the singular, of finding crucial local meanings in those awful events. It therefore serves, ultimately, to buttress the Tamil nationalist argument that, *in every instance*, those Tamils attacked were attacked *solely* because they were Tamil. For, if there was a local dimension to every attack that constituted the pogrom, as Kanapathipillai claims, then the 'riots' should have 'brought home' to Southern Tamils many other things besides the fact that they could not identify, or where not identified, as Sri Lankans.

In arguing thus, I do not seek to deny that the predicament of Southern Tamils is perhaps primarily produced by the Sri Lankan/ Sinhala state. My point is simply that limiting such identification— or 'blame'—to the Sinhala state is an intellectually inadequate and politically futile exercise. For, as hopefully was demonstrated in the previous section, while the Southern Tamil predicament must be seen

---

[96] For an excellent ethnographic account of (an event during) the pogrom, that doesn't subsume the local within the national, and which has inspired my own thinking, see Pradeep Jeganathan's ' "All the Lord's Men?" Ethnicity and Inequality in the Space of Riot', in Michael Roberts (ed.), *Collective Identities: Nationalisms and Protest in Modern Sri Lanka*, 2nd edn (forthcoming). It is not my purpose here to pursue this line of argumentation; but, clearly, an important method of contesting the nationalist narrative consists, of course, in telling 'local' or singular stories—and calling attention to their appropriation by nationalism, rather than to their self-evident contiguity with it.

[97] Kanapathipillai 1992, p. 321.

in the context of Sinhala nationalism, and of the failure of an operative post-colonial pan-Sri Lankan community—not necessarily conceived on a national/ist basis—to occupy the country; after TD, that is with regard to the women whose stories are examined here, this circumstance must also be situated within Tamil separatism's inability, or unwillingness, to include them in its own project. Thus my contention that Tamil nationalism after 1976 is a failed, at best deficient, response to Sinhala nationalism. In other words, and this bears repetition since this position may otherwise seem fallible before a naive and crude 'blaming the victims' style critique, I do not see Southern Tamils as victims of Tamil separatism, so much as see their *predicament*, their continuing dysphoria and homelessness, as the consequence of *both* Sinhala and Tamil nationalisms; of, indeed, the logic of nationalism as such.[98] This is a more productive way of claiming their stories for history: situating them outside a simple oppressor/victim binary allows one to locate what is enabling in even so dire a predicament.

In what follows, I read just two of the stories recounted by Kanapathipillai, of women survivors of the 1983 pogrom who, as women—who *because women*—can no longer perform their Tamilness (be Tamil in public). Their stories are, of course, responses to the Sinhala state; but they also must be understood as responses to being 'designated genocides'. These women can—and perhaps must—be seen as occupying 'emergent' spaces outside national identity; not in the Bhabhian sense of still being in search of their nations—they most decidedly are not—but of being denied the possibility of national belonging and looking elsewhere for an end to dysphoria. It is by calling attention to such spaces produced by the very logic of nationalism, and by articulating their political potential, that the critic, in collaboration with

---

[98] To those who would still respond to this statement by insisting that I 'blame the victim', I repeat: while the predicament of Southern Tamils cannot be understood outside the criminal record of the Sinhala nation-state, to say this is not to deny Tamil nationalism's own agency in contributing to this predicament. In other words, while the Southern (and every other) *Tamil*—the coding offered by the census—could be understood, though inadequately, as victim of the Sinhala state, *Tamil nationalism*—the ideology and political practice, which arose in part, but only in part, as response to this victimhood—cannot.

its occupants, can contest the project of nationalism. It is by seeking out and identifying these emergent spaces that don't stick out, by writing these stories that direct our attention to the failure of nation as community, that the critic—who also seeks to inhabit these spaces, who does inhabit them by writing the story—can contest the histories produced by nationalism. And thus pave the way—this task not being the sole province of the critic—for new stories, new spaces, and the imagination of more enabling notions of community. Which is why I find that nationalism undermines itself: not in a simple, linear, or even dialectical fashion, but in the sense that, since the logic of nationalism must produce exclusions, the critical act of collaboration with those expelled, of adding strength to their voices, and articulating their potential where necessary, enables (though without guarantee) its undermining.[99]

Before getting to these voices, one final comment on Kanapathipillai is needed. She found that, '*regardless of their political ideology they* [Southern Tamils] were identified as Tamils and not as Sri Lankans.'[100] That is, from the perspective of Sinhala nationalism, the distinction made by Tamil nationalism between Tamils and Tamil nationals—or, from the Southern Tamil perspective, one between Tamil nationals and Tamils demanding interpellation as Sri Lankan nationals—was not operative in southern Sri Lanka in July 1983. As argued earlier, there having being no Sri Lankan nationalism in evidence, there could not have been Sri Lankan nationals in 1983. Within the logic of Sinhala nationalism, every Tamil was a Tamil national(ist); and, in so far as it saw itself—or at least its pogrom—as a response to Tamil nationalism, all Sri Lankan Tamils (including the UpCountry) therefore became legitimate targets of Sinhala nationalist vengeance.

Saroja Solomon was one such target. Her house was destroyed, and property vandalized during the pogrom. She recalled the events of 1983, says Kanapathipallai, 'primarily in terms of the changing relationships with her neighbours.'[101] Some of them had helped her:

---

[99] To say this is not to suggest, of course, that *every* victim of nationalism occupies a potentially useful space.

[100] Kanapathipillai 1992, emphasis added.

[101] Kanapathipillai 1992, p. 323.

a (Sinhala) neighbour kept them in a room in his store while the 'mob'—which consisted, we are told, mostly of young men from outside the locality—attacked, damaged and looted her house; she called the neighbour's act one of 'unexpected kindness'; subsequently, another neighbour (Muslim) drove them to a refugee camp; and, after a while in the camp, she encountered an old (Sinhala) schoolfriend, who lived nearby, and whose own home became a refuge from life in the camp.

These are not insignificant happenings. Whether as the propagandist LTF or the academic Wilson, when Tamil nationalism tells the story of the pogrom, these acts of ordinary kindness that take on extraordinary significance at a moment like this, these assertions of faith in community at moments when there would appear to be no basis for such faith, these events that remind us that national affiliations *never* completely flatten out others, can find no place. For Tamil nationalism, 1983 is about Sinhala genocide; any events that may suggest otherwise must be repressed.[102] Which is precisely why the critique of nationalism demands that these stories be foregrounded. They may not appear to carry much weight when compared to the enormity of the violence; and it is, of course, a part of the narrative strategy of nationalism to deny meaning to these events, which are dismissed as purely local and, therefore, insignificant. But, an anti-nationalist reconstruction of those events must begin somewhere; and one can do worse than highlighting moments of community and connection—moments which clearly indicate the significance of the singular and non-aggregative moments that hint of other possibilities even in the midst of disaster.

To Solomon herself, says Kanapathipillai, 'the deteriorating relationship with her landlord crystallized the meaning of national events in

---

[102] The pogrom, of course, had an economic and a gendered dynamic, as much as it did a nationalist one. Gunasinghe has made a very persuasive argument for understanding those events as enabled, in part, by a crisis faced by a (petty-bourgeois) sector of Sinhala capital. Pradeep Jeganathan, 'A Space for Violence: The Location of a Sinhala Practice of Masculinity' (in this volume) argues, equally persuasively, that the pogrom was also enabled by a practice of Sinhala masculinity.

her everyday life;' the 'ethnic strife simply provided the pretext' for the 'landlord's interest in having the house vacated'.[103] One might wish to query this reading, or at least require its nuancing: would the landlord, for instance, have desired the house vacated if the tenant was not Tamil? Could he have successfully used the pogrom to evict a Sinhala or Muslim tenant? Speculating along those lines, however, would be a fruitless exercise. One might ask, instead: what is at stake in Solomon's denial of a national dimension to her predicament? How do we read, how should we respond, to the denial?

An answer requires quoting Kanapathipillai/Solomon at somewhat greater length:

> One may summarize Saroja's reactions to her Tamil identity by her poignant statement that '*to be Tamil is to live in fear*'. She remembered with *nostalgia* the times when she used to dress up in typical Tamil fashion. Now she avoids wearing a *pottu* ... The children, she said, resented her Tamil identity. Whenever she wore an Indian saree and a pottu they remarked, 'She is dressing to go out and get hit again'. *The fear of being identified as a Tamil* pervaded relations within the family, for although Saroja and her husband spoke in Tamil, the children spoke in Sinhalese, even at home. Saroja encouraged the children to identify themselves more and more with the Sinhala community and to hide all marks of a Tamil identity. 'I have told them,' she said, 'to marry persons from any ethnic community but the Tamil'. *Ensuring a better future* for the children, she felt, was to ensure that *they moved away from being identified as Tamils*.[104]

Broaching the issue of nostalgia, an important one for the study of nationalism, will be deferred till the conclusion of this essay. Here, a seemingly simple question suggests itself: what does Solomon, a Southern Tamil survivor of 1983 Sri Lanka, a Southern Tamil continuing to reside in post-1983 Sri Lanka, want? Simply answered, a 'better future'; for her, but more importantly for the next generation, her children.

The contours of this future are not known, or spelt out. Indeed,

---

[103] Kanapathipillai 1992, p. 327.
[104] Ibid., p. 328, emphasis added.

Solomon is much more certain as to what *she does not want: to be identified as Tamil*, to continue 'living in fear'.[105] Performing Tamilness—for instance, wearing the 'Indian saree'—in public would ensure such identification and, thus, a predictable and frightening future (at the hands of Sinhala nationalism); not doing so would make the future easier, more enabling, perhaps even better. Consequently, Solomon—and, more importantly, her children—stop performing Tamilness. This act carries with it a critique of the Sinhala state—which does not allow a non-apprehensive performance of Tamilness, which has not allowed Tamils a way of being Sri Lankan (nationals). But I would also insist on seeing in her move a critique of Tamil separatism: which, as I have argued, after 1983 effectively allows the (safe) performance of Tamilness—Tamil nationalism's avowed *raison d'être*—only within its geographic boundaries, the borders of its anticipated new country, and leaves all other (census category) Tamils to be victims of genocide.

But the question recurs: why does Solomon deny a connection, surely obvious, between her predicament and the national? Why does she insist upon a purely local significance to her predicament? Part of the answer must lie in the internalization of the Sinhala nationalist explanation of her oppression, which would have her guilty simply of being Tamil, and therefore complicitous with Tamil separatism. Solomon, therefore, is by no means a perfect figure, or untarnished exemplar; her position is confused, sometimes even self-contradictory, in need of clarification. Nevertheless, one can surely read in her denial a demand for telling the local story, for a renarrativization of the events of 1983 that does not stress the national/ist? Or, at the very minimum, cannot one find here a call for re-thinking the (Tamil) nationalist account of enabling community?

One can; and in order to do so most comprehensively, one must see Solomon as responding to Tamil nationalism both as a Tamil and as a woman. As we know, woman as primary signifier of national identity, of cultural difference, is a common trope of nationalism. Flora

---

[105] Cf. Jeganathan's argument in 'In the Shadow of Violence', referred to earlier, that 'Tamilness in southern Sri Lanka . . . is produced . . . in anticipation of violence' (Jeganathan, forthcoming).

Anthias and Nira Yuval-Davis have argued: 'Women do not only teach and transfer the cultural and ideological traditions of ethnic and national group. Very often they constitute their actual symbolic figuration.'[106] Or, as Fanon put it, somewhat more colourfully: to the national liberation struggle, the 'sari becomes sacred'[107]—a point, by the way, not lost on the LTTE; its women's wing made this demand, in 1985: 'It is important for women to take care in their dress, in their pottu and make-up. It doesn't mean that we are enslaved if we dress according to our tradition. Some married women say that it is expensive to wear saris. *This is not acceptable* . . . We are engaged in a struggle for national liberation.'[108]

The struggle for national liberation makes different demands on men and women. Women's dress represents both national identity and resistance; whereas male dress does not signify nation—bourgeois male apparel in urban Sri Lanka being unmarked by ethnicity or nationality. The public appearance alone of Tamil bourgeois men—wearing the ubiquitous shirt and pants—would not identify them as Tamil. By refusing to wear pottu and sari, by refusing to 'dress according to tradition', Solomon is not only hiding from the Sinhala nation-state, but also resisting Tamil nationalism—and calling into account the especial burden it, like every nationalism, places upon women.

Solomon's response to the post-1983 conjuncture also resists another gendered trope of nationalism: the mother as reproducer of the nation, woman as she who begets children and nurtures them into national belonging and consciousness. Indeed, as Assia Djebar has noted, it is solely as reproducer and nurturer that woman, as woman the being—as opposed to Mother the figure—is legitimated by nationalism: 'the mother seems, in fact, to have monopolized the only

---

[106] Flora Anthias and Nira Yuval-Davis, 'Introduction', in *Woman-Nation-State* (London: Macmillan, 1989), p. 9.

[107] Fanon 1991, p. 221.

[108] Quoted in Maunaguru, p. 169 (emphasis added). The terror in that passage must be noted: nationalism knows what is good for women, and will ensure that they understand and perform it.

authentic expression of a cultural identity.'[109] Solomon actively refuses such a role, encouraging her children to perform Sinhalaness in public *and private*, speaking to them in Sinhala inside the home, going so far as telling them not to marry Tamils and thus to not reproduce Tamilness. A similar refusal is made by the other Southern Tamil woman whose testimony I discuss, Kamala (whose surname has been witheld by Kanapathipillai). Kamala too had her house destroyed in 1983; she too benefitted from the help of neighbours, during and after the pogrom; and she too desired a better future for her children. Unlike Solomon, however, Kamala chose emigration as the resolution to her predicament; a solution at least in part determined by the fact that, again unlike Solomon, Kamala's identification with Sri Lanka was more active. This is how Kanapathipillai tells Kamala's story: 'Kamala had always seen herself as totally integrated with other ethnic groups in the country; yet she found herself a target of vicious violence during the riots. She found it difficult to come to terms with the ethnic polarization that she saw around her. She *refused to identify with the emerging Tamil nationalism*, which she considered chauvinistic, but neither could she cope with the Sinhala chauvinism that was beginning to emerge.'[110]

We know by now why Kamala could not have been a Sri Lankan national. What this particular instance illustrates particularly is that these women are not at home in the Tamil nation either. More generally, we can learn from this that national belonging is not determined by the subject's, or would-be national's, desire alone (something true, as we know, of all forms of collective belonging). The subject does not have a determining choice with regard to collective identity: she can always refuse to identify with a way of being (resist interpellation); or, of course, she can acquiesce, whether unwillingly or with enthusiasm. But she cannot produce her own identity by herself; the field of 'choices' is determined elsewhere. That we know: that individual subject does not produce ideology. But, what Solomon and Kamala point

---

[109] Assia Djebar, 'Postface', in *Women of Algiers in Their Department* (Charlosttesville: University of Virginia, 1992), p. 147.

[110] Kanapathipillai 1992, p. 333, emphasis added.

out to, in their resistance to being identified—or interpellated—as a Tamil national, is the inadequacy of the Althusserian notion of interpellation, which leaves no room for the 'subject' to resist or refuse 'ideology'. Their evasion of interpellation indicates that some notion of (reiterative) performativity, as the other side, as it were, of interpellation, is required both to comprehend the failure of interpellation, as well as to accommodate the possibility of change.

When faced with choices that are not choices at all, when faced with the impossibility of asserting an identity, the possibility of what Butler terms 'disidentification'—which could be understood in this context as halting the performance of identity as a matter of habit—assumes great significance. Its persistence, Butler argues, is 'crucial to the rearticulation of democratic contestation.'[111] Disidentification with (performing) Tamilness is what one finds with Solomon and Kamala after 1983, after the conjuncture identified with the Thimpu Declaration; because the only forms of Tamilness available to them in Sri Lanka—changing their residence to the Northeast and becoming Tamil nationals, or remaining as 'minorities' in Southern Sri Lanka and practising Jeganathan's 'tactics of anticipation of violence'—are not enabling options. Thus, disidentification must be read as constituting a crucial first step in the production of a new and alternative identity, if not of the actual possibility of being without it. For, what these two Southern Tamil women are attempting to articulate, if somewhat inchoately, is the need for ways of being untrammelled by being named or identified—perhaps they are even saying that *any mode of being predicated upon identification, classification and naming is claustrophobic and actually inhibits being.*

Unable to be Sri Lankan, refusing to be a Tamil national, Kamala, as said before, decided to emigrate (to New Zealand). According to Kanapathipillai, she did so for two major reasons: 'The first was the constant fear with which the children had to live after the 1983 violence. The second was the construction of their own identity as minorities, who would have to live in constant awareness of this fact, wherever

---

[111] Butler 1993, p. 5.

they chose to live.'[112] Kamala is also quoted as saying: 'If we have to live as minorities ... we might as well live in a place that promises security to the children.'[113] In other words, there is no security (home) in being deemed a minority; a minority is, by definition, homeless;[114] there is resistance here to the logic that would invest number with political significance—in this instance, minority status. At first glance, Kamala herself appears to accept such status, since she is unable to conceive of an alternative, and not only does she reject the majority (Tamil national) status the decision to migrate to Northeastern Sri Lanka would grant her, but decides to migrate to New Zealand, in the full knowledge that she would continue to 'live as a minority' in a new country. But it is, at best, a fraught acceptance: her statement, 'if we *have to* live as minorities,' should be read as containing a plea for more enabling conditions of being. As I have been arguing all along, it is the critic's responsibility to respond to this dysphoria, to such pleas, to see more enabling possibilities in what may initially appear as defeatism, pessimism or despair; or, in Butler's terms, to rearticulate the possibilities of democratic contestation.

But, before that, the question of motherhood. To quote Kanapathipillai once more: 'As in the case of Saroja, Kamala's children also identified their Tamil identity as the cause of much pain and suffering. 'After 1983 [said Kamala] the children were pestering us to change our names to a less Tamil sounding one. And also to get rid of the name board on our front gate.'[115]

Here, much more clearly than with Solomon, one finds a radical inversion of the role imposed upon mothers (and their children) by nationalism. Solomon resists Tamil nationalism by refusing to nurture her children into Tamilness, an act with which the children are actively complicitous, even comfortable. In fact, she actively seeks to nurture

---

[112] Kanapathipillai 1992, p. 336.

[113] Ibid., p. 338.

[114] This argument is developed in Aamir Mufti, 'Auerbach in Istanbul: Edward Said, Secular Criticism and the Question of Minority Culture', *Critical Inquiry* (forthcoming).

[115] Kanapathipillai 1992, p. 337.

her children into Sinhalaness, by encouraging them to speak the language and marry non-Tamils. In so far as she does so, one must see her as succumbing to Sinhala nationalism, or as being at best somewhat confused. What the critic finds enabling about her predicament is her desire for operative community—even if she cannot find it, or articulate its contours, herself. In contrast, what is significant with regard to Kamala's family is not that the mother would take her children away from the nation—although she does; here, rather, it is the children themselves who—when insisting that their name-board be changed etc.—would take their mother (and father) away from the possibility of belonging to the nation. According to the ideology of nationalism, children are supposed to inherit the nation; to fortify, foster and further it; to renew and rejuvenate it where necessary. Without children, nationalism cannot continue to be. But the Southern Tamil woman, and child, refuse, disdain, deny this disabling, if not oppressive, inheritance, refuse to regenerate this way of being, this community that does not provide security. A more radical negation of national belonging, of nationalism, of the nation as community, is difficult to conceive.

Conclusion: Against Nostalgia

Jean-Luc Nancy has contended that, 'Until this day, history has been thought on the basis of a lost community—one to be regained or reconstituted.'[116] If history is understood in its disciplinary sense, then such understanding is of relatively recent provenance; such history is the product of the Enlightenment. It is also the product of nationalism, just as much as it made nationalism possible by making it possible to give the nation a past (going back, in the—typical—Tamil case discussed here, to the 'dawn of history'). It is in that sense that both history and nationalism is about reconstituting lost community, or redeeming loss. About, in a word, nostalgia: for, to nationalism, the past is a destiny and a destination, the past is the horizon of the future. As we have seen with regard to the Tamil case, nationalism relies fundamentally

[116] Nancy 1991, p. 9.

in maintaining the possibility of restoring, if not resurrecting, an ideal from the past: explicitly, in the case of the TULF and the *Vadukoddai Resolution*, which justified its future, its promise to the Tamil people, in terms of resurrecting past community; and somewhat more implicitly with the LTTE and *Liberation Tigers and Tamil Eelam Freedom Struggle*. What unites both these manifestations of separatist Tamil nationalism is their reliance, to a greater or lesser degree, when justifying their claim for a Tamil nation-state in the future, upon an argument that it existed in the past.

But the question arises: can this lost community actually be restored? Not in the common sense that the past, however understood, cannot be replicated. Rather, in the sense that, what would happen to nationalism, what work would it have left to do, if it kept its promise to its people, restored community, took its nation home? If this happened, the task of nationalism would be complete. But we know that this does not happen; that one can identify nationalism after the state; that the task of nation-building is always an ongoing process; that, within the terms of the present argument, the domination, suppression, marginalization and exclusion of social groups continue. We also know, not by recourse to ontological phenomena but by definition, that if one can speak of nationalism *before* the state, that if instituting a state for its nation is just one of the (many) goals of nationalism, that one can also speak of nationalism *after* the state. This is not to argue that we are doomed to be always trapped within the suffocating grasp of nationalism—this essay is written against such pessimism—but that *nationalism is not a transformative politics or ideology*. This, by the way, was known to both Luxemburg and Fanon—thus their contention, implicit in the latter instance, about the fundamental incompatibility of nationalism and Marxism (an anti-nostalgic ideology if there ever was one).[117]

Nationalism, to repeat myself, is therefore not a transformative but—as Guha tipped us off—a profoundly conservative ideology (and

---

[117] Actually, Fanon was almost explicit about this, when arguing for instance about the necessity to move 'from national consciousness to political and social consciousness' (Fanon 1991, p. 203), but he did not articulate his position in these terms.

politics). It promises to restore lost community, but can never keep this promise; for, if it did, it would have exhausted its *raison d'être*. Indeed, the very logic of nationalism demands that it does not keep its promises—because it cannot: if nationalism is analogous to the Messiah, in this instance as the answer to all the problems, predicaments and pressures facing its nationals, then, as Fritzman points out, 'the Messiah only remains Messiah by not arriving.'[118] Nationalism's logic, in other words, demands that it conserve, nurture and foster nostalgia, not rebut or terminate it.

Resisting nationalism, therefore, requires resisting nostalgia. For suggestive—though far from perfect—instance of such resistance, one can turn to the example of Saroja Solomon. After 1983, if we recall, she stopped wearing the sari in an identifiably Tamil style, stopped wearing the pottu, stopped performing her Tamilness in public. She remembered the times she did so, we are told, 'with nostalgia'. Kathleen Stewart has argued that nostalgia arises and 'takes on the function . . . to provide some kind . . . of cultural form' in situations where 'there is no longer any place . . . to stand.'[119] If one understands by a 'place to stand', certainty and fixed identity, then this is where Solomon found herself after 1983—without certainty, dysphoric. But, unlike the nationalist, she does not respond to this by seeking to keep nostalgia alive, she does not seek 'some kind of cultural form', but actively resists it. She is prepared to give up what has been lost—though not without some regret and not, it is important to note, quite the same community claimed by nationalist nostalgia—rather than engage in an effort to search for and reconstitute it. She represents, in George's terms, 'the need to move beyond one's home [nostalgia] into . . . less comfortable spaces.'[120] So doing might, as Alexander warned, 'entrap or ensnare'; but one can also read Solomon's actions and non-actions as constituting a plea for what the critic can—perhaps must—recognize as 'being-in-common'.

---

[118] Fritzman 1993, p. 170.
[119] Kathleen Stewart, 'Nostalgia—A Polemic', in *Cultural Anthropology*, 3(3), 1988, p. 227.
[120] George 1996, p. 31.

Nancy has elaborated upon what this entails: 'Being *in* common has nothing to do with communion, with fusion into a body, into a unique and ultimate identity that would no longer be exposed. Being *in* common means, to the contrary, no longer having, in any form, in any empirical or ideal place, such a substantial identity, and sharing this ... "lack of identity".'[121]

Saroja Solomon and Kamala, though they are not a part of community that sees itself as unique or fused, do not share a 'lack of identity', either. Such ways of being are yet to be. What Solomon and Kamala demonstrate is that the only alternative to oppression need not be, as Lloyd and critics of that persuasion would have it, finding refuge in another form of oppression; they demonstrate that nationalism cannot be seen as liberatory or resistant in any emancipatory sense of the term, but that it is exclusionary, oppressive disabling community. They remind us that the past need not be a destiny;[122] and they demand the possibility, if not the necessity—without recognizing which, as we know, 'freedom' is not possible—of at least beginning to think of ways of being that are not nostalgic, that find their inspiration not in the problems of the past but in the predicaments of the present.

---

[121] Nancy 1991, p. xxxviii.
[122] I owe this point to Fritzman.

Toleration and Historical Traditions of Difference*

DAVID SCOTT

WHAT IS THE ethical-political ground on which to think—or rethink—the question of religious and ethnic difference in Sri Lanka today? How can we think through the justification of a commitment to pluralism and tolerance in contemporary Sri Lanka? What considerations of history and politics, and what considerations of culture and tradition, ought to govern our approach to the toleration of religious and ethnic difference? Indeed, how are we to conceptualize the very problem of toleration and pluralism *as such* as central problems in contemporary cultural-political discourse? Toleration, so it is often maintained, is a form of *active* forbearance that is neither a matter of mere licence, nor mere indifference; it constitutes, in other words, a *positive* attitude of forbearance in the face of fundamental (or at least strong and strongly held) moral disapproval. So that if, for instance, we grant that Sri Lanka is a plural—that is, multi-ethnic and multi-religious—society, is it enough to think of toleration in terms of the mere *accommodation* of existing difference by, say, the

---

*Earlier versions of this essay were presented at conferences at Harvard University, and Mansfield College at the University of Oxford, in November 1997 and January 1998 respectively. I am grateful to the late Neelan Tiruchelvam, Director of the International Centre for Ethnic Studies, Colombo, for inviting me to both, and to those participants who offered their comments and criticisms.

establishment of fundamental rights provisions and constitutional safeguards to protect actual cultural communities? Or is toleration to have a wider scope and an ethos of more *generative* significance that makes it responsive to, and critical of, the moment when difference hardens into injurious forms of exclusion? How, in short, are the demands for a common life, for a life of shared interdependence and mutual recognition, to be balanced against the demand of historical communities to live according to their own ways and their own languages?

These, it seems to me, are some of the fundamental questions that offer themselves to us in the Sri Lankan cultural-political present. One might well say, of course, that these are questions that are crucial to thinking through our postcolonial futures *anywhere*, because they are questions that raise issues central to the general crisis of our political modernities. This is a crisis, in many ways, of the legitimacy of the postcolonial state and the secular conceptual principles (of majoritarian democracy, of state-driven development, of liberal egalitarianism, of Lockean constitutionalism, etc.) through which it was established and rationalized. This crisis arises against the background of the collapse of the Bandung projects of nationalist and socialist development. Beyond the obvious differences that characterised these paths of Bandung (between the middle 1950s and middle 1970s), what they shared was the sense of a single criterion of evaluation and a single principle of adjudication for competing conceptions of the social, political and economic direction to be taken. This context has, over the last two decades or so, been fundamentally eroded. And it is in this unstable space where the old bases of consensus no longer hold that toleration emerges as the contemporary moral-political problem that it is.[1]

These considerations regarding the present are especially important in the context of contemporary Sri Lanka. The particular form of this crisis of legitimacy of the postcolonial state in Sri Lanka has of course been shaped by the civil war—now more than fifteen years old—between the armed forces of the Sri Lankan state and (in the main) the

---

[1] For a fuller discussion see my *Refashioning Futures: Criticism after Postcoloniality* (Princeton: Princeton University Press, 1999).

insurgent Liberation Tigers of Tamil Eelam (LTTE). The LTTE have been demanding a separate state in the North and East which Tamils think of as their traditional homelands.[2] Needless to say, the history of the conflict between the Tamils and the Sinhalas is an immensely complicated one, far too complicated to enter into here in any detail. A crucial chapter in that history, however, and one that has contributed deeply to the present predicament, is the story of the relationship between Buddhism and the politics of Sinhala community that authorises a privileged place in the nation-state for 'Sinhala–Buddhist' identity. The Sinhala–Buddhist demand for that embodiment, and the modern language of political order that has rationalised it, has contributed to the creation of a social, cultural and political climate inhospitable to, and intolerant of, the ways of life of other historically constituted communities.

There has, of course, been an important multi-faceted movement for peace in Sri Lanka. That movement arrived at a crucial juncture at the end of October 1997, when the administration of President Chandrika Kumaratunga tabled the long-awaited draft constitution in Parliament. This is perhaps the most significant effort in many years (perhaps the most important effort since the ill-fated Indo-Lanka Peace Accord of a decade before, in 1987) to bring the civil war to a just conclusion. But between then and now (May 1999) the draft constitution has little more than languished in parliamentary inertia. What it will take to urge the constitutional conversation on is by no means clear. This essay is intended as a contribution to that (constitutionalist) conversation; but it is also intended as a contribution to the attempt to *expand* the cognitive terrain in which that conversation takes place. Consequently, the question that interests me here is not *whether* war or peace, but *what kind* of peace? Central to this question is my worry that peace and tolerance among what are essentially historically

---

[2] The question of the politics of the LTTE is an issue of theoretical and moral complexity. I cannot enter into it here. It may be suggested, however, that characterizing its political project (to the extent that one can) has to take into account the radically altered context of global politics and political reasoning, and the transformed terms and options that these have called into being.

constituted communities cannot be reduced to a liberal debate about constitution-making, as important as this by itself may be.

What I propose to do in the course of this essay is the following: First, I will sketch out some of the assumptions that govern a prominent conception of the relation between identity and community in one historical tradition in contemporary Sri Lanka. My concern here is to try to understand the implications of these assumptions about religion and ethnicity for thinking through the cultural-political present. (Note that I do not assume here that either 'religion' or 'ethnicity' totalize the field of possible subject-positions in contemporary Sri Lanka. Surely they do not. What I *do* assume is that 'religion' and 'ethnicity' *in part* define the space of possible intervention in the present conflict because this is the terrain on which they have historically been constituted *as a conflict*.[3]) Second, I will outline some salient aspects of the liberal argument for toleration and pluralism. I shall say what I think the limits of the liberal model of toleration and pluralism are, and why I think it does not provide us with an adequate political vocabulary in which to think ourselves out of the predicament of the Sri Lankan present. I shall agree of course that a plural and tolerant society is a 'good' worth investing in, but I shall question the liberal justification of pluralism and toleration (and thus the background conceptions of these provided and endorsed in liberal accounts). And finally, and very briefly, I will indicate what I take the implications of these limits to be for thinking through the question of toleration and pluralism in our Sri Lankan present.

II

The question of Sinhala identity and Buddhist identity in contemporary Sri Lanka is very often posed in terms of history. There is a prominent argument according to which ethnicity and religion have for a very long time been constituent elements or features of the collective consciousness of the Sinhalas. So that, for example, it is said that

---

[3] I am grateful to Qadri Ismail for raising a question to me on this point.

whereas the term 'Sinhala–Buddhist' only came into common parlance in the early twentieth century, it actually 'reflects an ethnic cum religious identity, the origin of which can be traced to very early times.' And thus the 'intensity with which the Sinhalese identity is expressed in modern times appears to be the outcome of over two millennia of mainly conflictual contact with Dravidian neighbours, particularly the Tamils.'[4] The 'salient aspect of the Sinhalese ideological tradition', it is then argued on this basis, 'is its long-established and explicitly stated identification of the island with one ethnic group and one religious community—Sinhalese and Buddhist—which were considered constituent elements of a single identity.'[5] On this view, Sinhalas and Tamils have ever been at enmity with one another, and in this Tamils have been the 'alien' aggressors and Sinhalas the hapless 'victims' whose civilizations were systematically and maliciously destroyed by 'invading' South Indians. As a result, Sinhala–Buddhists have never been secure in their own island-home.

I have elsewhere expressed my reservations about this sort of story.[6] I shall repeat some aspects of my argument here, but only so much of it as will enable me to draw out some of the implications for an understanding of the challenge of toleration in contemporary Sri Lanka. I have suggested that in such stories regarding the supposed ancient hatred between Sinhalas and Tamils, concepts like 'religion', 'state', and 'identity', are treated ahistorically insofar as they are made to refer to a set of timeless social-ideological formations as defining (or as defining *in the same way*) for say third-century inhabitants of the island as for contemporary Sinhalas. This conceptual/ideological projection of the present onto the past (as a hermeneutic of the present) is possible only because these categories—religion, state, and so on—are the

---

[4] I have been quoting here from one protagonist of this view, K.N.O. Dharmadasa, *Language, Religion and Ethnic Assertiveness: The Growth of Sinhalese Nationalism in Sri Lanka* (Ann Arbor: University of Michigan Press, 1992), p. 2.

[5] Dharmadasa 1992, p. 19.

[6] See, 'Religion in Colonial Civil Society' in my *Refashioning Futures*. Much of this paragraph and the following four are compressed and slightly recast versions of an argument set out there.

authoritative and *normalized* categories through which Universal History has been written, and through which the local histories of the colonial and postcolonial worlds have been constituted as so many variations on a common theme about the progressive making of modernity.

A number of scholars (beginning with Wilfred Cantwell Smith) have argued that religion—understood as moderns understand it—as a demarcated system of doctrines-scriptures-beliefs, and that of its plural, 'religions', understood as rival ideological communities of such demarcated systems of doctrines-scriptures-beliefs, are modern European inventions, more specifically, early-modern ones. They begin their recognizable existence only in and through the theological disputes of the sixteenth and seventeenth centuries.[7] The important *postcolonial* issue for us therefore, is to understand the ways in which Europe, in its *colonial* project, altered the *conditions* of the lives of non-European peoples in such a way as to oblige *them too* to reconstitute themselves as members of one exclusive 'religious' community against (or in competition with) others. This is important because this alteration has played a central part in re-shaping both the modern lives we are now obliged to live, and the modern categories through which these lives are experienced and articulated.

In this context, it is interesting that—as John Ross Carter and Kitsiri Malalgoda have argued, for example—words representing the concepts 'religion' and 'Buddhism' in Sri Lanka are of fairly recent origin.[8] The point they are making is not that pious men and women in Lanka had not thought about the Buddha or his *dhamma* or the *sangha* prior

---

[7] See Wilfred Cantwell Smith, *The Meaning and End of Religion: A New Approach to the Religious Traditions of Mankind* (Minneapolis: Fortress Press, 1991[1962]); Peter Harrison, *'Religion' and the Religions in the English Enlightenment* (New York: Cambridge University Press, 1990); and Talal Asad, 'The Construction of Religion as an Anthropological Category' in his *Genealogies of Religion* (Baltimore: Johns Hopkins University Press, 1993).

[8] See John Ross Carter, 'A History of Early Buddhism', *Religious Studies* 13(3)(1977), pp. 263–87; and Kitsiri Malalgoda, 'Sinhalese Buddhism: Orthodox and Syncretistic, Traditional and Modern', *Sri Lanka Journal of Historical and Social Sciences* (n.s.) 2(2)(1972), pp. 156–69.

to British colonialism. The point rather is that they are not likely to have thought of this in terms of 'religion' understood in the modern sense of a natural, abstract, systematic *entity*, and thus are unlikely to have imagined themselves to possess one distinctive member of the family of such entities, namely, 'Buddhism'. Both Malalgoda and Carter (though with slightly different emphases) believe that it was probably during the early part of the nineteenth century and specifically through the encounter with Western missionaries that *agama* came to represent the concept 'religion' and *buddhagama* to represent 'Buddhist religion'. But whatever the exact date of coinage, it seems to be the case that by the middle of the nineteenth century, a reified, ideological entity 'Buddhism' or buddhagama was available for polemical, adversarial use, and was in fact mobilized and deployed in the series of *vadayas* (debates, controversies) carried on between representatives of the Buddhist and Christian communities between the middle 1860s and 1880s.[9]

In my view, whatever the importance of this story for the anti-colonial imaginary, the more profound significance of this confrontation for the postcolonial present we inhabit is not that the *bhikkhus* carried the day. Rather the significance is that it signaled that something new had emerged on the social and political horizon of colonial Sri Lanka: a propositional 'religion' called Buddhism or buddhagama available for modern ideological and organizational work, through a new kind of religious subject, in a newly invented colonial public sphere. The point here is that the bhikkhus did not themselves *choose* the epistemic-institutional terrain of their encounter with (or, if you like, resistance to) the Christian missionaries. But what is important to understand is that they clearly arrived at a point at which they were obliged to respond on the terrain chosen for them.[10] And the reason for this is that

---

[9] For a discussion see, Kitsiri Malalgoda, 'The Buddhist-Christian Confrontation in Sri Lanka, 1800–80', in *Social Compass* 20(2) (1973), pp. 171–200, and *Buddhism in Sinhalese Society, 1750–1900: A Study of Religious Revival and Change* (Berkeley: University of California Press, 1976).

[10] On my reading of it, this is the substance of the shift that Malalgoda records in his history of the emergence of 'Protestant Buddhism' in his magisterial work, *Buddhism in Sinhalese Society*.

their 'traditional' terrain was being systematically displaced by a new one, one that in definitive ways rendered the old options inefficacious. In other words, what is important to understand is that the adversarial confrontation between Christianity and Buddhism in the middle to late nineteenth century was taking place as colonial power was radically altering the very social and political field in which dispute *as such* could be conceived, negotiated and resolved.

My argument has been that the single most crucial moment for these transformations is the so-called Colebrooke–Cameron Reforms of the early 1830s.[11] The project of these reforms was to inscribe a *modern* secular (or *secularizing*) political rationality into the institutional and conceptual space of colonial Sri Lanka. By calling these reforms 'secularizing', I do not mean to suggest that they precipitated a *decline* in religion. (I am in fact suggesting that this conception of secularization-as-decline-of-religion is mistaken.[12]) I mean rather that these reforms led to *a new placement* of 'religion' in conceptual, institutional and social life. The Colebrooke–Cameron Reforms ought to be understood as initiating a process of secularization in the sense that with them a fundamentally new set of generative *conditions* begins to emerge in colonial Sri Lanka: a new social space (that of civil society as a differentiated field of seemingly self-sustaining institutions and organizations); a new social and conceptual object (that of 'religion'); a new sovereign discourse (that of reason as the adjudicating truth-discourse); and a new form of subject (that of a laity whose business it is to take positions on the assumed truth or untruth of religious propositions). These transformations fundamentally alter the game in which the problem of 'religion' and 'politics' can be thought and engaged. This is why for me, the crucial moment of Buddhism and modernity in colonial Sri Lanka is not the so-called Buddhist Revival of the latter part of the nineteenth century but the secularizing *conditions* produced by the Colebrooke–Cameron Reforms two or three decades

---

[11] I have discussed these at length in my 'Colonial Governmentality', in *Refashioning Futures*.

[12] For a useful critical discussion of secularization see C. John Sommerville, *The Secularization of Early Modern England: From Religious Culture to Religious Faith* (New York: Oxford University Press, 1992).

Toleration and Historical Traditions of Difference 291

earlier and the new political rationalities that made the Revival *itself*—as an ideological and organizational moment—possible.

To understand the implications *for the present* of what I am getting at here, let us move from the nineteenth century to the year 1956. In the narrative history of Sinhala–Buddhist nationalism 1956 is a watershed year. This is perhaps uncontroversial. It is the historical moment of the open expression of a politicized Sinhala–Buddhist identity of the kind with which we are now very familiar. It is in 1956 (and subsequently, and of course more dramatically, in 1958) that there occurs the first incidence of a form of organized violence that is inextricably linked to religion, ethnicity and politics *in a very modern way*. The story of '1956' is often told as the story of the convergence of a number of factors that had been gestating in the Sri Lankan polity since the Buddhist Revival. As Stanley Tambiah, for example, tells it in his controversial book:

> The year 1956 was historic, because it saw the political success of Sinhala Buddhist nationalism, which had remained latent for some time and began to gain momentum in the early fifties. There was a confluence of many concerns and aspirations which had a cumulative effect upon the elections held at this date. These concerns were the rehabilitation and restoration of Buddhism to its pre-colonial status; the shift from English language as a medium of administration (official language) and education to the indigenous mother tongues, especially the fostering by the Sinhalese of their national identity and their national culture.[13]

I do not entirely disagree with this account. It is certainly the case that during the first half of the twentieth century a number of activist Buddhist organizations emerged in the public sphere, and that by the early 1950s a certain Sinhala–Buddhist ideological and organizational momentum was gathering. Urmila Phadnis's much neglected book, *Religion and Politics in Sri Lanka*, provides the most detailed description and discussion of these organizations.[14]

At the same time, however, I am not so sure that this is an adequate

---

[13] See Stanley J. Tambiah, *Buddhism Betrayed? Religion, Politics, and Violence in Sri Lanka* (Chicago: University of Chicago Press, 1992), p. 42.

[14] See Urmila Phadnis, *Religion and Politics in Sri Lanka* (London: Hurst, 1976), especially chapters 4, 5, 6, and 7.

story. Or rather, I am not so sure about the adequacy of its *register*: the growth and development of an *ideological* and *organizational* formation. I am not at all sure, in other words, that what needs to be explained is the rise of an ideology and its forms of organization. It seems to me that there is in fact another story about '1956' to be told, namely the story of its conditions of possibility in the register of *political rationality*—that is, the reasons of power through which a conceptual and institutional space is deconstructed/reconstructed. This would be a story that links the political rationality inaugurated in the Colebrooke–Cameron Reforms of the early 1830s to the cultural-politics of the post-Independence period. And the central mediating link here are the Donoughmore Reforms of 1931.[15] Schematically, and simplifying considerably, where the Colebrooke–Cameron Reforms of a hundred years earlier sought to reorganize the colonial polity *in a modern direction* through the inscription of a liberal rationality (fashioning the kinds of economy, society, and subjectivity such a rationality depended upon), the project of the later reforms (their introduction of adult suffrage and the principle of territorial representation) was to *re-shape* that emerging modern order through the explicitly numerical ratio of territorial representation, to re-shape it, that is, on an understanding of democracy as a matter of numbers. So that by the 1950s, not only do you have a now normalized ideological object—buddhagama—and a proliferation of ideological organizations involved in the construction of a collective 'mass' identity around it, but you have a political reason that depends precisely upon the *incitement* and *mobilization* of just such identities in the majoritarian project of securing state power. In my view, therefore, S.W.R.D. Bandaranaike was not the opportunist he appears to be in the liberal accounts of this period.[16] He was himself a subject of the rationality of the new political game of representative democracy he had entered and was determined to exploit.

[15] For a more detailed discussion see my, 'Community, Number, and the Ethos of Democracy', in *Refashioning Futures*.

[16] For instance, James Manor, *The Expedient Utopian: Bandaranaike and Sri Lanka* (Cambridge: Cambridge University Press, 1989).

I should like to read the Tamil critique that emerges with S.J.V. Chelvanayakam and the Federal Party in the late 1940s as an incipient critique of this political rationality of liberal majoritarian representationalism.[17] When Chelvanayakam breaks with G.G. Ponnambalam and the All Sri Lanka Tamil Congress in 1949 (breaking as he does so with the accommodationism that had characterized official Tamil politics for many decades) and begins to articulate a claim for the autonomy of the Tamil nation, for Tamil self-government within a federal state, he is in effect trying to break the politico-epistemic hold of the majoritarian intolerance of this political reason. There is a genealogy waiting to be written of the discourse of 'federalism' in twentieth-century Sri Lanka, and of its connections to questions of pluralism and toleration. Suffice it to say for the present that I agree that dismantling the unitary state and establishing a federal structure would go a far way to ensuring a more livable pluralism and a more effective toleration, but I wonder whether this isn't the *beginning* rather than the end of an important dialogue. In my view the challenge of toleration is for something more fundamental, more far-reaching, than a federalist solution. The challenge, I think, is the fashioning of a more *pluralizing* political domain (one that offers more than the constitutional recognition of *existing* pluralities), a way of thinking a pluralist politics that, while perhaps federalist in its overall framework, is not statist in its logic, one that can accommodate both existing pluralities and resist the drive to the naturalization of an ideology of (ethnic/religious) difference. If this is the challenge then perhaps we shall have to rethink some aspects of the liberal discourse of pluralism and toleration in relation to which that federalism is being thought out.

III

Let me turn then to a discussion of some aspects of the liberal debate about toleration. I do not intend a comprehensive or even far-ranging discussion of the varieties of conception and defence of toleration

---

[17] On Chelvanayakam and Tamil nationalism see, A. J. Wilson, *S.J.V. Chelvanayakam and the Crisis of Tamil Nationalism, 1947–1977* (London: Hurst, 1994).

within liberalism.[18] What I am principally concerned to explore here are some of the limits of these models, and in particular the way in which liberal models of toleration depend upon the philosophical anthropology of moral individualism—the idea that 'the *source* of morality, of moral values and principles, the creator of the very criteria of moral evaluation, is the individual.'[19] Or, to put it another way, what I am interested in is the inability of liberal conceptions of pluralism and toleration to adequately deal with the question of *historical communities*, especially *postcolonial* historical communities. For what is politically and conceptually challenging about these communities ('religious' communities, 'ethnic' communities) is both the fact that their constitutive virtues may not be the virtues admired and commended in liberal traditions (that of liberal autonomy, for instance), and the fact that they are communities that have been subjected over long periods of time to *liberalizing* and *secularizing* reforms as part of the colonial project of restructuring them in modernizing directions. I shall explore the parameters of liberal tolerance by focusing on two liberal thinkers, Will Kymlicka and Chandran Kukathas. These liberal theorists argue in quite different directions about the matter of 'cultural' rights and their implications for toleration, but in the end they share what I shall regard as a limiting liberal premise regarding the moral and epistemological priority of the individual.

Before turning to Kymlicka and Kukathas, however, I want to make two framing observations. The first has to do with the contemporary

---

[18] For a useful way into the range of issues that characterize contemporary discourses on toleration, see the series of books that came out of the Morrell Project on Toleration at the University of York, Toronto. John Horton and Susan Mendus (eds), *Aspects of Toleration* (London: Methuen, 1985); David Edwards and Susan Mendus (eds), *On Toleration* (Oxford: Clarendon Press, 1987); Susan Mendus (ed.), *Justifying Toleration* (Cambridge: Cambridge University Press, 1988); and Susan Mendus, *Toleration and the Limits of Liberalism* (London: Methuen, 1989). See also, more recently, David Heyd (ed.), *Toleration: An Elusive Virtue* (Princeton: Princeton University Press, 1996); and Michael Walzer, *On Toleration* (New Haven: Yale University Press, 1997).

[19] Steven Lukes, *Individualism* (Oxford, Blackwell, 1973), p. 101, his emphasis.

political/conceptual context in which the problem of toleration has become so prominent a feature. This context is shaped, on the one hand, by the revival (so to put it) of liberalism and of liberal political theorizing over the last decade-and-a-half; and on the other hand, by the collapse of liberalism's main twentieth-century competitor, socialism, and Marxist political theorizing. This is the context in which the contemporary debate is being conducted, and in which the *moral force* of the ideal of liberalism's toleration is felt. In the middle 1960s when Herbert Marcuse wrote his famous essay on 'repressive tolerance', dedicated to his insurgent students at Brandeis University, his defence of a 'liberatory intolerance' depended upon the conceptual and politico-historical plausibility of a narrative of liberation.[20] This idea of liberation was of course sustained against the status quo by a rival conception of morality, grounded in a rival conception of the good society, and guided by a rival conception of reason.[21] These provided the radically alternative horizon in relation to which liberal tolerance could be criticised. By contrast, the present we inhabit appears to offer us no such alternative, no radical *outside* to the conceptual and political space normalized by liberalism's new hegemony. We have *all* to be liberals now. So, at least, liberalism's autobiography would have us believe.

The second observation has again to do with context, but this time the context that constitutes the implicit *background* of liberal political theorizing. The background question in discussions of toleration is this: How is the *liberal* state to accommodate difference, to face up to diversity? One underlying assumption, therefore, is the *prior* existence of a secular state and a secularized society populated by autonomous citizens living their diverse life-styles and privately pursuing their

---

[20] See Herbert Marcuse, 'Repressive Tolerance', in Robert Paul Wolff, Barrington Moore, Jr., and Herbert Marcuse, *A Critique of Pure Tolerance* (Boston: Beacon, 1965).
[21] See Marcuse's *An Essay on Liberation* (Boston: Beacon, 1969). Perhaps the most sustained argument in this tradition is the one found in Max Horkheimer and Theodor Adorno, *Dialectic of Enlightenment* (New York: Continuum, 1988).

multiple ends, who are now confronted with the influx of numbers of largely non-European (and often not-so-liberal) peoples making (not-so-liberal) claims on the resources of a liberal state rapidly retreating from welfarism. This, obviously, is the context of the north-Atlantic liberal democracies and the new discourse of multiculturalism. It is this cognitive-political context that sets the terms of the debate. So that whether the problem of toleration is posed in terms of the justification of requiring non-liberal cultural minorities to re-order themselves so as to admit the principle of individual liberty held by the 'host' society, or of obliging that community to allow dissident individuals to cast in their lot with the liberal majority if they so choose, the clearly approved *direction* is the liberal one. In consequence, the problem of toleration in postcolonial societies where the background assumption of a liberal state and a liberal majority population is harder to take for granted can only be a derivative one. I have a fundamental doubt about this kind of theorization.

Kymlicka is a particularly interesting liberal thinker because he wants to use the idea of autonomy to explore liberalism's ability to respond to the claims of cultural diversity. He has been justifiably critical of liberals like John Rawls or Ronald Dworkin for not adequately recognizing the disadvantages minority communities may face, and thus the claims of 'cultural rights' that seek to redress such disadvantages.[22] These communities may require special rights (regarding language, for example, or education) to protect them from decisions of the majority community that could have the unintended effect of undermining the viability of their culture. Kymlicka endorses such rights, arguing that this is consistent with—perhaps even required by—liberal equality. For him, culture is an important register of rights because it is the domain that provides the context in which meaningful individual choice is made.

---

[22] See Will Kymlicka, *Liberalism, Community, and Culture* (New York: Oxford University Press, 1989). To be fair, of course, Rawls has attempted to make some concession in this direction in his 1993 Oxford Amnesty Human Rights Lecture, 'The Law of Peoples'. See Stephen Shute and Susan Hurley (eds), *On Human Rights: The Oxford Amnesty Lectures, 1993* (New York: Basic Books, 1993).

However, Kymlicka insists that such protections or special safeguards for minority cultures are only justifiable insofar as the fundamental principle of individual autonomy is not violated. Indeed, for Kymlicka what distinguishes *liberal* from non-liberal tolerance is precisely its commitment to the principle that individuals have an inalienable interest in their moral capacity to assess and potentially revise their existing ends. This is why, for example, the millet system of the Ottoman Empire (a system that allowed Muslims, Christians, and Jews to organize themselves into more or less self-governing units), is not a persuasive model for him. He allows that this system had several praiseworthy virtues; it was 'generally humane, tolerant of group differences, and remarkably stable.' *But*, he goes on, 'it was not a liberal society, for it did not recognize any principle of *individual* freedom of conscience.'[23]

In Kymlicka's conception, liberalism has to think through the problem of minority rights in terms of two kinds of limitations. The first is that liberalism will not justify the demand of a minority culture to restrict the basic civil or political liberties of its own members. These are what he calls 'internal restrictions.' Liberals, Kymlicka argues, are committed to supporting the right of individuals to decide for themselves which aspects of their cultural heritage are worth passing on, and which not. As he goes on: 'Liberalism is committed to (perhaps even defined by) the view that individuals should have the freedom and capacity to question and possibly revise the traditional practices of their community should they come to see them as no longer worthy of their allegiance.'[24] The second limitation is that while liberals are more sympathetic to demands to reduce a minority culture's vulnerability to the decisions of the larger society—what he calls 'external protections'—these are only legitimate insofar as they promote equality between groups by rectifying disadvantages. In other words, Kymlicka's commitment to the priority of autonomy means that he is

---

[23] Will Kymlicka, 'Toleration and its Limits', in *Multicultural Citizenship: A Liberal Theory of Minority Rights* (New York: Oxford University Press, 1995), p. 157, emphasis in original.
[24] Ibid., p. 152.

willing to defend the right of minority cultures to maintain themselves as distinct, but *only* if 'they are themselves governed by liberal principles.'[25]

Chandran Kukathas, a thinker with equally strong liberal commitments, has taken issue with this argument of Kymlicka's.[26] Kukathas is particularly concerned with the way in which Kymlicka's idea of cultural rights and toleration is grounded in autonomy. The problem of course, as Kukathas rightly says, is that many non-Western cultures do not privilege autonomy, do not put a special premium on the individual's freedom to choose and revise their plans of life. What is entailed therefore in Kymlicka's argument, Kukathas charges, is that for special rights to apply to minority cultures, the internal moral structure of their community will have to be reorganized *in a liberal direction*. Kymlicka is bound to encourage liberalization. And therefore, far from having the effect of preserving the cultural context of choice, Kymlicka—like Mill—will be 'drawn down the path of interference.'[27] But as Kukathas argues, from the point of view of persons seeking to preserve the cultural integrity of their community this is obviously not going to be acceptable. To argue, as Kymlicka does, that it is possible to alter a non-liberal culture in a liberal direction without significantly destroying it, is 'to fail to take their culture seriously.' As he says: 'Culture is not simply a matter of colorful dances and rituals, nor is it even a framework or context for individual choice. Rather it is the product of the association of individuals over time, which in turn shapes individual commitments and gives meaning to individual lives—lives for which individual choice or autonomy may be quite useless. To try to reshape it in accordance with ideals of individual choice is to strike at its very core.'[28] What cultural communities very often want, he suggests, is really to be left alone to manage their own affairs. If there is going to be any reshaping they want to be able to

---

[25] Ibid., p. 153.

[26] Chandran Kukathas, 'Are There Any Cultural Rights'? *Political Theory* 20(1) (February 1992), pp. 105–39.

[27] Ibid., p. 121.

[28] Ibid., p. 122.

undertake it themselves, and as far as possible within the idiom of their own cultural practices.[29]

Against Kymlicka's view, Kukathas seeks to develop an account of liberalism in which the justification for toleration is detached from the assumption of the privilege of individual autonomy. Kukathas agrees with Kymlicka that 'the cultural health of minority communities' may indeed be something that liberals ought to be concerned about, but he sees no need for liberalism to modify or revise itself in order to meet this concern.[30] To the contrary, he maintains that what is necessary is to reassert the fundamental importance of the liberal principles of individual rights and individual liberty (and the core assumptions of individualism, egalitarianism, and universalism on which they rest), and reject the idea of cultural rights. No liberal needs to deny that individuals are invariably members of 'groups or associations which not only influence their conduct but shape their loyalties and their sense of identity.' What has to be denied, he stresses however, 'is the proposition that fundamental moral claims are to be attached to such groups and that the terms of political association must be established with these particular claims in mind.'[31]

From a liberal point of view, says Kukathas, the desire to live according to the practices of one's own culture has to be respected not, as Kymlicka thinks, because the culture has the right to be preserved, but because individuals have a freedom of association as well as a corollary freedom of dissociation. As Kukathas argues: 'If there are any fundamental rights, then there is at least one right which is of crucial importance: the right of the individual to leave a community or association by the terms of which he or she no longer wishes to live.'[32] This, he suggests, is a view of the rights of the individual that while assigning a good deal of authority to the cultural community does not accord it any *fundamental* rights. Unlike Kymlicka's individualism, Kukathas 'does not impose severe restrictions on what is to count as

[29] Ibid.
[30] Ibid., p. 107.
[31] Ibid., p. 110.
[32] Ibid., p. 116.

(a legitimate form of) human flourishing. It does not go on to suggest that human flourishing requires that the individual be capable of autonomy or have the capacity to choose his or her way of life on the basis of critical reflection on a range of options. Rather, it is content to accept that what matters most when assessing whether a way of life is legitimate is whether the individuals taking part in it are prepared to acquiesce in it.'[33] This is why the *only* fundamental right for Kukathas is the right of exit.

I think that Kukathas pushes the standard liberal conception of difference and toleration in a very challenging direction, one worth taking seriously if we want to think through the impasse of our Sri Lankan postcolonial present. For unlike Kymlicka, he is willing to give up the Enlightenment demand for a progressive convergence on a secular ideal of community grounded in and guided by a comprehensive and singular liberal reason. I think he is right to seek to bracket the assumed privilege of autonomy and to give more room to ways of life whose internal virtues the West may find unacceptable, even unassimilable. What this means is that whereas Kymlicka's plural society is ideally composed of liberal communities, Kukathas' need not be.

At the same time, however, it is to be noticed that for Kukathas' right of exit to be a substantial one, the wider society has ideally to be of a *certain* sort, namely, 'one in which the principle of freedom of association [is] upheld.' Non-liberal social formations are therefore largely ruled out: 'A society composed of tribal communities organized on the basis of kinship, for example, would not make the freedom of exit credible. . . . Exit would be credible only if the wider society were much more like a market society within which there was a considerable degree of individual independence and the possibility of what Weber called social closure was greatly diminished.'[34] It may

---

[33] Ibid., p. 124.

[34] Ibid., p. 134. Kymlicka himself comments on this curious caveat in his response to Kukathas. See his 'The Rights of Minority Cultures: Reply to Kukathas', in *Political Theory* 20(1) (February 1992), p. 143; and Kukathas' rejoinder, 'Cultural Rights Again: A Rejoinder to Kymlicka', in *Political Theory* 20(4) (November 1992), pp. 674–80.

well be wondered, then, whether in the end Kukathas too arrives at a liberal *limit* where his own individualist premises oblige him to endorse unproblematically a wider society 'embodying a liberal political culture' as the *privileged* (if not the only) horizon in relation to which pluralism, and the 'exit' rule that gives it meaning, can be thought out. I wonder whether, unwilling as he is to historicize and anthropologize the liberal foundation of individualism itself, and the constituent features that make it up, his best hope can only be for an exit into a mode of being-in-common that not only shelters this moral ideal but depends upon its epistemological centrality.[35]

IV

I want to find a way to other grounds than these for a commitment to toleration in contemporary Sri Lanka. I do not believe that Kymlicka and Kukathas define our only options. Or rather they are our seeming options only insofar as we buy their presumption of the primacy of individualism and the conceptions of culture that follow from it. The direction that seems to me worth exploring is one that sets aside the demand for a normative background of liberalism and opens itself to the possibility of contending non-liberal historical traditions of difference, none of which necessarily depend upon, nor principally defend, the primordiality of individualism.

I want to think of Sinhala, Tamil and Muslim communities as constituting historical traditions of difference. An historical tradition of difference is a distinctive moral community which has, over time, developed an argument (or an intersecting complex of arguments) about who it is, about how and why it has come to be who it is, and about what it takes to continue being who it is.[36] This argument (or

---

[35] Neither Kymlicka nor Kukathas acknowledge other traditions of liberty in the West in which the individual has not been taken so singularly to be the *only* subject of freedom. On this see, Quentin Skinner, *Liberty before Liberalism* (New York: Cambridge University Press, 1998); and James Tully, *Strange Multiplicities: Constitutionalism in an Age of Diversity* (New York, Cambridge University Press, 1995).

[36] Obviously, this conception of a tradition owes much to Alasdair MacIntyre, *After Virtue* 2nd edn. (Notre Dame: University of Notre Dame Press, 1984).

complex of arguments), moreover, has come historically to be *embodied* in practices and institutions through which distinctive moral selves are cultivated and in which the valued virtues of the tradition are inculcated and reproduced. An historical tradition of difference is not internally homogeneous. There are always diverse positions and points of view. This is precisely why it is an argument. What is shared, though, is what is held in common, what is argued *about*. Among Sinhalas, for instance, there are narratives that give point to what it means to be Sinhala. Many of these narratives turn on the figuration of the Buddha in a normative relation to the land of Lanka and the political power of the state. Some of these stories are authoritative in the sense that they are invoked and deployed in ways that seek to pre-empt a space for other narratives of identity. The extent to which they are actually able to do so, of course, depends upon the kinds of institutional practice into which they are inserted.

This is why in my view what we ought to be systematically exploring in Sri Lanka are ways and means of inventing, cultivating and institutionalizing cultural-political spaces in which such communities can formulate and articulate their moral-political concerns and their self-governing claims in the languages of their respective historical traditions. What this direction would entail is not a de-politicization of community, not the exclusion of Muslim, Tamil and Sinhala cultural values from the domain of public political life, but rather the fashioning of the institutional means of enabling tradition-bearing Tamils, Muslims and Sinhalas to be active participants in their own self-government. It is important to stress, however, that to think in these terms is emphatically *not* to assume that Muslimness, Tamilness or Sinhalaness (or whatever other identity is in question) is any *one* thing. I am not, as some might be inclined to think, advocating the communalization of institutions. Were I doing this I would be assuming, as the nationalists do, that there is an authoritative transcendental horizon from which *real* Sinhalaness, Tamilness, or Muslimness can be identified and represented. This is not my view. Kymlicka (and other liberals) are wrong to assume that the idea of an historical tradition entails the view that people's ends are fixed or are beyond 'rational' revision. To the

Toleration and Historical Traditions of Difference 303

contrary, the idea of an historical tradition entails the idea that people's ends *are* revisable, not however in relation to the cipher of autonomy, but in relation to, against the background of, in an argument with, the constitutive tradition that has produced them as subjects *of a certain sort* in the first place.

At the same time let me add that I am not saying (as the anti-essentialists do), that there is in fact *no* real Sinhalaness, Tamilness, or Muslimness. To the contrary this whole line of preoccupation with the idea of an epistemological vantage from which such supposed realness is to be determined should be set aside. What I am suggesting is that what constitutes the lived reality of these identities is, at the least, *an embodied historical argument* in which Sinhalas and Tamils and Muslims have respectively been engaged—among themselves (in the first instance), but also with each other. Conceiving of such traditions as ongoing embodied moral-political arguments, then, the project of toleration would be to find the modalities by which to enable both the relative sovereignty of these historical forms of life *and* to provide space for their mutual recognition and for stimulating and sustaining an intercultural dialogue between them. It is not enough, in other words, for Tamils, Sinhalas and Muslims to be able to argue within their own discursive traditions about who they are respectively and what they want, it is necessary to create overlapping public spaces (new overlapping domains of the political) in which these traditions meet, in which disagreement and discord can be voiced, claims and counter-claims negotiated, and accommodations, compromises—i.e. settlements (albeit temporary ones)—arrived at.

To sum up, I have sought to do no more than clarify, in a preliminary way, a doubt that liberal discourse on toleration is adequate to the task of thinking through the contemporary impasse in Sri Lanka. That liberal discourse, even where it has addressed itself to questions of cultural rights, depends too deeply on the priority of a certain kind of subject (private, secular, autonomous, self-adjudicating), and on the priority of a certain kind of social and institutional space (a background liberal state and liberal public culture). The challenge of toleration in contemporary Sri Lanka, however, is not that of enabling the individual subject of legal rights and private ends, but of finding ways of enabling non-liberal historical communities to embody their historically constituted traditions of difference in politically meaningful ways. I believe the fundamental questions are these: How can we begin to imagine organized spheres and practices of Sinhala–Buddhist self-determination that articulate in overlapping spaces of identity and difference with spheres and practices of Tamil and Muslim self-determination? What transformations in law, in our conceptions of consensus and dissent, in our notions of the state, in our understandings of political process, policy and administration, have to be imagined to facilitate the conceptualization of such over-lapping spheres, practices and articulations? To be sure, these are not questions with ready-made answers; but they are, in my view, questions worth asking.

Discussion: An Afterword on the New Subaltern

GAYATRI CHAKRAVORTY SPIVAK

THIS VOLUME IS a selection of papers from the 1995 Subaltern Studies Conference in Colombo. The theme of the volume is 'community, violence and gender'.

I had come to the conference from Bangladesh. I had experienced there the ways in which delegates for the non-governmental organizations forum, to be included in the (then upcoming) Fourth World Women's Conference, organized by the United Nations and to take place in Beijing, were being gathered, nation-state by nation-state. The incursion of non-governmental organizations into UN women's conferences was initiated at the 1994 UN conference on Population and Development in Cairo. In the wake of the disappearance of the Soviet bloc, it was of course a way of undermining nation-specific resistance in the name of international solidarity.

These convictions were strengthened by the experience of delegate-formation in the South. Asked to speak at the opening of the conference, I had therefore spoken of 'the new subaltern', the somewhat monolithic woman-as-victim who is the constituted subject of justice under (the now-unrestricted) international capitalism.

To chart the constitution of an ideological subject in a politico-economic interest is the work of interventionist cultural studies. The 'new subaltern' is a global model of such a subject, yet it is always and necessarily tried out on local scenes. In these remarks, I will first attempt to place, within an international or global frame, various nation-state versions of constituted subjects proposed in some of the essays in this volume.

In 'Hegemonic Spatial Strategies', for example, Satish Deshpande examines the change from Nehru (secularism) to Savarkar (Hindutva), and describes the *mise-en-scene* or setting for the new subject that Tejaswini Niranjana, in 'Nationalism Refigured', will see constituted in Maniratnam's films. Deshpande calls this the 'loosen[ing of] the nation-space from its moorings in alternative ideologies in order to relocate it within the framework of Hindu hegemony.'

In the context of the United Nations globality that puts together the new subaltern, the 'hegemony' is in the international feminist dominant. Such a staging can accommodate the 'feminists'—writing 'rape' into the law by implicitly presupposing patriarchal values—questioned by Nivedita Menon in 'Embodying the Self'. If we globalize Menon's scene, 'woman' would be seen as written into the law with an implicit presupposition of the values of the internationalization of capital, which may sometimes seem anti-patriarchal, especially if sexual difference is confused with gender. These women of the international dominant are a combination of 'the Englished' (read 'globalized') and the 'national-modern' proposed by Tejaswini Niranjana.

Indeed, grounds for such loose analogies, a combination of the global and the national defined in a peculiarly national interest, can be found, with appropriate variations, in the North as well as the South. And, after the Cold War, the national interest of the United States does increasingly masquerade as the global. This will be my second framing of the nation-state arguments in our volume.

If the 'Indian modernity' that is the condition and effect of Maniratnam's films is 'linked to the emergence of a new consumer economy supported by the ongoing reconstitution of the national imaginary,' the 'modernity' of the United States—represented in videographic news where 'audiences in the West are obliged to identify with an invisible but adamant moralistic perspective in which the United States is seen as superior'—is a displacement of the old doctrine of 'manifest destiny'.[1]

In the summer of 1999, at the time of this writing, the United States has been invited into that very Kashmir—scene of India–Pakistan conflict—scene also of *Roja*, one of the films discussed in Niranjana's essay, now contextualized by the fierce near-Fascist nationalism daily shown on Indian national television. These *in*cursions of US nationalism—a displacement of the doctrine of manifest destiny into geopolitical culture—have introduced other, more macrological discursive constitutions. These latter will have infiltrated and sublated (destroyed yet preserved) the infiltration of the abstract civil structures of parliamentary democracy by the movements of religion-as-majority and the personal-as-political—heterosexism-as-citizenship—that Niranjana points out. In the cultural sphere, details such as Niranjana's distinction between 'Englished' and 'Indian' modernity, and the definition of the latter as 'post-national-modern', may still be available to the localist and the specialist. They will not, however, be available to the great general audience, pedagogically and politically active, undergirded by the massive and dynamic US foundation culture—one thinks particularly of the Ford Foundation—involved in South Asia (and in the global South in general) at least since the National Defense Education Act of 1958, Title VI.[2] For that powerful and influential audience, the commanding power of a cruder theory of national identity—paradoxically receiving an alibi for the dismissal of class as too crude a model—will prevail. Qadri Ismail's essay 'Constituting Nation, Contesting Nationalism' indirectly addresses such problems by pointing at the contradictions in some left-leaning intellectuals' invocations of the nation.

In the geopolitical field, however, a yet cruder discursive re-constellation may become operative: ethnic cleansing. This volume contains

[1] Rey Chow, 'King Kong in Hong Kong' and Don Pease, 'US Imperialism: Global Dominance Without Colonies', both in Henry Schwarz and Sangeeta Ray (eds), *The Blackwell Companion to Postcolonial Studies* (forthcoming).

[2] In terms of the construction of a 'feminist' post-national-modern, I remain curious about the peculiar sequence featuring the song 'I will not give you a girl child' in Maniratnam's *Bombay!*

a lovely essay on the nearly ethereal politics of Saadat Hasan Manto's staging of the Partition of India—Aamir R. Mufti's 'A Greater Storywriter than God'. Ismail cites the recitation of the nostalgic account of the forcible adhesion—rather than partition—of a coerced Ceylon [*sic*], out of two honourably separate 'nations', Tamil and Sinhala. Ismail and Deshpande both show that, since the 1980s, the terminology of genocide has been used to exacerbate 'national' and 'subnational' conflict. (I use the quotation marks because I cannot agree with Ismail that 'the nation itself is [an] inoperative, oppressive, disabling community.' The problem is, precisely, that it is only too operative, too enabling, leading to liberation claims that seem the opposite of oppression.)

But 'ethnic cleansing' is a different order of business from 'Partition' or 'genocide', which is a term that was invented to accuse aberrant German Fascist anti-Semites, and by historical metonymy, to name this blot on the European past.[3] 'Ethnic *cleansing*', on the other hand, carries with it an aura of pre-Christian sacrificial cultures. It is a mobilization, once again, of the historical use of the argument from normative deviations to justify European intervention.[4] Its most potent use was, as usual, in Africa—in the case of Rwanda.[5] Now, with the US

---

[3] 'Nazism was not born in the desert. We all know this, but it has to be constantly recalled. And even if, far from any desert, it had grown like a mushroom in the silence of a European forest, it would have done so in the shadow of big trees, in the shelter of their silence or their indifference but in the same soil.' Jacques Derrida, *Of Spirit: Heidegger and the Question*, tr. Geoffrey Bennington and Rachel Bowlby (Chicago: Univ. of Chicago Press, 1989), p. 109.

[4] I have argued this in Chapter I of *A Critique of Postcolonial Reason: Toward a History of the Vanishing Present* (Cambridge and Calcutta: Harvard Univ. Press and Seagull Books, 1999). In the European context, Max Horkheimer argues this in the following way, which is to be related to the conviction of manifest destiny in the US national imaginary: 'The attempt to afford justification to every idea and every historical person and to assign the heroes of past revolutions their place in the pantheon of history next to the victorious generals of the counterrevolution, this ostensibly freefloating objectivity conditioned by the bourgeoisie's stand on two fronts against absolutist restoration and against the proletariat, has acquired validity in the Hegelian system along with the idealistic pathos of absolute knowledge.' 'On the Problem of Truth', in *The Essential Frankurt School Reader*, ed. Andrew Arato and Eike Gebhart (New York: Urizen Books, 1978), p. 418.

[5] V.Y. Mudimbe, born in what was then rural Belgian Congo, resigned in the 1960s

Discussion: An Afterword on the New Subaltern   309

intervention in Serbia—although the victims immediately being rescued were Muslims—the argument has been advanced to the fringes of Europe and cobbled to the relatively remote history of pre-European empires, with conveniently Muslim culprits.[6] This gives rise to a narrative riddled with contradictions. But has that ever been a problem when power is in need of adequate justification?

With the irrational and excessive loyalties of the non-resident Indian, I want to believe that such discussions will show up their absurdity upon this densely populated subcontinent. Yet the lineaments are clear. A relatively remote pre-European Islamic empire cobbled with the normative deviation of 'ethnic cleansing', requiring US intervention—military, political, as well as cultural, making-human, not the 'Muslim', as in *Roja*, but the redefined population of Kashmir, by geographical metonymy the entire population of the subcontinent. If Hitler was an 'aberration' causing the events that yielded the word 'genocide', it is Tito and Nehru—the good guys—who are considered aberrations here. The delicacies of subcontinental Partition studies may have to line up with the Human Rights pieties of an Alfredo Jaar (Rwanda) or the hysterical jingoism of a Susan Sontag (Kosovo).

Over against such macrologies, Ismail, Jeganathan and Menon, and by extension David Scott, ask for attention to the local. In this connection, I would like to say a word about the insistently local 'wild response' to anthropology offered by the nonresidential subcontinental, as claimed here by Pradeep Jeganathan in 'A Space for Violence'.

I hasten to add that 'wild response to anthropology' is not a term of derogation. Louis Althusser had laid out Lenin's 'wild response' to

---

from the Belgian Benedictine order, into which he was inserted by the colonials because of his forbidding intelligence, already evident in childhood, in protest against Belgian policy in Rwanda. How shall we square this with the notion of Rwandans' 'natural savagery' which accompanies notions of 'ethnic cleansing?' See also Mahmood Mamdani, 'From Conquest to Consent as the Basis of State Formation: Reflections on Rwanda,' *New Left Review* 216 (March/April 1996), pp. 3–36.

[6] The international press often carries news items to show that international Islam does not support NATO intervention in the Balkans. The history of Balkan Islam is crosshatched with the usual conflicts between reform, orthodoxy and divided nationalisms that form the red thread that runs through this volume.

philosophy in 'Lenin and Philosophy' in 1968, to describe, among other things, Lenin's insertion of politics into philosophy and vice versa: 'Everything which touches on politics may be fatal to philosophy, for philosophy lives on politics.'[7]

Earlier, it was the colonial subject's relationship to the colonizing culture that could have been described as a 'wild anthropology', rather more than mere mimicry or masquerade, however carefully theorized. For the exercise entered the production of the disciplines, with an unrecognized, and potentially destructive, entry of the political, as sketched by Althusser and shown here by Jeganathan.[8] If indeed that

---

[7] Louis Althusser, 'Lenin and Philosophy', in Gregory Elliott, ed., *Philosophy and the Spontaneous Philosophy of the Scientists & Other Essays* (New York: Verso, 1990), p. 173.

[8] It is a simple notion, adroitly thematized in Peter Dickinson's vaguely racist mystery novel *The Poison Oracle* (New York: Pantheon, 1974) where, incidentally, the minimal ethical agent is a trained chimpanzee: whereas the disciplinary anthropologist has difficulty entering the observed culture, colonized groups enter the culture of the colonizer with violent ease, destablizing and transforming it in the process. In the context of the discipline of literary criticism, I have linked this to the theory of the creative imagination as the inbuilt instrument of othering: 'People like Matthew Arnold yoke the power of the imagination to the indigenous upper class in the colonies. Under the impetus of a pedagogic incentive much stronger than merely academic, my ancestors othered themselves and became colonial subjects. When Wordsworth wants to become transparent so that he can enter the minds of persons who have been uncontaminated by the industrial revolution and become a conduit and actively enter the passions of the reader so that by exercising this othering through the imagination, the person who can no longer be excited without external stimulation because of the horrible factory life in cities, will get training in ethics, by robustly imagining the other; and Shelley says Roman law is 'poetic' in his enlarged sense, they are still figuring an experience of the impossible if they read with the whole soul. But, by the time Arnold and Pater write, that figure has been transformed into the institutional practice of producing the colonial subject. We have moved from figure to calculus. When Wordsworth or Shelley uses poetry as the subject of a proposition, or Coleridge uses imagination thus, they are describing faculties of the mind or mental phenomena. They are making a critique of individual will. They talk about the poetic sensibility as something which can in fact be unlike the individual will because it is given over to a principle and faculty of the subject which is larger than the outlines of the will. On the other hand, when Arnold uses the word "culture" as a subject of propositions, he does not have a theory of the mental theater at all. The study of perfection

produced the colonial subject, the 'wild response to anthropology' practised by the non-resident subcontinental, more the subject of what is called 'postcolonialism' than the actual citizens of the postcolonial state, is a turn or trick of writing without which 'abandoned to the simple content of its conclusions, the ultra-transcendental text will so closely resemble the precritical text as to be indistinguishable from it.'[9] (Thus the confusion between Subaltern Studies and an unexamined culturalism.) Jeganathan's piece is a brilliant and selfconscious example of that genre, undertaken by a disciplinary anthropologist. Chuni Kotal, a subaltern attempting to enter the discipline, as yet unmarked by the turns or tricks of such 'wildness', must be remembered as part of what remains uncleared as Jeganathan clears space for a violence beyond the discipline. Of her I will speak below.

Such local investigations are appropriately confined to micrologies, detail of word and gesture. Emboldened by that protocol, I will repeat here a point I raised at the conference.

We often claim that knowledge is caught in idiom. It has been further suggested that the madness of all decisions—incessantly translated into politics—is the substance of histories.[10] There is no decision below the declarative—and no violence greater than the translation of the declarative into performance via the imperative, however implicit or instantaneous. In the untranslatibility of idiom is the guarantee of the plurality of histories. In the difference between *mama baya nahe*— a declaration quoted in Jeganathan's essay as the semiotic correlative of the special space of violence that he discusses, and 'I have no fear', its rough English equivalent, for instance.

The subject of the Sinhala declaration is 'fear'—if *baya* is quite or

---

does not involve tapping a different *faculty* of the mind but a change in the reading list. But the colonial subject is reading with the whole soul—with politics in it.' Spivak, 'A Moral Dilemma', in *Red Thread* (Cambridge: Harvard Univ. Press), forthcoming. Niranjana notices the peculiar politics of students and teachers of English Honours.

[9] Jacques Derrida, *Of Grammatology*, tr. Gayatri Chakravorty Spivak (Baltimore: Johns Hopkins Univ. Press, 1976), p. 61.

[10] Derrida, *Politics of Friendship*, tr. George Collins (New York: Verso, 1997), pp. 219–20.

just fear. The 'literal' translation would be 'my fear is-not [third person singular of the negative]'. The statement is not about the 'I' but about the fear that travels, qualified by shifters. And 'I am afraid' does not translate as the positive of this negative (*mama bayahe*)—although there too it is *baya* rather than 'I' that is the subject.

There are translations of all kinds. From Jeganathan's translation in the narrow sense, from Sinhala to English, marked by idiomatic difference, I go to a more general—though not the most general—translation—a special declarative entailed by the Enlightenment—a subject of much concern for many essays in this volume.

The missing of the translation between the high Enlightenment and its colonial betrayal is reflected in the understanding of consensual rule-governed behaviour, as in road-crossing, defensive driving, chosen disease-preventive measures and, of course, all expectation of civic responsibility, as 'fear'. It would be a mistake, I think, to imagine that there are 'cultures' proper to the Enlightenment where such voluntary self-restraint is 'natural'. Yet the socio-political restraints that allow the myth of such self-restraint to flourish give way where a space for celebrating the failure of the Enlightenment contains a tendency toward that particular violence toward which Jeganathan points.

It is the ethical declaration of Ulysses faced with the Sirens that is given the lie by this dialectic of 'fear' and the special space of violence: 'you must bind me with harsh bonds, that I may remain fast where I am.'[11] For a Jon Elster, this 'imperfect rationality' is what 'takes care both of reason and of passion:' 'Man [*sic*] often is not rational, and rather exhibits *weakness of will*. Even when not rational, man knows that he is irrational and can *bind himself* to protect himself against the irrationality. This second-best or imperfect rationality takes care both of reason and of passion.'[12] Elster's brilliant and complex discussion remains confined to the level playing field of European history. For him 'culture' (never necessary to name except altogether incidentally

---

[11] Homer, *The Odyssey*, tr. A.T. Murray (Cambridge: Harvard Univ. Press, 1995), vol. 1, p. 461.

[12] Jon Elster, *Ulysses and the Sirens: Studies in Rationality and Irrationality* (Cambridge: Cambridge Univ. Press, 1979), p. 111. The rest of the quotations, all confined to these three paragraphs, are indicated in the text by page number alone.

as 'internalization of parental norms') (103) is by default continuous with the politics and economics of the state.

It is therefore unreasonable to expect Elster to conceive of the misfiring of translation, between Enlightenment and colony, that is under discussion here. The only loss he can imagine is of a 'sense of adventure': 'This second best or imperfect rationality takes care both of reason and of passion. What is lost, perhaps, is the sense of adventure.' (Thus he reveals, rather more than incidentally, that the European philosopher is susceptible to supplementation by 'baya', the denial of which would be a denial of the 'adventurousness' of the figure first sketched by Jeganathan.) Yet Elster does of course know that 'the crucial notion of the constituent assembly . . . as a real historical assembly seeking to bind its successors . . . is the closest analogy in society to the state of mind of Ulysses setting out on that dramatic part of his journey' (103). Further, 'in modern democracies a number of institutions can be interpreted as devices for precommitment . . . The central bank can be seen as the repository of reason against the short-term claim of passion' (90).

Elster also knows the scene of Ulysses and the Sirens has something to do with 'character-formation' (78). Using the language of agency, we can say that here the I speaks in its own name—not as the subject of affect but as the agent of knowledge: I will hear and know. I will willingly allow myself to be bound. This delayed gratification—upstream even from knowledge (although never fully; the revelation, by the *Gedankenschnelle* of global circulating capital, that the circuits of capital are also circuits of knowledge/information, is as much a repetition as a rupture)—is indeed the motor of the self-determination of capital from the fault of a weak European feudalism: the dialectics of Enlightenment.[13] It should be mentioned that the Sirens in the epic are not elaborated in the cliches of the seductive female. They speak clearly, in tones of proclamation, they offer fuller knowledge (*pleiona eidos*), and they claim knowledge of the entire events of the Homeric epic.

---

[13] The argument from weak European feudalism is taken from Samir Amin, *Unequal Development: An Essay on the Social Formations of Peripheral Capitalism*, tr. Brian Pearce (New York: Monthly Review Press, 1976) and is developed in chapter 1, *Critique of Postcolonial Reason*.

Ulysses thinks he hears the truth and wants to hear felicitously, by stopping. His past—Circe's advice against the Sirens and his rehearsal of it to his mates—and his future—getting home, 'know' this as lie. Ulysses is not 'afraid' of the Sirens. He prevents himself from being taken in by the present, by attending to it in the frame of its passing, in a robust mistrust of the intending subject. He attends to the future anterior, in Elster's words the 'past future' (67).[14]

It is this binding that is understood as mere 'fear' by Piyal, by Vikram, the players in Jeganathan's essay. When so understood, it is fear that is the subject, not 'I'—*mama baya nahe*, not 'I have no fear'. In this instantiation, Ulysses is derouted and goes to his death in the violent perjury of the Sirens. Yet the *mythos* is still of a return to an

---

[14] It should perhaps be mentioned that the ruse is suggested by Circe, in the mode of 'if you yourself have a will to listen' [*after autos akouemen ai k'ethelestha*]. The entire episode is reported by Odysseus to Arete, Nausicaa's mother. Odysseus further reports his reporting of the ruse to his mates, specifically calling it what the translator calls a 'rehearsal'. In that telling, the 'if' has been transformed into command—'me alone she bade listen to their voices' [*oion 'em enogei op' akouemen*]—intention tied to intent to obey. In the telling of the tale, the listeners identify with the people in Arete's husband's court, and with the mates, as they hear the singer as Odysseus report the past. Do they move with Odysseus as he reports Circe's direct speech? Does one remember that 'Homer' is iteration-specific as one claims a historical legacy? Paradoxically, a Shelley, a Freud, or an Elster must uncouple the narrative from its iteration in order to claim its logico-ethical persuasiveness. Indeed, the imaginative training of a community with an active oral epic tradition is what Aristotle shuts off by claiming imagination for tragedy: its 'vividness can be felt whether it is read or acted' (*Poetics*, tr. W. Hamilton Fyfe and W. Rhys Roberts, Cambridge: Harvard Univ. Press, 1991, p. 115). In terms of the ethical instantiation as such, a connection with Indic material can be made. In her well-documented study 'Parampurushartha Moksha', Tara Chatterjea distinguishes between Indic and 'Western' epistemes by suggesting, at least implicitly, that the latter is guided by nonsatisfaction (*asantosa*) of desire (in Amita Chatterjee (ed.), *Bharatiya Dharmaniti*, Calcutta: Allied Publishers, 1998, p. 54). She points out that, in certain authoritative moments in the former—such as Vyasa to Yudhisthira in the *Mahabharata*—*asantosa* is also recommended as a caste-specific social norm. What we are discussing here can be described in this idiom as willed self-binding or *samyama* in the interest of *asantosa*—non-satisfaction as *kama* or desire, for knowing—rather than use (being-used)—as having. Since Elster discusses an epic for instantiation of political philosophy, I hope I will be spared accusations of mere 'textualism' here.

original home. 'History'—whatever that means—has uncoupled that *mythos* from the wife spinning there for whose sake the seductresses must be known but avoided.[15] Hence Qadri Ismail gives us the tale of two women denying the fantasmatic nation, by dress code and by migration. The classic patriarchal story of Ulysses loosely covers the lineament of capitalist civil society—of which one of the most assiduous agents today is global feminism.

It is here that the detail of Flavia Agnes's essay is most interesting. She shows again and again how, in the Indian context, by defining middle-class Victorian England as the norm, so-called 'reform' undermined the possibility of holding and passing of property by and through women. The point is not to cling to 'unreformed' tradition. The point is to supplement 'reform' on to existing social inscription.[16]

As long as we imagine this persistent task of supplementation as a binary opposition, a 'reject[ion] as a whole' of what binds 'value' to measure, 'democracy' to 'statistical principle' (David Scott), 'law' to reason as 'patriarchy', we are open to Satish Deshpande's critique, concretized in the name of 'communalism' and 'secularism': 'against this drab and debilitating anonymity [the flattening effect of an even-handed secularism], communalism asserts the privileges of non-negotiable, uniquely different identities.' If on the other hand we suppose each to be the effortful postponement of the other—value/measure as

---

[15] In Homer, Odysseus is managed by women acting in the interest of Zeus and Poseidon. He is let go by the nymph Calypso at the behest of Athene. Circe warns him of the Sirens. It is the Sirens—heraldic proclaimers of lie as truth, double guardians of the paradox, the very mode of fiction—who are never imagined as selved others.

[16] The tendency to continue colonial habit into globalization is evident in the misfiring of translation between the Introduction and the first essay of *Gender Training: The Source Book* (Oxford: Oxfam, 1998), a text as politically correct as the demand for a uniform civil code or the legal redress for rape, as discussed in Agnes or Menon. The first example of the failure of a 'Development' project, as shown in *Gender Training*, is due to a lack of understanding that the women of rural Mahawali are as involved in the 'public' aspect of the project as the men. Yet, in the very next piece, which is a summary of the condition of South Asian women meant to serve as a master model for gender-training policy, the colonial middle class, predicated upon Victorian Britain, is taken as example, and the chief problem is diagnosed as the division into public and private.

the insistent pushing away of imagination in 'an extra-moral sense', juridico-political agency as the deferment of the open-endedness of subject-formation, we place the negotiating of the relationship between them outside of, though related to, mere disciplinary revisionism. To conflate the two is as useless as to place the two in opposition. It is not enough to prove that the active decisive rational supplementation of the fuzzily human, the supplementation by the universal of the collectivity of singulars is theoretically vulnerable. It seems necessary to admit that such vulnerability is the risk of responsibility. Decision thus requires persistent supplementation in view of 'what will have happened in spite,' let us say of a Nehru or rape reform, in other words the future anterior. Because we want to be free, when we write about political work, of this 'setting-to-work', we are obliged to propose solutions in highly abstract terms at the end of essays which, in the main part of their text, lay out the critique of the opposition in concrete detail.[17] Conclusions such as: 'repudiating this principle [of the measurement of betterness] in the name of a practice of political criticism and a practice of political conduct that seeks to connect us to refashioned forms of moral and political community' (Scott in the original version of his essay at the conference); 'to redraw the map of our body to make it accessible to new codes, to new senses of the self, so that at least some of these selves would be free of the limits set up by the body' (Menon).

If, however, we admit that 'setting-to-work' norms the formalization of academic writing beyond a facile theory-practice binary, then we may be able to think (or theorize) democracy as common sense (in the common sense) tells us: that it functions by way of the irreducible possibility of its diversified 'failures', among which must be counted, not only juridico-legal, political or yet ethico-moral transgressions, but the subject-agent *différance* itself. We will not then have to banish out of the house of theory the problem that besets yet bestows living: that the agent, a centralized part of the subject, can operate only as if

---

[17] For a discussion of 'setting-to-work' in this meaning, see Spivak, 'Appendix', *A Critique of Postcolonial Reason*.

Discussion: An Afterword on the New Subaltern 317

bigger than the whole. We rehearse the self-other rhythm as we are selves; the subject as (also) the agent's other. If this fact of life is not ignored, the *data* (givens) without which these essays could not have been written might acknowledge, in an irreducible double bind (opposition or conflation), a gift, at the origin, and without guarantees, which some call the fall into temporality named 'life'; and which constantly translates itself as the right to responsibility.

To hope that the absence of fear will have once again displaced itself, perhaps, as responsibility rather than the pride of consciences, Subaltern Studies studies the subaltern as writer of an impossible historical possibility, not only as an object of a new disciplinary opening. Surely that can be taken on board by the word 'separation' in what Dipesh Chakrabarty has so accurately described as the consequence of a 'rejection': '[Ranajit Guha's] gesture [the *rejection* of Eric Hobsbawm's category 'pre-political'] is radical in that it fundamentally pluralizes the history of power in global modernity and *separates* if from any universal history of capital.'[18]

If there is anything to be known about deconstruction, it is that you cannot will yourself to perform it. I am obliged, therefore, also to put a codicil on the desire, expressed in Menon's essay, 'radically to deconstruct this apparently universal, shared understanding of 'sexuality' to reveal the tenuousness of its foundations ... to emancipate ourselves from the very *meaning* of rape.' We will never be able to define rape satisfactorily enough for the law not to lean toward its transgression, if not in patriarchy then in the general vulnerability of a law that must always be open to correction. Simply put, we cannot take Foucault and Derrida's side *against* the feminists who work on the ground.[19] We can make Derrida and Foucault work for us only if we have learnt the

---

[18] Dipesh Chakrabarty, 'A Small History of Subaltern Studies', in *The Blackwell Companion to Postcolonial Studies*; emphasis mine. I have no idea if Chakrabarty had this in mind, of course.

[19] I do not agree with the interpretation of the particular Foucault passage from *Discipline and Punish* that Menon uses to substantiate her point that 'dominant modes of constituting the self ... are maintained and reinforced through the conventions of legal language,' but that is irrelevant, of course.

ground well enough to lose our conviction of their superiority *as well as*, on the other side, as it were, the self-evident invulnerability of the ground as such. The European philosophers are useful in so far as they are critics of the dialectics of the Enlightenment, and as they queer the norm.[20] They do indeed show that Ulysses is already bound, by the desire for the Sirens and the need for Penelope, among many other threads.[21] But that is only the negative of those dialectics. Then comes the impossible enterprise of teasing out what remains of the compromised other (than Enlightenment) systems, so that 'reform' supplements something other than the dominant that poststructuralism questions and mainstream postcolonial activists use. It is not enough to use a slogan—'*Izzat gayi kiski? Bhateri ki, Bhateri ki*'—as self-evident proof of a radical deconstruction that displaces honour or *izzat* (deconstruction argues the untranslatibility of idiom) from the body in ways cognate with Judith Butler's. To suggest that the subaltern produces high theory in an unmediated way is hopelessly romantic, I fear. I am back with Flavia Agnes, whose own style of activism is so strikingly different.

II

The remarks I had made at the 1994 conference came out of a local scene in Bangladesh that had touched the global—the impending World Women's Conference in Beijing—through the mediation of a local organization. Those remarks were not mechanically reproduced. What I cite below will finally carry the stamp of another local scene I enter from time to time, like all the interventionist intellectuals who make up this volume. First a few definitions.

---

[20] 'Queer' in the general sense is not identical with phenomenal 'homosexuality'. The latter was used as a concept-metaphor throughout the final Foucault. Derrida's *Glas* (tr. Richard Rand and John P. Leavey, Jr., Lincoln: Univ. of Nebraska Press, 1986), straddles the general and the narrow by placing the masters of modern European philosophy on the left hand side of the page and the criminal homosexual illegitimate Jean Genet on the right. To yoke such impulses to located feminisms involves steps that cannot be finessed by authority claims.

[21] Lacan as explained by Jacqueline Rose in 'Feminine Sexuality—Jacques Lacan and the ecole freudienne' (in *Sexuality in the Field of Vision*, London: Verso, 1986, pp. 68–81) must also be invoked here.

The value-form makes things commensurable. A mode of production is, strictly speaking, a mode of production of value. The colonial subject could be *measured* by colonial standards in his very subjectivity. To change Marx slightly, 'he carried the subject of colonialism.' Since 'subaltern' in the subcontinental use defines those who were cut off from the lines that produced the colonial mindset, s/he did not emerge in the colonial cultural value-form. Thus, considerations of cultural problematics in Subaltern Studies are not a substitute for, but a supplement to, Marxist theory.

This is the work of the 'wild anthropologist'.

In its early career, Subaltern Studies had not been informed by feminist theory as such. This volume is immersed in the feminist mode. It is from within this mode that the 'subaltern' must be rethought today. S/he is no longer cut off from lines of access to the centre. The centre, as represented by the Bretton Woods agencies and the World Trade Organization, is altogether interested in the rural and indigenous subaltern as source of trade-related intellectual properties or TRIPs. Many ways are being found to generate a subaltern subject asking to be used thus.[22] Marxist theory best describes the manner in which such 'intellectual property' is made the basis of exploitation in the arenas of biopiracy and human genome engineering. (In so far as the remote origin of subalternist theory was Ranajit Guha's *A Rule of Property for Bengal*, the wheel may be said to have come full circle.) But 'the agent

---

[22] See the difference in tone between the meetings to grab Alaskan Inuit schoolchildren and similar disenfranchised groups on the one hand, and the in-house meetings where agencies and telecommunication giants discuss economic policy on the other, for one example among many, at the Global Knowledge 1977 conference in Toronto. In the name of 'Veeramma', a subaltern who 'wants modern science', a young Indian sociologist excoriated an older Indian activist scientist at a recent New York conference. My earlier criticism, in Chapter 3 of *A Critique of Postcolonial Reason*, that while British colonial authorities and benevolent bhadraloks can impose a discursively inaccessible will on the burning widow, when a woman acts without such authority to spell resistance by bodily practice, the women in her own family ignore this in the space of two generations, related to this particular social tendency. I will speak of 'credit-baiting' later. This has been theorized as the subaltern being made to unspeak herself in Leerom Medlovoi *et al.*, 'Can the Subaltern Vote?,' *Socialist Review* xx.3 (July–September 1990), pp. 133–49.

of production' here is no longer the working class as produced by industrial or post-industrial capitalism.

This new location of subalternity is being covered over by the sanctioned ignorance of elite theory. Recently, Foucault's 'bio-power' is being brought up for revision. Paul Rabinow, the eminent Foucauldian, comments on genome engineering as a move from *zoe* to *bios* and commends Iceland—'the oldest democracy in Europe'—(ironically, one hopes) for having citizenry that voluntarily allows its DNA to be mapped.[23] Giorgio Agamben, referring to bio-power, uses the *zoe-bios* argument and cites Rabinow, although in the last sentence of his *Homo Sacer* he does announce a disciplinary catastrophe as a result of 'a being that is only its own bare existence . . . seiz[ing] hold of the very *haplos* [bottom line] that constitutes both the task and the enigma of Western metaphysics.'[24] One cannot quarrel with such general pronouncements. But in a more particular sphere, voluntary acceptance of the transformation of *zoe* to *bios* does not seem to us to be the last instance. The issue is the difference between dieting and starving, when the dieters' episteme is produced by a system that produces the starvers' starvation. In other words, although the 'agent of production' is not the working class, we must still heed the social relations of production of value. The issue is that some own others' *bios*-beings—human, animal or natural (the impossibility of listing them together must be postponed for the moment, since they can be owned in their data-being by similar patents)—and secure ownership by patenting, often fining and punishing those others for not having followed patenting laws in their subaltern past and thus having put up 'illegal trade barriers.' The issue, in other words, is one of property—and the subaltern body as *bios* or subaltern knowledge as (agri-) or (herbi-) culture is its appropriate object. Not only property, but Trade Related Intellectual Property.[25]

---

[23] Professor Rabinow read a chapter from his forthcoming *French DNA* at Columbia University on 28 October 1998. The string of adjectives for Iceland as a representative of the European Enlightenment was rather more fulsome.

[24] Giorgio Agamben, *Homo Sacer: Sovereign Power and Bare Life*, tr. Daniel Heller-Roazen (Stanford: Stanford Univ. Press, 1998), p. 188.

[25] From the disciplinary perspective, this might perhaps be seen as a displacement from the anthropological 'research object' (Christine Nicholls, 'Nicknaming and

Discussion: An Afterword on the New Subaltern 321

This new location of subalternity also requires a revision of feminist theory. The *genetically* reproductive body as the site of production questions feminist theories based only on the ownership of the phenomenal body as means of reproduction, and feminist psychological theories reactive to reproductive genital penetration as normality.[26]

Politically, this new understanding of subalternity leads to global social movements supported by a Marxist analysis of exploitation, calling for an undoing of the systemic-antisystemic binary opposition. In the domain of a specifically feminist politics, such a Subaltern Studies would require an engagement with global feminism. The subcontinental Subaltern Studies collective, of which I am a sometime member, does not necessarily endorse this understanding of the new subalternity. (It should perhaps be mentioned that this volume does not contain an essay by any of the members of the collective.) I am therefore taking the liberty of writing according to my own stereotype of 'myself' here, rather than describing Subaltern Studies as it is commonly understood.

The word 'woman' has been taken for granted by the United Nations, ever since the beginning of the large-scale women's conferences. In the domain of gendered intervention, today's United Nations is indeed international. Within a certain broadly defined group of the world's women, with a certain degree of flexibility in class and politics, the assumptions of a sex-gender system, an unacknowledged biological determination of behaviour, and an object-choice scenario defining female life (children or public life? population control or 'development?'), are shared at least as common currency. I begin to think it is a discursive formation, and oppositions can be generated within it.

Although the subaltern is outside of this commonality, there has been an attempt to access her within it by defining, not her way of acting, but her ways of suffering others' action. Its most overt tabulation was the six-point Platform of Action of the fourth world women's

---

Graffiti—Writing Practices at Lajmanu, N.T.: A Post-Ethnographic Sociological Fiction', sociology dissertation, Macquarrie Univ., Sydney, 1998, p. 362) to development economics.

[26] I have discussed the former in 'Diasporas Old and New: Women in A Transnational World,' *Textual Practices* X, ii (1996), pp. 264–66, n. 8. The latter is too pervasive to tabulate.

conference in Beijing.²⁷ There was something grand in the effort to bring the world's women under one rule of law, one civil society, administered by the women of the internationally divided dominant.

Even as we understand the Encylopedist grandeur of this design, we must also see that it is the exact impersonal structural replica of the grand design to bring the world's rural poor under one rule of finance, one global capital, again run by the internationally divided dominant. To use a technique from Michel Foucault, let us say this is the most 'rarefied' definition of globalization that we can grasp.

If the dominant is represented by the centreless centre of electronic finance capital, the subaltern woman is the target of credit-baiting without infrastructural involvement, thus opening a huge untapped market to the international commercial sector. Here a genuinely feminist politics would be a monitoring one, that forbids the ideological appropriation of much older self-employed women's undertakings, and further, requires and implements infrastructural change rather than practices cultural coercion in the name of feminism. Farida Akhter's intercession with Grameen Bank to cancel its agreement with Monsanto is a case in point.²⁸

---

²⁷ See, for one example among a multitude, the copious e-mails coming in everyday on the Women and Violence network.

²⁸ Farida Akhter, 'Monsanto-r Biruddhe Bikkhobh Protibad: BRAC o CARE-er Biruddhe Hunshiari,' *Chinta* VII.13 (Sept 15, 1998), pp. 36–9. Let me also quote two passages from mainstream US journalism to make the connection with intellectual property. (It is not that these things are unknown. It is just that the connection between Eurocentric discussions of biopower on the one hand and the emergence of the new subaltern as intellectual property on the other remains unmade.): 'I untied the purple mesh bag of seed potatoes that Monsanto had sent and opened up the Grower Guide tied around its neck. . . . The guide put me in mind not so much of planting potatoes as booting up a new software release. [*bios* into data] [T]he potatoes I will harvest come August are mine to eat or sell, but their genes remain the intellectual property of Monsanto, protected under numerous United States patents, including nos. 5,196,525, 5, 164,316, 5,322,938 and 5,352,605. Were I to save even one of them to plant next year—something I've routinely done with potatoes in the past—I would be breaking Federal law. The small print in the Grower Guide also brought the news that my potato plants were themselves a pesticide, registered with the Environmental Protection Agency. . . . A Monsanto agent can perform a simple test in my garden and

With the breakup of the welfare state, the earlier definition of the subaltern as one cut off from lines of social mobility increasingly applies to the metropolitan homeless, although the cultural argument is subsumed under a class-argument there. Yet, because of its generally postcolonial focus, 'nation' is still the word that resounds in Subaltern Studies as such.

The notion of 'nation' as back-formation from the Western European nationalisms that were at the helm of capitalist imperialism informed and displaced the prevailing discourses of dominant proto-governmentalities—the Mughals, the Marathas—already in existence in 'India', as well as the emergent ground of colonial subject-formation—most especially the *bhadralok* society of Bengal. Partha Chatterjee has prospectively narrativized the latter as departure manoeuvre-arrival, giving it an exceptionalist Indian scope, locating each stage by one prominent individual—only the first of bhadralok origin. He has further suggested that the exceptionalist narrative is an uneasy collection of fragments in its Bengali context.[29] It can certainly be concluded from his work that the notion of an Indian nation as a miraculating ground of identity, thought and action, leading to a political community, was not discursively available to the larger proportion of the immensely

---

prove that my plants are the company's intellectual property. The contract farmers sign with Monsanto allows company representatives to perform such tests in their fields at will. According to *Progressive Farmer*, a trade journal, Monsanto is using informants and hiring Pinkertons to enforce its patent rights; it has already brought legal action against hundreds of farmers for patent infringement' (Michael Pollan, 'Playing God in the Garden,' *The New York Times Magazine*, 25 October 1998). Now transfer the scene of ownership and legal action from the US (or Iceland) to subaltern space. One hopes that a book such as Mae-Wen Ho, *Genetic Engineering—Dream or Nightmare?: The Brave New World of Bad Science and Big Business* (Bath: Gateway, 1998), written by an interventionist scientist, will not be dismissed by the Eurocentric social philosophers for using a pre-critical epistemic vocabulary: 'the genetic determinist mindset that misinforms both practitioners and the public takes hold of people's unconscious, making them act involuntarily, unquestioningly, to shape the world to the detriment of human beings and all other inhabitants', p. 1.

[29] That is the logic of his *The Nation and its Fragments* (Princeton: Princeton Univ. Press, 1993).

diverse inhabitants of the subcontinent. To consider this in an evolutionist way is to consider European enrichment as nothing but a result of the survival of the fittest. K.N. Chaudhuri is not an avowed subalternist, but his *Asia Before Europe* is a good corrective for such methods of analysis based on such a view.[30]

The concept of nation is the fuzzy partner to the more abstract 'state'. (I am borrowing the word 'fuzzy' from the 'fuzzy set' theory of Lotfi Zadeh, 'sets that', in the words of Daniel McNeill and Paul Freiberger, 'calibrate vagueness'.[31])

Since 1989, the state has withered away some, since barriers removed between national economies and the functioning of global capital curtail redistribution and constitutional redress. (Marx had quietly moved from 'national economy'—*Economic and Philosophical Manuscripts*—to 'political economy'—*Capital I*—a fact obliterated by English translations.) And the globalizing agencies directly confront those to whom nation-think was not accessible—thus the subaltern— during the colonial era. The work of the non-Eurocentric 'social movements', seeking to turn globalization persistently toward that subaltern front (no longer merely an arithmetical sum of 'local' movements), away from capitalist ends, provides, however haphazardly, the goal of a loosely-based 'regional' political agenda that must remain, as I have already suggested, Marxist in its analysis of exploitation. The Gramscian 'war of manoeuvre'—non-teleological and innovative— was unaware of broader consequences in the Italy of the beginning of the century. With full-scale globalized capitalism, this by-now subalternist alternative describes the most viable way of constructive resistance. (Paul Virilio's binarization of 'the cut [*coupure*] between developed and underdeveloped countries [as] . . . *absolute* [and] *relative*' is therefore not sufficiently nuanced.[32]) The 'regional' focus is perhaps less

---

[30] K.N. Chaudhuri, *Asia Before Europe: Economy and Civilization of the Indian Ocean from the Rise of Islam to 1750* (Cambridge: Cambridge Univ. Press, 1990).

[31] Daniel McNeill and Paul Freiberger, *Fuzzy Logic* (New York: Simon & Schuster, 1993).

[32] Paul Virilio, *Open Sky*, tr. Julie Rose (New York: Verso, 1997), p. 71; translation modified.

Discussion: An Afterword on the New Subaltern 325

strong in the feminist aspects of these movements—reactive as they are to population control by pharmaceutical dumping, to the undermining of women's relationship to seed development and storage through biopiracy and monoculture, and to credit-baiting. The 'rejoinder' to the state offered by 'the international civil society' of powerful non-governmental organizations studies the subaltern in the interest of global capital, and cannot be called subalternist, although it is, to a very large extent, feminist in its professed interest in gender.[33] The outlines of this latter group bleed into the postcolonial feminist activists mentioned above.

It is therefore clear that, although the terrain of the colonial subaltern cannot be explained by capital logic alone, this cannot mean jettisoning the concept of class-formation as a descriptive and analytical category. The new subaltern is produced by the logic of a global capital that forms classes only instrumentally, in a separate urban sphere, because commercial and finance capital cannot function without an industrial component. Postfordism had taken away the organizational stability of the factory floor and thus taken away the possibility of class consciousness, however imperfect. International labour is racist and thus has no class-solidarity as such. The union movement in the United States is severely restricted and politically effective only in so far as it serves managerial interests. This is not the moment to find a 'rejoinder' to class—even as it must be recognized that not much can be done in its name, that it cannot produce an account of subalternity. Indeed, there is an 'exceptionalist' class-mobility among aboriginal subalterns.

In 'Deconstructing Historiography' I had suggested that the Subaltern Studies collective assumed a subaltern consciousness, however

[33] It is this basically post-state situation, ravaged by the 'passionate intensity' in the underbelly of nation-thinking, that calls up other kinds of 'rejoinders': NATO stepping in to preserve 'Western values,' as is being debated in October 1998, with reference to the situation where the Albanians in Kosovo are being 'ethnically cleansed' by the Serbs. (I have moved this narrative forward in my text.) By contrast, Subaltern Studies cautions against vanguard rationalist solutions imposed from above, right or left.

'negative', by a 'strategic use of essentialism'.[34] Subaltern Studies had no need of such apologetics, because they were not investigating subject-formation but historical agency, where the institutional validation of something like intention is at play.

In the context of the emergence of the new subaltern, the question of subaltern consciousness has once again become important, now displaced to the global political sphere, so that (a) knowledge can be made data and (b) a subaltern will for globalization can be put together as justification for policy.

It is around the issues of democratization and gender-and-development that the question of subaltern consciousness most urgently arises. This is because it is precisely those who were denied access to the lines leading to the European civil society mindset and to bourgeois-model female emancipation who are being diagnosed today by the international feminist dominant as culturally incapable of democracy and feminism, in the interest of the smooth global functioning of these issues. Thus 'democratization'—code name for the political restructuring entailed by the transformation of (efficient through inefficient to wild) state capitalisms and their colonies to tributary economies of rationalized global financialization—carries with it the aura of the civilizing mission accompanying transformative projects from imperialism to development. This aura carries over to the question of minority rights within developed civil societies, where it engages postcolonial radicalism of a more political sort. 'Consciousness' here does not engage subject-theory, deconstructive, psychoanalytic or otherwise. As in the case of the first subalternists, we are here on the level of social agency—institutionally validated action. The institutions concerned are democracy and development—politics and economics.

Opposition to parliamentary democracy in the name of cultural origin (as advanced by Lee Kuan Yew, Senior Minister of Singapore, or, at the other end of the spectrum and in speech after speech, by Farid Zakaria, the editor of the influential conservative journal *Foreign*

---

[34] Spivak, 'Deconstructing Historiography', in *In Other Worlds: Essays in Cultural Politics* (New York: Methuen, 1987), pp. 197–221.

Affairs) is an obviously meretricious position. Opposition to female emancipation in the name of cultural sanctions is as onerous. But, to produce a subject for democracy and development, must we then rely on crash courses in 'gender training' and 'election training', offered by the international civil society?[35]

As a partial cautionary tale relating to the subaltern agent of the democratic postcolonial state, I offer a narrative concerning a tiny group of one kind of subaltern. Here is my 'local', my special 'space'. I have gotten to know them well in the last ten years, after I gave up my apologetic formula for Subaltern Studies (which the collective did not need anyway): strategic use of essentialism. I found instead a different one emerging from my own subaltern study: learning to learn from below.

Let me first present a context that is remote from the new subalternity, for 'reasons' that are too complex for this broad-stroke Afterword. It is the context of the smallest groups among Indian Aboriginals, at last count roughly ninety million as a whole. I use 'Aboriginal' just this once for the general readership. Neither 'Aboriginal' nor 'tribal' fits the Indian case, because historically—and this invocation of history is to beg the question—there is no certainty about the authenticity of the Aryan settler/original inhabitants story, and the politics of the state hangs on its truth-claim. I will therefore use 'ST', short for 'Scheduled Tribe', as laid down in the Indian Constitution, and regularly used by the state and activists alike.

This much is provisionally noticeable in the history of the present. These are people occupying remnants of varieties of oral culture permeated by dominant Sanskritized literate cultures without benefit of literacy. This last not because of widely disseminated anthropological piety, but because these people are among the increasing numbers of the Indian poor. Upward class mobility is harder for them because of longstanding patterns of prejudice and therefore low-level graft works even better upon this terrain, destroying the possibility or attractiveness

---

[35] Election training is pretty standard. Gender training by Oxfam is organized at the University of Sussex.

of real education for the intelligent child, the prospective leader or, of course, the ordinary child, the backbone of the functioning future electorate. Votes are bought and sold here, en block and individually. The prevailing system of education is to memorize answers to antiquated questions relating to set books. The occasional human-interest story—of villagers establishing their own schools or NGOs joining a UN drive for schools must, first, be evaluated against this grid—if indeed it penetrates to the bottom layers of the diversified life of the Indian scheduled tribes.

There is something like an opening into 'women's history', even here. The sharp young girl, wading up through the muddy slugging currents of gendered rural politics, can aim for the reserved seats on the various organs of state government, generally to become pawns in the hands of veteran mainstream players. (As I know from frustrating attempts, it is almost impossible for them to enter middle-class educational institutions.) When they enter UN statistics as 'women entering politics' (see the Declaration of Mexico, 1975), the aporia of exemplarity is rather brutally crossed.[36] The single female out of the Lodha tribe who made it into university—studying, heartbreakingly, Anthropology—hanged herself under mysterious circumstances some years ago. Various rumors about illicit love affairs circulate even as self-styled subalterns and oral history investigators assure each other in print that the subaltern can, indeed, speak. This is the Chuni Kotal who must be remembered as we learn from examples of post-theoretical 'wild anthropology'.

I am not a historian. Here I am moving in an area—the task of writing the history of the Indian STs—which baffles the historian. I move upon this landscape in an attempt to learn to learn from below. I enter yearly increasing intimacies with female and male children and adults. I bear witness to the storying of the vanishing present, the piecing together of characters (I might as well beg the question and call them 'historical agents') so that a detailed sequence may seem to pre-exist.

---

[36] *The United Nations and the Advancement of Women (1945–1995)* (New York: United Nations, 1995), pp. 177–201.

Discussion: An Afterword on the New Subaltern   329

At the same time, I try to disengage from the children and the teachers some pedagogic principles for teaching democratic habits. An electoral democracy is historical.

Are men and women different here? Only in so far as some indefinite thing called tribal 'culture' has started to resemble the class-mobility patterns of the non-tribal poorer classes. The men get a greater opportunity to travel out and up through governmental and non-governmental possibilities, though they too are used. Our usual sex-gender system cliches work fine here.

But what about writing history in the usual way? I see no difference between men and women for that project. Anti-colonial tribal insurgencies have occasionally been recorded. A handful of tribals get pensions as fighters for Independence, in the parasitical 'terrorist movements', of course. Tribals emerge into history in the perspective of the drama of colonialism.

I should at once say that the ST communities in India are not everywhere equally deprived, although they are all objects of at least everyday racism and casteism. My point is that we are not yet ready to grasp the challenge of gender upon the terrain of the subaltern ST. Gender-consciousness here is in the detail of unglamorous teaching, by patiently learning *from* below, not in directly confronting the challenge of history by impatient 'gender-training' from above.

The confrontation of impatient urbanist tribal activism inaugurates a clash of discursive formations as abrupt as any colonial encounter.[37] Activists from the institutionally educated classes of the general national culture won a state-level legal victory against police brutality over the most deprived ST groups last year. In spite of the group's legal victory against the state, the ruling party, which notionally does not approve of police brutality, supports them *on the state level.* Nationally, since a different party is in power, the question will bring us to the Indian federal structure. The party in its general Indian context does not relate at all to this particular subaltern group. The ruling party *on*

---

[37] I suppress names to protect confidentiality. This is an aporetic situation, where state- and national-level resistance cannot stop because of the rupture with subalternity.

the local level, on the other hand, is trying to take its revenge against the group's victory over the police by taking advantage of three factors, one positive, two negative:

1. The relatively homogeneous dominant Hindu culture at the village level keeps the ST materially isolated through prejudice.
2. As a result of this material isolation, women's independence among the STs, in their daily in-house behaviour ('ontic idiom') has remained intact. It as not been infected by the tradition of women's oppression within the general culture.
3. Politically ('pre-politically?'), the general, supposedly homogeneous rural culture and the ST culture, are united in their lack of democratic training. This is a result of poverty and class prejudice existing nationally. Therefore, as I have said above, votes can be bought and sold here as normal practice; and electoral conflict is treated by rural society in general like a competitive sport where 'violence' is legitimate.

Locally, since the legal victory of the metropolitan activists against the police, the ruling party has taken advantage of these three things by rewriting women's conflict as party politics. An incidental quarrel among ST women has been used by the police to divide the ST community against itself. One side has been encouraged to press charges against the other. The defending faction has been wooed and won by the BJP and the Trinamul Congress, the latter a local offshoot of the general Congress party, out of favour nationally. In the absence of education in the principles of democracy (not merely training in election control, which is also lacking) and *in the presence of women's power, however, circumscribed*, police terror has been accepted as part of the party spirit by the ST community. This is a direct consequence of the educated activists' 'from above' effort at constitutional redress. If there should be a person holding the views that I am describing in this essay within this activist group—organized now as a tax-sheltered non-profit organization—who thinks, in other words, that there should be a real effort to connect and activate the tribals' indigenous 'democratic' structure to *parliamentary* democracy by patient and sustained efforts to learn to learn from below, s/he would thus be both impractical and a consensus breaker. The consensually united vanguard is never patient. In my view, agency within rule-governed behaviour, a definition even more 'upstream' than Ronald Dworkin's 'democracy for hedgehogs', must be persistently reined in by engaging with the subject, rather than imposing rules from above. It is interesting that one of the efforts at 'civilizing the tribal', denied access to 'good' schools by the ferociously slanted examination systems, is now to train them in organized sports through the national Sports Authority—arguably the best colonial-model training in law-and-order democracy.[38]

Given that it is womanpower separated from the dominant culture that is being used here, and given that the ST community is *generally* separated from access to disciplinary history, to focus on gendered history, as a less class-conscious feminist theory is liable to do, is irrelevant and counterproductive in this context.[39]

The earlier work of the Subaltern Studies collective had met the general challenge of nationalist history by trying to deduce subaltern consciousness from the texts of the elite. Legal proceedings, where the subaltern gives witness or testimony, had been particularly productive for them. Are intimate interventions in subaltern education part of the documentation of Subaltern Studies? A resident teacher-trainer gets into the grain of their lives. Yet is that a requirement for good history writing, after all? Could it not stand in the way?

Julia Kristeva quotes the eighteenth-century French thinker Montesquieu to steer a clear evolutionary path from family-consciousness to state-consciousness. In her forthcoming book *Speaking through the Mask,* Norma Claire Moruzzi shows that such a story leaves out the postcolonial migrant, whose historical sequence and scenario are

---

[38] I have written at greater length on the imbrication of subject and agent in Spivak, 'A Dialogue on Democracy,' in David Trend (ed.), *Radical Democracy: Identity, Citizenship, and the State* (New York: Routledge, 1995), pp. 209–22.

[39] Kamala Visweswaran, *Fictions of Feminist Ethnography* (Delhi: Oxford Univ. Press, 1996) is a thoughtful study of related problems.

rather different. When we come to subaltern groups such as ST minorities within the postcolonial state, however, the lines become impossibly confused.

Investigation of agency must concentrate on society, on the outside world. If we come to the subaltern ST women's inner world—given our class-, cultural-, and, yes, 'historical' difference, although I am so close to them, I can only dimly imagine the enormity of assuming that I could enter a continuity with their specific pattern of working with the mind-body divide, which is my understanding of an inner world. ('Inner' and 'outer' here are shorthand terms appropriate to the readership of this anthology.) A disciplinary anthropologist computes this from the outside, to make it understandable to other anthropologists. And yet, I keep hoping that, while I work at my teacher training, understanding will perhaps have come to me in the way of fiction, a compromised way that history cannot challenge. I therefore think it is important that women of the international mainstream, such as we are, define and accept the challenge of women's history, again and again, in order to correct and deflect male domination. But if one is working for the subaltern, one cannot get a grip on it except through a do-gooding that presupposes 'above'. The work of training half-educated rural teachers, educating the educators by learning the principles from below, is for the remote possibilization of a living democratic culture in the classroom of subaltern children, protecting the girls by improvised tactics. This is to break subalternity not into hegemony but into a citizenship *without history*. If someone in our position and with our interests accepts the challenge of women's history as a goal, the specific kind of historylessness of the Aboriginal falls into an evolutionist primitivism that I will not accept. My non-acceptance is immaterial here. Once access is established by national activists, the furious metropolex of Calcutta will win and 'they' will be produced as 'we' were.

Yet, if one is as post-theoretical as this volume, one must keep imagining and presuming a challenge *to* history. In my own case, training in disciplinary literary criticism is of help, as feminist theory for Menon, film studies for Niranjana, anthropology for Jeganathan. I try to set the 'literary' to work. I must, however provisionally, keep the binarity between history and fiction alive. Ever since 'Deconstructing Historiography' I have tried to undo it and historians have advised against it. I now see their point, partly and as follows: Mainstream 'Indian' culture is as distant from the aboriginal subaltern in India as is Aristotle. Echoing Aristotle, then, one might keep reciting that history tells us what happened and fiction what may have happened and indeed may happen. (I am sure other similar models can be found by non-Europeanist literary critics.) The uneven entry of my pre-adult students' future children into the historical record will be along paths that I cannot make myself imagine. I have lost track here, in the interest of learning rather than knowing, using rather than remaining within the comfort of describing with coherence for disciplinary access alone. Paradoxically, a classroom where you teach the reading of fiction as such—learning from the singular and the unverifiable—is a training ground for this. Here, too, of course, the scholar cannot draw the direct line to social action as public policy.

Hopeless? Perhaps. But without this nothing can undo the divisions put in place in the colonies by the Enlightenment and still conserve the best legacy of the subaltern. The 'encounter with apartheid' made Mahmood Mamdani ask: 'How to transcend the urban-rural divide?'— but he wrote a book about it.[40] That divide is the gap we live in, a gap which keeps apart the production of definitive and elite knowledge on the one hand and any hope of educating the subaltern educators on the other. To look into the gap is as hopeful as it is hopeless, at least.

A Postscript. A year later, the division in the ST settlement is sharper. Among the two women on 'the other side' one has moved her entire extended family to another tract, which has now received the name of 'outside place'—*bahirdi*. The other has alienated five families and allegedly become a resident 'entertainer' for the police. Six children from the alienated families have stopped coming to school. Five men from 'this side' have been arrested (as 'dacoits') without charges and

---

[40] Mamdani, *Citizen and Subject: Contemporary Africa and the Legacy of Late Colonialism* (Princeton: Princeton Univ. Press, 1996), p. ix.

face the law's delay, sometimes by decades. The national movement flourishes, only connected with this devastation by way of arrangements for further remote-control high-level litigation.

A group of dancing ST women and men from 'this side' returned an hour ago in great triumph from what had seemed an embarrassingly 'colonial' handicraft fair in Calcutta, there in the shadow of eminent personages from the state government and the metropolitan culture sphere. Witnessing their elation in this desolate place, I wonder if a brutally civilizing mission is not, after all, more than half the answer; for a planned education of the educators forgets that 'there is no document of civilization which is not at the same time a document of barbarism.'[41]

---

[41] Walter Benjamin, 'Theses on the Philosophy of History', in *Illuminations*, tr. Harry Zohn (London: Fontana, 1973), p. 248.

Glossary

afsana	tale; short story
chandiya	tough guy; thug
dupatta	shawl or scarf
ekatmata yajna	ritual event for purposes of forging unity
gata-pramukh	leader of a sub-branch
ghagra-choli	long skirt with blouse (Hindi)
ghazal	a metrical poem, conventionally on love, often sung
goriya	a significant altercation; blows may be exchanged
guti-kama	a beating
haldi	turmeric
homa	fire offering; sacrifice
islahi	reformist
jan adesh yatra	pilgrimage to collect the people's mandate
jati	local variant of 'caste' (varna)
kanyadan	ritual marking the giving of one's daughter in marriage
kar sevak	religious volunteer; community worker-cum-warrior

karta	male head of the family
kotha	brothel
kumkum	a red preparation for making cosmetic marks on the forehead
kurta	shirt
lajja-baya	shame; fear
langa-davni	ankle-length skirt with a half sari draped across the left shoulder (Kannada)
maha-arti	large gathering for worship involving a chant and lighting lamps
maulavi	learned man; teacher
mehr	a marriage portion settled on the wife, or paid to her family before the marriage; dowry
nikahnama, kabin nama	marriage contract
pitrabhoo	(lit.) fatherland
punyabhoo	holy land
qanun	law
ratha yatra	ceremonial procession led by a chariot
sanduwa	a minor altercation
sannyasi	ascetic; renouncer
sansiya	a wandering tribe, often referred to as gypsies
sanskriti	culture
saptapadi	the seven steps round the sacred fire concluding the marriage ceremony
sathin	female attendant; social-service worker
shakhas	(lit.) branches (*gata-shakhas* = sub-branches)
shalwar	loose trousers worn by women
sharafat	courtly or well-born manner
sharif (pl. *ashraf*)	noble; high-born
shulka	fee; payment; tariff

sindoor	vermilion applied by married women to the hair parting
stridhan	wealth or property belonging exclusively to a woman
tavaif	dancing girl; prostitute
valiya	an altercation or fight that may not result in blows
vivahahoma	sacred fire offering at a marriage ceremony

Index

Abdulhaq, Maulvi 9n
Abeysekera, Charles 216n, 246
Adorno, Theodor 295n
Advani, L.K. 150n, 203
Agamben, Giorgio 320n
Agarwal, Bina 80n
Agnes, Flavia 67n, 70, 70n, 82, 82n, 83, 84, 84n, 85n, 86, 86n, 92, 92n, 100n, 101n, 109n 106, 315, 315n, 318
Ahmad, Aziz 8n
Ahmad, Imtiaz 31n
Ahmad, Nazir 10
Akhter, Farida 322, 322n
Alexander, Jacqui 217, 217n
Aligarh Movement 8n, 9n
All India Progressive Writers' Association (AIPWA) 2, 7n, 11, 34
Althusser, Louis 44, 44n, 233n, 309, 310n
Ambrose, Carole G. 84n
Amin, Samir 313
Amin, Shahid 139n

Anand, Mulkraj 11, 12, 22
Anderson, Benedict 9n, 169n, 214, 214n, 228, 229, 229n, 230, 237, 237n, 248n, 253, 255n, 257
Anderson, Michael 79n
Anthias, Flora and Nira Yuval-Davis 275
anthropologist 332; 'wild' 319
anthropology/anthropological 39, 40, 328; category 45; colonial 48; knowledge 42; objects 39, 40; scholarship 49; significance and limits 57, 61, 64, 65; Sri Lankan 40, 41, 41n; theory 43
anthropologyland 38, 52
Appadurai, Arjun 40n, 46n, 50n, 210n, 211n, 212n
Array, J.P. 89n
Arunima, G. 81n
Ashk, Upendra Nath 7
Askari, Muhammad Hasan 7
Atwood, Margaret 257, 257n
Auliya, Nizamuddin 19

Ayodhya 172, 178, 190, 193, 197, 203

Babri Masjid 140, 160, 172, 190-1, 198n, 201
Backward Castes 142n
Bajrang Dal 138n
Balibar, Etienne 169n, 173, 173n, 215, 215n
Bandaranaike, S.W.R.D. 216, 292
Bannerjee, Gooroodas 114, 114n,
Barth, Frederik 189n
Bartholomeusz, Tessa 233n
Basu, Kaushik 182n
Baxi, Upendra 81, 81n
Bedi, Rajinder Singh 7
Beg, Mirza Rajab Ali 10
Benegal, Shyam 152
Bhabha, Homi 236n, 247
Bhalla, Alok 17n
Bharatiya Janata Party (BJP) 138, 164n, 191n, 192, 196n, 198, 330
Blackstone, William 116-17, 124
Bomaya, Bhawna 160n
Bombay film industry 2, 5, 7
Bourdieu, Pierre 169n
Boyle, Christine 99n
Breckenridge, Carol 167n
Brennan, Timothy 9n
Bromley, P.M. 117
brothels 13, 14, 15, 18, 23, 28, 30, 31
Brown, Mick 78n, 100n
Brownmiller, Susan 74, 74n
Bumiller, Kristin 79, 92, 92n
Burn, E.H. 118n
Butler, Judith 103, 103n, 239, 278, 318

Carter, John Ross 288, 288n

Chakrabarty, Dipesh 40n, 139n, 255, 317, 317n
Chakravarthy, Venkatesh 157
Chakravarti, Uma 199n
Chander, Krishan 7, 34, 35
Chandra, Bipan 182
Chandra, Sudhir 4n
Chatterjee, Bankimchandra 26
Chatterjee, Partha 3, 3n, 5n 26, 28n, 65n, 167n, 177n, 180n, 183n, 184n, 189n, 198n, 212n, 214, 231, 231n, 237, 244, 245, 245n, 255, 323
Chatterji, Suniti Kumar 8n,
Chaudhuri, K.N. 324
Chelvanayagam, Samuel James 225n, 293
Chow, Rey 307n
Chughtai, Ismat 6
cinema, commercial 139, 144, 152; femininity in 145; popular 138-9, 142; South Indian 150n
Clark, T.W. 10n
Cohn, Bernard 38, 38n,181n
Colebrook-Cameron Reforms 290, 292
colonial archives 48; discourse 48, 49; era 324; India 5, 31, 32, 33; powers 236; project 288; public sphere 289; rule 120; Sri Lanka 290; state 183; struggle 252; subjects 311
colonialism 21, 50; British 229, 289
Comaroff, Jean and John 52, 55n
communal: fury 258; identities 176
communalism 16, 159, 1634, 183, 199, 200n, 208, 211, 315; Hindu 167-8, 177n
communities, Christian 289; cultural 284; historical 304;

identity and 286; imagined 167–8, 175, 176n, 229n; national 176; postcolonial 294; Sinhala 285, 301, 302
Congress party 330; politics 4
conjugal rights 132, 134
Coppola, Carlo 6n
Cornell, Drucilla 77, 77n,
Cornwall, Andrea 52n
Cossman, Brenda 98n
courtesans/prostitutes 4, 5, 6, 15, 16, 23, 24, 25, 26, 27–30; *see also* Manto
coverture 107, 108, 113, 117

Dalmia, Vasudha 8n
Daniel, Valentine 249n
Das, Veena 41n, 143n, 198n, 199n, 202n, 268n
de Alwis, Malathi 37, 51, 51n, 55n, 105, 212n
de Certeau, Michael 169n
de Silva, Chandra 225n, 233n
Deleuze and Guattari 35, 35n, 210n
Derrida, Jacques 239n, 308n, 311n, 317, 318n
Desai, S.T. 112n
Deshpande, Satish 167, 185n, 209n, 306, 308
Dhareshwar, Vivek 141n
Dharmadasa, K.N.O. 287n
divorce 114, 116, 135; law of 108
Diwan, Paras 108n
Djebar, Assia 275, 276n
Dube, L. 115n
Dumont, Louis 182
Duriappah, Alfred 244
Dworkin, Andrea 76
Dworkin, Ronald 296, 331

Elster, Jon 312, 312n, 313, 314, 314n

Faiz, Faiz Ahmad 6
Fanon, Frantz 247n, 275, 275n, 280
feminine/femininity: identity 140; models of 149; new 145; redefinitions of 145
feminism 68, 138; and Independence 140; global 315, 321
feminist(s) 74, 81, 83, 86, 88, 91, 99, 102, 141, 150; activists 66, 72, 95; analyses 101, 163; critics 226–7; critique of nationalism 218; critiques 93, 104; discourse 71, 75; discussions 97; lawyers 71, 89; legal practices 67; legislation 101; movements 325; points of view 92; politics 66, 103, 165–6, 322; practice 79, 96, 103, 104; propaganda 84; rape and 306; theories 321, 331–2
Fineman, Martha A. 78
Fort William College 10
Foucault, Michel 20, 20n, 79, 79n, 170, 170n, 171, 171n, 317, 318n, 320, 322
Freitag, Sandria 79n, 207n
Fritzman, J.M. 235, 235n, 281n
Frug, Mary Joe 98n

Gamburd, Geraldine 38n
Gandhi, Indira 4, 202n
Gandhi, Mahatma 8, 183, 194, 203
Gellner, Ernest 214n
gender: class and 168; issues 159; the modern and 138; questions and 141; training 329; violence and 305
Genet, Jean 318n

George, Rosemary 219
Godse, Nathuram 183
Gopalakrishnan, Adoor 152
Govindacharya, K.N. 198
Gramsci, Antonio 261n, 324
Guha, Ranajit 199, 199n, 212, 214, 215n, 219, 280, 319
Guha, Sumit 79n
Gunasinghe, Newton 40n, 216n, 227, 246n, 272n
Gunawardana, R.A.L.H. 227
Gupta, Dipankar 200n

Haider, Qurratulain 10
Halberstam, Judith 218n
Hali, Altaf Husain 8, 9n
Hansen, Thomas Blom 196n
Harvey, David 169n
Hasan, Zoya 5n, 199n
heterotopia 170–1, 174, 175 187–8, 196
Heuze, Gerard 200, 202n
Heyd, David 294n
Hindu communalism 192, 199–200, 206; culture 330; customs 123; fundamentalism 161; hegemony 167, 306; laws 80; marriage 131; Marriage Act 79, 80, 132, 135; pantheon 172; power 196; religion 181, 182; right 187, 189; temple 172; woman 140
Hinduism 177
Hindus 25, 28, 199n, 205; and Muslims 161
Hindutva 159, 172, 178, 180–1, 184, 186–9, 192–4, 196n, 198, 202–3, 207; and globalisation 208, 211; worldview 195
Hingorani, Anand T. 9n

Hobsbawm, Eric 233, 233n, 234, 248n, 255n, 317
Hoole, Rajan 220n
Horkheimer, Max 295n, 308n
Howe, Adrian 78n

identity, Buddhist 287; religious 287; Sinhala 286
imperialism 174; and colonialism 175
Indian Divorce Act 128, 133
Indian Penal Code 88
Indian Succession Act 129
Iqbal, Mohammad 6
Ismail Qadri 51n, 212, 229, 286, 307, 315
Ispahani, Mahnaz 1n

Jafri, Ali Sardar 34
Jalal, Ayesha 230n
Jayasekera, P.V.J 238n
Jeganathan, Pradeep 37, 41n, 51n, 105, 167n, 213n, 269n, 272n, 274n, 277, 311, 314
Jharkhand 185
John, Mary 167n
Johnson, Sharon 77
Joshi, Murli Manohar 191n, 192

Kanapathipillai, Valli 268–80 *passim*
Kapferer, Bruce 42, 42n, 43, 43n, 45, 46n
Kapur, Naina 77, 83n, 96n, 101n
Kapur, Ratna 98n
Kashmir 307, 309; militancy 159, 161; problem 154–5; situation 165; yatra 204
Katayayana 112, 113n
Kaviraj, Sudipta 4n, 26n, 186n, 187n, 189n

Kazmi, Fareed 5
Kesavan, Mukul 5n
Khan, Syed Ahmed 9n,
Khan, Zoya 17n
King, Christopher 8n
Kishwar, Madhu 81n
Kristeva, Julia 331
Kukathas, Chandran 294–304 *passim*
Kumar, Radha 79
Kumaratunga, Chandrika 285
Kymlicka, Will 294–304 *passim*

Lacan, Jacques 318n
law, ancient 112; ancient Hindu 111; Anglo-Islamic 110; binary logic of 81, 102; canon 116; children and 78; Christian 111; common 117; Continental 115; contract of 110; criminal 85; delay in 334; discourse of 67–9, 104; elasticity of 90; English 124, 130; family 116, 119; Hindu 114, 121, 125, 128, 129, 130–5; Judaic 115; logic of 67; matrimonial 106, 130; Muslim 109–10; personal 111, 119; Roman 113, 115; statutory 119; transformations in 304
Lefebvre, Henri 169n, 173
legal: codes 315n; discourse 78, 79, 81, 97, 98,102; language 79; reform 136; rights 304; system, Continental 118; system, Indian 107, 119,122; systems 120; systems, ancient 107–8; systems, English 108; systems, Islamic 109; systems, matrimonial 133
Lelyveld, David 9n

Lenin 248, 248n, 253, 309; and philosophy 310
Liberals/liberalism 283–304 *passim*
Lindisfarne, Nancy 52n
Lloyd, David 11n, 29n, 254, 255n, 256
LTTE 212–80 *passim*, 285, 285n
Lukacs, G. 1, 2, 3n, 11, 12, 34, 34n
Lukes, Steven 294n
Luxemburg, Rosa 222, 222n, 223, 229, 247, 280

MacIntyre, Alasdair 301n
MacKinnon, Catharine 74, 74n, 75, 75n, 76, 78n, 83n, 86, 98, 99n
Malalgoda, Kitsiri 266, 288n, 289, 289n
Malkote, Rama 167n
Mamdani, M. 309n, 333, 333n
Mandal Commission 141, 142, 142n; opposition to 143, 143n, 144, 149, 150n, 156; women and 142, 144
Mandelbaum, David 181
Manegold, Catherine S. 99n
Maniratnam 307n; films of 136–66 *passim*
Manor, James 292n
Manto, Saadat Hasan 1, 1n, 2, 2n, 3, 7, 12–19, 19n, 22, 23n, 25–6, 31, 35, 36, 308; nationalism and 29; prostitutes of 32, 33; relations with Progressive writers 3; stories of 3, 4, 6, 21, 24, 28; women and 13, 17, 30
Manu 112, 113n, 114
Marcuse, Herbert 295, 295n
Marx, Karl 209, 230, 260, 260n, 261n, 319, 324

Marxism 247; 247n, 280; Althusserian 239n; contemporary 255
Marxist 248, 254; analysis 321; critics 227; intellectuals 222; nationalism 246, 253; response 242; theory 222, 229, 295, 319
Marxist-Leninist 249
masculinity 39, 52, 53, 56, 58, 61; Sinhala practice of 37–65 *passim*
Matrimonial Causes Act 133
Maunaguru, Sitaga 218n
McClintock, Anne 226n
McNeill, Daniel 324n
Mehboob (film-maker) 4
Mendus, Susan 294n
Menon, Nivedita 66, 306, 315, 316, 317n, 332
Meyer, Eric 45
minorities/minority 35; cultural 296; Muslim 241; identity 147; rights 106
Miraji 6
Mirza, Saeed 150
Mitakshara 112, 113
Mitter, Partha 5n
modernities/modernity 11, 12, 139, 148, 158–9; colonialism and 30; global 317; Indian 145, 307; national 143; political 284; Sri Lankan 41
Mohammad, Khalid 144
Mohanty, Chandra 217, 226n
Mowitt, John 222n
Mufti, A. 308
Mufti, Aamir R. 1, 3n, 35n, 278n
Mukherjee, Geeta 94
Mukherjee, Hrishikesh 150
Mukund, K. 114n
Muslim/s 5, 195, 239n, 241, 259, 265, 273, 302–3, 309; communalism 206; community 206; cultural organization 192; culture 4; elites 25; fanaticism 190; minorities 4, 27n; rights 194; separatism 8, 31; violence 201
Muslimness 26, 27

Naidu, Ratna 196n, 204–5, 206n
Nairn, Tom 254n
Nancy, Jean-Luc 224n, 279, 279n
Nandy, Ashis 186n
Narayan Swamy, M.R. 244
nation 159, 184, 210; and belonging 33; and modernity 142; as community 214, 271; as mother 26, 27, 33, 176; constituting the 227; idea of 170; Indian 323; modernist 174; space 167, 168, 173, 181; state 237, 306; Tamil 212–82 *passim*
national: culture 13; identity 28, 270; imaginary 139; integration 162; interest 141; modern 139, 141, 144, 147, 160; modernity 13, 30; movement 334; realism 34; security 141
nationalism 4, 6, 8, 22, 26, 27, 140, 152, 153, 157, 162, 164, 164n, 175; anti-colonial 165, 213n; Buddhist 291; cinema and 138; claims about 213; contesting 268, 307; culture and 30; European 324; Fascism and 307; feminist critiques of 218; ideology of 279; logic of 222; love and 158; motherhood and 15, 16, 32; romantic secularism and 166; romance of 150;

Sinhala 212–82 *passim*; Tamil separatist 212–82 *passim*
nationalist 28, 164, 169, 177; claims 227; devices 176; discourse 4, 5, 176, 180, 182; history 331; identity 5; inventions 254; love 158; movement 185; Muslims 31; projects 284; realism 11; spatial strategies 166–212 *passim*; subjects 25; texts 24; thought 177n; 245
Nehru, Jawaharlal 3, 11, 28n, 177n, 182, 183, 184n, 187, 194, 306, 309, 316; and Mahalanobis 185
Nehruvian developmentalism 168; discourse 3; era 182, 183, 184, 186; nation space 185, 186, 188; nationalism 153, 154; secularism 28; state 138, 157
Niranjana, Tejaswini 139, 139n, 141n, 307, 332

Obeysekere, Gananath 46, 47, 50, 50n, 51, 64, 227, 246n
Oldenburg, Veena T. 26n
Other Backward Castes 141

Pandey, Gyanendra 27n, 163n, 189n, 199n
Pandian, M.S.S. 157
Parker, Andrew 5n, 226n
Parsi Marriage and Divorce Act 129
Partition of India 2, 6, 7n, 10, 13, 27n, 34, 35, 36, 187, 308; stories 13; studies 309
Patel, Sujata 199n
Patnaik, Arun Kumar 153n
patriarchal attitudes 91, 164, 306; family structures 112; Hindu and Muslim 165; society 95

Phadnis, Urmila 291, 291n
polygamy 130–2
Ponnambalam, G.G. 293
Ponnambalam, Satchi 223n
postcolonial activists 318; feminists 325; future 284; issues 288; modern 141, 144, 158, 165, 307; nations 323; societies 296; state 311, 332
post-national-modern 144, 149, 158,165, 307
Prabhakaran, Velupillai 244
Premchand 6, 7, 11, 35
Pritchett, Frances 8n,
prostitutes, *see* courtesans
Purewal, Jasjit 77, 83n, 101n

Qasmi, Ahmad Naseem 7

Rabinow, Paul 320
Rai, Amrit 8n
Raipuri, Akhtar Hussain 7n, 9n
Rajadhyaksha, Ashish 148n, 189, 189n
Rajagopal, Arvind 190n
Ram Janmabhoomi 172, 190–1
rape 81, 83, 86, 87, 97; and abduction 80; and feminists 306; and fraud 87; and law 83,104; and rights 96; and sex 74; attempts 71; cases 67, 70, 82, 85, 91, 93, 100; Canadian legislation and 71, 72, 74; conceptions of 73; custodial 70, 82; definitions 69, 70, 71, 72, 75, 77, 101; feminist analyses of 77; law 84; law, draft amendment to 72n, 73, 74, 74n, 75, 78, 83, 89n 90, 90n 97, 97n 101n, 102n; male 78; marital 88;

meaning of 104; reform 316; sex as 76; story 85; trial 84, 91, 92, 93; victims 100; women and 74, 93
Rashtriya Swayamsevak Sangh (RSS) 138n, 164n, 197, 201, 205
Rawls, John 296, 296n
Rithambhara, Sadhvi 191n
Roberts, Michael 46n, 47, 48n, 269n
Rogers, John 48, 49
Rose, Jacqueline 318n
Rosen, Hannah 105
Russell, Ralph 10n
Rusva, Mirza Muhammad Ḥadi 4, 26

Sahni, Bhisham 17n
Said, Edward 29n, 174, 221n, 221n, 231n
Saksena, Ram Babu 9n, 10n
Sangari, Kumkum 199n, 226n
Sangh Parivar 138, 203
Saradamoni, K. 115n
Sarkar, Sumit 188n
Sarkar, Tanika 89n, 188n, 199n, 201
Sarshar, Ratan Nath 10
Savarkar, V.D. 168, 176, 178, 178n 179, 179n, 180, 181, 182, 183, 187n, 188, 190, 306
Schrijver, Joke 45n
Schwarz, Henry 307n
Scott, David 20n, 40n, 43, 43n, 46n, 52n, 212n, 283, 309, 315
Scott, Joan 256
secular 140n; conditions 290; nationalism 183, 186, 193
secularism 12, 31, 138, 139, 154, 156, 158, 159, 162, 188, 306, 315,
Sedwick, Eve 214, 214n,
Seevaratnam, N. 264
Seshan, T.N. 150n
sex/sexual/sexuality 29, 68, 102, 135–6; and women 87; assault 70–3, 88, 96–9, 100, 104; children and 91; consensual 89, 91; deconstruction of 99; experience 67; female 86, 91, 94, 95; morality 95; nature of 70, 99; space for 57; violence and 66–105 *passim*
Sharar, Abdulhaleem 10
Shetty, Sandhya 5n, 26n
Shiv Sena 161n, 196n, 199n, 200, 201, 201n
Sinfield, Alan 232n
Sinhala: culture 49; history 212–82 *passim*; society 42, 43, 47, 50–2, 61
Sivanandan 220n
Skinner, Quentin 301n
Smart, Lucy Carol 74n 85, 85n, 86
Smith, Wilfred Cantwell 288
Smriti/Smritikars 112–14, 119, 123
Soja, Edward 169n
Somerville, C. John 290n
Soviet Writers Congress 11
Spencer, Jonathan 44n, 45n, 46
Spivak, Gayatri Chakravorty 5n, 174n, 233n, 305, 311n, 316n, 326n
Srinivas, M.N. 114n
Srinivas, S.V. 156n
Stalin, Joseph 253n, 254
Stewart, Kathleen 281n
Stirrat, R.L. 46, 46n, 47
Stridhan 113, 122

subaltern 29, 79; and elite 21; as writer 317; consciousness 326; crowds 203; education 33; life 28; 'new' 305–34 *passim*; struggles 21; women 324
subalternity 325, 329n
Subrahmanyam, S. 182n
Suhrawardy, Shaista Akhtar Banu 10n
Sultana, Nasreen 160n

Tambiah, Stanley 291, 291n
Temkin, Jennifer 72n
Tennent, James Emerson 46n
Thackeray, Bal 150n, 200n
Tharu, Susie 139n, 141n, 143n, 147n, 153n
Thomadsen, Nancy Sweet 78n
Thorner, Alice 199n
tolerance, and Sri Lanka 283–304 *passim*
TULF 212–80 *passim*

Uberoi, Patricia 176n
Upadhya, C. 114n
Urdu 4, 6, 10, 11; afsana and 1, 3; literary culture and literature 6, 7, 8, 30, 34, 35; lyrics 7; short story 12; writers 7, 13, 35; Urdu-Hindi conflict 7

Vaid, Sudesh 226n
Van der veer, Peter 180n, 181, 181n, 203n
Vanaik, Achin 188n
Vance, Carol S. 76n
Vasudevan, Ravi 155n
violence 47n, 48, 49; against women 66–105 *passim*; and gender 305; anthropological 41, 44; anti-Tamil 40; collective 45; sexual 100; Sinhala 43; space for 39, 42, 50–1, 53–4, 57, 59, 61–2, 64, 309
Virilio, Paul 324
Vishwa Hindu Parishad (VHP) 138n, 191n, 192, 204
Vishwanathan, Gauri 143
Visveswaran, Kamala 40n, 331n

Wallerstein, Immanuel 169n, 173n, 210n, 215n
Walzer, Michael 294n
Wakankar, Milind 20n, 213n
Weber, Max 300n
White, Hayden 258n
widows/widowhood 108, 111, 113, 117, 122, 125; inheritance of 126; remarriage 124, 127; rights 111
Williams, Raymond 226
Wills, Claire 29n, 33n
Wilson, Alfred J. 28, 219, 220, 220n 225n, 227n, 239n, 240n, 267, 267n, 293n
woman/women: as nation 24, 139, 157, 158; conflicts and 330; economic rights of 106, 108; marriage and 106–37 *passim*; Muslim 161; marital rights of 129; politics and 24
women's history 328; organizations 106; property rights 107, 117, 118, 119, 120–2, 125–6, 128; rights 106, 112, 114, 115, 117, 123, 136; subordination 119

Yajnavalkya 112

Zaheer, Sajjad 6

GPSR Authorized Representative: Easy Access System Europe, Mustamäe tee 50, 10621 Tallinn, Estonia, gpsr.requests@easproject.com

www.ingramcontent.com/pod-product-compliance
Lightning Source LLC
Chambersburg PA
CBHW072120290426
44111CB00012B/1722